DBS Library

75365

Pearson New International Edition

Social Media Marketing

Tracy Tuten Michael Solomon
First Edition

D1152246

DBS Library
13/14 Aungier Street
Dublin 2
Phone: 01-4177572

PEARSON®

Pearson Education Limited
Edinburgh Gate
Harlow
Essex CM20 2JE
England and Associated Companies throughout the world

Visit us on the World Wide Web at: www.pearsoned.co.uk

© Pearson Education Limited 2014

All rights reserved. No part of this publication may be reproduced, stored in a retrieval system, or transmitted in any form or by any means, electronic, mechanical, photocopying, recording or otherwise, without either the prior written permission of the publisher or a licence permitting restricted copying in the United Kingdom issued by the Copyright Licensing Agency Ltd, Saffron House, 6–10 Kirby Street, London EC1N 8TS.

All trademarks used herein are the property of their respective owners. The use of any trademark in this text does not vest in the author or publisher any trademark ownership rights in such trademarks, nor does the use of such trademarks imply any affiliation with or endorsement of this book by such owners.

- 4 Dec 2014

ISBN 10: 1-292-02353-8
ISBN 13: 978-1-292-02353-3

British Library Cataloguing-in-Publication Data
A catalogue record for this book is available from the British Library

Printed in the United Kingdom by Ashford Colour Press Ltd.

Table of Contents

The Horizontal Revolution

LearningObjectives

When you finish reading this chapter you will be able to answer these questions:

1 What are social media? How are social media similar to traditional media?

2 What are the major zones associated with social media?

3 What is Web 2.0 and what are its defining characteristics? How does Web 2.0 add value to Web 1.0?

4 How does the Social Media Value Chain explain the relationships among the Internet, social media channels, social software, and the Internet-enabled devices we use for access and participation? In what activities do individuals participate using social media?

5 What is social media marketing? What role does participation play in social media marketing?

6 What marketing objectives can organizations meet when they incorporate social media in their marketing mix?

GO

From Chapter 1 of *Social Media Marketing*, First Edition. Tracy L. Tuten, Michael R. Solomon.
Copyright © 2013 by Pearson Education, Inc. All rights reserved.

Greetings, Digital Native

When you woke up this morning, what was the first thing you did? Sure, you may have taken a moment to gulp down some juice or coffee, but odds are you also checked your cell for texts that came in overnight. Maybe you went straight to your Facebook page to check on posts about last night's party. Perhaps you called up today's issue of the *New York Times* on your iPad to see what's going on in the world. Or maybe you wanted to boast about those new shoes you bought so you posted your credit card transactions to your network on Swipely.

Face it—you're a **digital native**. If you're a typical student, you probably can't recall a time when the Internet was just a static, one-way platform that transmitted text and a few sketchy images. And, believe it or not, in the last century even *that* crude technique didn't exist. You may have read about this in a history class: People actually sent handwritten letters to each other and waited for printed magazines to arrive in their mailboxes to learn about current events!

The term *digital native* originated in a 2001 article by Marc Prensky entitled "Digital Natives, Digital Immigrants."[1] He tried to explain a new type of student who was starting to enter educational institutions. These students—students like you—were born in an era in which digital technology has always existed. You and your fellow digital natives grew up "wired" in a highly networked, always-on world. It's an exciting time—but it continues to change so constantly that we need to study it carefully.

Today the Internet is the backbone of our society. We call the current version that allows users to interact with senders **Web 2.0**—we've moved from a fairly simple one-way communications device (that's Web 1.0) to an interactive social system that's available to most of us 24/7. Widespread access to devices like personal computers, digital video and audio recorders, webcams, and smartphones ensures that consumers who live in virtually any part of the world can create and share content. Whether you're 18 or 80, odds are you're already participating to some extent in this wired world.

Information doesn't just flow from big companies or governments down to the people; today each of us communicates with huge numbers of people by a click on a keypad, so information flows *across* people as well. (Hint: How many Facebook friends do you have?) That's what we mean by a **horizontal revolution**. This fundamental change in the way we live, work, and play is characterized in part by the prevalence of social media. **Social media** are the online means of communication, conveyance, collaboration, and cultivation among interconnected and interdependent networks of people, communities, and organizations enhanced by technological capabilities and mobility.[2] Does that sound like a complex definition? It is … because social media exist within a complex and rapidly advancing environment. We'll dive deep into the social media environment, but first let's explore the makings of a social media life—*your* life.

Living a Social (Media) Life

The Internet and its related technologies make what we know today as social media possible and prevalent. Every day the influence of social media expands as more people join online communities. Facebook, a social utility that offers **synchronous interactions** (which occur in real time, such as when you text back-and-forth with a friend) and **asynchronous interactions** (which don't require all participants to respond immediately, such as when you email a friend and get an answer the next day), photo sharing, games, applications, groups, e-retailing, and more, has as of the time of this writing more than 800 million active users.[3] If Facebook were a country, it would be the third most populated in the world. Do you wonder why we called Facebook a social utility? A community that got its start as a social network, Facebook offers functionality far beyond basic relationship building. It competes with social channels ranging from video and photo sharing to blogs to e-commerce sites.

People aren't just joining social communities. They are contributing too! YouTube users upload more than 35 hours of video every single minute of every day. That's roughly equivalent to 176,000 full-length movies uploaded weekly. In just 30 days on YouTube, more video is broadcast than in the last 60 years on the CBS, NBC, and ABC broadcasting networks combined.[4] Google the phrase "social media stats" and you'll see mind-boggling facts and figures about the number of people who use social media, what they're doing (and when) with social media, and their reach and influence. We've done that for you in Table 1.

TABLE 1

Mind-Boggling Social Media Stats

- It took radio 38 years to reach 50 million listeners. TV took 13 years to reach 50 million users. The Internet took four years to reach 50 million people. In under 9 months, Facebook added 100 million users.
- Social media activity has overtaken porn as the number one online activity.
- 80 percent of companies use LinkedIn as their primary recruiting tool.
- 25 percent of search results for the world's top 10 brands point to user-generated content.
- If you were paid $1 for every time an article was posted on Wikipedia, you would earn $36.58 per hour.[1]
- About 76.8 percent of Facebook users reside outside the United States.[2]
- 1 out of 6 couples who married last year met on a social media site.[3]
- Approximately 1 billion pieces of content are shared on Facebook daily.[4]
- 40 percent of Twitter usage is from mobile devices and 17 percent of users have tweeted while on the toilet.[5]

[1] Wikipedia, "Wikipedia: Modelling Wikipedia Extended Growth," May 9, 2011, http://en.wikipedia.org/wiki/Wikipedia:Modelling_Wikipedia_extended_growth, accessed May 25, 2011.

[2] N. Gonzalez, "Check Facebook," May 24, 2011, www.checkfacebook.com/, accessed May 24, 2011.

[3] Chadwick Martin Bailey, "The Evolution of Dating: Match.com and Chadwick Martin Bailey Behavioral Studies Uncover a Fundamental Shift," April 2010, http://blog.cmbinfo.com/press-center-content/?month=4&year=2010, accessed May 24, 2011.

[4] Facebook, "Press Statistics," 2011, www.facebook.com/press/info.php?statistics, accessed May 24, 2011.

[5] K. Kasi, "Twitter's Mobile Usage Exploding," January 12, 2011, www.dotcominfoway.com/blog/twitters-mobile-usage-exploding, accessed May 24, 2011.

Social Behavior and the Philosophy of Participation

When we introduced the definition of social media earlier, we admitted it's a complicated idea. It's difficult to fully capture the realm of social media because of the expansive nature of sites, services, and behaviors that are a part of this rapidly expanding digital universe. There are simply too many social websites, too many things we can do online, and increasing access using a variety of devices to grasp it all at once.

More generally, however, we can think of social media as the way digital natives live a social life. To sum things up, it's all about a **culture of participation**; a belief in democracy: the ability to freely interact with other people, companies, and organizations; open access to venues that allows users to share content from simple comments to reviews, ratings, photos, stories, and more; and the power to build on the content of others from your own unique point of view. Here's just a brief look at some of the things you might do with social media.

- Post a status update about plans for the weekend.
- Create a blog to share your favorite recipes.
- Coordinate a book club meeting and negotiate a group discount on the book's purchase price.
- Instant message or voice chat with friends to carry on a synchronous conversation online.
- Share a micro-post to recommend an article to your friends.
- Make your own animated video and share it.
- Keep a travel diary of a trip abroad complete with photos, videos, journal entries, and destination ratings.
- Find people you used to know and reconnect with them.
- Entertain yourself and your friends with short social games.

This list could go on and on. Our point? Social media enables active participation in the form of communicating, creating, joining, collaborating, working, sharing, socializing, playing, buying and selling, and learning within interactive and interdependent networks. It's an exciting time to be around!

Social Media Zones

The word **media** has multiple meanings, but for our purposes we'll simply use it to refer to means of communication.[5] The media we use may range from **mass media** (means of communication that can reach a large number of individuals) such as broadcast, print, and digital channels, to **personal media** (channels capable of two-way communications on a small scale) such as email, surface mail, telephone, and face-to-face conversations. Social media cross the boundaries of mass and personal media, so they enable individuals to communicate with one or a few people as well as to thousands or even millions of others.

Communication travels using a **medium** (or **channel**) such as word-of-mouth, television, radio, newspaper, magazine, signage, Internet, direct mail, or telephone. Within each medium, marketers can choose specific **vehicles** to place a message. For instance, within the medium of television, marketers may choose *How I Met Your Mother* as one vehicle to broadcast their message. *Cosmopolitan* and *BusinessWeek* are vehicles for the magazine medium. Social media also have a set of online channels with numerous vehicles within each channel.

Part of the complexity of social media is due to the sheer quantity of channels and vehicles, with new ones coming online all the time. These options are easier to compare and contrast if we group similar channels together. In so doing we can conveniently organize the social media space into four zones. Figure 1 illustrates the four zones of social media channels, and we've organized the book around these groupings:

- Zone 1 is Social Community.
- Zone 2 is Social Publishing.
- Zone 3 is Social Entertainment.
- Zone 4 is Social Commerce.

Figure 1

Social Media Zones

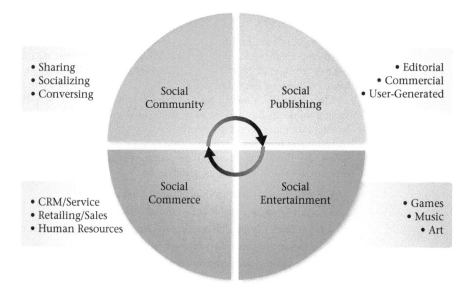

You'll note as we discuss various uses of social media for personal and commercial purposes that some areas overlap two or even more zones. That's the nature of social media. All social media are networked around relationships, technologically enabled, and based on the principles of shared participation.

Zone 1: Social Community   **Social communities** describe channels of social media focused on *relationships* and the common activities people participate in with others who share the same interest or identification. Thus, social communities feature two-way and multi-way communication, conversation, collaboration, and the sharing of experiences and resources. All social media channels are built around networked relationships, but for social communities the interaction and collaboration for relationship building and maintenance are the primary reason people engage in these activities.

Many of the channels in which you already participate likely reside in this first zone. The channels in the social community zone include **social networking sites, message boards** and **forums**, and **wikis**. All emphasize individual contributions in the context of a community, communication and conversation, and collaboration.

For example, *social networking sites (SNS)* are online hosts that enable site members to construct and maintain profiles, identify other members with whom they are connected, and participate using various services the site offers. There are a variety of services common to SNS; the focus is on the individual communication and collaboration within the context of connections in the community. Profiles enhance the ability of members to develop a **social identity** using a profile picture or avatar, basic information, and other customizable options. Members maintain a **social presence** in the community that indicates their availability, mood, friend list, and status. **Connections**, whom we might call *friends, followers,* or *fans,* communicate and share content in a variety of ways including *direct messages* (akin to email within the social networking site), *wall posts* (posts to a profile, visible to others), and *chat* or *instant messaging (IM)* options. Thus, SNS offers both synchronous and asynchronous forms of communication, and the resulting content may be either permanent or temporary.

There are hundreds of SNS vehicles operating at present, including Bebo, Friendster, and Orkut. LinkedIn is the leader in the area of professional networking. The most famous social network is Facebook. We differentiate Facebook from typical SNS though, because of the expansive nature of its offerings. Facebook defines itself not as a social network (although it did begin as one, and retains networking functionality), but as a **social utility**. Facebook's applications span all four zones of social media.

Forums are perhaps the oldest venue of social media. Essentially they are interactive, online versions of community bulletin boards. They focus entirely on discussions held among members. Members establish profiles as they do in SNS and participate by posing content including questions, opinions, news, and photos. Others then respond and extend the conversation as they post responses; this results in a **threaded discussion**. There are thousands upon thousands of forums active online, most oriented around a common interest. For example, RC Universe (www.rcuniverse.com) is a vibrant community of remote-control hobbyists.

Wikis are collaborative online workspaces that enable community members to contribute to the creation of a useful and shared resource. Wikis can be about anything and everything. A wiki could be created by a family community to share and update family history, or by an appliance manufacturer that is trying to develop the perfect user manual. The software that supports the wiki enables multiple members to collaborate, edit, make comments, and share a variety of content.

Zone 2: Social Publishing   **Social publishing** sites aid in the dissemination of content to an audience. The channels of social publishing include blogs, microsharing sites, media sharing sites, and social bookmarking and news sites. **Blogs** are websites that host regularly updated online content that may include text, graphics, and video. Blogs may be maintained by individuals, journalists, traditional media providers, or organizations, so they feature a wide range of topics. Thus, there are blogs that operate much like an online news source or magazine, a tabloid, or simply as an online personal diary. Blogs are social because they are shareable; they include the option for readers to leave comments that can result in threaded discussions related to specific posts. Several services are available for formatting and hosting, including Blogger, WordPress, Posterous, and Tumblr.

Microsharing sites, also called **microblogging sites**, work much like blogs except that there is a limit to the length of the content you can post. A **microshare** could include a sentence, sentence fragment, embedded video, or link to content residing on another site. Twitter, the most well-known microsharing vehicle, limits posts to 140 characters. Others include Twingly, identi.ca, and Laconica.

Media sharing sites, like blogs, host content but also typically feature video, audio (music and podcasts), photos, and presentations and documents rather than text or a mix of media. Media sharing sites host content searchable by the masses, but within each vehicle are options for following content posted by specific people. Thus, media sharing sites are also networked. Here are some prominent vehicles within different types of media:

- Video sharing : YouTube, Vimeo, and Ustream
- Photo sharing: Flickr, Snapfish, and Photobucket
- Music and audio sharing: iTunes, Live365, and Podcast Alley
- Presentations and documents: Scribd, SlideShare, SplashCast, BrightTalk, and SlideBoom
- Social bookmarking services (i.e., sharing links to other sites): Diigo and Digg

Zone 3: Social Entertainment   The zone of **social entertainment** encompasses channels and vehicles that offer opportunities for play and enjoyment. These include social games and gaming sites, socially enabled console games, alternate reality games (ARGs), virtual worlds, and entertainment communities.

At this stage in the development of social media, **social games** are by a substantial margin the most advanced channel in the social entertainment zone. These are hosted online and include opportunities for interaction with members of a player's network as well as the ability to **statuscast** (post updates to one's status) activities and gaming accomplishments to online profiles. Examples of social game vehicles include Bejeweled and Mafia Wars.

Virtual worlds are three-dimensional communities where people participate as **avatars**—digital representations of themselves that can take pretty much any form the person desires. Second Life and Web Alive are examples of virtual world vehicles.

Yet another aspect of social entertainment is **entertainment communities**. MySpace, once the leading social network, now defines itself as a social entertainment service. Why? Its value lies in the network of musicians and bands and their music offered on the site. Though social entertainment is still developing as a channel, we anticipate that social entertainment communities will develop around other traditional areas of entertainment in the near future—film, art, and sport.

Zone 4: Social Commerce   Our fourth zone is **social commerce**. Social commerce refers to the use of social media to assist in the online buying and selling of products and services. Social commerce leverages social shopping behaviors when online shoppers interact and collaborate during the shopping experience. Social commerce channels include **reviews and ratings** (on review sites or branded e-commerce sites), **deal sites** and **deal aggregators** (aggregate deals into personalized deal feeds), **social shopping markets** (online malls featuring user-recommended products, reviews, and the ability to communicate with friends while shopping), and **social storefronts** (online retail stores that sometimes operate within a social site like Facebook with social capabilities).

In addition, organizations can socially enable aspects of their traditional e-commerce websites by using tools such as **Facebook Connect** (a Facebook tool that allows users to log in to other partnering sites using their Facebook identities) and **Share applications** (tools that let users share what they are reading or doing on their status feeds). Examples of review and rating vehicles include Epinions and Yelp. Groupon is an example of a deal vehicle. Yipit, DailyFlock, and 8coupons are deal aggregators. Etsy is an example of a social shopping market. Levi's Friends Store is an example of a social storefront. Figure 2 illustrates the four zones of social media marketing along with several vehicles prevalent in each zone.

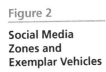

Figure 2

**Social Media
Zones and
Exemplar Vehicles**

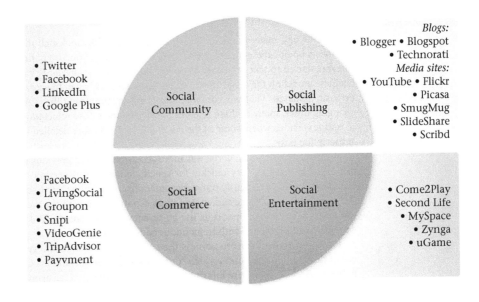

Learning
Objective 3

Web 2.0: The Defining Characteristics of Social Media

Chances are you've heard the term Web 2.0 before, but just what is it? This phrase most often is attributed to Tim O'Reilly, a thought leader on the future of technology. In a 2005 article entitled "What is Web 2.0?" O'Reilly wrote, "Web 2.0 refers to developments in online technology that enable interactive capabilities in an environment characterized by user control, freedom, and dialogue."[6] Web 2.0 offers a cost-effective solution that provides access to rich data; the collective wisdom of its users; access to micromarkets; software that operates on multiple platforms (mobile phone, PDA, computer) and beyond (cloud computing); and user interfaces that are easy, accessible, and interactive. Wow! That's a lot of breathtaking features to absorb at once. Let's take a look at the most important distinguishing features of Web 2.0.

The Web Is the Platform

The first feature of Web 2.0 relates to the value of social software and multiple Internet-enabled devices for social access. The focus is on delivery of service over software—this means that we don't necessarily have to purchase a software program via CD or download and physically install it on each of our computers. **Cloud computing** is a general term for anything that involves delivering hosted services online. A big chunk of Google's business model is based on this concept. Google aims to offer software for nearly every task, often at no cost to users, with the same anytime, anywhere accessibility of the Web itself. The Google Documents software that enables multiple users in different locations to work on the same file is an example of social software. More recently Amazon has gotten into the cloud business via its Cloud Player that enables music lovers to store their tunes on the company's servers and then lets them access the tunes on multiple devices.

Web 2.0 reaches well beyond the personal computer today. The Internet is no longer hardware-specific, tied to a physical device in a static location. Rather, we access the Web via tablet PCs and laptops, mobile phones, iPads, and PDAs. This also means that users interact with Web 2.0 services and applications in a host of different situations, locations, and times.

User Participation, User-Generated Content, and Crowdsourcing

Wherever this icon appears in the margin, please go to the website **www.zonesofsmm.com** for an example of the topic discussed.

Back in the day, many parents pointed with pride to a big bookshelf that displayed several rows of big, musty books; these bound encyclopedias contained a good bit of the world's knowledge. As the Internet started to take off, venerable publishers like *Encyclopedia Britannica* suddenly found their business model on the verge of extinction as consumers began to access information (which could be easily updated) via their computers rather than thumbing through heavy books. To adapt to changing times, many of these reference books (some rather reluctantly) converted their offerings to online versions where some of the content is free but more detailed information is available on a subscription basis.

Although the online material was more accessible than in previous formats—especially because the reader can search very quickly for specific entries—this version of an encyclopedia still is a Web 1.0 creature. It primarily transfers content from an authoritative source (the experts who write the topic entries) to a large audience of users. Contrast that with the Web 2.0 evolution that enabled the development of Wikipedia as the go-to encyclopedia source. Wikipedia is a "crowdsourced," easily updatable resource with tremendous added value to users.

Crowdsourcing means to harness the collective knowledge of a crowd to solve problems and complete tasks. Internet users search for information with *Britannica Online*; Internet users create, publish, rate, edit, and share information with Wikipedia. A small army of zealous volunteers serve as "editors" who verify others' entries—and they do so for personal satisfaction only. A single person would not have the resources or knowledge to publish an exhaustive, stellar online encyclopedia, but a mass of individual experts can.

There are many examples one could give of the evolution from Web 1.0 to Web 2.0, all with an enhanced role for the audience as the most distinguishing feature. Whereas earlier iterations of the Web focused on this digital platform as a publication medium, Web 2.0 is characterized by how it enables user participation. If an online site, service, or tool enables conversation, content augmentation via commenting, rating, editing, and sharing via the Web (whether accessed via mobile phone, PDA, or computer), it's a part of the Web 2.0 landscape.

As communication is empowered by the capabilities of Web 2.0, we enter the most recent evolution in the history of communication—the horizontal revolution we described at the beginning of the chapter. Communication is no longer one to many, mass, and vertically oriented. Instead, communication is now multi-way and multi-directional and publishers, the media, and individuals share the power. *This shift is critical to what it means to communicate using social media.* Web 2.0 levels the playing field between producers and consumers. It invites each of us to be **co-creators** in product design, delivery, pricing, and promotion. This means that users have a say in what producers and marketers offer in the marketplace.

User-Defined Content

Sites rely on users rather than pre-established systems to sort content. **Taxonomies** are classifications that experts create; for example, you may have learned (and perhaps forgotten) the classic system that biologists use to categorize organisms (the Linnaean taxonomy) that places any living thing in terms of Kingdom, Phylum, Class, Order, Family, Genus, and Specie. In contrast **folksonomies** are sets of labels, or **tags**, individuals choose in a way that makes sense to them, as opposed to using predefined keywords.

Tagging refers to the process social media users undergo to categorize content according to their own folksonomy. This process creates a **tag cloud** that not only enables others to search and retrieve information using tags that also make the most sense to them personally but also provides information about the popularity of the tags used. For example, many people tag photos of nature with the tag *happiness*. This suggests that those people associate this emotion with images of nature.

Amazon organizes its shopping site according to a taxonomy of product categories. These include categories such as (1) books; (2) movies, music, and games; and (3) computer and office products. Within books, one can further browse by genres such as nonfiction, literature and fiction, children's books, biographies, and more. These categories are part of an established taxonomy. However, Amazon also empowers its users to organize and classify its offerings using their own tags. These tags are entirely user-generated so users can search their own tags and the tags of others. The popular novel *The Girl Who Kicked the Hornet's Nest* by Stieg Larsson is categorized by Amazon's taxonomy as Books: Literature & Fiction: Contemporary. It is categorized by users' folksonomy tags as *murder trial, Swedish, strong women, mystery, conspiracy, adventure,* and *can't wait to read.* Visitors to Amazon's site can use its search engine to find this book using either Amazon's established taxonomy, or search "can't wait to read."

Network Effects

In Web 2.0, each additional user adds value for all users. Economists refer to this as a **network effect.** Amazon's ability to recommend books to you based on what other people with similar interests have bought gets better as it tracks more and more people who enter search queries and make purchases. When you're visiting a new city and want to find a great restaurant on Yelp you feel more comfortable with a place that 1,000 diners recommend than 1 that only 10 users rate. You get more value from Facebook as more of your friends also use the network. Network effects enable organizations to leverage the value of crowdsourcing. Organizations use crowdsourcing to benefit from the collective wisdom of crowds, but the network effect ensures that there is sufficient participation for the crowdsourced solution to be a good one.

Scalability

Suppose a new café opens in your town; it holds only 10 tables but offers a homemade cheesecake that is to die for. As diners sample the cake, they text and tweet about it and suddenly hordes of other people turn up to check it out. The owner didn't anticipate this response and had baked a limited number of cheesecakes for the evening. She has to turn people away; she's a victim of her own success. Her problem: The café is not scalable.

Scalability means to be able to grow and expand capacity as needed without negatively (or at least minimally) affecting the contribution margin of the business. Many concepts work well until the number of users grows beyond the system's capacity. At that point, system failures occur. If you've ever been at a virtual rock concert in Second Life, you've experienced issues with scalability. As long as there aren't too many avatars jamming at the concert, the system functions well. However, if too many try to enter the space, crashes occur because the grid can't accommodate so many users in one area. This is an example of how network effects can be both positive and negative for organizations building a Web 2.0 offering. Network effects not only enhance value but also tend to consume massive resources.

Scalability is an issue for organizations that offer services with limited resources. But it's also an issue related to monetization. If a system requires substantial new investment as users adopt it, the break-even point for return on investment is delayed even as it appears to be a success. BitTorrent, a peer-to-peer file sharing company, is an example of a company that side-stepped the issue of limited resources by designing its system in a way that ensured it was scalable. Rather than adding servers to accommodate growing user demand, BitTorrent's system relied upon the users as servers. BitTorrent enables its users to download large files including movies quickly. If it stored the data and provided the download processing power, it would be limited by the number of users and bits it could download at any point in time given its server capacity. However, BitTorrent works by gathering bits of the files simultaneously from all of its users who have that file in their hard drives. This innovation enabled BitTorrent to solve the scalability dilemma and use the network effect to its advantage.

Perpetual Beta

Web 2.0 is always changing, always responding to the needs of the community. It is in part characterized by a state of being in **perpetual beta**. In the world of innovations, the term *beta* is used to denote a product in testing. The label enables developers to introduce new features in products even if testing and refinement are not yet complete. In "the old days" we would write the code for a program and put it out in the market. If it had glitches (and most did) we might modify the code when we launched the next release. Users had to bide their time as they waited. For example, many businesses elected not to upgrade to Microsoft's Windows Vista office software. Instead they waited several years for Windows 7; the newer version addressed flaws people found in the earlier program. In Web 2.0, many online services improve and evolve constantly as providers operate in a near constant state of continuous improvement. Google Labs offers numerous services with beta labels for Google users including Google Knol, Google FollowFinder, and more.

Reputation Economy

In Web 2.0 users trust other users as a source of knowledge. As we noted earlier, many active contributors to social media platforms do not get paid a salary—but they do benefit because they earn the respect and recognition of other users. This positive feedback creates a **reputation economy** where the value that people exchange is measured in esteem as well as in dollars, euros, or pounds. Consider the value of rankings and ratings offered by other users as you make shopping decisions. Amazon reviews, eBay's reputation rankings, and other similar forms of collective ratings serve as credibility scores for what we can trust online.

One analyst referred to this ratings system, and other situations where decision making is decentralized to the online masses, as **radical trust**. This term refers to the trust bestowed on others when organizations shift control to their consumers and users. The trust is radical because those participating are not vetted; anyone and everyone online can participate in making decisions, creating and editing content, disseminating knowledge, and rating content quality. The trust enables organizations to expand beyond their own in-house resources and expertise but also puts them at risk: Will the actions taken by the masses be positive ones? Why would such trust be extended? In part, it's because of the reputation economy. Everyone can participate, but everyone is also charged with policing the content. Further, those who participate gain a form of "street cred" as power users; their reputations are at stake.

Web 2.0 is basically a term that encompasses all the ways that the Internet has developed since the early (Web 1.0) days. These advances make possible the world we know today as social media. Because social media is not possible without this infrastructure, it is the first supporting component we identify in the Social Media Value Chain that we'll talk about in the next section. Importantly, several characteristics of Web 2.0 extend throughout social media. Social media are *networked*, built on connected and interdependent *communities*, and *co-created*.

Learning
Objective **4**

The Infrastructure of Social Media

The environment of social media is like a volcano that suddenly erupts without warning. Within a few short years we've seen an ever-expanding domain of activities, channels, technologies, and devices that are changing how we think about our lives (for example, in the old days a "friend" was someone you actually knew in person!). As a student of social media marketing, recognizing the parameters of the field and how the pieces of the puzzle fit together will benefit you as you develop skill at devising social media strategies and tactics. The **Social Media Value Chain**, shown in Figure 3, organizes this complex environment into its core components.

The value chain illustrates the core activities of social media users and the components that make those activities possible. As a social media user, you are empowered to participate in any way you'd

Figure 3

The Social Media Value Chain

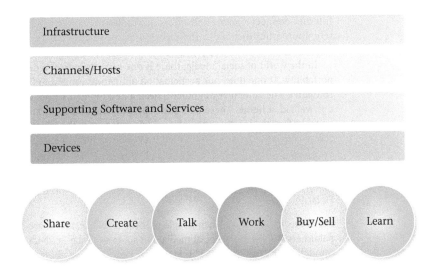

like, from just "lurking" on a site to scripting, filming, and uploading your own video stories. Those activities are made possible by the underlying *infrastructure* of the Internet. Just as in the physical world where we need infrastructure in the form of roads, railroads, TV transmitters, and trained people to operate and maintain these structures, in digital environments the pieces that make up Web 2.0 are crucial. These include the **social software** that provides the programming we need to carry out these activities, the **devices** (iPads, smartphones, computers) we use to access them, and of course the people whose contributions provide the content we all access. Let's take a closer look at each of these elements.

Social Software

So far we've learned that the social media environment supports many Web 2.0 core activities. But much of what we are able to create or do online is due to a host of **social software** applications. These are computer programs that enable users to interact, create, and share data online. For virtually everything you'd like to do online, there is a social software program (or several) that can help you accomplish the activity. Interested in planning an event? Use an event planner and invitation service like eVite.com. Want to keep a notebook of wedding ideas that you can share with your bridesmaids? Use Evernote.com. Need to keep a newsfeed of all the latest happenings at your school? Use Paper.li or Google Alerts. Social software can facilitate interaction, content creation, sharing, syndicating, saving, analyzing, filtering, sorting, and searching data online. Such tools are certainly useful to individuals, communities, entrepreneurs, and businesses. Examples include Audacity (for producing podcasts and other sound files), Xtranormal (for video production), and Prezi (for presentations).

You've heard the phrase "There's an app for that!" Those **apps,** also known as **widgets** (usually downloadable or embeddable), are types of social software. In addition to apps, social software also encompasses application service sites that we call **social services.** Importantly, social software exists to facilitate *all* social media channels. There are applications for social community activities, publishing, entertainment, and commerce.

Devices

Devices are pieces of equipment we use to access the Internet and the range of activities in which we participate online. We utilize hardware devices like tablet PCs, iPads, smartphones,

Internet-connected game consoles, and traditional laptops and desktops for access, but we also rely upon other devices in the creation of social content. In addition to those already mentioned, we can add webcams, flip cams, and digital cameras.

In the world of social media, there is one key attribute of a device that is extremely valuable—portability. At one time, our participation online was limited to the times when we had access to a computer. The computer might have been a desktop in a school computer lab, or if we were lucky, one we had at home. These days many people have access on multiple devices and in many locations. In fact, the location might be anywhere we go as the adoption of smartphones with Internet access increases. Just think—of the more than 800 million Facebook members, 350 million access Facebook on their mobile phones. And those who use Facebook mobile are twice as active on Facebook as are those who don't.[7]

People

Social media work only when people participate, create, and share content. Journalists, editors, and publishers still matter in social media, but so do everyday individuals. People support social media through their participation. This is why we hear so much about **citizen journalists** (amateurs who post about newsworthy events) and **citizen advertisers** (people who share their views about a product or service even though they're not affiliated with the company). Bloggers represent a unique hybrid form of "netizens" in that they may create and share content professionally or personally. Publishing a blog is surely a bigger commitment to sharing content than is posting a status update to your Facebook wall, but both actions generate content and add value to the social media environment.

Show Me the Money!

As wired individuals, we've come to rely on many of the social sites and services available online. And for marketers, social media have created one of the most exciting and efficient opportunities to reach target audiences. But have you ever thought about how those social sites earn revenues? Most sites

 ## THE DARK SIDE OF SOCIAL MEDIA

Is social media a wolf in sheep's clothing? Are users so addicted to their laptops, smartphones, and iPads they can't live without them? In Korea, obsessive video gaming already is a big problem; several gamers have actually died because they wouldn't stop playing long enough to eat or drink. The Korean government has established a network of "boot camps" to treat young Internet addicts. In the United States a facility in Washington state called ReSTART offers a similar service to patients like one who spent every waking minute playing "World of Warcraft" and flunked out of the University of Iowa as a result.[8]

A recent project illustrates just how tough a media-free life might be for digital natives. At the University of Maryland, 200 students were challenged to give up their "toys" for 24 hours. That's right, just one day and night with no text messaging or laptops. No Gchatting, no tweeting. e-mail and (shudder) no Facebook. The blogs they wrote about their harrowing experiences betray the signs of addiction: "In withdrawal. Frantically craving. Very anxious. Extremely antsy. Miserable. Jittery. Crazy." One student confessed, "I clearly am addicted and the dependency is sickening." The central role social media plays in relationships resulted in feelings of isolation and boredom, even though the participants were still living on a bustling campus. One person wrote, "I felt quite alone and secluded from my life. Although I go to a school with thousands of students, the fact that I was not able to communicate with anyone via technology was almost unbearable."[9]

Can we have too much of a good thing? Is social media a drug that can addict us?

still feature free access and a buffet of valuable tools and services. Yet those organizations invested in potentially extensive development costs and time, hosting costs, and ongoing maintenance. Though it's standard business practice to invest capital to pave the way for future profitability, how do these organizations earn revenue if many of the platforms are free to use?

Business Models and Monetization

Just like other businesses, social media providers (whether they are social communities, utilities, software providers, or game and app developers) need a **monetization strategy**. This plan is part of a company's overall **business model**—the strategy and format it follows to earn money and provide value to its stakeholders. For example, Google derives most of the revenue from its widely used search engine (where you "google" a term to locate relevant online links) from the fees it charges advertisers to put their messages on the results pages. In contrast, eBay makes most of its money by taking a cut of the proceeds each time a seller fills an order from a buyer on its merchandise pages. Two different business models; both ways to return value to the sponsoring organization.

For decades now, media providers (e.g., the big networks, ABC, NBC, CBS, and Fox) and media conglomerates (e.g., Disney, Viacom, and Time Warner) relied heavily on a business model we call the **interruption-disruption model**. The goal is to create programming that is interesting enough to attract people to watch it or listen to it. Then, when they have your attention, they interrupt the programming to bring you a commercial message. They sell ad space to marketers who want to gain the attention of a targeted audience, and the audience allows this to happen in return for access to programming they want. The monetization strategy relies upon attracting as many people as possible to the content; the more who pay attention (or who at least tune in even though they may not be paying attention), the more the programmer can charge for the right to insert messages in that vehicle.

In the age of Web 2.0, many online sites still use this same strategy (did you notice the text ads delivered alongside your Facebook newsfeed today?), but they also recognize the need to find other ways to earn revenues. Importantly, the **revenue stream** (a revenue stream is a source of income) that will ultimately replace the model of "ad space as revenue" probably won't be paid access by subscribers or members. Though hundreds of thousands of households pay monthly for cable access, the resistance to paying for programming is strongly ingrained among many consumers. The exception is when the content is superior to what you can get by other means—and you're willing to pay a premium to receive it without being exposed to ad messages. Anyone who pays a monthly fee to subscribe to XM/Sirius Radio's hundreds of music, talk, news, and sports channels understands this model.

Psychic Income

Should you have to pay for online content? Believe it or not, way back in the old days (that is, before 1999) it never occurred to consumers that they should *not* pay for content. That's when a college student named Shawn Fanning introduced the Napster site that enabled music lovers to share tracks for free. That party lasted only 2 years before legalities caught up with the service, but by then the cat was out of the bag. Now, many people (not to point fingers, but especially college students) believe that "information wants to be free," and they gravitate toward technology that enables them to download songs, newspapers, and yes, even textbooks without cost.

As attractive as that sounds, in the long run an entirely free world probably isn't feasible. Remember the old expression "there's no such thing as a free lunch." At the end of the day, *someone* has to pay for content and services. Music artists and novelists (and yes, even textbook authors) can't create and receive nothing in return (for long, anyway). However, the currency that we exchange doesn't necessarily have to be money. For example, if you post a restaurant review on Yelp you won't get a check in the mail for your comments. But you may get "paid" by the satisfaction of sharing your foodie opinions with the uneducated masses. You may even receive a rating on some sites that designates you as a star reviewer. These are forms of **psychic income** (perceived value that is not expressed in monetary form) that help to grease the wheels of social media.

The 5th P of Marketing

Social media offers marketers opportunities to reach consumers where they work and live. Just as in the other aspects of our lives we've already discussed, the element of participation is key in this context also: *Social media enables consumers to have more of a say in the products and services that marketers create to meet their needs.*

Let's take a step back: **Marketing** is the activity, set of institutions, and processes for creating, communicating, delivering, and exchanging offerings that have value for customers, clients, partners, and society at large.[10] The classic view is that organizations accomplish these goals through a **marketing mix** that includes the so-called **4 Ps**: Product, Price, Promotion, and Place (or distribution).

As social media marketing techniques continue to sprout around us, today we need to add a fifth P: **Participation**. It's fair to say that just as social media is changing the way consumers live on a daily basis, so too these new platforms transform how marketers go about their business. Whether our focus is to improve customer service, maintain customer relationships, inform consumers of our benefits, promote a brand or related special offer, develop a new product, or influence brand attitudes, new social media options play a role. **Social media marketing** is the utilization of social media technologies, channels, and software to create, communicate, deliver, and exchange offerings that have value for an organization's stakeholders.

Marketing Communication: From Top-Down to Bottom-Up

Just as the horizontal revolution changed the way society communicates, the advent and adoption of social media changes the way brands and consumers interact. Traditional marketing focuses on **push messaging** (one-way communication delivered to the target audience) using a large dose of broadcast and print media to reach a mass audience. There are minimal opportunities for interaction and feedback between customers and the organization, and what is possible is facilitated by **boundary spanners** (employees who interact directly with customers) who operate in service roles. The brand message is controlled in a top-down manner by brand leadership within the organization.

Believe it or not, when the Internet first began to catch on there were many skeptics who declared it was just a fad! Even as digital technology developed in the 1990s and beyond, marketers still essentially applied the traditional 4Ps model to reach customers. Over time they embraced the Internet as an environment for promotion and distribution. **E-commerce** began to blossom as an alternative to other forms of promotion such as television or radio. Consumers increasingly began to learn about products online—and to purchase them online as well. E-commerce sites are websites that allow customers to examine (onscreen) different brands and to conduct transactions via credit card.

This explosion in e-commerce activity was a boon to manufacturers, retailers, and nonprofit organizations because it offered greater speed, cost efficiencies, and access to **micromarkets**. A micromarket is a group of consumers once considered too small and inaccessible for marketers to pursue. Suddenly it became feasible for even a small company that offered a limited inventory to reach potential customers around the globe. The Internet enables efficient access to these markets, and in turn allows customers to search for very specialized products (e.g., music tracks by bands that recorded bassline music in Sheffield, England, between 2002–2005, or steampunk science fiction novels written by K. W. Jeter). This allows marketers to offer **niche products** that appeal to small, specialized groups of people.

As it became clear that the Internet was not going to go away, marketers flocked to cyberspace. However, most of them still applied the familiar model of the 4 Ps to the digital domain. This form of marketing, **tradigital marketing**, is characterized by improvements in interactivity and measurement, but it retains the primarily vertical flow of power in the channels of communication and distribution. Digital online messages made it possible for consumers to respond directly to an online **display ad** by clicking through to the e-commerce website. **Search advertising** grew during this time too, making it possible for online advertising to target both mass and niche audiences. Direct marketers widely adopted email marketing as a complement to direct mail and telemarketing. Despite these developments, modes of communication were still primarily vertical, one-way "mass communication," largely impersonal, and delivered from one to many. Whether you read the front page of the *New York Times* online at www.nytimes.com or peruse the physical newspaper at your kitchen table, the content from the publisher is delivered vertically through the channel of communication.

Both traditional and tradigital marketing work on the basis of the interruption-disruption model we discussed earlier. This means that the source of a communication delivers messages to audiences whether they want to receive them or not, and regardless of whether these messages are directly relevant to their unique needs. By design, an advertising message interrupts some prior activity: A commercial for Axe body deodorant suddenly appears during the latest episode of MTV's *Jersey Shore,* or perhaps a pop-up bubble asks you to click on a link to learn more about low rates on car insurance while you browse a website.

Why would Internet users tolerate these disruptions as they surf the Web? For the same reason television viewers and radio listeners have for decades. The ad as interruption provides a stream of revenue for the media provider, which enables this sponsor to provide the content of interest at little or no cost to the audience. Television programming exists to draw audiences, which enables the network to sell space to advertisers who wish to reach that audience. The audience in turn accepts the presence of the advertising in order to consume the desired programming. This "you scratch my back and I'll scratch yours" relationship also describes traditional Internet advertising: Before you can watch a full episode of *Gossip Girl* on your laptop, you might sit through a 15-second ad for Verizon Wireless. Just like television and radio broadcasting, the Web 1.0 Internet relies upon the interruption-disruption model to earn revenue.

In contrast, social media empowers consumers. It isn't enough to interrupt the consumer experience and steal a few moments of attention. With social media marketing, the ability for consumers to interact and engage with brands is greatly enhanced. Social media channels give consumers unparalleled access. Consumers discuss, contribute, collaborate, and share—with brands and with each other. The culture of marketing has shifted to an informal one focused on the belief that customers are in control. Marketing guru Peter Drucker once famously said, "The purpose of a business is to create a customer." With the reach and community influence of social media, we can expand this definition: The purpose of a business is to create customers who create other customers.[11] *That Participation in the process is the new fifth P of marketing.*

In the few years of social media's existence, social media marketing has expanded rapidly as much for its efficiency given its low absolute costs as for its potential business applications as a tool for garnering customer attention, managing customer relationships, developing new product ideas, promoting brands, driving store (online and off) traffic, and converting consumers to customers. Social media are not a substitute for traditional marketing communications, but they are also more than a complement to traditional methods. This shift from traditional to tradigital to social media is illustrated in Figure 4.

Learning Objective **6**

Social Media Achieves Marketing Objectives

As social media marketing has accelerated over the last few years, the objectives organizations can accomplish also have expanded. Figure 5 shows these objectives cross a range of marketing activities that include promotion and branding, customer service, relationship management, retailing and commerce, and marketing research. Just as the digital lives of consumers intersect across

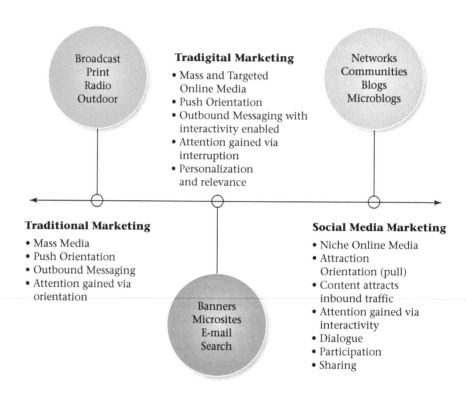

Figure 4

The Evolution of Marketing Communications

Source: Based on David Armano (May 21, 2009), *Social Engagement Spectrum,* http://darmano. typepad.com/logic_ emotion/2009/05/social-engagement-spectrum.html, accessed November 8, 2011.

Broadcast
Print
Radio
Outdoor

Tradigital Marketing
• Mass and Targeted
  Online Media
• Push Orientation
• Outbound Messaging with
  interactivity enabled
• Attention gained via
  interruption
• Personalization
  and relevance

Networks
Communities
Blogs
Microblogs

Traditional Marketing
• Mass Media
• Push Orientation
• Outbound Messaging
• Attention gained via
  orientation

Banners
Microsites
E-mail
Search

Social Media Marketing
• Niche Online Media
• Attraction
  Orientation (pull)
• Content attracts
  inbound traffic
• Attention gained via
  interactivity
• Dialogue
• Participation
• Sharing

the four zones of social media, brands reach consumers in those same spaces to build awareness, promote themselves, and encourage users to try them. Let's take a closer look at some of the ways they do this.

Promotion and Branding Marketers have many possible techniques to promote goods, services, ideas, places, or people. Though there are potentially dozens of specific promotion objectives marketers may seek to accomplish, there are two overarching objectives relevant to the use of social media marketing as part of a brand's promotional mix:

1. Extend and leverage the brand's media coverage, and
2. Influence the consumer throughout the decision-making process.

Figure 5

Brand Applications Across Social Media Zones

Social Community
Building Brand/Consumer
Relationships
Promoting a Presence
Marketing Research

Social Publishing
Blogging
Sharing Branded Content
Advertising/PR
Re-sharing

**Social
Media
Marketing**

Social Commerce
Buying and Selling
Servicing
Managing
Converting to Transactions

**Social
Entertainment**
Enabling Play
Branded Entertainment

When it comes to acquiring space in media to distribute brand messages, marketers have access to three core types of media: (1) paid, (2) owned, and (3) earned. Marketers are assessed monetary fees for **paid media**, including purchasing space to deliver brand messages and securing endorsements. Paid media are traditionally the purview of **advertising**, defined as the paid placement of promotional messages in channels capable of reaching a mass audience. **Public relations**, the promotional mix component tasked with generating positive publicity and goodwill, may also utilize paid media in the form of sponsorships. Television commercials, radio ads, magazine print ads, newspaper ads, billboards, Internet display ads, and **search engine marketing (SEM)** all represent examples of paid media that may be incorporated in a brand's promotional plan. Other emerging formats include paying for messages in online games like Happy Pets or offering branded virtual goods to inhabitants of virtual worlds. And traditional sales promotions such as coupons and contests get a new life on social media platforms.

Owned media are channels the brand controls. Corporate websites and e-commerce sites, corporate blogs, advergames, and ARGs all represent forms of owned media. Just as Best Buy's brick-and-mortar retail stores are owned and controlled by the organization, so is its website.

Earned media are those messages that are distributed at no direct cost to the company and by methods beyond the control of the company. **Word-of-mouth (WOM) communication** (called **influence impressions** in social media) and publicity are important forms of earned media. Companies release content through press releases and paid channels, participate in community events and causes, create stunts designed to generate media attention and buzz, and offer exceptional service quality, all with the hope that a brand message will spread. Table 2 explains the forms of paid, earned, and owned media possible in each of the zones of social media marketing.

TABLE 2

Types of Media

Zone	Paid Media	Earned Media	Owned Media
1: Social Communities	• Ads	• Conversations in communities • Shared content • Influence impressions • Likes, followers, fans	• Controlled profiles
2: Social Publishing	• Endorsements • Branded channels in media sharing sites	• Embeds • Comments • Shares • Links • Search rankings	• Corporate blogs • Brand-controlled media sharing sites
3: Social Entertainment	• Ads in games	• In-game interactions	• Advergames and branded ARGs
4: Social Commerce	• Sales promotions	• Reviews and ratings • Recommendations and referrals • Group buys • Social shopping interactions	• Social storefronts

A major objective related to using social media marketing for promotional purposes is to assist in moving the consumer through the purchase process. Marketers target various stages of this cycle to increase brand awareness, enhance brand liking and image, build brand equity, incite desire, and move consumers to action. They can influence consumer attitudes and movement through the process with promotional messages targeted throughout the social media channels. Let's take a brief look at how this works at each stage of the purchase process.

1. *Increase Awareness:* Brands can increase awareness with social media marketing by maintaining an active presence in the social spaces where target consumers "live." That means engaging in social communities and publishing content as well as encouraging word of mouth communication and consumer reviews. It may even include social entertainment.

2. *Influence Desire:* Social media promotions can be used much like advertising, catalog marketing, and feature events to persuade consumers to recognize a sense of desire. The fashion brand Black Horn posts each new collection on Facebook, Flickr, and YouTube. Visitors can tour pictures of its designs, fresh from each photo shoot. It's like being in the pages of *Vogue.*

3. *Encourage Trial:* Social media can even be used to support sampling and loyalty programs. **Sampling** means to offer a free trial of a product; these are usually mailed to consumers' homes or distributed in stores or on the street. Social media can be used to recruit interested prospects to qualify for samples. Emergen-C, a health supplement, used this tactic to promote free samples. Whenever a user on Twitter tweeted something like "need energy" or "need to focus" Emergen-C sent a tweet requesting the person's mailing address. A couple of days later, the tired tweeter received a gift of three samples.

4. *Facilitate Purchase:* Social media serves as a distribution channel and venue for many sales promotion incentives including deals and group offers. Many customers "like" or follow brands in social networks in order to qualify for special deals. Here's a recent tweet from Best Buy: "Save $330 on an LG 32" Class HDTV + Wireless Adapter package: http://bbyurl.us/t3s via @BestBuy_deals." Kohl's distributes thousands of coupons by posting announcements on its Facebook Fan Page. Fans visit the page, download the coupon, and store traffic increases.

5. *Cement brand loyalty:* Social media venues offer engaging activities for consumers that can ensure they spend more time with the brand, hopefully resulting in higher levels of brand loyalty. Look no farther than social games that offer rewards for the most loyal visitors. That's just what FourSquare does. Starbucks "mayors" earn one dollar off a cup of coffee when they visit. Tasti D-Lite, a regional ice cream chain, went even further when it developed its social media loyalty program.[12] Customers use TreatCards—which also double as gift cards—to earn points for purchases, and those that opt in to the social media bonuses automatically earn additional points. Twitter and Foursquare accounts are updated each time the card is swiped and points are earned or redeemed. As a customer earns points, he or she can redeem them for free cones.

Customer Relationship Management and Service Recovery   Despite all the hype we hear constantly hear about how social media is the "new advertising," in fact there also are other applications where these techniques will play an increasingly important role. For one, customer relationship management, or CRM, also finds a home here. CRM practices focus on what we do with a customer after the first sale; it's far more difficult (and expensive) to attract new customers than to keep old ones. That's why many organizations work hard to maintain contact with their customers and to provide additional products and services to them over time. Often they rely on sophisticated databases that keep an ongoing record of what a person buys and other pertinent information so that he or she will receive customized follow-up messages and offers that are likely to meet unique needs.

Because of this digital focus, it's not surprising that CRM lends itself to social media applications. **Social CRM** embraces software and processes that include the collective intelligence of a

BYTES TO BUCKS

Perhaps the best way to illustrate how marketing objectives can be pursued with social media marketing is to kick things off with pizza (things always go better with pizza). Domino's Pizza is one company that has successfully integrated social media into its marketing strategy. Let's take a look at how Domino's Pizza developed its product based on insights gained from social media, responded to a public relations crisis, earned publicity with its social media campaign, increased brand exposures on social media networks and media sharing sites, and incorporated user-generated content into its advertising and promotions. Domino's utilized social communities, social publishing, and social commerce channels in its campaigns and generated earned media from consumers.

Our story begins badly—with an amateur video that may make you swear off pizza forever. In April 2009, two Domino's Pizza employees filmed themselves violating several health-code standards and posted the videos on YouTube. The violations, pranks in the eyes of the two employees, were gross—they made nasal mucus sandwiches and sent them out for delivery, among other disgusting acts. In short time, the video had over a million views on YouTube, references to it were showing up on search engine rankings for Domino's, and there were posts on Twitter about it. Because social media communications travel far and wide fast, attitudes toward the brand plummeted quickly.[13]

Domino's decided to fight fire with fire as the company used social media to respond to the crisis. It created a Twitter account (@dpzinfo) to address comments people were posting, and the CEO made a statement that was posted to YouTube. By responding and doing so quickly, Domino's was able to demonstrate concern for its customers and to inform the customer audience of the steps being taken to correct for any health hazards. This segment of Domino's story illustrates how an organization can use social media marketing as part of its public relations work when it monitors cyberspace for issues and responses to crises in real time.

But Domino's didn't stop there. It continued to monitor customer comments about the brand and the product it represents. User comments about the pizza posted on social networking sites and blogs called the pizza "boring, bland, mass-produced cardboard." By monitoring and analyzing social media content, Domino's learned its pizza didn't taste as good as it could. The company responded by gathering data from customers on their taste preferences using focus groups and social media monitoring. The data were analyzed and chefs were brought in to create a new,

better-testing pizza. Social media helped the company in its product development work.

That's not all. Domino's launched its Pizza Turnaround campaign, an integrated campaign with advertising using broadcast and Internet, videos on media sharing sites, activity in social networks, and public relations work involving taste tests, pizza reviews on popular shows, and press coverage of the campaign. The company was active on Twitter, Facebook, and YouTube, generating and responding to content. Hashtags for #pizzaturnaround and #newpizza were used to track coverage and aid search. The commercials aired on television and on YouTube. The jewel of the campaign was a 4-minute documentary on the redesign of the Domino's pizza including crust, sauce, and toppings, created by the well-known agency Crispin Porter + Bogusky. In this portion of the case, we can see Domino's integration of social media with other advertising media as well as interaction between the brand and its target audience in social communities. The brand also built its own identity in social communities, which helped to build brand awareness and enhance the brand's image. A microsite, "Pizza Turnaround," carried links to all the coverage and a live Twitter feed of posts related to Domino's and its new pizza. Although this aspect of Domino's marketing strategy focused on exposing the brand's message and building positive affinity for the brand, and driving sales of the new pizza, it still included a research and measurement component.[14]

But wait—there's more! Domino's next step was to invite its fans (those convinced of the company's sincerity and now its quality and deliciousness) to share their own pictures of the pizzas they order from Domino's. This new stage of the campaign, called "Show Us Your Pizza," also got its own microsite that explained the rules of the contest. Anyone can upload photos of Domino's pizza to the Show Us Your Pizza gallery. Winning entries (based on viewer votes) win $500. The third angle to Domino's response works to create a community of Domino's fans. Images can be "liked" and tweeted. The positioning for the campaign is based on the Photo Promise—Domino's promise to be transparent in marketing its food. How can you be sure that the pizza you receive looks just as good as the one in the ad? People just like you took the pictures. All the while Domino's has maintained its presence on Twitter and Facebook, using the sites to continue to monitor and respond. In addition, both sites are used regularly to offer sales promotions including special deals and contest opportunities.[15]

firm's customers to more finely tune the offer and build intimacy between an organization and its customers.[16] When brands embrace social CRM, they use social media as it was meant to be used. Why do we make this claim? Just as we learned that earned media can be garnered from creative and interactive social messages, companies that do a good job at maintaining strong brand to customer relationships will benefit from earned media, as those customers share information and recommendations with their networks.

It's ideal when all of our interactions with customers are positive. Unfortunately, things sometimes go wrong. When they do, today's social consumers won't hesitate to share their nasty experiences with others on social platforms. They'll vent their frustrations in the most public of ways. A great example is the sad story of one man's plane trip that resulted in a busted guitar that went viral on YouTube (United Breaks Guitars video on YouTube).[17] After he tried unsuccessfully to get United Airlines to repair or replace his guitar, this disgruntled passenger created his own version of the story and set it to music—the video he uploaded about his experience was viewed nearly 10 million times. Obviously this was not a happy event for the airline. This illustration of the potential negative impact on a firm's image underscores how important it is for organizations to take customers' complaints seriously (especially those who are inclined to post about their experiences). It is also vital to have a plan in place to initiate **service recovery** when things do go wrong (and they will). This term refers to the actions an organization takes to correct mishaps and win back dissatisfied customers.[18] One helpful set of guidelines that some companies use is known as the **LARA framework**:[19]

- **Listen** to customer conversations.
- **Analyze** those conversations.
- **Relate** this information to existing information within your enterprise.
- **Act** on those customer conversations.

Service recovery typically has to happen quickly if it's going to have any impact. A firm that can identify a problem in the system (e.g., a product recall, a snowstorm that will ground flights) can nip it in the bud by letting customers know that it's aware of the issue and is taking steps to address it. That's a big reason why social media can play such a big role in CRM: The platforms they can use allow them to communicate quickly and efficiently to large groups of customers or to customize messages to individuals who require follow-up. For example, companies such as Carphone Warehouse, Zappos, Best Buy, and Comcast have turned to Twitter to conduct their social CRM: They can monitor trending topics and preempt problems if they find that a lot of people are tweeting about them (in a bad way). If necessary they can send their own tweets to explain what happened and provide solutions.

Marketing Research   Social media opens exciting new windows for marketing research. Whether collecting insights for the discovery stage of the creative process or gathering ideas for new product development, social media provide new tools to listen to customers as they discuss their lives, interests, needs, and wants. And, organizations can crowdsource their problems; they can ask the market to assist them in solving problems, creating ads, and developing new products. Which channels of social media are relevant for social media market research? Potentially all of them, but profile data, activities, and content shared in social communities and content shared via social publishing vehicles are especially valuable for researchers.

Retailing and E-Commerce   The last major application for social media marketing is that of retailing and e-commerce. We've already shared ways that brands can incent trial and purchase using social media promotions. If you are like most consumers, you've used your share of online ratings and reviews before you made a purchase decision. But did you know that you can go shopping in social storefronts or shop on e-commerce sites that enable real-time chat with your friends? That's right. Groups of friends can shop together even when everyone is online—and not necessarily in the same physical location. When brands use social media marketing as a retailing space, create a venue for and/or encourage consumer reviews and ratings of products, and enable applications that help friends shop together online, we're solidly in the social commerce zone.

Social Media Jobs

Now you've seen how social channels are used by people and businesses. As organizations learn the value of social media for marketing, new jobs are developing to accommodate the need for skilled social media marketers. Interested? Consider the list of social media jobs in Table 3.

TABLE 3

Jobs in Social Media

Job Title	Job Duties
Social Media Editor	Build and maintain our content distribution network by way of social media channels.
	Participate in real-time conversations that surround our content and brand, answer comments, be a mediator.
	Create content for various social media and marketing channels that align with corporate communications goals and calendars.
	Schedule and organize multiple projects that generate content on a daily basis.
	Tag and title content, with an understanding of how the words chosen impact natural search traffic and rankings via recurrent optimized content.
Social Media Marketing Manager	Create and execute social media marketing campaigns.
	Analyze trends in social media tools to increase the use of social media directing consumers to our sites.
	Strategize with marketing team to include and utilize social media as an alternative marketing tool.
Marketing and Communications Associate	Manage key strategic messages, ensuring precise coordination with mission, vision, and positioning. Ensure accuracy, timeliness, and consistency of tone. Integrate messages into all communication formats with particular emphasis on social media and the website.
Project Social Media Manager	Manage the strategy, planning, and execution of the social media initiatives of the brand.
	Work interdepartmentally to select, develop, and promote social content and experiences.
	Consistently report on performance metrics of social media initiatives.
	Monitor and respond to the fan community, as appropriate.

(continued)

TABLE 3

Continued

Job Title	Job Duties
	Optimize the fan experience across social platforms.
	Assist in the continued development of social media strategy.
	Help educate other departments throughout the company on social media.
Social Media Communications Manager	Build and maintain all social media platforms, including Facebook, Twitter, and new/emerging platforms such as location-based social media.
	Establish and grow relationships with key influencers in the digital space, such as bloggers, highly followed personalities, influential YouTube reviewers, etc.
	Lead all digital outreach efforts behind key efforts such as new apps, new original series, priority entertainment verticals, etc.
	Manage all communications with PR team and agency.
	Build and manage Brand Ambassador program.
	On an ongoing basis, measure and report performance of all marketing activities and assess against goals, identify trends and insights, and optimize plan based on these insights.
Social Media Coordinator	Support the day-to-day management and execution of the social media initiatives of the brand.
	Assist in the promotion and development of social content and experiences.
	Handle data entry and tracking of the performance metrics of social media initiatives.
	Monitor and respond to the fan community, as appropriate.
	Support the optimization of the fan experience across social platforms.
Online Communications and Social Media Director	Drive high-profile social media strategies to raise visibility and buzz for the company's major business initiatives, products, and services.
	Develop and implement strategies for the company's official social media channels and platforms.
	Manage PR and social media agencies and vendors to maximize results.
	Shape the company's approach to social media in the short and long term while educating and counseling colleagues, business units, and leaders on social media opportunities, best practices, and key learnings.
	Serve as an external spokesperson and official company representative both for press and within social media channels engaging with bloggers, customers, partners, and prospects on an ongoing basis.

Job Title	Job Duties
	Develop and nurture relationships with relevant consumer and industry media and influencers.
	Analyze online buzz and discussions as well as emerging social media tools and platforms to develop innovative ideas, programs, and appropriate messaging/response.
	Work with brand marketing teams, legal, business units, and corporate affairs colleagues.
Social Media Communications Specialist	Develop social media strategies and plans to integrate into marketing mix; perform continual updates and adjust plans accordingly to meet business needs.
	Maintain internal communications calendar to consistently deliver new dynamic content to consumers throughout the year.
	Work with cross-functional teams to deliver a consistent brand voice and message across all social media platforms (e.g. Twitter, Facebook, YouTube, blog posts).
	Strategize and collaborate with creative team to incorporate captivating social networking features into design templates and content, with distribution through various channels (blog posts, viral video campaigns).
	Research and advise creative team and communications team on trends and best practices involving new media and communications tools.
	Build and maintain content distribution lists by way of social media channels.
	Contribute to public relations activities and efforts by monitoring news on social networks; assist with producing reports of results.
	Compile key metric reports (e.g., tonality, number of fans and followers) on a monthly/quarterly basis that measure effectiveness on social media platforms including competitors.
	Establish an implementation strategy for leveraging third-party content to enrich the overall user experience and keep the community fresh for frequent visitors.
	Generate titling of content and tags; optimize tags on feeds to include shared sites, search engines, and keyword optimization; understand how words chosen impact natural search traffic and rankings via recurrent optimized content.
	Train customer service representatives on how to respond to customer service issues via Twitter; monitor quality of responses and provide guidance on best practices.
Social Media Intern	Construct and implement social media strategy for the brands' Facebook, Twitter, and YouTube accounts, which will include editorial management and development, blogging, posting, and monitoring website user-generated activity, user experience optimization, and potential development and management of third-party relationships.
Social Media Strategist	Drive strategy, planning, and execution of social media strategies to increase brand visibility, reputation, engagement, and social footprint.

(continued)

TABLE 3

Continued

Job Title	Job Duties
	Develop innovative, comprehensive, and actionable approach for establishing and expanding presence on social networks and perform day-to-day tasks including listening, brand monitoring, social activities, and competitive research.
	Conduct research, monitor, and provide recommendations to enhance social presence and customer engagement.

Source: Used by permission of SimplyHired.com.

Chapter Summary

What are social media? How are social media similar to traditional media?

Social media are the online means of communication, conveyance, collaboration, and cultivation among interconnected and interdependent networks of people, communities, and organizations enhanced by technological capabilities and mobility. Like traditional media, social media include several channels, and within each channel there are specific vehicles. For example, television is a broadcast media and *The Today Show* is a vehicle within the medium of television. Social communities are a channel of social media and LinkedIn is a vehicle.

What are the major zones associated with social media?

The major channels of social media include social communities, social publishing, social entertainment, and social commerce. Each channel incorporates networking, communication functionality, and sharing among connected people, but they each have a different focus. Communities are focused on relationships. Publishing features the sharing and promotion of content. Entertainment channels are geared to fun and shared uses of social media. Commerce addresses the shopping functionality of social media applications.

What is Web 2.0, and what are its defining characteristics? How does Web 2.0 add value to Web 1.0?

Web 1.0 provided Internet users with easy access to information, entertainment, and communications tools, but in many ways it was akin to shifting existing programming from traditional media like television broadcasts and magazines to new media online. There were benefits to consumers, but Web 2.0 fundamentally changed the consumers' role as well as the role of providers in delivery information, entertainment, and communications tools. Web 2.0 adds value because it ramps up what we called the "Fifth P") of marketing: participation. When consumes engage in an ongoing dialogue with other people and with companies their stake in the process increases—this results in more satisfying outcomes for producers and customers. Tim O'Reilly, a leader in technology innovations, defined Web 2.0 as developments in online technology that make interactive possible as it offers users control, freedom, and the ability to participate in a dialogue. Several characteristics support the meaning of what is Web 2.0: (1) Web as platform, (2) user participation and crowdsourcing, (3) user-defined content, (4) network effects, (5) scalability, (6) perpetual beta, and (7) the reputation economy.

How does the Social Media Value Chain explain the relationships among the Internet, social media channels, social software, and the Internet-enabled devices we use for access and participation? In what activities do individuals participate using social media?

The Social Media Value Chain explains that social media is made up of core activities and supporting components. The core activities include the things people do with social media such as converse, share, post, tag, upload content, comment, and so on. The support components include the Web 2.0 infrastructure, social media channels, social software, and the devices we use to interact with social media.

What is social media marketing?

Social media marketing is the use of social media to facilitate exchanges between consumers and organizations. It's valuable to marketers because it provides inexpensive access to consumers and a variety of ways to interact and engage consumers at different points in the purchase cycle.

What marketing objectives can organizations meet when they incorporate social media in their marketing mix?

There are several marketing objectives achievable utilizing social media marketing techniques. Branding and promotion, research, and customer service and relationship management objectives are all viable using social media.

Key Terms

advertising
apps
blogs
business model
cloud computing
connections
crowdsourcing
deal aggregators
deal sites
devices
digital native
display ad
earned media
entertainment communities
Facebook Connect
forums
horizontal revolution
interruption-disruption model
LARA framework
marketing
media
media sharing sites
medium

message boards
microblogging sites
micromarkets
microshare
microsharing sites
monetization strategy
network effect
niche products
owned media
paid media
perpetual beta
psychic income
public relations
radical trust
reputation economy
revenue stream
reviews and ratings
sampling
scalability
search advertising
search engine marketing (SEM)
social commerce
social entertainment

social games
social identity
social media
social media marketing
Social Media Value Chain
social networking sites
social presence
social services
social shopping markets
social software
social storefronts
social utility
tag cloud
tags
taxonomies
tradigital marketing
vehicles (media)
virtual worlds
widgets
wikis
word-of-mouth (WOM)
    communication

Review Questions

1. How do you define social media? Social media marketing?
2. What are the supporting components of the Social Media Value Chain?
3. Identify the characteristics of Web 2.0.
4. What is the meaning of crowdsourcing?
5. Explain the difference between a taxonomy and a folksonomy. What role does tagging play in creating folksonomies?
6. What does perpetual beta mean for software users?
7. What are the implications of the radical trust adopted by organizations using social media?
8. What are the four zones of social media? How do social media compare to traditional media?
9. Explain the concept of psychic income.
10. What are the characteristics of social ads?
11. How can brands use social media to develop earned media value?
12. What is social CRM? How is it different from traditional CRM?

Exercises

1. What is a monetization strategy? Visit Twitter.com and explain how Twitter monetizes its business. Do the same for FourSquare.
2. Replicate the University of Maryland study discussed in the "The Dark Side of Social Media" feature. Abstain from all social media for 24 hours. That's right—no texting, no e-mailing, no Facebook. Keep a record of your unwired day and then produce a blog post about your experience.
3. Should online services like Facebook and Google Docs be free? Poll your classmates and friends (including your social network) to find out what they think should be free. Use an online tool such as PollDaddy or SurveyMonkey to conduct your poll. What do the results say about the possible monetization strategies available to social media providers?
4. Create an account at About.Me or Flavors.Me. Your account will serve as the basis for your social footprint. Begin to link your existing social media accounts to your footprint page. Identify other social communities in which you should develop profiles.

Notes

1. Marc Prensky, "Digital Natives, Digital Immigrants," *On the Horizon* 9, no. 5 (October 2001): 1-6.
2. There are several definitions of social media proposed by experts in the field. In preparing this definition, we've aggregated the most commonly referenced characteristics of social media and also sought to align the definition with those of traditional media.
3. Facebook statistics, www.Facebook.com/press/info.php?statistics, accessed November 15, 2010.
4. Chloe Albanesius, "YouTube Users Uploading 35 Hours of Video Every Minute," *PCMag.com*, November 11, 2010, www.pcmag.com/article2/0,2817,2372511,00.asp, accessed November 15, 2010.
5. The Free Dictionary, www.thefreedictionary.com/medium, accessed.
6. Tim O'Reilly, "What is Web 2.0?" *O'Reilly Media*, September 30, 2005, http://oreilly.com/web2/archive/what-is-web-20.html, accessed December 31, 2010.
7. Facebook statistics, www.Facebook.com/press/info.php?statistics, accessed November 21, 2010.
8. "Center Tries to Treat Web Addicts," *New York Times,* September 5, 2009, www.nytimes.com/2009/09/06/us/06internet.html, accessed May 13, 2010.
9. Quoted in Jenna Johnson, "Fighting a Social Media Addiction," *Washington Post,* April 26, 2010, http://voices.washingtonpost .com/campus-overload/2010/04/fighting_a_social_media_addict .html, accessed May 13, 2010.
10. American Marketing Association, "Definition of Marketing," www. marketingpower.com/aboutama/pages/definitionofmarketing.aspx, accessed December 31, 2010.
11. Shiv Singh, "Social Influence Marketing Trends for 2010," January 21, 2010, www.slideshare.net/shivsingh/social-influence-marketing-trends-2967561?from=ss_embed, accessed December 31, 2010.
12. Jennifer Van Grove, "Twitter and Foursquare Become the New

Loyalty Program at Tasti D-Lite," *Mashable*, January 13, 2010, http://mashable.com/2010/01/13/tasti-d-lite-tastirewards/, accessed September 7, 2010.

13. Stephanie Clifford, "Video Prank at Domino's Taints Brand," *New York Times*, April 16, 2009, http://www.nytimes.com/2009/04/16/business/media/16dominos.html, accessed September 7, 2010.

14. Kipp Bodnar, "B2B Social Media Lessons from Domino's Pizza Turnaround Campaign, Social Media B2B," January 4, 2010, http://socialmediab2b.com/2010/01/dominos-pizza-turnaround-campaign/#ixzz0ysPSdwLd, accessed September 7, 2010.

15. "Domino's Pizza Continuing Transparency ... This Time Through Photography," *PR Newswire*, July 5, 2010, www.prnewswire.com/ dominos-pizza-continuing-transparency, accessed September 7, 2010.

16. Michael Fauscette, "What Is 'Social' CRM Anyway?" January 26, 2009, www.mfauscette.com/software_technology_partn/2009/01/what-is-social-crm-anyway.html, accessed September 8, 2010.

17. Josh Bernoff, *Empowered* (Cambridge, MA: Harvard Business Press, 2010).

18. Maria Ogneva, "Why Your Company Needs to Embrace Social CRM," *Mashable*, May 21, 2010, http://mashable.com/2010/05/21/social-crm/, accessed September 7, 2010.

19. Maria Ogneva, "Why Your Company Needs to Embrace Social CRM," *Mashable*, May 21, 2010, http://mashable.com/2010/05/21/social-crm/, accessed September 7, 2010.

Strategic Planning with Social Media

From Chapter 2 of *Social Media Marketing*, First Edition. Tracy L. Tuten, Michael R. Solomon.
Copyright © 2013 by Pearson Education, Inc. All rights reserved.

Strategic Planning with Social Media

LearningObjectives

When you finish reading this chapter you will be able to answer these questions:

1 Where does social media marketing planning fit into an organization's overall planning framework?

2 What are the three phases of social media marketing maturity? How does social media marketing change for companies as they shift from the trial phase to the transition phase and eventually move into the strategic phase?

3 What are the steps in social media marketing strategic planning?

4 What are the characteristics of good strategic marketing objectives?

5 How does a social consumer profile differ from other content a campaign team needs to understand its target market?

6 How can organizations structure themselves to support social media marketing?

7 What are the key components of an organizational social media policy, and why is it important to have such a policy in place?

GO

Learning
Objective 1

Wherever this icon
appears in the margin,
please go to the
website **www.zonesofsmm.com**
for an example of the topic
discussed.

Strategic Planning and Social Media Marketing

GM's Buick division is buying into social media, big time. When the company introduced its new Regal model in 2010, it strategically utilized several different social media tools and coordinated these with more traditional tactics to maximize the campaign's impact. Its slick website, MomentOfTruth.com, provides real-time commentary on its latest car. The site scours the Web for anything people post about the Regal, filters out the bad words, and reprints commentary on a 3D billboard that displays YouTube videos, Flickr photos, tweets, comments from the car's Facebook wall, and experts' blogs.

Buick promotes this collection of social media outputs with digital advertising and public relations efforts. It advertises on car enthusiast sites and on social networks such as LinkedIn to reach opinion leaders. Buick is further integrating the campaign as it runs TV commercials that include the site's URL so that people who are actively shopping for a new car will check it out.[1]

For marketers like those at Buick, **strategic planning** is the process of identifying objectives to accomplish, deciding how to accomplish those objectives with specific strategies and tactics, implementing the actions that make the plan come to life, and measuring how well the plan met the objectives. The process of strategic planning is three-tiered, beginning at the corporate level, then moving to the business level, and lastly moving to the functional areas of the organization, including marketing. Planners first identify their overall objectives (e.g., "raise consumer awareness of our brand by 10 percent in the next year") and then develop the specific tactics they will use to reach those goals (e.g., "increase our spending on print advertising in targeted publications by 15 percent this year"). A **marketing plan** is a written, formalized plan that details the product, pricing, distribution, and promotional strategies that will enable the brand in question to accomplish specific marketing objectives. Figure 1 provides a sample of an overall marketing plan structure.

On second thought, what's wrong with jumping right into the game? Why should we take the time to plan? Although it's tempting to just follow our instincts, it turns out there is tremendous value in planning. Dumb luck and sweat takes you only so far. Planning ensures that an organization understands its markets and its competitors. It helps to ensure that organizations are aware of the changing marketplace environment. When organizational partners participate in the planning process, they are better able to communicate and coordinate activities. Planning requires that objectives are set and agreed upon, which improves the likelihood of those objectives being met. It enhances the ability of managers to allocate

Figure 1

The Structure of a Typical Marketing Plan

The Marketing Plan OUTLINE	QUESTIONS the Plan Addresses
A. PERFORM A SITUATION ANALYSIS 1. Internal Environment	• How does marketing support my company's mission, objectives, and growth strategies? • What is the corporate culture and how does it influence marketing activities? • What has my company done in the past with its: Target markets? Products? Pricing? Promotion? Supply chain? • What resources including management expertise does my company have that make us unique? How has the company added value through its offerings in the past?
2. External Environment	• What is the nature of the overall domestic and global market for our product? How big is the market? Who buys our product? • Who are our competitors? What are their marketing strategies? • What are the key trends in the economic environment? The technological environment? The regulatory environment? The social and cultural environment?

(continued)

31

Figure 1

Continued

The Marketing Plan OUTLINE	QUESTIONS the Plan Addresses
3. SWOT Analysis	• Based on this analysis of the internal and external environments, what are the key Strengths, Weaknesses, Opportunities, and Threats (SWOT)?
B. SET MARKETING OBJECTIVES	• What does marketing need to accomplish to support the objectives of my firm?
C. DEVELOP MARKETING STRATEGIES 1. Select Target Markets and Positioning	• How do consumers and organizations go about buying, using, and disposing of our products? • Which segments should we select to target? If a consumer market: What are the relevant demographic, psychographic, and behavioral segmentation approaches and the media habits of the targeted segments? if a business market: What are the relevant organizational demographics? • How will we position our product for our market(s)?
2. Product Strategies	• What is our core product? Actual product? Augmented product? • What product line/product mix strategies should we use? • How should we package, brand, and label our product? • How can attention to service quality enhance our success?
3. Pricing Strategies	• How will we price our product to the consumer and through the channel? How much must we sell to break-even at this price? What pricing tactics should we use?
4. Promotional Strategies	• How do we develop a consistent message about our product? How do we best generate buzz? • What approaches to advertising, public relations, sales promotion, and newer forms of communication (such as social networking) should we use? • What role should a sales force play in the marketing communications plan? How should direct marketing be used?
5. Supply Chain Strategies	• How do we get our product to consumers in the best and most efficient manner? • What types of retailers, if any should we work with to sell our product? • How do we integrate supply chain elements to maximize the value we offer to our customers and other stakeholders?
D. IMPLEMENT AND CONTROL THE MARKETING PLAN 1. Action Plans (for all marketing mix elements)	• How do we make our marketing plan happen?
2. Responsibility	• Who is responsible for accomplishing each aspect of implementing the marketing plan?
3. Time line	• What is the timing for the elements of our marketing plan?
4. Budget	• What budget do we need to accomplish our marketing objectives?
5. Measurement and Control	• How do we measure the actual performance of our marketing plan and compare it to our planned performance and progress toward reaching our marketing objectives?

limited resources using established priorities. Perhaps most of all, planning enables success to be defined. Success or the lack thereof becomes a measurable outcome that can guide future planning efforts.

It's increasingly common for organizations to include a heavy dose of social media in their marketing plans. One recent survey of Canadian executives reported that 90 percent (yes, 90 percent) use social media to communicate with customers. One in five respondents went so far as to say they now consider social media the "most important means for communicating with the public"—beating out broadcast media, email, regular mail, and the telephone. Another survey of executives worldwide found that over half now use social media to maintain contact with their customers.[2] This upward trend will continue in the coming years.

It makes sense to include social media marketing in a brand's marketing plan. Social media can be a delivery tool to build buzz and word of mouth communication. It can efficiently deliver coupons and other special promotional offers. Social platforms can be the primary venue for the execution of contests and sweepstakes. They can collect data to build databases and to generate sales leads. Social media also can serve as an efficient channel to manage customer service relationships and to conduct research for new product development.

Because the creative applications related to social media are somewhat unique, we will suggest an approach for developing an in-depth social media marketing strategy much as advertising plans (also known as **integrated marketing communications (IMC) plans** or **marcom plans**) provide in-depth detail on the execution of the (traditional) promotional portion of a brand's marketing plan. Figure 2 provides the structure of a social media marketing plan. We'll begin this process as we explore the strategic development of social media marketing plans. Then we'll cover the steps in strategic planning for social media marketing. Finally, we'll discuss structural approaches organizations can take to be prepared to execute their plans.

Figure 2	**The Social Media Marketing Plan Outline**

A Social Media Marketing Plan	**I. Conduct a situation analysis and identify key opportunities**
	   1. Internal Environment
	     a. What activities exist in the overall marketing plan that can be leveraged for social media marketing?
	     b. What is the corporate culture? Is it supportive of the transparent and decentralized norms of social media?
	     c. What resources exist that can be directed to social media activities?
	     d. Is the organization already prepared internally for social media activities (in terms of policies and procedures)?
	   2. External Environment
	     a. Who are our customers? Are they users of social media?
	     b. Who are our competitors? What social media activities are they using and how is social media incorporated in their marketing and promotional plans?
	     c. What are the key trends in the environment (social, cultural, legal and regulatory, political, economic, and technological) that may affect our decisions regarding social media marketing?
	   3. SWOT Analysis
	     a. Based on the analysis, what are the key strengths, weaknesses, opportunities, and threats (SWOT)?
	
	 II. State objectives
	   1. What does the organization expect to accomplish through social media marketing? (promotional objectives, service objectives, retail objectives, research objectives)

(continued)

Figure 2

Continued

III. **Gather insight into target audience**
  1. Which segments should we select to target with social media activities?
  2. What are the relevant demographic, psychographic, and behavioral characteristics of the segments useful in planning a social media marketing strategy?
  3. What are the media habits, and especially the social media habits of the segments?

IV. **Select social media zones and vehicles**
  Which mix of the four zones of social media will be best to accomplish our objectives within the resources available?
  1. Social community zone strategies
     a. What approach to social networking and relationship building should we use? How will we represent the brand in social networks (as a corporate entity, as a collection of corporate leadership, as a brand character)? What content will we share in this space?
  2. Social publishing zone strategies
     a. What content do we have to share with audiences? Can we develop a sufficient amount of fresh, valuable content to attract audiences to consume content online?
     b. What form should our blog take?
     c. Which media sharing sites should we use to publish content? How should we build links between our social media sites, owned media sites, and affiliates to optimize our sites for search engines?
  3. Social entertainment zone strategies
     a. What role should social entertainment play in our social media plan? Are there opportunities to develop a customized social game or to promote the brand as a product placement in other social games? Is there an opportunity to utilize social entertainment sites such as MySpace as an entertainment venue?
  4. Social commerce zone strategies
     a. How can we develop opportunities for customer reviews and ratings that add value to our prospective customers?
     b. Should we develop retail spaces within social media sites? If we socially enhance our own e-retailing spaces, what applications should be used?
     c. How can we utilize social commerce applications like group deals to increase conversions?

V. **Create an experience strategy encompassing selected zones**
  1. How can we develop social media activities that support and/or extend our existing promotional strategies?
  2. What message do we want to share using social media?
  3. How can we encourage engagement with the brand in social spaces?
  4. How can we encourage those who engage with the brand socially to act as opinion leaders and share the experience with others?
  5. In what ways can we align the zones used as well as other promotional tools to support each other? Can we incorporate social reminders in advertising messages, in store displays, and other venues?

VI. **Establish an activation plan**
  1. How do we make the plan happen?
  2. Who is responsible for each aspect of implementing the plan?
  3. What is the timing of the elements in the plan?
  4. What budget do we need to accomplish the objectives?
  5. How do we ensure that the plan is consistent with the organization's overall marketing plan and promotional plan?

VII. **Manage and measure**
  1. How do we measure the actual performance of the plan?

Three Phases of Social Media Marketing Maturity

Learning
Objective 2

If you keep up with industry news, you might be tempted to think that *every* brand has a social media strategy. Each day seems to bring new stories about a marketing campaign with social media elements. On ads, storefronts, and business cards, we see "Follow me" calls to action as organizations large and small flock to Twitter and Facebook.

Although it seems everyone is talking about social media, it's one thing to claim you *use* social media and quite another to say you have a *strategy* that incorporates social media. In the former case, a group can turn to social media activities to stage **stunts** (one-off ploys designed to get attention and press coverage) or as **activation tools** to support other marketing efforts. For example, when Skittles let its social media presence take over its website, that was a stunt. But when Starbucks runs social media promotions, it integrates these promotions with the overall campaign in place.

As organizations develop in their **social media marketing maturity**, they plan systematically to ensure social media marketing activities are consistent with their marketing and marketing communications plans and are capable of meeting specific marketing objectives. By this we mean that as a result of time and experience we tend to see that applications that start as one-time "experiments" often morph into more long-term and carefully thought-out elements that the organization integrates with all the other communication pieces it uses to reach customers.

However, many marketers currently use social media marketing tactics without that level of maturity. A major study of marketers in both Europe and North America found huge differences in the level to which respondents use social media and integrate it with their other initiatives. Many still just experiment with baby steps (like creating a Facebook page) rather than include social media as a fundamental component of their marketing strategy.[3] Figure 3 illustrates just how varied these efforts are.

Companies are eager to jump into the social media game, but many are still in the process of figuring out just how these approaches can go beyond the novelty stage and actually help them to meet their objectives. That's the key message in a recent report from marketing research firm Marketing Sherpa. Its 2010 *Social Media Marketing Benchmarking Report* surveyed 2,300 marketers. The findings suggest that marketers are spread among three phases (trial, transition, and strategic) of social media marketing adoption. In 2010, 40 percent of the organizations included in Marketing Sherpa's study reported that their social media activities resided in the transition phase. Thirty three percent acknowledged they were experimenting in the trial phase, and 23 percent were advancing, learning and adapting towards the strategic phase. Marketing Sherpa calls this a social media marketing maturity life cycle, and as we can see in Figure 4 it looks a lot like a traditional product life cycle. Let's take a closer look at each phase.

Trial Phase   The **trial phase** is the first phase of the adoption cycle. Organizations in the trial phase test out social media platforms, but they don't really consider how social media can play a role in the overall marketing plan. In these early days, most groups focus on learning to use a new form of communication and exploring the potential for social media as a venue.

It isn't necessarily a bad thing to test the waters of social media. Companies need, especially early on, to experiment—to play in the sandbox, so to speak. Doing so helps them to brainstorm ideas to use social media and understand what it takes to succeed in this brave new world. However, the problem with the trial phase is that many companies do not treat it as an exploratory stage of what is really a multi-stage process. Instead they just jump right in and only focus on cool new ways to communicate.

Pizza Hut is one example of a company that initially focused on a platform rather than a strategy. The company published a press release announcing a new job opening for a "Twitern"—an intern

Figure 3

**Social Media
Marketing
Activities**

Source: Used by permission
of Marketing Sherpa.

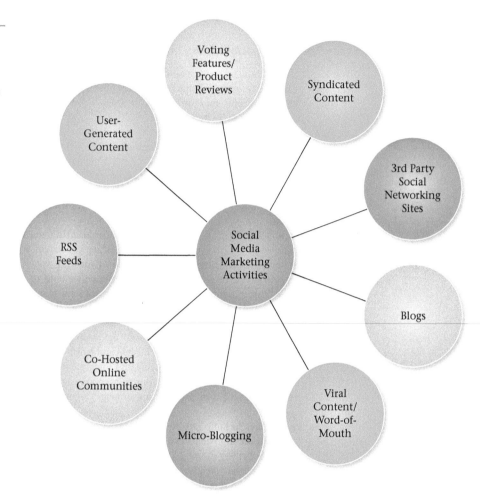

Figure 4

**Maturity Lifecycle
for Social Media
Marketing**

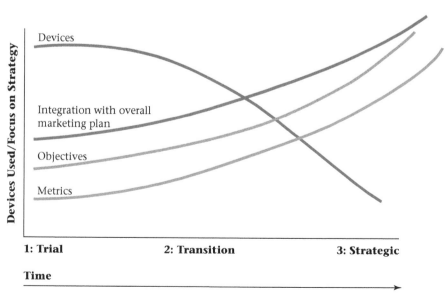

who would manage the brand's Twitter presence. Creating a job to manage a brand's social media presence could be a strategic thing to do. But in this case, Pizza Hut used the press release as a stunt to make fun of the acronyms twitterers commonly use. The ploy to be seen as a hip, Twitter-aware brand got Pizza Hut named as one of the nine worst social media mistakes of 2009 by the well-known blogger @MediaPhyter (aka Jennifer Leggio). Thousands upon thousands of brands have Facebook pages and Twitter accounts—many of them abandoned. Why? They were created during a trial phase that never developed into the next stage.

Transition Phase   As organizations mature in their use of social media marketing, they enter a **transition phase**. During this phase, social media activities still occur somewhat randomly or haphazardly but a more systematic way of thinking starts to develop within the organization. As Marketing Sherpa learned, the majority of organizations are in a transition phase.

The Beall's chain of Florida department stores is typical of a company in transition. The retailer operates over 80 brick-and-mortar locations. In the caveman days of, say, 2005, here's how Beall's would have built a campaign to promote its retail outlets: The chain used traditional advertising methods including print ads, radio and television commercials, and online advertising. It would publish notices of seasonal sales and coupons in the Sunday newspaper display ads or in circulars inserted in the paper. Its website would feature on-sale brands, particularly those for which the brand earned cooperative advertising dollars from the manufacturers.

This site was pretty sophisticated for the time; it invited visitors to shop online so they could order much of the same merchandise they saw on store shelves from the comfort of home. Beall's would run display ads that rotated on Internet portals such as Yahoo! while other popular websites routed traffic to the store's website. Advertising sought to drive **traffic** to the chain's physical locations and websites (advertisers use the term *traffic* to mean consumers who visit a client, not cars that drive there). Like other department store chains, Beall's employed additional marketing elements such as captivating in-store merchandising (e.g., stylishly dressed mannequins), competitive pricing, and in-store sales associates to drive sales. Beall's also had a public relations initiative to ensure that local newspapers featured specific stores when they ran news stories on fashion trends and community events.

Fast forward to today. Beall's embraces social media to communicate with its core audience of female shoppers. The company recently hired a social media director and revamped the entire way it relates to customers. Despite its geographic limits in terms of store locations, Beall's targets customers who live well beyond its home state of Florida. Even though it doesn't operate any stores outside the state, the retailer boasts a loyal national following because of its dynamic e-commerce site at www.bealls.com.

But Beall's goes well beyond traditional e-commerce strategies to reach its base. A major component of its promotional efforts is its Facebook fan page. It's updated several times a day and includes many multimedia components such as commercials and fan videos. Beall's uses social media as a sales promotion delivery channel; each day the company posts Facebook fan coupons online so that followers can print them and share them with their networks. To get a good snapshot of how the company utilizes social media tools, see Figure 5. As Beall's strategy matures, its social media footprint will probably expand, much as yours will. Where in the social space should Beall's expand next? Perhaps a YouTube Florida Fashion channel? A virtual department store in Second Life? An iPad app?

Strategic Phase   When an organization enters the final **strategic phase**, it utilizes a formal process to plan social media marketing activities with clear objectives and metrics. Social media are now integrated as a key component of the organization's overall marketing plan. Paint company Benjamin Moore is one of the few firms that has entered the strategic phase. As we move forward we'll share insights from Benjamin Moore's social media campaign to show why.

Figure 5

Beall's Social Media Mix

For a regional retailer, Beall's has established a strong presence in social media, boasting nearly 50,000 fans on Facebook. Facebook and the BeallsFlorida.com website serve as Bealls' social media hubs, connecting activities across online channels.

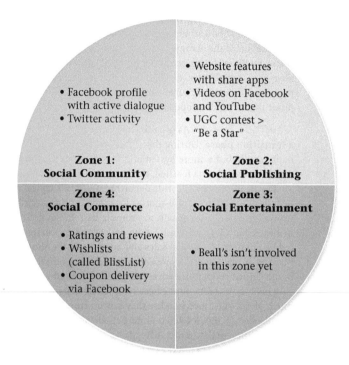

Zone 1:
Social Community

- Facebook profile with active dialogue
- Twitter activity

Zone 2:
Social Publishing

- Website features with share apps
- Videos on Facebook and YouTube
- UGC contest > "Be a Star"

Zone 4:
Social Commerce

- Ratings and reviews
- Wishlists (called BlissList)
- Coupon delivery via Facebook

Zone 3:
Social Entertainment

- Beall's isn't involved in this zone yet

Learning Objective 3

Social Media Campaigns: The Strategic Planning Process

Those organizations that have moved beyond the trial and transition phases of social media marketing maturity develop strategic plans for social media that incorporate components of the social media mix as channels to accomplish marketing objectives. As we saw in Figure 2, the process consists of the following steps:

- Conduct a situation analysis and identify key opportunities.
- State objectives.
- Gather insight into and target one or more segments of social consumers.
- Select the social media channels and vehicles.
- Create an experience strategy.
- Establish an activation plan using other promotional tools (if needed).
- Execute and measure the campaign.

Situation Analysis

The first step in developing the plan is much the same as it is in the creation of traditional strategic plans—research and assess the environment. Good social media planning starts with research on the industry and competitors, the product category, and the consumer market. Once this research is compiled, strategists try to make sense of the findings as they analyze the data in a **situation analysis**.

The situation analysis details the current problem or opportunity the organization faces; it often includes a **SWOT analysis** to highlight relevant aspects of the firm's internal and external environment that could affect the organization's choices, capabilities, and resources. This acronym refers to *strengths, weaknesses, opportunities*, and *threats* that the firm should consider as it crafts a strategy. The **internal environment** refers to the strengths and weaknesses of the organization—the controllable elements inside a firm that influence how well the firm operates. The **external environment** consists of those elements outside the organization—the organization's opportunities and threats—that may affect its choices and capabilities. Unlike elements of the internal environment that management can control to a large degree, the firm can't directly control these external factors, so management must respond to them through its planning process.

A key aspect of the external environment is the brand's competition. Analyzing competitive social media efforts and how the target market perceives those efforts is a must-do in social media marketing planning. You can use an internal system or a **cloud service** (a social software service offered online "in the cloud") such as RivalMap (www.rivalmap.com) to organize competitive information and to monitor news and social activity. When you use RivalMap, you can maintain a search of competitive activity and news mentions online for a small fee.

A competitive social media analysis should answer the following questions:[4]

- In which social media channels and specific vehicles are competitors active?
- How do they present themselves in those channels and vehicles? Include an analysis of profiles, company information provided, tone, and activity.
- Who are their fans and followers? How do fans and followers respond to the brand's social activity?

Importantly, marketers have many approaches to solving problems and taking advantage of opportunities. Here we are concerned with the organization's use of social media, but still, the planner should ask the question, "Given the situation and the problem identified, is social media marketing the appropriate approach?" Especially for organizations that are still in the trial phase, it's tempting to focus on social media "gimmicks" even if other less trendy tactics might in fact be more effective. So, a word of caution: Social media often provides effective solutions to marketing problems, but beware of blindly using these tools. In other words, don't be "a hammer in search of a nail!"

 # THE DARK SIDE OF SOCIAL MEDIA

As is true with other marketing activities, understanding the external environment includes a consideration of how the theme or outcome of a social media campaign might resonate with broader issues in a culture—either positively or negatively. The viral nature of some social media vehicles means they have the potential to encourage copycat behavior on a huge scale in a very short time. Sometimes this means a campaign will backfire if some people feel it endorses actions that aren't in the best interests of participants.

Smirnoff encountered this problem when a drinking game called "icing" went viral. Although the company denies that it instigated the game, for a brief period in 2010 thousands of young people were "iced." Many college students were involved; celebrities such as the rapper Coolio, the actor Dustin Diamond, and members of the rock band The National also participated. The icing game is simple to play: Hand a friend a Smirnoff Ice malt beverage and he has to immediately drop to one knee and drink the whole bottle—unless he is carrying a bottle himself, in which case the attacker must drink both bottles. Amid much criticism for encouraging excessive drinking, Smirnoff's parent company Diageo stated, "Icing is consumer-generated, and some people think it is fun. We never want underage 'icing' and we always want responsible drinking." Although sales of Ice took off (especially among younger men) in the short-term, the fad put Diageo in a delicate position. No company—not even one that sells alcohol—wants to be seen as encouraging binge drinking.[5]

To see how the early stages of the strategic planning process work in the real world, let's return to our "poster child" for social media, Benjamin Moore & Co.[6] With a history going back to 1883, you might be tempted to think of the brand as old-school. Recognized as a manufacturer of high-quality premium paints and finishes, Benjamin Moore has weathered many changes in the "build" and "home improvement" industries. However, the recent past has been difficult for the brand as it faced a challenging external environment and limited internal resources for brand building. As the United States dealt with a debilitating housing and construction slump, sales of paints and finishes declined. Not only did demand fall, but buyers were more price-sensitive, eager to save money wherever possible as they scooped up cheaper paints at home improvement warehouses. As a premium paint brand, the company was hesitant to discount on price—though the leading competitor priced its product at $23 *less* per gallon.

To add salt to the wound, other premium paint brands had much bigger budgets for promotional spending. But here's a case where an apparent weakness presents an opportunity: Necessity is the mother of invention, as the saying goes. Because they had high budgets to buy advertising in traditional media, competitors had not yet tapped social media as a promotional channel. For instance, Duron Paint and Valspar both had Facebook pages, but both brands had under 200 friends and low levels of activity. Benjamin Moore's media budget was already a drop in the bucket compared to that of the competition, and its agency, Cramer-Krasselt, was tasked with a further reduced budget in 2010.

Although the external environment painted a dark picture, two bright spots stood out. First, design professionals adore Benjamin Moore. Open any issue of *House Beautiful, Southern Living*, or *Traditional Home* and you'll see Benjamin Moore paints featured time and time again. The brand had never used these features as a form of testimonial in its paid media, but it was a part of the brand's back story.

Second, end customers were fiercely loyal and highly vocal. Research into these two audiences revealed that Benjamin Moore was what some advertisers (particularly those at the Saatchi & Saatchi agency, where the term originated) called a **lovemark**—a brand that commanded passionate loyalty from its target market. Indeed, a study of design professionals showed that 80 percent would choose Benjamin Moore over any other paint. And, a study of conversations in social media spaces found that 95 percent of online conversations about Benjamin Moore were positive.

Table 1 illustrates a partial SWOT analysis for Benjamin Moore. Two important elements in the situation were a limited media budget combined with heavy media spends by the competition.

TABLE 1

Benjamin Moore's SWOT Analysis

Strengths:	Weaknesses:
• Loyal customers • High brand equity • Unsolicited testimonials from design community • Quality products • High levels of earned media in traditional media outlets	• High price point • Limited media budget
Opportunities:	**Threats:**
• Social media as a cost-efficient channel • Do-it-yourself mentality combined with fear of choosing the wrong color by end consumers • Competitors focused on traditional media or in trial stage of social media marketing	• Declining demand in hard-hit industries • Competition with large media budgets and lower-priced products

The Cramer-Krasselt team decided to counter these liabilities with a social media campaign that it hoped would leverage the client's strengths in terms of brand equity, and the potential to build a strong share of voice in social media channels. **Share of voice** is the percentage of advertising for a brand compared to competing brands.

Learning Objective **4**

Identify Social Media Marketing Objectives and Set Budgets

In this stage of the process, the planner elaborates on what is expected of the social media campaign and what financial and human resources are available to meet those objectives. An **objective** is a specific statement about a planned social media activity in terms of what that activity intends to accomplish. The content of the objective will vary based on the situation and the problem at hand. For instance, the campaign may be designed to amplify other marketing communication efforts the organization uses. Let's say, for example, the brand co-sponsors a concert series. This series is an event marketing strategy built into the overall marketing communications plan. But the organization realizes that promoting the event using social media can build pre- and post-event buzz. In this case, the objective (to create heightened awareness of the event among target customers) relates to other activities in the organization.

The basic assumption is that the campaign can accomplish desired marketing objectives. What are some examples of the basic marketing objectives social media marketers pursue? Here are some important ones:

- Increase brand awareness.
- Improve brand or product reputation.
- Increase website traffic.
- Amplify or augment public relations work.
- Improve search engine rankings.
- Improve perceived customer service quality.
- Generate sales leads.
- Reduce customer acquisition and support costs.
- Increase sales/sales revenue.

Figure 6 summarizes how social media can help to accomplish specific objectives, and it also illustrates that this effectiveness is influenced by the sophistication of the organization in terms of social media applications.

In this stage of planning, it's important to state the objectives in a way that will help the planner to make other decisions in the planning process and eventually to measure the extent to which the objective was accomplished at specific points into the campaign. A well-stated, actionable objective should include the following characteristics:

- Be specific (what, who when, where)
- Be measurable
- Specify the desired change (from a baseline)
- Include a time line
- Be consistent and realistic (given other corporate activities and resources)

Here's an example of an actionable objective: *To increase site stickiness in the retail areas of our site by 100 percent (from 5 minutes browsing to 10 minutes per site visit) with the addition of social commerce sharing applications by the end of the third quarter of 2012.* The statement of the objective should include specific elaboration on the individual goals the brand wishes to achieve over the course of the campaign, taking care to state these goals such that they are specific, measurable, realistic, and time-lined.

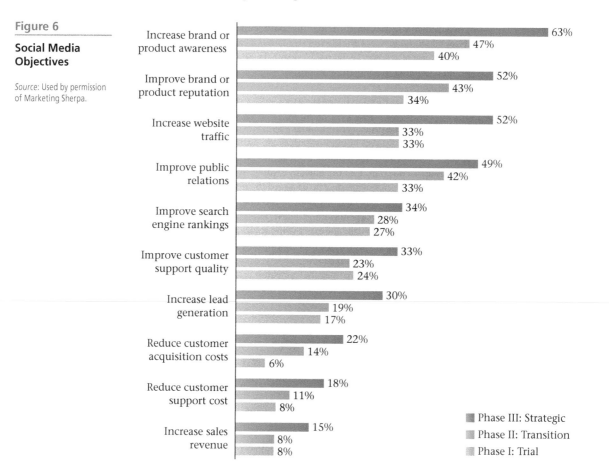

Figure 6

Social Media Objectives

Source: Used by permission of Marketing Sherpa.

Why the focus on resources? You've probably heard businesspeople say that the main benefit of social media marketing is that it's free. When brand managers work with agencies to plan traditional advertising campaigns, the cost of media placement can seem overwhelming. With that as a point of comparison, one can see why many might think of social media marketing as the free alternative to advertising.

There's just one problem: *Social media is not free.* In planning a social media campaign, a budget must be allocated that ensures sufficient resources to accomplish the goals—just like in a traditional ad program. Granted, the media costs often are much lower compared to, say, a national television campaign. But there are other costs associated with social media. Charlene Li, a leading social media strategist, once said, "Social media trades media costs for labor costs."

What does Li's comment mean? To a large extent, the social communities in which brands engage consumers are indeed free to play spaces in terms of *media costs.* But there are other costs we must take into account. Content must be generated, shared, and managed, and the time it takes requires funding. Strategies in some social media channels of our social media framework require development costs (in-house or with a vendor or agency) such as customizing profiles and developing social games, branded applications and widgets, and microsites. At the end of the day, there's no such thing as a free lunch!

As Figure 7 shows, most organizations to date allocate only a small portion of their marketing budgets to social media. But most companies, regardless of industry, plan to increase monetary allocations to social media marketing activities as the popularity of these new applications starts to take off.[7]

Figure 7

Marketing Budget Allocated to Social Media

Source: Used by permission of Marketing Sherpa.

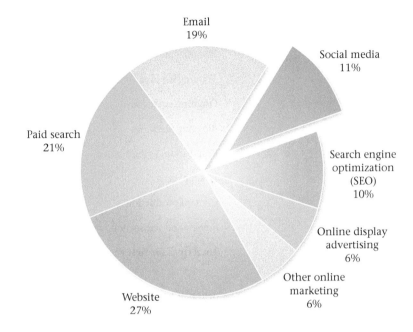

Email 19%

Social media 11%

Paid search 21%

Search engine optimization (SEO) 10%

Online display advertising 6%

Other online marketing 6%

Website 27%

Where will this money be spent? Primarily organizations are staffing for content management, ensuring that time is available for content development, blogging, and monitoring of social channels. In addition, organizations not only are creating internal positions to manage social media marketing, they also are hiring agencies, consultants, and service providers. The job of **social media manager**, akin to that of a brand manager, is becoming more commonplace. This person has the role of overseeing, managing, and championing the social media strategy internally. Agencies and other providers can supplement the work of the social media manager (or team) with ideas, ways to integrate social media marketing with the rest of the brand's marcom plan, technical expertise, and measurement.

As with everything else in business, the budget is critical—without funding, the organization can't initiate or maintain the campaign. How much should it allocate? When it comes to social media campaigns, budgets run the gamut from a few hundred to hundreds of thousands of dollars (particularly for complex campaigns like those associated with global alternate reality games).

Many companies approach social media marketing budgets as a percentage of their ad spends, which in turn are assigned by planners within the organization according to one of several formulae. The **percentage of ad spend** method assigns a set portion of the overall advertising budget for the organization to social media activities. Some use a variation, where they allocate a percentage of online marketing funding to social media.

Two other methods are used by companies. The **competitive parity method** uses competitors' spending as a benchmark. Like advertiser share of voice, competitive parity is based on the belief that spending the same or more on social media marketing will result in a comparable change in share of attention for the brand. When it comes to social media, though, share of voice takes on a new dimension; social media includes conversations about the brand from other sources. In contrast, with advertising, increasing share of voice is simply accomplished by purchasing more media time for advertisements.

With social media marketing, the costs of different approaches and platforms vary widely, and even a large spend may not result in widespread buzz or content sharing and viral spread. The resulting share of voice depends in part on the extent to which fans and friends share the message with their own networks. Lastly, the **objective-and-task method** considers the objectives set out for the campaign and

TABLE 2

TABLE 2

An Illustrative Budget for a Corporate Blog

Start-up costs	
Planning and development	$25,000
Training for blogger	$10,000
Ongoing costs (annual)	
Blogging platform	$25,000
Brand-monitoring service	$50,000
IT support	$3,000
Content production	$150,000
Review and redirection	$20,000
Total costs for first year	**$283,000**

determines the cost estimates for accomplishing each objective. This method builds the budget from a logical base with what is to be accomplished as the starting point. Table 2 provides an example of the budget an organization might develop to support the creation and maintenance of a corporate blog.

Benjamin Moore's campaign sought to increase share of voice in social communities using cost-efficient media outlets and to leverage the company's stellar relationship with the design community to reach out to end consumers.

Learning Objective 5

Profile the Target Audience of Social Consumers

Social media marketing plans, like any marketing plan, must target the desired audience in a meaningful and relevant manner. To do this requires the development of a **social media profile** of the target audience. The target market for the brand will have been defined in the brand's marketing plan in terms of demographic, geodemographic, psychographic, and product-usage characteristics. The target audience's social profile will take this understanding of the market one step further. It will include the market's social activities and styles such as their level of social media participation, the channels they utilize and the communities in which they are active, and their behavior in social communities.

The strategic planner must assess what it means to speak to the audience in the social media space. Who is the core target? How can we describe the key segments of that core target? To whom will the conversations in social media be directed? Of which social communities are the consumers a member? How do they use social media? How do they interact with other brands? The insights from the consumer profile that was done for brand's overall marketing and marcom plans will be useful to understand the overall profile of the target market.

However, the planner also must understand how and when his or her customers interact in online social communities, as well as which devices they use to do so. In developing a consumer profile, the planner may plot out a typical day for the social media user as well as gather information on the Internet activities of the audience. This is a bit like charting a sample lifestream for a target market over at least a brief period of time.

Let's see how Benjamin Moore went through this profiling process. Its strategy included the targeting of two existing markets (industry professionals and end consumers) with different media (social) and message strategy (a functional appeal delivered in the context of a relationship). The industry professionals primarily were interior designers but also included architects and contractors. These people already know the Benjamin Moore brand and perceive it as the premium choice among paints and finishes.

End consumers included people doing remodeling, renovation, and new construction projects. These end consumers may be do-it-yourselfers, or they may be working with or interested in working with a designer. Importantly, while many consumers are interested in home décor, many feel intimidated by the many decisions they need to make. They may struggle with visualizing the end result and worry about the investment needed to make their decorating dreams a reality.

Although the company wanted to expand its presence in two separate segments, both industry professionals and the end consumers it identified include well-educated professionals with financial resources. They have a strong and growing presence in social media communities and they tend to use the Internet to gather information prior to making decisions. Though they may not be "techies," both target markets have access to multiple devices including desktop and/or laptop computers, smartphones, and tablets.

Select Social Media Channels and Vehicles

Once the organization understands who it wants to reach, it's time to select the best **social media mix** to accomplish this. The zones of social media make up the channel and vehicle choices available for a social media mix. Similar to a more traditional marketing mix, the social media mix describes the combination of vehicles the strategy will include to attain the organization's objectives. For example, a fund-raising campaign for a college sorority might be based on a social media mix of a Facebook page, a Twitter blast, and a Foursquare check-in competition at the local sorority house.

The social media mix options lie among the four zones we've already discussed: relationship development in social communities, social publishing, social entertainment, and social commerce. Within each zone are many specific vehicles that may be best-suited to reach a certain audience. For instance, to meet the desired objectives and the social media patterns of a target audience that includes college students, the planner may determine that the campaign should include social networking, social publishing, and social games. The media vehicles might include Facebook, YouTube, and Flickr. Social publishing may utilize a corporate blog and document sharing sites such as Scribd. The brand may choose to utilize an existing social game such as Retail Therapy. You've seen examples of social media mix choices brands made as they developed effective social media campaigns. It's also a good idea at this stage of planning to map out how the campaign will build earned media and utilize paid and owned media synergistically. See Figure 8 for a look at how Benjamin Moore used social media channels for its "Experts Exchange" campaign.

Create an Experience Strategy

If we were planning an advertising campaign, the next step would be to identify a creative message strategy. **Message strategy** refers to the creative approach we will use throughout the campaign. This should flow from the brand's **positioning statement**—a single written statement that encapsulates the position the brand wishes to hold in the minds of its target audience. Positioning statements succinctly capture the heart of what the brand is and what the sponsor wants it to become. Reviewing the position is a necessary step in preparing a social media marketing strategy, because the social media activities the campaign plans and executes need to consistently support the desired message.

Can you identify the brands that go with these positioning statements?[8]

1. The computer for the rest of us

2. Networking networks

3. The world's information in one click

4. Personal video broadcasting network

Answers: (1) Apple, (2) Cisco, (3) Google, (4) YouTube

Figure 8

**Benjamin Moore's
Social Channels**

- Facebook profile
- *Experts Exchange*
  on Facebook
- Forums within
  Experts Exchange
- Twitter dialogue

**Zone 1:
Social Community**

- "Living in Color
  with Sonu" blog
- YouTube videos
  - How to videos
  - UGC contest videos
  - Expert interviews
    with designers
  - Advertisements republished
- Flickr photostream

**Zone 2:
Social Publishing**

**Zone 4:
Social Commerce**

**Zone 3:
Social Entertainment**

- Coupons shared
  via Facebook

- BM isn't operating
  yet in this zone

*paid media
drive traffic*

Owned Media:

- BenjaminMoore.com
- Living in Color blog
- Facebook profile and
  Experts Exchange posts
- YouTube channel
- Flickr photostream
- Retail storefronts

Paid Media:

- Magazine ads in
  *Elle Décor, House
  Beautiful, Traditional
  Home, Real Simple,
  Country Living*
- Co-branding with
  Pottery Barn

*valuable content plus interaction
in owned media space seeds
creation of earned media*

Earned Media:

- Influence impressions generated throughout social web
- Influence posts shared via Benjamin Moore's social experts
- Questions and comments posted by brand fans to Facebook Wall
  and to Experts Exchange, and as comments to social publishing
  on blog, YouTube, and Flickr.

The message strategy should also be appropriate to meet the campaign's objectives. It is developed from a **creative brief**—a document that helps creatives channel their energy toward a sound solution for the brand in question. In planning for social media marketing campaigns the design process works similarly; the planners create a brief to guide the development of the campaign. But—because unlike traditional media, social media focus on interactive experiences, social sharing, and engagement—the brief has a somewhat different structure and goes by a different name. Some planners call this document an **experience brief**.

The concept of an experience brief evolved from the work of website developers who consider the direct impact on users when they design site architecture, imagery, copy, and other site features. Griffin Farley, a strategy planner at BBH in New York, uses a different term. He describes the planning document for social media as a **propagation brief**.[9] He explains that propagation planning means to plan not for the people you reach, but for the people that *they* will reach. In other words, traditional advertising promotes a message to a passive audience, and that audience is the target. Social media invite an interactive experience with an audience of influencers who will then share the brand's message and invite others to the experience. To develop a social experience worthy of participation and worthy of sharing, social media planners ask and answer several questions.[10] The answers become the basis for the brief:

- **What are the campaign goals and/or communication tasks?** Objectives have been set for the campaign and the use of social media identified as a possibility. Here the planner reviews these decisions and provides a succinct overview of the goals.

- **How is the brand positioned? What is unique and special about its position in the marketplace?** As in a traditional creative brief, any campaign work should leverage the brand's positioning strategy and build on the brand's strengths.

- **Who is the target audience?** You've profiled the target already. Now consider what you want the audience to do. Do you want them to talk to the brand? Create and share content? Spread the message to their network? On what devices (e.g., iPad, smartphone, desktop) will they interact with your brand? What could you offer of value in exchange for their cooperation?

- **Is there another group of people who can persuade the target audience to follow them?** This group is your *influencers*—the people who will propagate your message. Why would these people want to share your message with others? What's in it for them?

- **What are the existing creative assets? How can the brand's creative foster a social experience?** Most brands already have some **creative assets** that drive their paid and owned media. For example, a well-known and popular brand spokescharacter such as the GEICO gecko is a creative asset that the insurance company has developed in its traditional advertising, so he might be employed in a social media campaign to give the company a head start in terms of consumer recognition as it tries to break through the clutter of competing messages. The planner should list the creative assets that already exist and identify the assets he or she still needs to extend the brand's story. How can the creative assets already available be used and/or leveraged in a social media context?

- **How can we integrate with other branded media being used by the organization, and how long do we have to execute?** This is a question that references how the campaign can integrate best with the brand's paid and owned media.

- **What experiences are possible given target market needs and motives, the available channels, and the creative assets? How can we design these experiences to maximize device portability and access?** Creative used in social media campaigns should inspire activity and interactivity. These questions ask what types of activities could be engaging for the target audience using multiple devices and worth sharing with their network.

- **What content will be needed?** Social media are content-driven. What content will be relevant to the campaign and what will be the source? Comments? Questions and polls? Video? Images? Stories? Apps?
- **How will experience engagement be extended and shared throughout the social channels?** For instance, will engagement activity auto-post to status updates (e.g., "Tracy likes Cole Haan")?

After the planner goes through the process of **discovery** and **briefing** to provide these "must-knows" to the creative team, the creative team will then enter the stage of **ideation** or **concepting**. Discovery is the term used to describe the research stage of the plan. Planners may rely on secondary and primary research as they seek to discover insights that will be useful to the creative team. These insights will be presented to the team during the briefing. The creative team will spend time brainstorming ideas and developing possible concepts for the campaign. Eventually the chosen ideas will be further refined and designed, and **prototypes** or mockups will be developed. These preliminary executions can then be used for internal review, usability testing, and other pre-testing.

When a brand begins to interact in social spaces, a key decision is how to represent the brand's **social persona**. This means planners need to define how the brand will behave in the social Web, what voice will be used, and even how deeply the brand will interact in the social space with customers. The decisions made should support the brand's position in the market. To introduce that persona, brands have several creative options. They may involve humanizing the brand (again, think of the GEICO gecko); showing a vulnerability to the customer and working as a steward to customer service (think Dell); or providing a value to the customer whether that value be function, information, or entertainment (think Nike). In Benjamin Moore's case, the brand's position is the choice of experts and the social persona that supports that position is brand as corporate entity.

Additionally, the makeup of the brand's social persona may vary. Benjamin Moore's is singular as a unified corporate brand. Other brands, such as Zappos, utilize different employee voices in social communities so the online retailer's persona is the sum of its employees. Still others have represented the brand with a person, but with a single individual charged with the brand's social reputation. Scott Monty, who represents Ford in its social media communications, is an example of this form of social persona. Lastly, the brand's mascot may take the social stage as Travelocity has done with its Roaming Gnome. Some brands present themselves as funny, comedic, thought leaders, and friends. There is no right or wrong social persona—it should ultimately be a social representation of the brand's position and of course be consistent with how the brand presents itself in other contexts. Many consumers have a built-in "BS alarm" that goes off when a brand tries to be something it's not.

So, what did Benjamin Moore's creative team at Cramer-Krasselt plan? Research during the discovery stage showed Benjamin Moore's planner that everyday people want to have beautiful homes but are fearful of color and making bold design choices. Even those who wouldn't hire a designer would love to get a designer's opinion. They want ideas for beautiful design choices and some kind of "safety net" to be sure they're not making decisions they will later regret. These consumers are hungry to learn about decorating, color selection, design, and paint.

As we've seen, the industry already loved Benjamin Moore, and the brand needed a way to leverage the enormous loyalty it commanded. The team devised a strategy to guide the campaign: "Those who know more, know Benjamin Moore." The natural executional device was to feature experts—designers, architects, and contractors—who all endorsed the Benjamin Moore brand. Several design and paint experts—recognizable and well-known design stars—were invited to participate in a campaign named *The Experts Exchange*. In doing so, the brand integrated authority-based testimonials into the **creative message strategy**.

Executed as a Facebook application, the campaign highlights the experts who share their own portfolio and who are available to answer questions end consumers pose on Benjamin Moore's Facebook page. These amateur designers can also upload their own project photos for feedback and kudos. Site visitors connect with sanctioned experts, and they also have access to dozens of designers and painting contractors who are available to share their knowledge. The participating designers in turn get a forum to show off their portfolio and to promote their own consulting services. Anytime there's a post—from designer or end user—the activity is shared on the contributor's wall feed to alert their network. An Events tab highlights sales events and other in-store activities. In addition, Benjamin Moore's Facebook wall shares news of what's happening on the Experts Exchange and provides links to YouTube videos and blog posts by the experts. The Twitter stream from Benjamin Moore likewise promotes links to the Facebook page, YouTube channel, and the Flickr photostream. The brand's website includes links to all the social media aspects and accompanying traditional advertising in the form of print and video executions that feature eight of the star designers. Not only does the campaign leverage every consumer participant's network through the sharing of activities, it also works in a business-to-business context as it reinforces brand choice and provides value to the industry participants.

The agency also developed a traditional print campaign to increase brand awareness and drive traffic to the Facebook application. The print ads illustrated the experts featured in a *Vanity Fair*–style portrait. The headline, "Paint with the very best," pays homage to the celebrity experts, while it emphasizes Benjamin Moore's product superiority. In addition, online rich media units and television spots feature these same experts as they provide unscripted commentary on their experience with Benjamin Moore.

Integrate with Other Promotional Components and Establish Campaign Timeline

Traditional media campaigns typically live a designated lifespan with timing tied to the accomplishment of specific objectives. For social media, though, campaigns are not necessarily events with fixed start and stop dates. Conversations in communities continue over time, and a brand's social media marketing presence should do this as well. This is particularly true for brands that rely on social media for customer service and customer relationship management. Some of the most famous social brands, like Dell and Zappos, are "always on" with their social media campaigns. They aim to project a constant presence in the communities in which they participate. Other organizations use a mix of short-term and ongoing social media. Benjamin Moore, for instance, will maintain its social media activity but may shift the focus of the work from the "Paint with the best" message at some point.

Other brands implement a social media marketing campaign for a specific period of time. Consider the movie *Eat Pray Love* starring Julia Roberts that opened with great fanfare in 2010. Columbia Pictures relied heavily on social media for the movie launch. The timing of the social media marketing strategies and tactics were tied to the launch date for the movie in theatres; this allowed time for people to spread the word, talk about the book, and make plans to see the movie. The marcom plan for *Eat Pray Love* included the usual television commercials on network and cable, magazine ads in a variety of magazines including *Real Simple* and *Oprah,* and banner ads and rich media across popular Internet sites. In addition, the launch included a heavy dose of social media: An active Facebook fan page, an interactive *Eat Pray Love* scrapbook that invited fans to share a picture that epitomizes their own personal journal, three social games—*Eat Pray Love Sudoku, WordSearch,* and *SCVNGR* (an adventure-themed, geosocial mobile game), and a *Share Your Story* appeal for fans to share the answer to one striking question, *What is one thing in life your friends said you could/would never do, but you did it anyway?*

$ BYTES TO BUCKS

Social media marketing can work in tandem with other elements of an organization's promotional strategy and can even amplify the impact of those elements. Pizza Hut recently announced a plan to use Foursquare as a sales promotion and loyalty tool. Pizza restaurants have long relied on coupons to drive business and encourage demand for specific products at specific times. They traditionally deliver these coupons to customers as freestanding inserts in newspapers, downloadable coupons on the brand's website, and in mailers. Pizza Hut's social media strategy, in part, will use the social game of Foursquare as a loyalty tool and coupon delivery device. Players will be encouraged to check in at Pizza Hut locations. *Mayors* will receive free breadsticks with the purchase of a large pizza.[11] A mayor is a person with the most check-ins at a location in the last 60 days. Thus, the tactic encourages and rewards regular patronage at unique Pizza Hut locations.

Execute and Measure Outcomes

In the final stage of the strategic planning process, we implement the plan and measure the results. There are *metrics* we can use to assess the effectiveness of social media campaigns. The data gathered on all aspects of the social media plan are used to provide insight for future campaigns.

As we've seen, many organizations are still "social media wannabes." They're at an early stage in the process and feeling their way in a new environment. So perhaps we can forgive them for the common mistakes they tend to make. Here are some of the biggest offenders:

- **Staffing:** The initial imperative when it comes to social media marketing is to simply get there—to have a presence in the community of interest. But focusing on presence can result in brand assets that are underutilized and underperforming in terms of the objectives set for the campaign. Organizations in the trial and transition phases tend to focus on establishing Facebook profiles and Twitter accounts, or perhaps on planning a poorly executed UGC (user-generated content) contest. These companies take a "if you build it, they will come" *Field of Dreams* approach, without addressing ways to build and maintain traffic and interest. Ultimately though, social media marketing is built on the community, content, and technology inherent to social media. To make it successful, the brand must be active in the space—and that means committing staff time to posting, responding, and developing content.

- **Content:** A related issue is the failure to introduce new, fresh, and relevant content. Developing interactivity, emphasizing relevance, monitoring the asset for needed maintenance, responding to visitor feedback, and providing new content will keep the asset fresh and inspire a curiosity to return among the core audience. Importantly, these components of successful social media marketing require an ongoing commitment of human resources.

- **Time Horizon:** Social media works differently than does traditional advertising, and may require patience before results are delivered. Although a television campaign can utilize a heavy buy early in its media plan to incite near immediate awareness and build momentum, social media is just the opposite. It can take months for a social media campaign to build awareness (and there are plenty of social media failures that never gained traction). Assuming the plan itself is sound, organizations must be patient while the community embraces the content and the relationship. Although the results may take longer to see, the overall effectiveness and efficiency of the social media model can be well worth the patience and resources required.

- **Focus of Objectives:** It's not uncommon for organizations to focus on action steps rather than desired outcomes from social media. In other words, they take a short-term tactical approach rather than a long-term strategic approach. An inappropriate objective might read: "Increase engagement by responding to comments on Twitter and Facebook within 24 hours of posting, posting three status updates per business day, and adding links to social media accounts on the corporate blog." Do you see the error? The emphasis is on the action steps the social media manager will complete (tactical) but there's no focus on what the social media activities should *do* for the brand. There is no value in doing social media marketing for the sake of social media—the value lies in accomplishing marketing objectives. Social media is more than the "flavor of the month"—it has the potential to provide lasting and measurable benefits when it's done right.

- **Benefits to Users:** Social media lives or dies on the quality of the content a platform offers to users. That content must add value to the social community. A social media marketing plan answers the question, "How will we distribute our content using social media channels?" But it also must answer other questions: How can we engage our target audiences in social media communities? What content is valued by our audiences? Do they want content that informs? Entertains? How can we develop an ongoing stream of relevant, fresh content?

- **Measurement:** Organizations fail to properly measure results. Marketing consultant Tom Peters famously observed, "What gets measured gets done." As social media marketing has developed, some evangelists have encouraged new disciples to keep the faith, emphasizing the growth and popularity of the media as reason enough to develop a presence in the space. In the long term, that's just not good enough. For organizations to succeed in social media marketing, measurement is critical. Measuring outcomes ensures that the organization is learning from what worked and what didn't. Importantly, as organizations begin to shift more marketing dollars from traditional advertising to social media marketing, managers will seek out comparisons on metrics such as ROI (Return On Investment) between social media and other media options.

Learning
Objective 6

Develop a Planning Structure in the Organization

So there we have it—a framework to plan a social media marketing campaign. But just how does the planning and execution of a campaign get done—and who does it? These jobs didn't even exist 5 years ago; many organizations are scrambling to create a structure that will enable their people to take advantage of these new methods.

Social media personnel can cross several areas of a company's organizational chart. Who has responsibility for the planning, execution, and evaluation of social media marketing strategies? Who should be involved in social media marketing activities? Should there be limitations to social media use within the company? Especially for large companies, different divisions and units may pursue a variety of tactics, ultimately resulting in a disparate collection of pages across social media sites—many ultimately abandoned. Some accounts are abandoned as the campaign component comes to a close. Others quit perhaps due to lack of time, staff, or funding—or simply because their need to explore the space waned over time.

Learning
Objective 7

The Social Media Policy

Companies need to develop, adopt, and publicize a **social media policy** among employees. A social media policy is an organizational document that explains the rules and procedures for social media activity for the organization and its employees. Just like you, many employees are already engaged in social media. They may be active on social networking sites and microsharing tools like Facebook and Twitter. While employees may use social media to communicate with friends and access entertainment opportunities (maybe even when they're supposed to be working!), there's a good chance they will mention their employers and maybe even vent about office politics or shoddy products.

Managing that risk is a must for companies. And many companies will recognize that these employees can act as powerful brand ambassadors when they participate in social media. As we mentioned, Zappos takes advantage of the fact that many of its employees participate in social media vehicles—and these enthusiastic team members promote the company in the process.

Of course, there's no guarantee that an employee (at least on his or her own time) will necessarily say only glowing things about the company. Brands use formal documents to ensure that the company is protected in a legal sense and also to encourage employees to participate in ways that are consistent with the brand's overall strategy. Here are excerpts from three companies' policies:[12]

- *Microsoft:* If you plan to tweet about any professional matters (such as about the business of Microsoft or other companies, products, or services in the same business space as Microsoft), in addition to referencing your alias@microsoft.com email address, whenever possible use the service's profile or contact information to assert that you are a Microsoft employee and/or affiliated with a specific group/team at Microsoft.

- *Sun Microsystems:* Whether in the actual or virtual world, your interactions and discourse should be respectful. For example, when you are in a virtual world as a Sun representative, your avatar should dress and speak professionally. We all appreciate actual respect.

- *Intel:* Consider content that's open-ended and invites response. Encourage comments. You can broaden the conversation by citing others who are blogging about the same topic and allowing your content to be shared or syndicated. … If you make a mistake, admit it. Be upfront, and be quick with your correction. If you're posting a blog, you may choose to modify an earlier post—just make it clear that you have done so.

The Word of Mouth Marketing Association (WOMMA) developed a quick guide to designing a digital social media policy, shown in Figure 9. Its purpose is to guide how the organization, its employees, and agents should share opinions, beliefs, and information with social communities.[13] Not only is it good business, it can also help prevent legal problems. The WOMMA guide encourages organizations to make several decisions and include those in an organization-wide social media policy. Organizations must decide upon:

- *Standards of conduct:* Standards of conduct in a social media policy refer to the basic expectations for employee behavior in social communities. At a minimum, WOMMA recommends that the standards require that all online statements about the business be honest and transparent. Deceptive, misleading, or unsubstantiated claims about the organization or its competitors must not be issued. Further, good manners must be used in social communities (no ethnic slurs, personal insults, rumors, lies, or other offensive statements).

- *Disclosure requirements:* Transparency is key in online communities. Employees must disclose that they are affiliated with the organization. If they are receiving material compensation or gifts in exchange for posting, this must be disclosed. Disclosing affiliations ensures that readers can still find the posts credible and trustworthy. WOMMA recommends that bloggers include a simple statement: "I received [insert product name] from [insert company name] and here is my opinion. …" In addition, when using posts on social networks, WOMMA recommends that the poster use **hashtags** to disclose the nature of relationships reflected in the posts: #emp (employee/employer), #samp (free sample received), #paid (paid endorsement).

- *Standards for posting intellectual property, financial information, and copyrighted information:* Many of the potential legal problems within social media relate to the inappropriate sharing of information. No organization is immune to these issues; consider the embarrassing revelations the U.S. government had to deal with when a rogue organization called WikiLeaks posted thousands of confidential cables and emails that went into great detail about the country's diplomatic relationships. WOMMA recommends that organizations keep all intellectual property and private financial information confidential. Prior to posting copyrighted information, appropriate permissions should be collected.

Figure 9

Key Aspects of the WOMMA Disclosure Form

Source: http://womma.org/ main/Quick-Guide-to-Designing-a-Social-Media-Policy.pdf, accessed September 2011.

Personal and Editorial Blogs

- I received _____ from _____ sent me _____

Product Review Blogs

- I received _____ from _____ to review
- I was paid by _____ to review

Additionally for product review blogs, WOMMA strongly recommends creating and prominently posting a "Disclosure and Relationships Statement" section on the blog fully disclosing how a review blogger works wit h companies in accepting and reviewing products, and listing any conflicts of interest that may affect the credibilit y of their reviews.

Providing Comments in Online Discussions

- I received _____ from _____
- I was paid by_____
- I am an employee [or representative] of_____

Microblogs

Include a hash tag notation, either:

- #spon (sponsored)
- #paid (paid)
- #samp (sample)

Additionally, WOMMA strongly recommends posting a link on your profile page directing people to a full "Disclosure and Relationships Statement." This statement, much like the one WOMMA recommends for review blogs, should state how you work with companies in accepting and reviewing products, and listing any conflicts of interest that may affect the credibility of your sponsored or paid reviews.

Status Updates on Social Networks

- I received_____ from_____
- I was paid by_____

If status updates are limited by character restrictions, the best pract ice disclosure requirement is to include a hash tag notation of either #spon, #paid or #samp. Additionally, WOMMA strongly recommends posting a full description or a link on your social network profile page directing people to a "Disclosure and Relationships Statement." Note that if an employee blogs about his or her company's products, citing the identity of the employer in the profile may not be a sufficient disclosure. Bloggers' disclosures should appear close to the endorsement or testimonial statement they are posting.

Video and Photo Sharing Websites

Include as part of the video/photo content and part of the written description:

- I received_____ from_____
- I was paid by_____

Additionally, WOMMA strongly recommends posting a full description or a link on your video and/or photo sharing profile page directing people to a "Disclosure and Relationships Statement."

Podcasts

Include, as part of the audio content and part of the written description:

- I received_____ from_____
- I was paid by_____

Additionally, WOMMA strongly recommends posting a full description or a link directing people to a "Disclosure and Relationships Statement."

An Organizational Structure to Support Social Media

Who "owns" social media within an organization? Some brands assign the responsibility to a discipline "silo" such as the marketing department, whereas others rely upon a **center of excellence model** that pulls people with different kinds of expertise from across the organization to participate. Intel and American Express both follow the center of excellence model. This eliminates the internal political issues relating to who in the company has primary responsibility for social media so it's easier to integrate social media applications with other marketing initiatives.

Aside from the organizational structure to support social media marketing efforts, businesses must make decisions on the level of resources to dedicate. Social media is an ongoing conversation across potentially several communication vehicles. Some businesses dedicate multiple employees to manage the conversation calendar whereas others assign a single person. The organizational task is to assign the least number of resources needed internally and then supplement those resources with help from the organization's social media agency resources.

There are three basic models for social media structure: centralized, distributed, and combination.[14]

1. In the **centralized structure**, the social media department functions at a senior level that reports to the CMO (Chief Marketing Officer) or CEO and is responsible for all the social media activations. The potential problem here is that all social media activity may not be adequately represented. Is customer care going to be good if social media marketing is housed under marketing rather than customer service?

2. In the **distributed structure**, no one person owns social media. Instead, all employees represent the brand and work social media into their roles. This is implemented through training and used across the organization. The danger here is that the tools can end up off message. Best Buy uses this model: The store chain is decentralized because everyone in the organization has a role in social media, as the "twelpforce" (the name Best Buy assigned to its social media evangelists) demonstrates. Any employee can sign up to respond to customer queries on Twitter. However, Best Buy does have a well-developed social media policy in place to guide employee behavior in social communities.

3. The **combination structure** involves both centralized best practices and decentralized execution. The brand establishes a committee of social media leaders to make decisions on the social media position and voice, and these details are disseminated to the company at large. But from there, each division is left to incorporate social media into its own executions. Kodak and IBM follow this model. IBM even used a wiki to crowdsource the guidelines for a company blog.

Chapter Summary

Where does social media marketing planning fit into an organization's overall planning framework?

Social media marketing should be planned as part of an organization's marketing plan. Like integrated marketing communications plans, organizations may also develop stand-alone plans offering greater social media marketing.

What are the three phases of social media marketing maturity? How does social media marketing change for companies as they shift from the trial phase to the transition phase and eventually move into the strategic phase?

The three phases of social media marketing maturity are trial, transition, and strategic. In the trial phase, organizations are pursuing social media tactics in an ad hoc manner, with a focus on gaining experience in social media. The tactics are not well linked to the organization's overall marketing plan and may be haphazardly executed. Organizations in the transition phase think more systematically about how to plan social media activities that support marketing objectives. When an organization enters the final strategic phase, it utilizes a formal process to plan social media marketing activities with clear objectives and metrics. Social media are now integrated as a key component of the organization's overall marketing plan.

What are the steps in social media marketing strategic planning?

The social media marketing strategic planning process consists of the following steps:

- Conduct a situation analysis and identify key opportunities.
- State objectives.
- Gather insight into and target one or more segments of social consumers.
- Select the social media channels and vehicles.
- Create an experience strategy.
- Establish an activation plan using other promotional tools (if needed).
- Manage and measure the campaign.

What are the characteristics of good strategic marketing objectives?

A well-stated, actionable objective should have the following characteristics:

- Be specific (what, who when, where)
- Be measurable
- Specify the desired change (from a baseline)
- Include a time line
- Be consistent and realistic (given other corporate activities and resources)

How does a social consumer profile differ from other content a campaign team needs to understand its target market?

The target market for the brand will have been defined in the brand's marketing plan in terms of demographic, geodemographic, psychographic, and product-usage characteristics. The target audience's social profile will take this understanding of the market one step further. It will include the market's social activities and styles such as their level of social media participation, the channels they utilize and the communities in which they are active, and their behavior in social communities.

How can organizations structure themselves to support social media marketing?

There are three basic models for social media structure: centralized, distributed, and combination. In centralized structures, the social media department functions at a senior level that reports to the CMO or CEO and is responsible for all the social media activations. In the distributed framework, no one person owns social media. Instead all employees represent the brand and work social media into their roles. This is implemented through training and used across the organization. The combination approach involves both centralized best practices and decentralized execution. The brand establishes a committee of social media leaders to make decisions on the social media position and voice, and these details are disseminated to the company at large. But from there, each division is left to incorporate social media into its own executions.

What are the key components of an organizational social media policy, and why is it important to have such a policy in place?

Policies may include several guidelines such as standards of conduct, disclosure requirements, and standards for posting intellectual property, financial information, and copyrighted information.

Key Terms

activation tool	external environment	share of voice
briefing	hashtags	situation analysis
center of excellence model	ideation	social media marketing maturity
centralized structure	internal environment	social media policy
combination structure	lovemark	social persona
competitive parity method	marketing plan	strategic phase
concepting	message strategy	strategic planning
creative brief	objective	stunts
creative message strategy	objective-and-task method	SWOT analysis
discovery	percentage of ad spend	traffic
distributed structure	positioning statement	transition phase
experience brief	propagation brief	trial phase

Review Questions

1. Why do some organizations enter the trial phase without planning and research? Is there value in getting social media experience before social media marketing becomes part of the marcom plan?
2. Explain the three phases in the social media marketing maturity life cycle.
3. What are the three forms of organizational structure used by companies embracing social media marketing? What are the pros and cons of each?
4. Explain the seven steps in the social media marketing strategic planning process.
5. What approaches to budgeting can be used by organizations planning for social media marketing?

Exercises

1. Visit www.thecoca-colacompany.com/socialmedia/ where you'll find Coca-Cola's social media policy. You can also visit www.digitalbuzzblog.com/coca-cola-launches-new-social-media-policy/ to watch a video on the introduction of Coca-Cola's policy. Identify the three key components WOMMA recommends be included in a corporate social media policy. How could the policy be improved?
2. Identify a social media campaign for a favorite brand. In what experiences does the campaign invite you to take part? Does the campaign include share technologies to ensure your activities are shared with your network?

Notes

1. Karl Greenberg, "Buick Aggregates Feedback on its Regal," *Marketing Daily*, July 30, 2010, www.mediapost.com/publications/?fa=Articles. showArticle&art_aid=132866&nid=117102, accessed August 17, 2010; www.momentoftruth.com/#/everyone, accessed August 17, 2010.
2. Erik Sass, "The Social Graf: Social Media Is Here to Stay (Just Look at History)," *Social Media & Marketing Daily*, August 17, 2010, www.mediapost.com/publications/?fa=Articles. showArticle&art_aid=133945&nid=117666, accessed August 17, 2010.
3. Unica, "The State of Marketing 2010," www.unica.com/survey2010, accessed August 10, 2010.
4. J. David Goodman, "Popular New Drinking Game Raises Question, Who's 'Icing' Whom?" *New York Times*, June 8, 2010, www.nytimes.com/2010/06/09/business/media/09adco. html?_r=1&adxnnl=1&emc=eta1&adxnnlx=1280768445-DD4x8h5JjKx+rdSynxAVaA, accessed December 18, 2010.
5. *A Step-by-Step Guide to a Successful Social Media Program*, MarketingProfs, 2009, p. 9.
6. Case study provided by Benjamin Moore and Cramer-Krasselt.

7. eMarketer, "Using Social Media Strategically," December 21, 2009, www.emarketer.com/Article.aspx?R=1007430, accessed August 7, 2011.

8. Leslie Jump, "Marketing Artifacts: Brand Positioning Statements?" February 7, 2007, www.marketerblog.net/2007/02/marketing_artif .html, accessed August 11, 2010.

9. Griffin Farley, "Propagation Planning," May 3, 2010, http://griffin-farley.typepad.com/propagation/, accessed December 1, 2010.

10. Adapted from Griffin Farley, "Revised Propagation Planning Brief," May 3, 2010, http://griffinfarley.typepad.com/propagation/ 2010/05/ revised-propagation-planning-brief.html, accessed December 1, 2010.

11. "Pizza Hut and Foursquare Offer Discounts for 'Mayors,'" *PRNewswire*, August 9, 2010, www.prnewswire.com/news-releases/ pizza-hut-and-foursquare-offer-discounts-for-mayors-100264499 .html, accessed August 11, 2010.

12. Kimberly Smith, *A Step-by-Step Guide to a Successful Social Media Program*, Marketing Profs, 2010, P. 9.

13. "The WOMMA "Quick Guide" to Designing a Digital Social Media Policy," WOMMA, http://womma.org/main/Quick-Guide-to-Designing-a-Social-Media-Policy.pdf, accessed December 31, 2010.

14. Kunar Patel, "You're Using Social Media: But Just Who Is Overseeing It All?" *Advertising Age*, February 22, 2010, http://adage.com/digital/ article?article_id=142221, accessed December 31, 2010.

DUBLIN BUSINESS SCHOOL

LIBRARY

Social Consumers

From Chapter 3 of *Social Media Marketing*, First Edition. Tracy L. Tuten, Michael R. Solomon.
Copyright © 2013 by Pearson Education, Inc. All rights reserved.

Social Consumers

LearningObjectives

When you finish reading this chapter you will be able to answer these questions:

1. How are our lives reflected online? In what ways are individuals involved in the four zones of social media?

2. How and why does digital culture play a role in consumer behavior?

3. Why are consumers drawn to social media activities?

4. Which bases of segmentation are relevant to target wired consumers in a social media context?

5. What are the most important segments of social media consumers? What do they tell us about targeting users of the social Web?

GO

Digital Identity: You Are What You Post

Facebook? YouTube? Flickr? Twitter? Which of these sites do you make a part of your digital life? What are you sharing? Thoughts, opinions, activities, photos, videos? When and from where? On the go with a mobile device? From a fixed location using a stationary computer? These days, the answer is most or all of the above. Our online activities and the information we post document our **digital identity**—the way we represent ourselves via text, images, sounds, and video to others who access the Web.

Learning Objective 1

Social Touchpoints in a Wired Life

Perhaps in a typical day you wake up using an alarm clock app on your smartphone. After you snooze the alarm, you might check your News Feed on Facebook Mobile. If you still subscribe to cable and have a television, you might turn on *The Today Show* while you get ready for morning classes. When Matt Lauer asks for your reaction to today's breaking news, you turn to Twitter to post your opinion—or if you are an innovator, you might use your Google TV to respond right from your television console. You leave home and head for school. In the car, you have less access to devices than at home, but still stay connected with your smartphone or even an Internet-enabled car if you drive a new Ford (but don't text when you drive!). Here too are many applications with social implications—you might search for reviews on the best place for coffee along your route, or the cheapest source of gas. When you get to class, your professor might ask you to work collaboratively in a wiki on a class assignment or bookmark research for a group project. Shopping later (or during a lecture)? Use an app such as FourSquare and you might score valuable coupons for savings while you shop. See what we mean? Everywhere you go, as long as you have an Internet-enabled device, social media can be a part of your daily life. The opportunities exist as **social media touchpoints.** You can see the possibilities for these touchpoints in Figure 1.

Social Footprints

A footprint is the impression or mark an object makes when it occupies a physical space. Depending upon the surface material, the impression may remain some time after the indentation was created—when a budding graffiti artist happens upon a patch of drying cement, the rest is history! Similarly, a **social footprint** is the mark a person makes when he or she occupies digital space. As we visit websites and web communities, we leave a digital trail behind. This social footprint may be subtle or obvious depending upon the quantity and frequency of visits and the activities in which we participate. For example, when you visit your friend's Facebook profile and learn that she's a fan of Juicy Couture, you learn something about what matters to her. This information is one aspect of her social footprint.

Figure 2 illustrates a social footprint for one person, Gary. It's clear in this example that the footprint's owner, an artist in Richmond, Virginia, has a sizeable presence on Facebook. There he interacts with friends and colleagues, posts personal messages, and sometimes promotes gallery showings and art for sale. Gary also publishes his film work on the media sharing site YouTube. As he adds photography to his multimedia productions, he frequently uses his iPhone to capture images and upload them to Flickr and Facebook. He further promotes the content he's published by microblogging on Twitter. Gary also posts images and written observations to his blog, Naked Doodles, hosted on Blogger. He utilizes the social shopping functions of apps such as Snipi on his iPad, which help him to keep track of items he might want to purchase and enable him to run price comparisons across the Web before he does. Over time it's likely that Gary will continue to expand his digital footprint as he becomes involved in other social communities, posts his physical where

Figure 1

A Social Life

Throughout the day, social media users touch a variety of devices, channels, and sites for many different reasons. Whether checking the weather forecast, getting the latest news, relaxing with your friends while watching favorite videos, or trying to get a deal on a pizza, social media is increasingly a part of our daily lives.

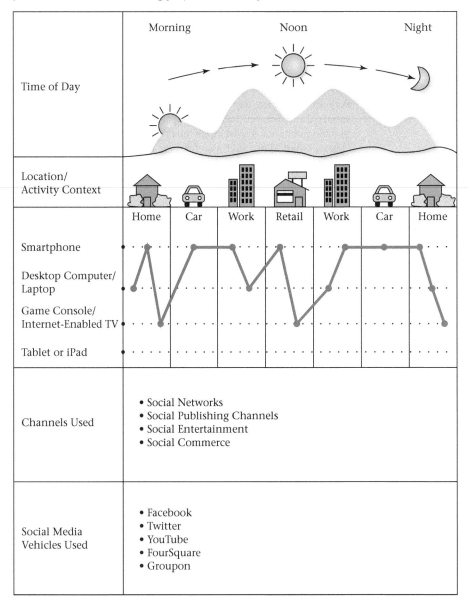

Source: Based on Ken Martin and Ivan Todorov, "How Will Digital Platforms Be Harnessed in 2010, and How Will They Change the Way People Interact with Brands?," *Journal of Interactive Advertising* 10, no. 2 (Spring 2010), http://jiad.org/article132, accessed November 17, 2010.

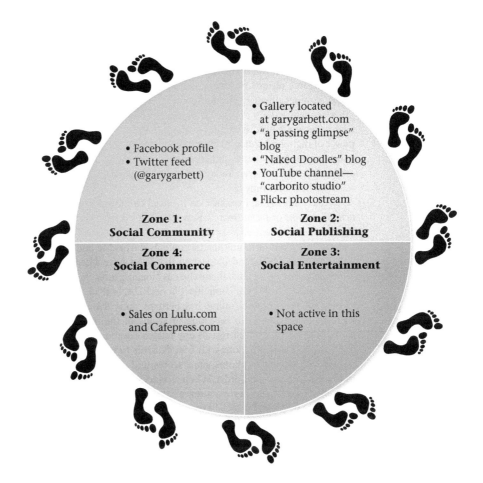

Figure 2

One Consumer's Social Footprint

- Facebook profile
- Twitter feed (@garygarbett)

Zone 1: Social Community

- Gallery located at garygarbett.com
- "a passing glimpse" blog
- "Naked Doodles" blog
- YouTube channel— "carborito studio"
- Flickr photostream

Zone 2: Social Publishing

Zone 4: Social Commerce

- Sales on Lulu.com and Cafepress.com

Zone 3: Social Entertainment

- Not active in this space

abouts on Foursquare, designates his favorite bands on Rank 'Em, and subscribes to news and entertainment feeds using aggregators such as Paper.li. Across all four zones of social media, Gary leads a *very* social digital life as he continues to deposit footprints.

You may or may not leave as many footprints as Gary, but you certainly leave your share. Like Hansel and Gretel who dropped breadcrumbs to mark their way in the forest, you leave traces as you interact online and especially as you share social content. Have you ever "liked" a site, an article, or a product? Footprints. Did you ever shop online? More footprints. Comment on YouTube videos? Download podcasts from iTunes or upload pictures on Flickr? That's right . . . more footprints. And guess what: You're certainly not alone in this particular forest. Lots of people other than your BFFs are interested in these electronic tracks. Savvy marketers follow them to see where you've been and to predict where you are headed and what you might want when you get there. This knowledge helps them ensure that when you do arrive they will be ready to serve you customized, targeted ads and offers that meet your needs. More on that later.

Lifestreams

Lifestreams are time-ordered streams of entries and posts. Whereas your social footprint is the mark you leave after you occupy a specific digital space, your lifestream is the ongoing record of

Wherever this icon appears in the margin, please go to the website **www.zonesofsmm.com** for an example of the topic discussed.

your digital life. Think of it as an electronic résumé that chronicles what you've done in words and pictures. However, there's a really important difference: Your lifestream also includes information you might not want a potential employer, friend, or romantic partner to see!

What pieces make up a lifestream? Depending upon the zones of social media a person uses, this electronic résumé may include blog posts; lists; status updates; photos of events and experiences; announcements; reflections; and interactions with family, friends, colleagues, and strangers. It is essentially a diary of your life online. A graduate student named Eric Freeman first coined this term as he wrote his dissertation in computer science at Yale University in 1997. He envisioned the power of digital recording to eliminate the hassles of personal recordkeeping. Freeman developed a software program that would, in simplistic terms, maintain a time-ordered series of records with easy search and retrieval. Today the lifestream concept has come to more generally describe our recorded lives over time.

Because our digital lives are tied to social communities, lifestreams are sometimes called *social activity streams* or *social streams*. Several online services such as Tumblr, Posterous, HootSuite, and Flavors.Me tout themselves as **lifestream aggregators;** they provide an easy way for users to share and organize their own multimedia content. Flavors.Me pulls user content from other sites including Facebook, Twitter, and Blogger so that users have a central hub to represent their life online. Tumblr and Posterous pitch themselves as blogging tools for the masses, with multimedia posts you can easily share from your computer, phone, PDA, or iPad.

Facebook, as a social utility, has perhaps done the best job of recording the lifestreams of its members. Whether on Facebook or at any of the million websites integrated with Facebook Connect, a member's Wall reveals any related Facebook activity. Depending upon your activities, the Wall records interactions with friends, visits to websites, online purchases, notes and journals, mobile uploads, shared photos, game scores, and more—all time- and date-stamped and presented in reverse chronological order. Whereas Gary's footprints showed us his individual activities over several social sites, his lifestream reveals the order of his activities, provides a context for them, and catalogs the whole of his social experience over time.

To summarize, your *digital footprint* leaves evidence of where you are and where you've been. Your *lifestream* is the journal of your digital life. Taken together, they make up your digital identity. When you look at this evidence, we think you'll agree: *You are what you post!*

Your Social Brand

You deposit social footprints throughout the social communities you visit. Many social communities require registration as a member of the community in order to access services and join in community activities. Your username in social communities is a **handle** or nickname, just like those truck drivers used on their old-fashioned CB radios. It may be a pseudonym or your real name. Although many digital natives use pseudonyms that can hide real identities and maintain some privacy, others choose handles that describe something about them in shorthand as they try to build a following. We can think of these IDs as our **digital brand name.** Rather than hide one's identity, they heighten the meaning associated with one's name. For example, digital media guru Jennifer Leggio, a prominent blogger for ZDNet, uses the handle "mediaphyter" to represent her social digital footprint.

One of your first strategic decisions as you build your social presence is to choose your digital brand name. You need to decide whether to use your own name, a handle, or more than one name depending on the application (one of this text's authors uses the handle "brandacity" on professional posts and her real name on personal posts). Your choice is important. You make a trade-off between recognition and privacy, because if you pick a distinctive digital brand name it will be easier for others to identify your physical identity also.

Once you've made that decision, you'll need to ensure that you aren't **handle-squatting.** This term refers to the use of a digital brand name by someone who really doesn't have a claim to the brand name. Sometimes another person may have a legitimate claim to the name—many of us have names that are not unique. For instance, there are hundreds of men named David Jones in the world. In that case, use of the handle doesn't constitute squatting. On the other hand, a quick search of Twitter for actor Hugh Jackman turns up several people listings, including @RealHughJackman, @JackmanHugh, @HughJackman, and @H_Jackman, among others. Only one is the "real" Hugh Jackman—the others are probably handle-squatting.

Next, you should find out whether your desired username is available in the many social communities. Visit Username Check (www.usernamecheck.com) to find out. This handy service will check for registrations at several popular social sites and report whether your handle is available. At that point, you may want to revisit your handle selection or, if your preferred handle is free, start registering to be sure your social brand stays yours!

Learning
Objective **2**

The Life of a Digital Consumer

OK, you're starting to expand your social footprint. Already, you've audited community membership in networks such as Facebook and media sharing sites such as YouTube. As we continue, you'll be adding to your footprint and socially streaming your activities. But have you thought about how your digital life has changed over time? A few years ago, your footprint might have included the time you spent on WebKinz or other kids' virtual world sites such as Club Penguin or Habbo Hotel. Back then (in the good old days!) you may have sent more emails and spent hours gabbing on the phone, whereas now you focus on text messages and IMs. This shift is called **digital primacy.**[1] It reflects a change in the culture of wired individuals like you—digital natives—who turn *first* to digital channels for communication, information, and entertainment.

When PBS's *Frontline* set out to make a documentary about life in the digital age the network partnered with *Smith*, an online magazine known for its memoirs in six words, to challenge visitors to pose six-word insights on their digital lives. The following posts are a small sample of what people wrote. To see more visit www.pbs.org/wgbh/pages/frontline/digitalnation/participate . What do these musings say about the impact of a digital world on the way we think about ourselves?

Digital Natives, Digital Immigrants

Countless connections, never a soul meeting

140 characters cannot encapsulate my status

Tweets, keyboards, and mice: my frenemies

My thumbs weren't made to type

Needed to find myself. Used Google

Afraid my phone's smarter than me

Because you are a digital native, your day-to-day experiences differ immensely from that of your parents—digital immigrants who grew up without Web 2.0 technology.

In part, your status as digital native or immigrant is a generational by-product. Natives didn't choose to be more active online and utilize more digital gadgets in their daily lives—they were simply born at a time when society adopted these technologies. Beloit College's *Mindset List* publishes each year a list of observations about that year's entering freshmen class. The list draws from experiences you, as a digital native, will find commonplace, but that immigrants will find surprising, shocking, and sometimes even disappointing. As a digital native, for example, you may not have ever searched for a library book using a card catalog—or you may not even know what such a catalog is!

In contrast, immigrants do have a choice. They choose to what extent they will become socialized into the digital culture, or go down swinging in defense of their right to write letters on paper or get their news from printed newspapers. The word *culture* is a critical indicator of the difference between natives and immigrants. No matter the time spent in digital environments, immigrants will always feel like outsiders looking in. As immigrants experience new technologies, they experience a sense of culture shock. They adopt some digital technologies but eschew others.

And, immigrants may use the technologies quite differently than their native counterparts. Consider the actions of many "clueless" parents: A mother and her daughter attend a high school basketball game together (if the daughter allows herself to be seen with Mom). The daughter uses her smartphone to snap pictures at the game and upload them to Facebook from her mobile Facebook app. Mom, a digital immigrant, takes pictures at the same game with a camera (even though her phone also has a camera), and then prints hard copies at a kiosk at a nearby drugstore. The daughter keeps a photo album on a photo-sharing site such as Flickr, Snapfish, or Shutterfly, whereas Mom is an avid scrapbooker even though she could just store (and tag) all of her pictures online.

Diffusion of (Digital) Innovations

How can we encourage digital immigrants to embrace the brave new world of social media? How likely is it that different types of consumers will change their stripes as new technologies become more commonplace? To help us approach these questions let's review a classic (pre-digital) perspective on how people deal with new products and new ways of doing things.

Roger's **diffusion of innovations** theory presents characteristics of innovative products that explain the rate at which people are likely to adopt these new options.[2] These characteristics include:

1. The relative advantage of the innovation (i.e., does it provide a greater benefit than the existing alternatives?)
2. The ability to observe and try the innovation
3. The innovation's compatibility (how easily it can be assimilated into the person's life)
4. The innovation's simplicity of use

Most consumers won't adopt a new product just for the sake of trying something new. They will weigh the costs and benefits associated with adoption—does the product solve a problem? Does it work with other products consumers already own? Do they see other people using it? Can they try it without risk? Is it easy to use or is there a learning curve involved in the adoption process? To the extent that marketers can make an innovation better, while also making it easy to integrate, try, use, and see in use, the faster consumers will accept the new product.

Kodak's advertising campaign for its Kodak EasyShare digital cameras targets digital immigrants by focusing on the *simplicity* characteristic. Kodak wants consumers to see how easy it is to share digital images with its new camera. Its theme, "the real Kodak moment happens when you share," and the supporting elements of the campaign (with a heavy dose of social media) are designed to encourage digital immigrants to adopt a new Kodak EasyShare camera and to use social media sites, including the Kodak-sponsored www.kodakmoments.com, as sharing channels.[3] What's so phenomenal about EasyShare cameras? They feature "share" buttons that automatically send the selected image to the Kodak-Gallery, Flickr, Facebook, or via email. That's right—it's that easy to share pictures! For digital immigrants, this feature solves a problem. They may see mobile uploads of photos on Facebook pages, and they want to join in. The Kodak product design ensures they can be a part of the social experience.

Great idea, right? How do we know this campaign targets immigrants over natives? That's easy. The campaign features references to the venerable phrase "Kodak moments." The inclusion of this phrase in campaign pitches began in the early 1960s and continued off and on until the early 1990s. It's a campaign theme that only digital immigrants would recognize. By using it, Kodak appeals to the nostalgic nature of anyone who has ever tried to capture and save a special moment with a photograph. Importantly, though, Kodak's campaign doesn't turn its back on you, the digital native. By including many forms of social media in its campaign and soliciting user-generated photos for its gallery, Kodak also reaches tech-savvy natives.

As you can see, understanding the digital culture of a target audience can play a role in product design as well as promotions, as it did in the Kodak Moments case. But even so, whether digital immigrants or natives, people vary in their attitudes, behaviors, and preferences. This is true offline *and* online. When it comes to managing their digital lives, no two people are alike.

A Wired World

The *World Internet Usage Statistics* site estimates that there are just over 1.7 billion Internet users worldwide. Asia hosts the most Internet users with 42.6 percent of the world's online population, followed by Europe with 23.1 percent and North America with 13.6 percent. According to the Pew Internet & American Life Project in 2009, 74 percent of Americans were online (it's safe to assume that percentage is even higher today). Although North America lags behind Asia and Europe in percentage of total users, it has the highest Internet **penetration rate,** the measure of the percentage of a population with Internet access. Asia's penetration rate is just 19.4 percent and Europe's is 52.0 percent. Australia makes up a measly 1.2 percent of all Internet users, but boasts a 60 percent penetration rate.

Table 1 summarizes who is online in the United States and who isn't (yet). As you might expect, younger people are more likely to be active online. Fully 93 percent of teens and young adults aged 12–29 are online, compared to 81 percent of adults aged 30–49 and 70 percent of adults aged 50–64. It's only when we consider elderly groups that we see a lack of Internet penetration—just 38 percent of adults 65 and over are online. Even so, this means more than one out of every three "senior citizens" surfs the Web!

Thousands of people join the online world every day. What's more, their quality of access has improved dramatically. Just a few years ago, you had to dial in to a slow connection to get online, while today most of us have high-speed access via cable modems and DSL-enabled phone lines. We've gotten used to the luxury of seeing pages load in seconds and many of us just assume that we can jump online almost anywhere we travel (even on airplanes). In addition, Internet access has gone mobile for many as we continue to snap up wireless devices such as netbooks and smartphones. These changes in access to the Internet equate to increased access to target audiences for social media marketers. In other words, our **reach** is now extensive online. Reach refers to the percentage of the target audience that can be accessed using a form of media. In the early days of the Internet, reach was small and the medium was not considered as attractive.

TABLE 1

Pew Chart of Generations Online

The Pew Internet & American Life Project is a think tank devoted to monitoring the increasingly digital lives of Americans. Its research provides an unbiased and holistic view of digital life in the United States, as it seeks to provide a sort of census on Internet adoption and activities for Americans of all backgrounds.

Generations Online 2010: Summary

The following chart shows the popularity of Internet activities among Internet users in each generation.

90–100%	40–49%
80–89%	30–39%
70–79%	20–29%
60–69%	10–19%
50–59%	0–9%

Key: % of Internet users in each generation who engage in this online activity

Millennials Ages 18-33	Gen X Ages 34-45	Younger Boomers Ages 46-55	Older Boomers Ages 56-64	Silent Generation Ages 65-73	G.I. Generation Age 74+
Email	Email	Email	Email	Email	Email
Search	Search	Search	Search	Search	Search
Social network sites	Health info	Health info	Health info	Health info	Health info
Use SNS	Get news	Get news	Get news	Get news	Buy a product
Watch video	Govt website	Govt website	Govt website	Travel reservations	Get news
Get news	Travel reservations	Travel reservations	Buy a product	Buy a product	Travel reservations
Buy a product	Watch video	Buy a product	Travel reservations	Gov't website	Gov't website
Instant Message (IM)	Buy a product	Watch video	Bank online	Watch video	Bank online
Listen to music	Social network sites	Bank online	Watch video	Financial info	Financial info
Travel reservations	Bank online	Social network sites	Social network sites	Bank online	Religious info
Online classifieds	Online classifieds	Online classifieds	Online classifieds	Rate things	Watch video
Bank online	Listen to music	Listen to music	Financial info	Social network sites	Play games

(continued)

Millennials Ages 18-33	Gen X Ages 34-45	Younger Boomers Ages 46-55	Older Boomers Ages 56-64	Silent Generation Ages 65-73	G.I. Generation Age 74+
Gov't website	IM	Financial info	Rate things	Online classifieds	Online classifieds
Play games	Play games	IM	Listen to music	IM	Social network sites
Read blogs	Financial info	Religious info	Religious info	Religious info	Rate things
Financial info	Religious info	Rate things	IM	Play games	Read blogs
Rate things	Read blogs	Read blogs	Play games	Listen to music	Donate to charity
Religious info	Rate things	Play games	Read blogs	Read blogs	Listen to music
Online auction	Online auction	Online auction	Online auction	Donate to charity	Podcasts
Podcasts	Donate to charity	Donate to charity	Donate to charity	Online auction	Online auction
Donate to charity	Podcasts	Podcasts	Podcasts	Podcasts	Blog
Blog	Blog	Blog	Blog	Blog	IM
Virtual worlds	Virtual worlds	Virtual worlds	Virtual worlds	Virtual worlds	Virtual worlds

Source: Kathryn Zickuhr, *Generation 2010*, Pew Internet & American Life Project, December 16, 2010, http://pewinternet.org/Reports/2010/Generations-2010/Activities/Summary .aspx, accessed December 31, 2010. Used by permission of Pew Internet & American Life Project.

Learning
Objective 3

What We Do Online

For decades, Westerners spent most of their media time watching television. Now, those who are connected spend about the same amount of time online instead of being glued to the Boob tube. Consumers perceive the Internet as the most essential of all media. Table 2 provides a list of the most common activities people engage in online. When we look at this list, it is easy to see how user behavior drives marketing efforts online. For example, Internet users spend much of their time emailing, so many advertisers send **permission emails.** Permission emails are the direct mail of the digital age—they are personalized email offers sent to individuals who "**opt in**" to receiving marketing communications. Opting in is an agreement activity in which an individual gives his or her permission for the source to send relevant messages.

These advertisers might also embed **display ads** in some email sites. Display ads are advertisements shown on websites. They may be simple **banner ads** that appear above, below, or on the side of a site; **rich media ads** that include streaming video; or **text ads** that present short, clickable headlines. If you use Google's email client, Gmail, you've likely noticed the text ads that appear along the side of your email inbox.

Another popular activity is **online search,** which simply means using a search engine to find information using key words. Millions of us instinctively check **search engines** such as Google and Yahoo! to answer almost any kind of question—so much so that the word "Google" has become a verb as well as a noun. Search engine advertising leverages that behavior by presenting display ads associated with the search terms entered by the user.

TABLE 2

**Participation Rates
in Popular Online
Activities**

Source: Adapted from *Pew
Internet & American Life
Project, Online Activities/Total,*
www.pewinternet.org/
Static-Pages/Trend-Data/
Online-Activites-Total.aspx,
accessed December 31, 2010.
Used by permission of Pew
Internet & American Life
Project.

Activity	Percent of Internet Users
Send or read email	94%
Use a search engine to find information	87
Look for information online about a service or product you are thinking of buying	78
Get news	75
Go online just for fun or to pass the time	72
Buy a product	72
Watch a video on a video sharing site such as YouTube or Google Video	66
Use an online social networking site such as MySpace, Facebook, or LinkedIn	61
Look for information on Wikipedia	53
Use online classified ads or sites such as Craigslist	53
Send instant messages	47
Upload photos to a website so you can share them with others online	46
Play online games	35
Read someone else's online journal or blog	32
Rate a product, service, or person using an online rating system	32
Post a comment or review online about a product you bought or a service you received	32
Share something online that you created yourself	30
Pay to access or download digital content online	28
Categorize or tag online content such as a photo, news story, or blog post	28
Post comments to an online news group, website, blog, or photo site	26
Download a podcast so you can listen to it or view it later	21
View live images online of a remote location or person, using a webcam	17
Use Twitter or other status-update service	17
Create or work on web pages or blogs for others, including friends, groups you belong to, or for work	15
Take material you find online—such as songs, text, or images—and remix it into your own artistic creation	15

Activity	Percent of Internet Users
Download or share files using peer-to-peer file-sharing networks, such as BitTorrent or LimeWire	15
Sell something online	15
Create or work on your own web page	14
Create or work on your own online journal or blog	14
Participate in an online discussion, a listserv, or other online group forum that helps people with personal issues or health problems	7
Visit virtual worlds such as Second Life	4

Why We Login

Web users increasingly participate in social networks such as Facebook, play online social games (turn-based, multiplayer games designed to be played within social networks) such as Farmville within the network community, comment on the posts of friends, update status messages, and share content. Likewise, brands are joining in on these sites as they add content and try to converse with consumers. What's your motivation for the time you log on social networks? Chances are there are many reasons that drive you to visit these sites. Some of these motives probably seem like no-brainers, but others may surprise you. These are the most common impulses researchers have identified:

- **Affinity impulse**: Social networks enable participants to express an affinity, to acknowledge a liking and/or relationship with individuals and reference groups. When you use Facebook to stay in touch with high school friends and to make new friends, you are responding to the affinity impulse.

- **Prurient impulse**: People may feel a curiosity about others and want to feed this interest—this is known as the prurient impulse. Online, we can satisfy our curiosity by "following" people on Twitter and visiting their profiles. Surely it is the prurient impulse that led nearly 5 million Twitter users to follow Ashton Kutcher's daily tweets while millions of others relentlessly track the ups-and-downs of actress Lindsay Lohan—will she prevail, or crash and burn?

- **Contact comfort** and **immediacy impulse**: People have a natural drive to feel a sense of psychological closeness to others. Contact comfort is the sense of relief we feel from knowing others in our network are accessible. Immediacy also lends a sense of relief in that the contact is without delay. Do you feel lost without your mobile phone? Do you feel anxious if you haven't checked Facebook recently? When you reply to a message, do you keep checking for a response? These are indicators of your need for contact comfort and immediacy.

- **Altruistic impulse**: Some participate in social media as a way to do something good. They use social media to "pay it forward." The altruistic impulse is also aided by the immediacy of social media, and this value has been played out in the **immediate altruistic responses (IAR)** of social media users to aid calls during crises such as the earthquake relief for Haiti or Japan.[4] Individuals want to do good and do it quickly—social media makes it easier to contribute in the form of a cash donation or a service to the community.

THE DARK SIDE OF SOCIAL MEDIA

As people spend more time screen to screen and less face to face, it's inevitable that our relationships will center less on the physical world and more on the online experience. **Contact comfort** refers to the psychological relief we feel when we are assured of the accessibility of companions in our network. The concept is based on the early work of the psychologist Harry Harlow, who found that monkeys were motivated by contact comfort, even more so than by food. A classic experiment involved two groups of baby monkeys that had been removed from their mothers. They were exposed to two types of "surrogate mothers," one made out of terrycloth and one made of wire. Some of these "mothers" provided milk from a bottle whereas others did not. The babies clung only to the wire structures that provided milk—but they attached themselves to the soft terrycloth "mothers" whether or not this resulted in being fed.

Whether it's a soft piece of downy terrycloth or the reassurance that your friends are online to give you advice, what happens when we are deprived of this contact comfort? Some researchers and public policymakers are concerned about the growing threat of **social media addiction**, a psychological dependency and recurring compulsion to engage in social media activity. It is in part characterized by the limited amount of time addicts can go before checking in on their favorite social media sites, suggesting a need for **contact immediacy**. This term refers to the speed at which we can communicate and deliver messages even from afar. The immediacy of social media communication channels have made many of us impatient with the delays we associate with more traditional modes such as email and mail. It remains to be seen how the shortened attention span digital media encourages will impact our ability to absorb information that doesn't include these updates (e.g., traditional college lectures!).

- **Validation impulse**: Social media focuses intently on the individual. You can share as much or as little of your opinions and activities, and comment on those of others. This focus on the self highlights the validation impulse, in other words, feeding one's own ego. Andy Warhol famously said, "In the future, everyone will be world famous for 15 minutes." The legendary artist and visionary understood even way back in 1968 that the media had the power to spotlight almost anybody and everybody. For better or worse, it looks like Warhol was right. With social media, anyone anywhere in the world can earn worldwide fame for a brief time. The only catch is that with social media, the fame probably won't last even 15 minutes.

  As attention spans continue to diminish, we focus on one "micro-celebrity" but before you can say "Twitter" we're on to the next. Take for instance, the story of Sarah Killen (her Twitter handle is @LovelyButton). On March 5, 2010, Conan O'Brian announced he would follow one person and only one person on Twitter, whom he would choose at random. That person was Sarah Killen. When Conan first followed Sarah, she had three followers. Within 24 hours, 16,000 people were following her. In that same period of time, she was interviewed by magazines and talk shows ranging from *MTV News* to *New York* magazine. Sarah's fame lasted more than 15 minutes, but not much more—news stories peaked on March 6 and were over by March 10. Still, for those who want a stab at the brass ring, social media activity, especially in the form of publishing one's own content, can validate one's sense of self-importance and ego.

Learning Objective 4

Market Segmentation: Slicing the Social Media Pie

Marketers are rapidly adopting social media marketing strategies and techniques, but social media marketing will work only to the extent that these new media platforms can reach the customers organizations want to talk to in the digital space. And, just reaching people isn't the only issue: Not all social media users are the same. Just as there are segments of consumers in the overall marketplace, there are segments within the population of social consumers. For example, we've already seen that there are important differences between digital natives and digital immigrants. Understanding these segments and how their attitudes and behaviors differ is a critical component to devise an effective social media marketing strategy.

Although it may seem like everyone is online, and most everyone is on Facebook, the extent to which a person's life is digital varies based on their lifestyle, personality, demographics, and even their geographic and economic conditions. These characteristics represent the bases of segmentation marketers use when they divide a population into manageable groups. **Market segmentation** is the process of dividing a market into distinct groups that have common needs and characteristics. Marketers use several variables as the basis to segment markets. Let's briefly review each and try to understand how these variables translate into the online world.

Geographic Segmentation

Geographic segmentation refers to segmenting markets by region, country, market size, market density, or climate. For example, North Face can expect to sell more parkas to people who live in winter climates whereas Roxy will move more bikinis in sunny vacation spots. Geographic segmentation will become increasingly relevant to social media marketers, not only due to location-based targeting based on a business's distribution channel, but also because social media increasingly incorporates **GPS technology**, a satellite system that provides real-time location and time information.

This innovation should aid local businesses who can use the technology to target specific people based on physical presence. Services such as Foursquare (Gowalla is a similar competitor) position themselves as geo-targeted social media. In other words, Foursquare is part social network, part GPS tracking system. Users log in via their smartphones and other Wi-Fi-enabled mobile devices and "check in" to their location. From there they can see if they have friends nearby (both services will import friends from Facebook and other accounts), and also see links to local businesses. This is where segmentation strategy comes into play.

Geographic segmentation via social media is relevant to local businesses that want to increase retail traffic in physical store locations. As Foursquare members check in, local businesses in that area can reach out to them with special offers and interactive promotions such as free drinks or discounts. There are awards for checking in to business venues most recently and most frequently; these instill a sense of loyalty among users. Importantly for the local merchants who use the service, Foursquare offers a business "dashboard" that includes metrics on the number of check-ins, the times of day people check in, the most recent visitors, and the most frequent visitors.[5] Of course, the offers require consumer cooperation—without check-ins, the promotions won't be effective. So are wired consumers checking in? Indeed they are. A recent study from JiWire, a Wi-Fi provider, found that 65 percent of Wi-Fi users said they frequently use apps that require they provide their physical location.[6] When it comes to community merchants, social is local.

Demographic Segmentation

When marketers employ **demographic segmentation** they utilize common characteristics such as age, gender, income, ethnic background, educational attainment, family life cycle, and occupation to understand how to group similar consumers together. General Mills creates specialized campaigns for different demographic segments, such as when it launched QueRicaVida.com as an online platform for Latina moms.

How can demographic segmentation benefit social media marketers? Let's take a look at a campaign from Huggies, a brand of diapers Kimberly-Clark manufactures. How would you describe Huggies' target market demographically? That's easy—primarily female, between the ages of 20 and 40, and in the parenting (early) years of the family life cycle. Traditionally, a brand such as Huggies would target young mothers with daytime, network television commercials and print ads in magazines such as *Parenting*. If the brand wanted to test the social media environment, it might sponsor a "precious babies" photo contest where it would ask parents to submit pictures of their babes in Huggies brand diapers on a microsite, and then encourage all participants to vote for the most popular image.

In this case, though, Huggies has taken a very different route; its strategy highlights the importance of considering demographic characteristics. Here's an overview of the campaign. Huggies® sponsors a MomInspired ™ Grant Program that will award $15,000 grants to mothers with product ideas that address an unmet need of parents.[7] Mothers can share ideas on the Huggies MomInspired microsite, which also features the proposals of other inspired moms, a tweet stream from moms, and detailed resources to ensure inspired mothers understand how to write a winning business proposal. As you'll see later in the book, brands can use traditional media to activate social media initiatives, or can use social media to activate traditional communications plans. For Huggies, the campaign is 100 percent social: Online publicity, tweets, Facebook updates on its Fan Page, StumbleUpon traffic on its microsite, and a "share" button support the campaign. Huggies relies on mothers in the know to tell other mothers about the opportunity.

Is this campaign an effective way to reach the Huggies' target market? The approach is clearly targeted to mothers and does so in a way that suggests the Huggies brand really understands the challenges of motherhood. It goes beyond the basic love and pride a mother feels for her child to the underlying motives and needs that face mothers. This is a key component of demographic targeting. It's about more than the basic facts. The marketer takes the demographic knowledge and uses it to understand the needs of the market.

Psychographic Segmentation

Psychographic segmentation approaches slice up the market based on personality, motives, lifestyles, and attitudes and opinions. These variables may be used alone or combined with other segmentation bases such as demographics. Psychographics tend to provide the richest picture of a consumer segment in that the descriptions of psychographic segments help marketers to know the real person making the consumption decisions. When BMW wanted to understand how different types of people think about cars, its research identified segments such as "upper liberals" (socially conscious, open-minded professionals who prefer the roominess and flexibility of SUVs), "post-moderns" (high-earning innovators such as architects, entrepreneurs, and artists who like the individualistic statements made by driving convertibles and roadsters), "upper conservatives" (made up of wealthy, traditional thinkers who like upper-crust, traditional sedans), and "modern mainstream" (family oriented, up-and-comers who want a luxury brand but likely can't afford more than the lowest-end model). Using this segmentation scheme as an anchor, BMW created vehicles for several categories and then expanded its product line to capture additional segments via its acquisitions of Rolls-Royce and the Mini Cooper.[8]

Let's consider a practical application of psychographics in the social media space. The greeting card industry has experienced declining sales for some time now. Today fewer people send holiday greeting cards; many instead send email and e-cards to loved ones on holidays. A large-scale study by Unity Marketing identified four psychographic segments among greeting card buyers. Unfortunately for the greeting card industry, a segment called "Alternative Seeker," the largest and fastest growing group the study identified, is also the most eager to find an alternative to the traditional card.[9] Alternative Seekers view social media as an answer to staying in touch with friends and family on both a daily basis and on special occasions such as birthdays and holidays.

Unity's report warns that greeting card companies are at risk as people turn to social media as a replacement to traditional cards. Obviously as consumers' reliance on the U.S. Postal Service continues to drop, this is not good news for traditional greeting card companies. But this change presents an opportunity for others. Hallmark, the market leader in the greeting card industry, creates new product offers for Alternative Seekers such as the Hallmark Social Calendar, a Facebook application, and the Hallmark Mobile Greetings mobile app. The Social Calendar enables Facebook users to track birthdays and other holidays and get reminders, but it does something even more enticing. With the

BYTES TO BUCKS

Marathon runners are a special breed. Before the 2010 New York Marathon, the tens of thousands of these dedicated (or crazy?) athletes received an email asking them to participate in a new social networking project spearheaded by actor Edward Norton, who is also an avid runner. They were invited to participate in a fund-raising site he started with three partners called crowdrise.com. The platform enables people to easily set up a page for a cause they support and then reach out to others in their social networks to contribute. The actor observed, "The '60s were the era of people realizing they could rally together to express their priorities. [Social networking offers] a new way of getting people together to create power in numbers." And, he notes that it can help users express themselves through the causes they support. The idea for Crowdrise and its partnership with the New York City Marathon both originated during the 2009 Marathon, when Norton ran to raise money for a charity in Kenya. Prior to that event he held daily contests for donors on his Twitter account and raised $1.2 million for a wilderness reserve. This experience showed him the fund-raising potential of social networking; now celebrities such as actor Seth Rogen and musician Flea (bassist for the Red Hot Chili Peppers) as well as many everyday people use Crowdrise to involve people in a variety of causes.[10]

Social Calendar, you can send "Wall Wishes," virtual gifts, and other greetings Hallmark style! What's more—it's free. With Hallmark's Mobile App, you can send mobile-to-mobile MMS greetings.

Benefit Segmentation

Benefit segmentation groups individuals in the marketing universe according to the benefits they seek from the products available in the market. For example, in the auto industry people who buy hybrids and electric cars look for different benefits from a car than those who buy muscle cars or SUVs.

What benefits do consumers want from their interactions with brands in social media environments? There are competing schools of thought on this issue. Some industry experts argue that consumers want to have meaningful relationships with the brands they use frequently, and particularly with those brands they consider lovemarks. This term refers to brands that inspire passionate loyalty in their customers. Kevin Roberts, CEO of Saatchi & Saatchi, originated the concept; his agency looks for ways to deepen bonds with consumers and thus cultivate these lovemarks. Saatchi & Saatchi even maintains a website that encourages people to nominate the brands that inspire them in different categories. For example, brands in the beverage category include Guinness, Inca Kola, and Boost Juice.[11] You can nominate your own favorites at www.lovemarks.com.

If Roberts and others are right, brands can use social media engagement with customers to build the relationship—conversing, sharing, caring, and interacting in each other's lives over time (just like people do). Do consumers make friends with brands? If we use the growing trend of online "friending" as an indicator, the answer is yes. According to Razorfish, a leading digital marketing agency, 40 percent of online consumers have become a friend or fan of a brand on a social networking site. Even more have interacted with brands in other ways; 70 percent report having read a corporate blog, 67 percent watch branded videos on YouTube, and 65 percent play a branded game online.[12]

Consumers may also seek help from trusted brands to help them manage their lives. The research firm trendwatching.com suggests that time-starved consumers who use mobile Wi-Fi–enabled devices turn to brands to help them take care of life's requirements more efficiently. Brands that can provide this benefit to consumers are called **brand butlers**.[13]

The growing popularity of mobile apps provided by brands, such as the GEICO Glovebox app, are examples of how brands can serve as butlers. This app enables customers to view their insurance card with their phone, pay their insurance bill, report accident information, find instructions for what to do in roadside crisis situations, and call for taxis and rental car reservations. By making activities that are sometimes necessary but always a hassle to consumers easy and accessible, GEICO provides a benefit to its time-starved customers. The idea of seeking out brands to serve in the role of brand butler is consistent with a key principle of marketing—that of offering value to customers. Brands that provide supporting services via social media add value to their product offering.

Besides wanting an emotional bond and valuable services, consumers may also want to simply save money. Razorfish's *Feed* report found that 44 percent of those who follow a brand on Twitter and 37 percent of those who had friended a brand on Facebook did so exclusively to be privy to special deals and offers. The popularity of location services such as FourSquare supports this reasoning; as we've seen, users are rewarded with deals when they check in with local business venues. Brands with successful track records in the social media space often use these platforms to aggressively offer incentives that motivate people to choose the brand because they can save money. Take Jet Blue, for instance. To celebrate its 10th anniversary, it promoted $10 fares on Facebook, targeting Facebook users who were fans or friends of JetBlue and those who had a vacation-related status message on their Walls.[14]

Jet Blue's campaign is an example of a **sales promotion;** an initiative that seeks to motivate buyer behavior during a limited period of time by offering a discount or prize. Sales promotions are a tried-and-true tool; we see them all around us in the form of coupons, sweepstakes, and contests. The social media space is fertile ground to extend these techniques, though sometimes danger lurks on this road. Ironically, because of the viral nature of social media, marketers can be *too* successful if they offer a promotion that spreads wider than originally intended. A key principle of Web 2.0 is scalability. If a social service or campaign can't scale, it won't be sustainable. That's when brands trade short-term successes for long-term losses. This is exactly what happened to Subway when the sandwich franchise launched a promotion to give away one million free subs. The online campaign drew such a heavy response that the promotion hit the one million mark in just 3 days. The parent company shut down the free coupon registration at that point—but individual franchisees had to deal with irate customers who showed up to claim their free sandwich.[15]

Behavioral Segmentation

Behavioral segmentation divides consumers into groups based on how they act with regard to a brand or a product category. For example, knowing how much of a product a group uses and how often they purchase that product can be useful information—especially because "heavy users" often differ quite a bit from occasional users. And, even though these hard-core customers usually are a minority of the total customers that patronize an organization, they often account for a lot of its sales. In fact, marketers rely on a rule of thumb we call the **80/20 Rule:** Twenty percent of a brand's customers purchase 80 percent of its products. This ratio is not set in stone, but it often is surprisingly accurate.

This idea of a hard-core minority is very important in the social media area. Quite simply it reminds us how key a brand's dedicated fan base can be to success or failure. These heavy users tend not only to use the product; they also are the most likely candidates to blog about it, retweet articles to their network on Twitter, or friend it on Facebook.

Furthermore, in the context of interactive advertising online, behavioral targeting means delivering relevant display ads based on the behaviors we exhibit as we surf the Web. **Behavioral targeting** relies on the use of software and Web analytics, as well as cookies and IP addresses, to create a profile of individual behavior marketers then use to deliver relevant ads. For example, a Facebook user who has just viewed the price of flights to New York City on Expedia might then be shown a display ad that announces discounts on Broadway theater tickets. This strategy is especially useful for brands that advertise within social communities because the community provider is privy to a database of information on user demographics and interests. For instance, Gather, a social network for older intellectuals, targets ads placed on its site using online behavior within the community.

Generally advertisers rely on **ad networks** to manage behavioral targeting for them. Ad networks are basically media brokers that partner with websites in order to access information about their visitor traffic and then sell space on the websites to their advertisers. The tracking process uses **cookies**, small pieces of data that are dropped onto consumers' hard drives, to track searches, site visits, clicks, and even the contents of electronic shopping carts. This is where things get sticky.

Though behavioral targeting online is more effective than non-targeted advertising, the industry faces privacy concerns from regulators and consumers. The Federal Trade Commission threatened to regulate the practice if the industry couldn't govern itself in the protection of consumers' right to privacy. At issue—some consumers do not want their actions tracked and others may not even realize it's happening.

Marketers generally prefer to self-regulate rather than risk an increase in government monitoring and centralized enforcement of violations. Also, they don't want to raise what they term the **privacy salience** among wired individuals. This means they hope to address people's concerns about privacy violations before their user base revolts out of fears that companies are intruding into their personal lives.[16] The "mini-revolution" against Facebook exemplified this problem—large numbers of users were not happy about Facebook's privacy settings and talked about deleting their Facebook accounts.[17]

To address the issue, 12 major companies met in 2009 in conjunction with the Interactive Advertising Bureau (IAB) to develop self-regulatory advertising principles. Since then, the group produced a governing document for the industry with seven guiding principles based on consumer education, transparency, consumer control, data security, changes to existing behavioral advertising policies, care of sensitive data, and accountability.[18] In addition, these advertisers agreed to participate in the "Advertising Option Program" to include an icon on all display advertising it served to consumers based upon their behavioral data.

Learning Objective 5

Social Media Segments

Because social media is such a new area, marketers are still figuring out just how to use it, and to what extent they should rely on these platforms when they identify their target markets and try to communicate with them. One brand may add a social media piece to a broader strategy when it creates a Facebook page, whereas another may replace virtually all of its traditional advertising with "new media" messages. Decisions regarding just how much to rely on social media and how to design programs that will be effective require us to understand as much as we can about just who participates in social media and how they may differ from one another. We need to address these questions:

- In what online communities do these consumers participate?
- What activities do they participate in online and in social communities, specifically?
- What role does social technology play in their lives? Is it for keeping in touch with friends and family, a productivity tool, a stress reliever?

Knowing the answers to these questions will help you to ensure that the social media marketing strategies and tactics you plan have a shot to resonate with the target market. There are countless examples of social media marketing campaigns that have failed. In fact, Gartner, a research firm specializing in technology, claims that half—that's right, 50 percent—of social media campaigns fail.[19] Why the huge number of bombs? Probably a major reason is simply that the social strategy is not matched to the target audience. A contest that requires players to upload original video content will not succeed with a target market that primarily consumes content but does not create its own. A promotion for a free song download offered on Twitter will not work if the band's fans tend to hang out on MySpace instead. A stunt from Skittles to feed live streams from social media communities to its website will not appeal to parents if the live feed includes profanity inappropriate for their children.

How then should we identify and define social segments? The segmentation schemes of consumers participating in social communities online are still in their infancy. We'll take a look at three typologies of digital consumers, each of which offer insights into the lives of social consumers. Then we'll view a typology specifically about Twitter users that may provide some insight about our motives to participate in social communities.

Social Technographics

Forrester Research introduced the concept of **social technographics,** based on research it conducted on the social and digital lives of consumers. This work became the foundation for a book, *Groundswell,* by Charlene Li and Josh Bernoff.[20] From that first study, Forrester identified six types of people (of those online) based on how those people use and interact with social media. Because the types reflect increasing levels of involvement in social media, Forrester used a ladder image to illustrate the segments (see Figure 3). The system classifies people into the types based upon their social activities within the last month. The types are not exclusive—some people fit into more than one category based on their activities. Still, the ladder is indicative of the level of involvement in social media a person has reached given their activities. Forrester continues to collect data as social media further penetrates our culture, and to study the social technographics of specific groups including businesses.

Creators are categorized as such because—guess what?—they create content. They add value to the social Web and their social communities as they contribute content to be shared with others. Of wired consumers, 24 percent are creators. User-generated content (UGC) is one of the defining cornerstones of the social Web. What constitutes creating content? UGC may refer to a broad range of content ranging from video, photos, blogs, vlogs, comments, podcasts, forum discussions, online product reviews, wiki contributions, and consumer-generated advertising. The technographics profile categorizes people as creators if they recently published a blog entry, wrote and posted an article online, maintained a personal web page, and uploaded video or audio they created to a site such as YouTube. In other words, creators are those who at least in part provide the ammunition with which the rest of the social community interacts.

Forrester added **conversationalists** to the social technographic ladder in 2010 as the company recognized that people (33 percent of wired consumers) were *talking* through social media and doing so frequently (at least weekly). What does this mean? Simply, conversationalists maintain discussions with their friends via Twitter and Facebook updates and comments. Generally, conversationalists are the youngest of the segments, and more likely to be female.

Critics are reactors to content, rather than creators of content. They interact socially primarily by posting comments, ratings, or reviews and editing wikis. Although critics are not creating original content at the same level as creators, their contributions are highly valued in their social communities. Reviews and ratings are among the most utilized sources of information in the social Web. Critics are more than consumers of content; they embellish the content others contribute and thus create **consumer-fortified media,** also known as *augmented content.* Forrester estimates that in 2009, 37 percent of online participants were critics.

As we move down the technographics ladder, the segments become less responsible for content and more involved in the *consumption* of content. Of course, creators and critics are also consumers of content, but they are defined more by their contributions than by their consumption.

Collectors tend to be efficient and organized users of social content. They use **RSS feeds** (syndicators of content that send content directly to subscribers) to receive regular updates on the information they want; bookmark and share online content; add tags to content such as bookmarked articles, photos, and videos; and "vote" for content. Though collectors are not contributors in the sense that creators and critics are, their social activities ensure that they are regular consumers of content and help the communities to which they belong by sorting and rating the content others

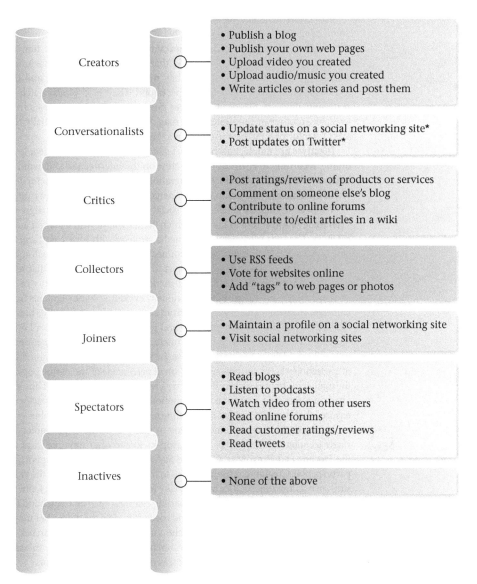

Figure 3

Social Technographic Ladder

Source: 2011 Social Technographics® For Business Technology Buyers,http://forrester.typepad.com/groundswell/2010/01/conversationalists-get-onto-the-ladder.html, accessed May 28, 2011.

Creators
- Publish a blog
- Publish your own web pages
- Upload video you created
- Upload audio/music you created
- Write articles or stories and post them

Conversationalists
- Update status on a social networking site*
- Post updates on Twitter*

Critics
- Post ratings/reviews of products or services
- Comment on someone else's blog
- Contribute to online forums
- Contribute to/edit articles in a wiki

Collectors
- Use RSS feeds
- Vote for websites online
- Add "tags" to web pages or photos

Joiners
- Maintain a profile on a social networking site
- Visit social networking sites

Spectators
- Read blogs
- Listen to podcasts
- Watch video from other users
- Read online forums
- Read customer ratings/reviews
- Read tweets

Inactives
- None of the above

Groups include people participating in at least one of the indicated activities at least monthly. *Conversationalists participate in one or more of the indicated activities at least weekly.

post. Collectors may not give the social audience a cool new video on YouTube, or publish poetry on WeBook, but they do add value when they help to organize content in a way that benefits the social network as a whole. Collectors make up just 20 percent of the social population.

Joiners represent fully 59 percent of online Americans (according to 2009 Forrester data). Why are joiners such a popular group? Joiners are people who maintain a profile on one or more social networking sites and who visit those sites on a regular basis. Joining is fun. Joining is easy. It takes advantage of the enhancements available in Web 2.0 technologies and social software that makes it simple for even technophobes to participate in social networks.

Spectators (estimated at 70 percent of those online) sit on the periphery of social communities. Some people call these types **lurkers** because they consume the content of others, while they keep their own identities at a distance. Spectators do a lot of things that others do—they consume content. What makes them unique is that they are *primarily* consumers of content. They don't create, augment, share, or join in. They mostly just read, watch, and listen. What activities then are the activities that characterize spectators? They read blogs, watch videos, listen to podcasts, read online forums, and read customer ratings. In essence, spectators treat online content like that available in other media—television, magazines, and radio. Essentially they still consume one-way Web 1.0 information; they just do it in a Web 2.0 environment.

Inactives are online, but they aren't social participants. Some people (about 17 percent of those online, according to Forrester) spend time on the Internet and still avoid social communities. Being inactive is largely a by-product of generation. Of those users in developed countries worldwide who are in the under 35 age group, only 10 percent fall into the inactives category.

When an organization develops a social media marketing campaign, it can use Forrester's Social Technology Profile Tool to identify which tactics will fit with its target audience's social media usage category. The idea is to match your media strategy with how your target market uses social media to maximize the likelihood you will connect with your intended customers.

For example, it wouldn't be too smart to set up a UGC contest that requires entrants to film and upload their own video if your target market is composed primarily of spectators. Or at the other extreme, there is the danger of unintentionally excluding some segments from the experience. Unilever launched an initiative that solicits ads from consumers for several of its brands, including Ben & Jerry's, Dove, and Axe. The winners win cash and prizes, as well as a trip to a London film festival. However, the campaign focuses on creators. The microsite only provides information for video creation rules and uploading guidelines. Judges will choose the winners. There are no planned participation routes for the other technographic segments. Only a small percentage of the online population are creators, whereas the market for brands such as Ben & Jerry's and Dove is quite broad. Thus, even though Unilever developed an interesting social media promotion with an experienced partner, the company unwittingly ensured that about 76 percent of its online target audience won't be able to engage.

 Unilever's campaign reminds us that in many cases the target audience will include more than a single technographic type. For this reason it's key to offer multiple ways to participate. For example, the Doritos and Pepsi Max *Crash the Super Bowl* contest offers opportunities for several forms of participation. Creators contribute videos to the contest site and share the videos on other media sharing sites such as YouTube. Critics rate and vote on the videos submitted. Conversationalists talk about the videos. Collectors share the video links using channels such as Twitter and Facebook and tag the videos so that others can find them. Joiners and spectators view the videos but may not help to promote them. Still, they add to the overall impact of the contest because brand awareness for Doritos and Pepsi Max increase and joiners and spectators may not have been exposed to the messages prior to the Super Bowl event had it not been for the creators, conversationalists, and collectors.

Pew Internet Technology Types

The Pew Internet & American Life Project published a paper called "The Mobile Difference."[21] As increasing numbers go online and participate in social communities from mobile devices, this Pew report sought to better understand consumer views of mobile Internet access. In the study, participants were asked about their attitudes toward a variety of online activities as well as their motives. What resulted was a typology of 10 digital lifestyles for the American consumer. In this scheme, digital lifestyle groups are based on two characteristics: (1) whether they hold a positive or negative view of **digital mobility** and (2) relationships with assets (gadgets and services), actions (activities), and attitudes (how technology fits in their lives).

Pew defines digital mobility in terms of whether the individual welcomes mobility as a way to further delve into digital communications or keeps Internet communication technologies at a distance. Five groups have an increasing reliance on mobile technologies as a way to connect with others online; the other five groups are "stationary" in their use of Internet communications. The research suggests that when it comes to social media strategies, marketers should target those with positive views of mobility. The use of social media is associated with their use of the Internet and mobile devices whereas the stationary groups are less likely to be heavily engaged in social media. Table 3 summarizes the 10 groups Pew identified.

TABLE 3

Pew Internet Technology Types

Source: Adapted from John Horrigan, "The Mobile Difference," Pew Internet & American Life Project, March 2009, http://pewinternet. org/Reports/2009/5-The-Mobile-Difference-Typology. aspx, accessed March 27, 2010. Used by permission of Pew Internet & American Life Project.

Motivated by Mobility

- **Digital collaborators** (8 percent of U.S. adults): Digital collaborators have the most gadgets of any group and use them to work, play, create, and share by visiting social networks with their mobile devices. Fifty-four percent have posted user-generated content online and 18 percent have an avatar. Key demographics: mostly male, late 30s, well-educated, relatively high incomes.
- **Ambivalent networkers** (7 percent of U.S. adults): Ambivalent networkers use mobile devices to visit social networks and for texting, but they also feel like people need breaks from so much connectivity. Fifty-four percent of ambivalent networkers have a social network profile and 25 percent blog, according to the study. Key demographics: male (60 percent), young (late 20s), ethnically diverse.
- **Media movers** (7 percent of U.S. adults): Media movers create content such as photos and share them on social networks using their mobile devices. For them, digital is all about being social and connecting with others. Forty-six percent have a social network profile. They are managers of content and have a high attachment to the Internet. Key demographics: male (56 percent), mid-30s, family oriented, middle income.
- **Roving nodes** (9 percent of U.S. adults): This group wants to be connected but primarily for work. They use texting and email and rely upon their mobile devices for productivity. Social networking is not a key concern. Thirty-two percent have a social network profile, but overall this group relies on voice communication, texting, and email for communication. Key demographics: female (56 percent), late 30s, well-educated, high incomes.
- **Mobile newbies** (8 percent of U.S. adults): This group is relatively new to mobile connectivity to the Internet. Overall, they are more focused on old media than new. Key demographics: female (55 percent), 50s, lower educational and income levels.

Stationary Media Preferred

- **Desktop veterans** (13 percent of U.S. adults): Content to use desktop computers with high-speed Internet access. Key demographics: male (55 percent), mid-40s, well educated relatively high incomes.
- **Drifting surfers** (14 percent of U.S. adults): Infrequent online users who wouldn't mind giving up the Internet and their mobile phone. Key demographics: female (56 percent), early 40s, middle income.
- **Information encumbered** (10 percent of U.S. adults): This group suffers from information overload. They prefer old media such as television to the Internet. Key demographics: men (66 percent), early 50s, average education, lower-middle income.
- **Tech indifferent** (10 percent of U.S. adults): This group is made up of light users of the Internet who would be willing to give up their digital connectivity. Key demographics: female (55 percent), late 50s, lower income.
- **Off the network** (14 percent of U.S. adults): This group is made up of people who do not use the Internet and do not have mobile phones. They may have had some experience in the past, but did not choose to continue participation. Key demographics: low-income seniors.

Figure 4

Anderson Analytics' Social Media Users and Nonusers

Sources: Anderson's website and also published at Jennifer Van Grove, "What Type of Social Media User Are You?," *Mashable. com*, June 15 2009, http:// mashable.com/2009/07/15/ social-media-users/, accessed June 21, 2011. Used by permission of Anderson Analytics, LLC.

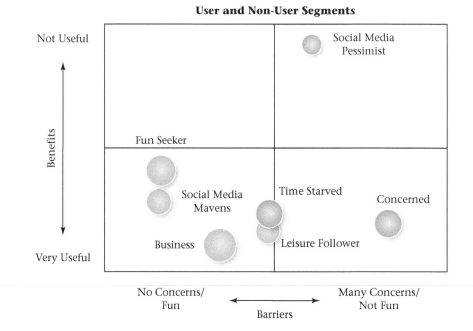

Anderson Analytics: Users and Nonusers

Another description of social media users is provided by Anderson Analytics. This typology plots segments along two axes: the perceived benefits of using social media and the perceived barriers to using social media.[22] Figure 4 illustrates the segments that reflect both social media users and nonusers. Users include fun seekers, social media mavens, business, and leisure followers. Nonusers include social media pessimists, concerned, and time starved. Only the social media pessimist truly finds social media to lack utility benefits. The concerned feel the negatives outweigh the benefits while the time-starved have barriers too great to overcome.

The Anderson Analytics model of social behavior is more limited in its applicability than the other models we've presented. Its value exists primarily in understanding the types of barriers consumers face as they adopt and explore social media communities. In particular, this work reminds us that in many cases time is an issue—whether it's saving time because of the "always on" aspect of social media or wasting time when a user feels it will take too long to learn and adapt to the new platform. The time-starved segment in particular may describe those stationary consumers who have not fully adopted mobile technologies. The concerned are especially worried about the downside of social media such as privacy violations, cyberbullying, and cyberstalking—issues we'll address later.

Microblog User Types

Our last model of social segmentation was suggested by Kevin Hillstrom, CEO of MineThatData.[23] Twitter is a service for microblogging, the posting of short messages. Hillstrom analyzed posts (called "tweets") on Twitter as (1) original statements, (2) responses to the statements of others, or (3) re-posts (retweets) of the statements of others. Consistent with prior work that showed most microblog posts originated from a small percentage of members, Hillstrom found that the **Pareto Principle** describes the productivity of microblog members.[24]

You may not think you know what that means, but it turns out you do. Remember our discussion about the 80/20 Rule? This term refers to the same thing as the Pareto Principle: Roughly 80 percent of events come from 20 percent of the causes. Consistent with our observations about the importance of heavy users, Hillstrom found that 25 percent of users accounted for more than 80 percent of the posts. In fact, 5 percent accounted for more than 40 percent of the posts. What's most interesting to our discussion of social segments, though, is Hillstrom's identification of four user types. These four user types can be viewed on a two-by-two matrix ranging from whether a user posted few or many posts and whether the posts were reposted content or original content.

Although Hillstrom's typology is focused on microblog behaviors and segments, it mimics behaviors we observe in many online communities. Power players such as the *elite* are considered influencers in social communities like Digg, because those users provide content for the masses. *Difference makers* participate only when they see clear value. They may be managing their own time/benefit analysis in terms of how they dedicate time to participating in communities, with a focus on saying less but making what they say count. *Knowledge seekers* use the community to learn and grow. This is definitely a behavior present in many communities, though it is perhaps more visible in communities like LinkedIn. Lastly, *attention seekers* exist in every community, online and offline.

Chapter Summary

How are our lives reflected online? In what ways are individuals involved in the four zones of social media?

Increasingly our lives are spent online checking email, shopping, banking, watching videos, playing games, and socializing in social networks. This is illustrated in the activities revealed in Table 2. In zone 1, consumers interact and communicate with others in their networks. In zone 2, we publish our own content as well as consume the content produced by others (both commercial and user-generated). If you've watched videos on YouTube, you've spent part of your online activity in zone 2. Playing games online is a major activity of zone 3 and shopping online is a prelude to zone 4.

How and why does digital culture play a role in consumer behavior?

Culture has changed as Internet access around the world increases, and particularly so in areas with high penetration rates. Those consumers, the wired ones, have experienced a shift to digital primacy, a cultural change by which consumers turn first to digital channels for content over traditional media. Despite this shift, wired consumers still differ from one another in many ways. One prime cultural divide is between those known as digital natives and the older digital immigrants. Digital natives are those who have always known a life with digital technology. Digital immigrants have been socialized into the digital way of life, but may still experience culture shock and feel less fluent in dealing with innovations.

Why are consumers drawn to social media activities?

There are several motivations for consumer participation in social media activities. The affinity impulse is our need to acknowledge a liking or relationship with individuals or reference groups. The prurient impulse is the curiosity we feel—curiosity that can be fed by observing social media activity. Contact comfort is our need to feel close to others. The immediacy impulse is our need to have contact without delay. The altruistic impulse is the need to do something good for others. The validation impulse is the need to feed our own egos.

Which bases of segmentation are relevant to target wired consumers in a social media context?

The traditional bases of segmentation marketers rely upon still are useful in social media applications. Geographic segmentation is segmenting by market location or location characteristics. In particular, social media tools with geo-targeting such as FourSquare are useful to businesses that employ geographic segmentation. Demographic segmentation includes common personal characteristics such as age, gender, income, and educational attainment. Benefit segmentation is based on the benefits consumers seek from products. Some brands are developing mobile apps to provide added value to consumers; we call these branded applications brand butlers. Behavioral segmentation uses consumer behavior as the basis for segmentation. Online, behavioral segmentation utilizes cookies and IP addresses to track online activity and serve targeted ads based on the data. Psychographic segmentation utilizes personality, activities, interests, and opinions to categorize individuals. Many of the existing social media segmentation schemes available to date are psychographic in nature.

What are the most important segments of social media consumers? What do they tell us about targeting users of the social Web?

Several typologies of digital consumers exist including the social technographics profiles from Forrester Research, Pew's Internet technology types, Anderson Analytics' user and nonuser profiles, and Hillstrom's typology of microbloggers. Each provides insight into online social behavior.

Key Terms

80/20 Rule	digital collaborators	online search
ad networks	digital identity	opt in
affinity impulse	digital mobility	Pareto Principle
altruistic impulse	digital primacy	penetration rate
ambivalent networkers	display ads	permission emails
banner ads	drifting surfers	privacy salience
behavioral	geographic segmentation	prurient impulse
segmentation	GPS technology	psychographic
behavioral targeting	handle	segmentation
benefit segmentation	handle-squatting	reach
brand butlers	immediacy impulse	rich media ads
collectors	immediate altruistic	roving nodes
consumer fortified media	responses (IAR)	RSS feeds
contact comfort	inactives	sales promotion
contact immediacy	information encumbered	search engines
conversationalists	joiners	social footprint
cookies	lifestream aggregators	social media addiction
creators	lifestreams	social media touchpoints
critics	lurkers	social technographics
demographic segmentation	market segmentation	spectators
desktop veterans	media movers	tech indifferent
diffusion of innovations	mobile newbies	text ads
digital brand name	off the network	validation impulse

Review Questions

1. Define digital primacy. Do your media choices reflect the claim of digital primacy? Explain.
2. What is the difference between a social footprint and a lifestream?
3. Digital natives and immigrants are both online and involved in social media activities. What is the key difference between digital natives and digital immigrants?
4. Define the major variables marketers use to segment consumers, and provide an example of how each variable can be applied in a social media application.

5. Identify the five characteristics that explain the rate at which individuals adopt innovations.
6. What is a lovemark?
7. Describe the seven types of people characterized by the social technographics ladder. Which of the types is the most important to marketers using social media marketing? Why do you say so?
8. Why is the concept of mobility relevant to social media marketers?
9. What differences exist between the Pew Internet technology types who are motivated by mobility and those who prefer stationary media?
10. What is privacy salience? Why is it of concern to social media marketers?

Exercises

1. Begin a social footprint audit. Make a list of your online memberships. Start by "googling" yourself to find out where you've left your mark online.
2. Visit our URL and take the social technographics survey. How do you anticipate your segment will shift as you continue in this course?
3. Find an ongoing social media marketing campaign. Assess the components of the campaign in terms of whether and to what extent it offers a participation route for the social technographics segments. How could the campaign be improved to better engage people of varying levels of social media involvement?
4. Visit Twitter and read the stream of user posts (this is known as the tweet stream) for a few minutes. Select several posts and identify whether those posts fit the profiles of elite, difference makers, knowledge seekers, or attention seekers. How are you able to identify them?
5. Visit *Smith* at www.smithmag.net and contribute six words on your digital life. What do the other entries you see on the site tell you about how people think about this?
6. Visit www.usernameaudit.com and audit your own preferred handles. Once you've selected an available handle, begin to register your handle with the social sites in which you wish to be involved.

Notes

1. *Feed: The Razorfish Digital Brand Experience Report*, 2009, http://feed.razorfish.com/downloads/Razorfish_FEED09.pdf, p. 17, accessed August 7, 2011.
2. Everett M. Rogers, *Diffusion of Innovations* (New York: Free Press, 1962).
3. Stuart Elliott, "Modernizing the 'Kodak Moment' as Sharing," *New York Times,* April 25, 2010, www.nytimes.com/2010/04/26/business/media/26adco.html?src=busln, accessed August 7, 2011.
4. Scott Brown, "Scott Brown on How Twitter + Dopamine = Better Humans," *Wired*, April 19, 2010, www.wired.com/magazine/2010/04/pl_brown_karma/, accessed August 7, 2011.
5. Erick Schonfeld, "FourSquare Becomes More Business Friendly," *Tech Crunch,* April 22, 2010, http://techcrunch.com/2010/04/22/foursquare-business-friendly/, accessed August 7, 2011.
6. "Location-Based Content Draws Local Users," *e-Marketer*, May 18, 2010, www.emarketer.com/Article.aspx?R=1007700, accessed August 7, 2011.
7. Matthew Yeomans, "Huggies Taps Mothers for Social Media Invention," *The Big Money Blog*, May 14, 2010, www.thebigmoney.com/blogs/c-tweet/2010/05/14/huggies-taps-mothers-social-media-invention, accessed May 17, 2010.
8. Neal E. Boudette, "Navigating Curves: BMW's Push to Broaden Line Hits Some Bumps in the Road," *Wall Street Journal*, January 10, 2005, p. A1.
9. "Changing Demographics and Psychographics of the Greeting Card Market Reveal New Opportunities—and Challenges—for Card Marketers and Retailers," *Market Wire*, February 4, 2010, www.marketwire.com/press-release/Changing-Demographics-Psychographics-Greeting-Card-Market-Reveal-New-Opportunities-Challenges-1112522.htm, http://www.marketwire.com/press-release/changing-demographics-psychographics-greeting-card-market-reveal-new-opportunities-challenges-1189051.htm, accessed August 7, 2011.
10. www.crowdrise.com/about/how-it-works, accessed December 18, 2010; Amy Wallace, "Prototype: Online Giving Meets Social Networking," *New York Times*, September 4, 2010, www.nytimes.com/2010/09/05/business/05proto.html?src=me&ref=business, accessed December 18, 2010.
11. Lovemarks, www.lovemarks.com/index.php?pageID=20015&lmcategoryid=17&additions=2&require=100, accessed May 21, 2010.
12. *Feed: The Razorfish Digital Brand Experience Report* 2009, http://feed.razorfish.com/downloads/Razorfish_FEED09.pdf, p. 9, accessed August 7, 2011.
13. "Time-Starved Consumers Seek Brand Butlers," *Marketing Charts*, March 29, 2010, www.marketingcharts.com/direct/time-starved-consumers-seek-brand-butlers-12437/?utm_campaign=rssfeed&utm_source=mc&utm_medium=textlink, accessed.

14. Christopher Heine, "Facebook Ads Provide Big Win for JetBlue's $10 Campaign," *ClickZ*, May 12, 2010, www.clickz.com/3640312, accessed May 18, 2010.

15. Karlene Lukovitz, "Quiznos Free Sub Promo Hits Snag," *Marketing Daily*, February 27, 2009, www.mediapost.com, accessed March 2, 2009.

16. "Privacy 2.0, A World of Connections: A Special Report on Social Networking," *The Economist*, January 20, 2010, pp. 12–13.

17. Courtney Mills, "Facebook Privacy Issues Getting Worse," *WebProNews*, May 25, 2010, www.webpronews.com/blogtalk/2010/05/25/facebook-privacy-issues-getting-worse, accessed May 25, 2010.

18. "Self-Regulatory Principles for Online Behavioral Advertising," *Interactive Advertising Bureau*, 2009, www.iab.net/media/file/ven-principles-07-01-09.pdf, accessed June 21, 2011.

19. Caroline McCarthy, "Analyst: Half of 'Social Media Campaigns' Will Flop," *CNET news*, October 6, 2008, http://news.cnet.com/8301-13577_3-10058509-36.html, accessed December 20, 2010.

20. Charlene Li and Josh Bernoff, 2008. *Groundswell: Winning in a World Transformed by Social Technologies,* (Cambridge, MA: Harvard Business Press, 2008)

21. John Horrigan, "The Mobile Difference," Pew Internet & American Life Project, March 2009, http://pewinternet.org/Reports/2009/5-The-Mobile-Difference-Typology.aspx, accessed March 27, 2010.

22. Jennifer Van Grove, "What Type of Social Media User Are You?," *Mashable*, July 15, 2007, http://mashable.com/2009/07/15/social-media-users/, accessed March 30, 2010.

23. Kevin Hillstrom, "#Blogchat: An Analysis of Twitter User Behavior," January 12, 2010, www.minethatdata.com/Kevin_Hillstrom_MineThatData_BlogChatAnalysis.pdf, accessed March 30, 2010.

24. Bill Heil and Mikolaj Piskorski, "New Twitter Research: Men Follow Men and Nobody Tweets," *Harvard Business Review Blog Network*, June 1, 2009, http://blogs.hbr.org/cs/2009/06/new_twitter_research_men_follo.html, accessed March 30, 2010.

Digital Communities

LearningObjectives

When you finish reading this chapter you will be able to answer these questions:

1 What are the characteristics of online communities? How do ideas travel in a community?

2 In what ways do opinion leaders develop in communities? How do these influentials influence others?

3 What role does social capital play in the value of social media communities? What types of ties do we have to others in our communities?

4 How has social media leveled the playing field and created a source of power for consumers?

GO

From Chapter 4 of *Social Media Marketing*, First Edition. Tracy L. Tuten, Michael R. Solomon.
Copyright © 2013 by Pearson Education, Inc. All rights reserved.

Learning
Objective 1

Wherever this icon
appears in the margin,
please go to the
website **www.zonesofsmm.com**
for an example of the topic
discussed.

Online Communities

Though infrastructure, channels, devices, and social software make social media possible, people like you make it a living, breathing part of everyday life. Social media is first and foremost about *community*: the collective participation of members who together build and maintain a site. We've previously asked you to audit your own participation in social media. You built an early iteration of your social footprint. Chances are that you already participate in Facebook or other social networking sites. Maybe you post comments to a blog on music or fashion, or perhaps you take on the role of an orc or a warrior in a multiplayer game such as World of Warcraft or Everquest. If so, you're one of the millions of people worldwide who are part of online communities. Defining exactly what an online community is and what it isn't has been a difficult task for researchers. Though different approaches exist, we'll refer to **online communities** as a group of people who come together for a specific purpose, who are guided by community policies, and who are supported by Internet access that enables virtual communication. Here is a brief sampling of online communities; there may be some out there just waiting for you!

- MyLife
- LiveJournal
- Tagged
- Last.fm
- LinkedIn

In some ways, online communities are not much different from those we find in our physical environment. The *Merriam-Webster Dictionary* (online version, of course) defines **community** as "a unified body of individuals, unified by interests, location, occupation, common history, or political and economic concerns." In fact, one social scientist refers to an online community as a **cyberplace** where "people connect online with kindred spirits, engage in supportive and sociable relationships with them, and imbue their activity online with meaning, belonging, and identity."[1]

Networks: The Underlying Structure of Communities

When we first presented the social media value chain to you, we emphasized that all of social media is networked. Though there are sites wholly dedicated to social networking *all social communities are social networks*. Networks underlie the premise of social media. So, before we move on, let's cover the basics of social network theory.

A **social network** is a set of socially relevant nodes connected by one or more relations.[2] **Nodes** are members of the network. Members (who we also refer to as **network units**) are connected by their relationships (or **ties**) with each other. Relationships are based on various affiliations such as kinship, friendship and affective ties, shared experiences, and shared hobbies and interests. When we think of community, we tend to think of people, but members of a network can be organizations, articles, countries, departments, or any other definable unit. A good example is your university alumni association. The association is a community of networked individuals and organizations. Social networks are sometimes called **social graphs**, though this term may also refer to a diagram of the interconnections of units in a network.

Nodes in a network experience **interactions**; these are behavior-based ties such as talking with each other, attending an event together, or working together. If you chat online with a prospective dating partner on Match.com, you are a node engaging in an interaction with another node (hopefully a node, but not a nerd …). And, if that actually works out and you participate in an online forum that shares experiences about wedding photographers in your area, you engage in interactions with other nodes who are also getting hitched. Interactions are participative in nature—they are shared activities among members in the network.

Flows occur between nodes. Flows are exchanges of resources, information, or influence among members of the network. On Facebook you share news, updates about your life, opinions on favorite books and movies, photos, videos, and notes. As you share content, you create flows from among those in your network. In social media these flows of communication go in many directions at any point in time and often on multiple platforms—a condition we term **media multiplexity**. Flows are not simply two-way or three-way, they may be sent toward an entire community, a list or group within a network, or several individuals independently. Flows of communication also occur outside the community platform. While the online community exists within a web space, the flows of communication may extend to other domains such as emails, text messages, virtual worlds, and even face-to-face **meetups** where members of an online network arrange to meet in a physical location.

For marketers, flows are especially important because they are the actionable components of any social network system in terms of the sharing of information, delivery of promotional materials, and sources of social influence. The extent of this social influence (where one person's attitudes or behavior change as a result of others' attempts) varies depending upon the power or attractiveness of other nodes.

Social object theory suggests that social networks will be more powerful communities if there is a way to activate relationships among people and objects. In this perspective an *object* is something of common interest and its primary function is to mediate the interactions between people. All relationships have social objects embedded in the relationship. In the online world, a site such as Facebook provides venues for several object formats to ensure that relationships can thrive within the site's framework. One factor that drives Facebook's stunning success is that it offers so many objects for users to share; these include events, family and friends, quizzes, and so on. Other social networking sites (SNSs) provide a more specialized or focused set of objects. For example, consider how each of the following SNSs incorporates objects as part of its mission. On Flickr users participate because they want to share photos. These images are the objects that give meaning to the platform and motivate people to visit. Video is the social object around which YouTube centers. On Diigo, the objects are URLs. On Foursquare, the objects are places. On Dogster, the objects are our canine companions.

Object sociality, the extent to which an object can be shared in social media, is clearly related to an audience's unique interests—by virtue of tying the site relationships to a specific object such as photos of people's dogs or bookmarked websites that provide details about the history of alternative music. The audience becomes specialized at least to a degree. Importantly, though, SNSs oriented around object sociality are likely to be **passion-centric**. That is, the people who join those communities probably not only share an interest in the object in question; chances are they are passionate about the object. We all know people who devote countless hours to a hobby or who (to an outsider) seem insanely obsessed about the fine details of *Star Wars* characters, vintage wines, or warring guilds in World of Warcraft.

In industry terms, sites designed around object sociality are known as **vertical networks**. The term refers to the narrow, deep focus of SNSs that differentiate themselves because they center on some common hobby, interest, or characteristic that draws members to the site. These vertical networks do not attract the same traffic typical of general sites, but one might argue that the members are more involved because of the common interest that initially brought them to the site. They function much like so-called **niche markets** in the physical world. The term *niche* refers to marketplaces that offer a relatively small number of items to buyers who tend to be loyal to these outlets (for example, big-and-tall men's stores or bicycles built for two).

It's a Small World After All

Chances are you've heard of the game *The Six Degrees of Kevin Bacon*. It's based on the principle known as the **six degrees of separation**; an observation that everyone is connected to everyone else by no more than six ties. This statement comes from the mathematical model known as a **small-world**

network, which illustrates that most nodes in a social graph are not directly linked to one another—instead they are indirectly connected via neighbors. The principle is highly relevant in social media marketing, where sources of influence can flow throughout the network easily and quickly. It is this connectivity that has given rise to viral marketing where a message such as a joke or bizarre YouTube clip quickly spreads among members of a network. Social networks also have the characteristic of being "**scale free.**" This means that the more connections someone has, the more likely they are to make new ones.

Characteristics of Online Communities

All communities, whether they exist online or in the physical world, share important characteristics: Participants experience a feeling of membership, a sense of proximity to one another (even though in online groups other members' physical selves may be thousands of miles away), and in most cases some interest in the community's activities. Members may identify with one another due to a common mission (e.g., a Twitter campaign to donate money for Japan earthquake relief) or simply because they come from the same neighborhood or belong to the same sorority (e.g., Classmates.com connects people who attended the same high school).

Communities help members meet their needs for affiliation, resource acquisition, entertainment, and information. Above all else, communities are social! Whether online or offline, they thrive when the members participate, discuss, share, and interact with others as well as recruit new members to the community. Members do vary in their degree of participation, but the more active the membership, the healthier the community.

Social media provide the fuel that fans the fires of online communities. In the Web 1.0 era, people visited a lot of websites to get content that interested them. But these really weren't communities—the flow of information was all one way. In today's Web 2.0 environment all that has changed as interactive platforms enable online communities to exhibit the following basic characteristics.[3]

Conversations Communities thrive on communication among members. Though social media provides an online space for what are essentially digital conversations, these conversations are not based on talking or writing but on a hybrid of the two. The immediate nature of the written word is perceived more like a spoken conversation even without the soundtrack. For this reason if you communicate with a friend via AIM or Facebook chat, you may feel that you actually "talked" to her.

Presence Though online communities exist virtually rather than at a physical location, the better ones supply tangible characteristics that create the sensation of actually being in a place. This is particularly true for virtual world communities that include three-dimensional depictions of physical spaces, but it also applies to visually simplistic online communities such as message board groups. **Presence** refers to the effect that people experience when they interact with a computer-mediated or computer-generated environment.[4] Social media sites enhance a sense of presence when they enable interactions among visitors or make the environment look and feel real.[5]

Virtual communities do not develop and thrive without a foundation of commonality among the members. Just as your offline communities are based on family, religious beliefs, social activities, hobbies, goals, place of residence, and so on, your online communities also need commonalities to create bonds among the members. These groups come together to allow people to share their passions, whether these are for indie bands, white wines, or open-source apps. Communities are made up of people who share some reason to join together. As we said, this basis can be a location, a shared characteristic, a hobby, an occupation, or any number of other activities that people share.

Community content (whether simple dialogue, shared recipes, event photos, or something else entirely) is generated, shared, consumed, fortified, and promoted by community members. The contributions of members add value for the general membership group. Community members seek out ways to be connected. The site encourages new members to connect. It's critical to encourage participation among new members; these contributions continue to build the value of the platform for all members. If a social media site starts to lose visitors it resembles a deserted mining town in the Old West—empty saloons, banks, and stores with (digital) tumbleweed blowing across the streets.

Democracy   The political model of most online communities is democratic (that's with a small d, not the Democratic Party); leaders emerge due to the reputation they earn among the general membership. In this context **democracy** is a descriptive term that refers to rule by the people. The leaders are appointed or elected by the community based on their demonstrated ability to add value to the group. For instance, in the online community 4chan, an online bulletin board devoted to the sharing of images related to and discussion of Japanese anime, members widely acknowledge that the person who posts under the name of "moot" is a leader. His leadership comes from his role in the creation of the community as well as from his ongoing participation and the quality of his contributions. Even though leaders emerge in online communities, the power structure of the community is decentralized. Majority rule applies. New leaders can emerge as they choose to escalate their levels of involvement.

Because of the horizontal structure of social media (remember, this is all part of the horizontal revolution), we typically find that control over what appears on the platform shifts from a small elite to the larger mass. **Media democratization** means that the members of social communities, not traditional media publishers such as magazines or newspaper companies, control the creation, delivery, and popularity of content.

Standards of Behavior   Virtual communities need **norms**, or rules that govern behavior, in order to operate. Some of these rules are spelled out explicitly (e.g., if you buy an item on eBay you agree that you have entered into a legal contract to pay for it) but many of them are unspoken. Without these rules, we would have chaos. Imagine the confusion if a simple norm in the offline world such as stopping for a red traffic light did not exist!

In the online world people also need to observe norms and they may arouse others' anger when they don't. A simple example is the practice of **flaming** when a POST CONTAINS ALL CAPITAL LETTERS TO EXPRESS ANGER. Some norms such as flaming are pretty minor; they just help ensure a more pleasant online experience. Others relate to more serious matters; they help ensure protection for those who participate in terms of fair use of information (such as posting content that belongs to others), privacy, and etiquette. Two issues in particular are important in this context:

- **Open access sites** enable anyone to participate without registration or identification. This can be valuable for participation on sensitive topics as well as for ease of use. However, open access also lowers the barriers for misbehavior because it ensures anonymity to users. Just as people tend to "act out" at a costume party when no one knows who they really are, visitors to these sites may post things they might avoid if others knew their real identity.
- The **social contract** is the agreement that exists between the host or governing body and the members. You engage in a social contract when you indicate agreement to a "terms of use" clause for a site. Social contracts set forth expectations for user behavior as well as for the host or governing body. Some sites such as Facebook, however, come under fire when they make changes to the social contract without user input. The specific concern is typically for the protection of membership privacy.

Level of Participation   For an online community to thrive, a significant proportion of its members must participate. Otherwise the site will fail to offer fresh material and ultimately traffic will slow. Participation can be a challenge though, because most users are "lurkers." Researchers estimate that only 1 percent of a typical community's users regularly participate and another 9 percent do so only intermittently. The remaining 90 percent just observe what's on the site, so they don't add a lot of value—other than adding to the number of "eyeballs" the site can claim when it tries to convince advertisers to buy space. Sound familiar? This disparity roughly parallels the larger pattern we often observe in marketing contexts called the 80/20 Rule. As we saw in the last chapter, roughly 20 percent of a brand's users buy 80 percent of the product. Marketers label these faithful "heavy users." In many groups or consumer segments, a relative handful of people account for most of the activity; this hard-core group often is the most valuable for organizations to touch because they are the real movers and shakers.

How can a site convert lurkers into active users? The easier it is to participate, the more likely it is that the community can generate activity among a larger proportion of visitors. In part this means ensuring that there are several ways to participate that vary in terms of their ease of use. Facebook is an example of an online community that has figured out how to offer several forms of participation. Members can post status updates (very easy), make comments, upload photos, share notes and links, play social games, answer quizzes, decorate their profiles, upload videos, and create events (a bit harder), among other forms of participation. There is a way for everyone to participate actively in the community.

How Ideas Travel in a Community

Like a steel chain, communities are more than the sum of their links. Network structure and composition also play a role in the community's ability to support its members. Whether online or offline, a community has a **culture** that includes shared knowledge, myths, norms, and language.

We see evidence of community culture in the memes that evolve within the community. A **meme** is a snippet of cultural information that spreads person to person until eventually it enters the general consciousness. These snippets may include songs, phrases, ideas, slang words, fashion trends, or shared behaviors. For example, when the TV show *The Apprentice* caught fire a few years ago, its trademark term "You're fired!" made the rounds very quickly.

It's easy to understand how a meme spreads if you use the medical analogy of a virus: Memes spread among consumers in a geometric progression, just as a virus starts off small and steadily infects increasing numbers of people until it becomes an epidemic. The leap from person to person occurs as people share and imitate the meme. The memes that survive over time tend to be distinctive and memorable. The most enduring ones evoke earlier memes that may relate to legends and well-known stories and tales. For example, the *Star Wars* movies evoke prior memes that relate to the legend of King Arthur, religion, heroic youth, and 1930s adventure serials.

Because of the viral nature of memes, they typically spread rapidly. A bit later in the chapter, we'll shed more light on just how these ideas are able to spread geometrically across many kinds of people. For instance, Facebook memes include the popular "25 Things You Didn't Know About Me" and the use of several expressions such as FML ("f##k my life"), and texters often include shorthand phrases such as LOL. In fact, FML made Facebook's Top Ten in its Facebook Memology list for 2009.

Some memes "infect" numerous kinds of people and truly take on a life of their own—at least until the next meme takes over. *Rickrolling* is a great example: This term describes a prank that involves sending someone a link to click on—but when they do they're instead taken to a link to Rick Astley's campy video of his 1987 hit song "Never Gonna Give You Up" on YouTube. The first rickroll happened in 2007 when visitors to the YouTube trailer for the video game Grand Theft Auto IV were instead served Astley's video. YouTube got in on the fun itself for April Fool's Day 2008 when the site rickrolled every user who viewed a clip on its homepage.[6] Rick Astley performed an in-person rickroll at the Macy's Thanksgiving Day Parade in 2008 and live rickrollings have popped up since at university basketball games and at protest events.[7] With its large population, Facebook is an ideal online location for memes to develop. Table 1 explains the steps in creating a meme in Facebook.

TABLE 1

How to Create a Facebook Meme

Source: Adapted from Dan Zarella and Alison Driscoll, April 3, 2009, "The Anatomy of a Facebook Meme," *Mashable.com*, April 3, 2009, http://mashable .com/2009/04/03/ facebook-meme/, accessed December 31, 2010.

- **Create and invite people to an event or a group**
  - Keep the event public
  - Make it searchable
  - Allow others to invite and allow invitees to post videos, links, and photos
  - Keep wall open to allow discussion; participate yourself
  - Upload image

- **Post a note**
  - Tag friends in it so they will be notified of the new note; it will also post to their profile for other friends to see
  - Publish to profile and mini feed
  - Set up automated notes to pull from a blog or other RSS feed
  - Add an image

- **Post on walls and update status**
  - Update your own status with links and write on friends' walls with links to content you wish to share so others can view

- **Tag photo and/or video**
  - Tag with any friend to alert them that you have posted new photos and they're in them
  - Keep photo album settings open; this ensures that their friends who you don't know can see them as well

- **Send a message**
  - Segment friends into the largest group size allowed by Facebook
  - Send bulk message(s) with links to content; include crucial information

BYTES TO BUCKS

Big rewards await those who can identify memes or create new ones. A case in point: Ben Huh, a young entrepreneur who dipped into his own savings and bought a quirky site from two Hawaiian bloggers—the hugely successful *I Can Has Cheezburger*, which pairs photos of cats with quirky captions. He realized that there's a huge demand for content that satisfies people's quirky craving, and now he's expanded his empire—The Cheezburger Network—to include 52 sites that serve up all kinds of offbeat humor. These include *Fail Blog* for photos and videos of disastrous mishaps and *There I Fixed It* where people post photos of bad repair jobs. The network employs more than 40 people who scour the Web for new ideas to post. They are essentially meme miners who monitor cyberspace for themes that emerge on forums, blogs, and video sites. As the creator of a video series called "Know Your Meme" explained, "Cheezburger figures out what's starting to get popular and then harvests the humor from the chaff. Things like Lolcats and Fail are easy to make, easy to spread, and hit on an emotional level that crosses a lot of traditional boundaries." The network takes its work seriously—it receives more than 18,000 submissions every day but accepts only about 1 percent of them. Of course, no one can guarantee that a meme will take off, and Cheezburger yanks about 20 percent of the sites it puts up—including Pandaganda, which collected images of pandas looking comically evil and sinister.[8]

Group Influence and Social Capital

Although consumers get information from personal sources, they do not usually ask just *anyone* for advice about purchases.[9] If you decide to buy a new stereo, you will most likely seek advice from a friend who knows a lot about sound systems. This friend may own a sophisticated system, or may subscribe to specialized magazines such as *Stereo Review* and spend her free time browsing through electronics stores. However, you may have another friend who has a reputation for being stylish and who spends his free time reading *Gentleman's Quarterly* and shopping at trendy boutiques. You might not bring up your stereo problem with him, but you may take him with you to shop for a new fall wardrobe.

Learning Objective 2

Everyone knows people who are knowledgeable about products and whose advice others take seriously. We call this individual an **opinion leader**; a person who is frequently able to influence others' attitudes or behaviors.[10] Clearly, some people's recommendations carry more weight than others. Opinion leaders are extremely valuable information sources because they possess the social power we discussed earlier in the chapter:

- They are technically competent so they possess expert power.[11]
- They prescreen, evaluate, and synthesize product information in an unbiased way, so they possess knowledge power.[12]
- They are socially active and highly interconnected in their communities.[13]
- They are likely to hold positions of leadership. As a result, opinion leaders often have legitimate power by virtue of their social standing.
- They tend to be similar to the consumer in terms of their values and beliefs, so they possess referent power. Note that although opinion leaders are set apart by their interest or expertise in a product category, they are more convincing to the extent that they are *homophilous* rather than *heterophilous*. **Homophily** refers to the degree to which a pair of individuals is similar in terms of education, social status, and beliefs.[14]
- Effective opinion leaders tend to be slightly higher in terms of status and educational attainment than those they influence but not so high as to be in a different social class.
- Opinion leaders are often among the first to buy new products, so they absorb much of the risk. This experience reduces uncertainty for the rest of us who are not as courageous. Furthermore, whereas company-sponsored communications tend to focus exclusively on the positive aspects of a product, the hands-on experience of opinion leaders makes them more likely to impart *both* positive and negative information about product performance. Thus, they are more credible because they have no "axe to grind."

A recent reexamination of the traditional perspective on opinion leadership reveals that the process isn't as clear-cut as some researchers thought.[15] The original framework is called the **two-step flow model of influence**. It proposes that a small group of *influencers* are responsible for dissemination of information because they can modify the opinions of a large number of other people. When the authors run extensive computer simulations of this process, they find that the influence is driven less by influentials and more by the interaction among those who are easily influenced. These people communicate the information vigorously to one another and also participate in a two-way dialogue with the opinion leader as part of an **influence network**. These conversations create **cascades** of information, which occur when a piece of information triggers a sequence of interactions (much like an avalanche), as shown in Figure 1.

Learning Objective 3

Social Capital

When people form community relationships these affiliations allow them to accumulate resources that they can "trade" for other things. In the offline business world, we clearly see how

Figure 1

An Influence NetworkA message originates at Level 1 and is sent by the influencer to his or her contacts (Level 2). The message may travel on from some Level 2 contacts to their contacts (Level 3), and so on.

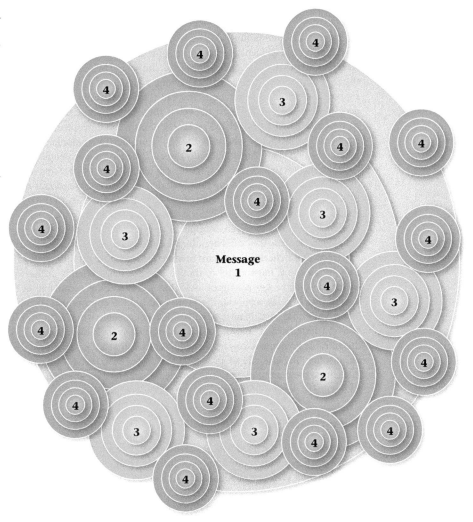

this process works in the golf subculture. Although many people do love to hit that ball around, the reality is that a lot of business is transacted on the course and executives profit from their membership in this community (some business schools even offer academic courses on "golf etiquette"!).

We call these resources **social capital** because their value flows to people as a result of their access to others.[16] The resources may be actual or virtual, and they may be held by a group or individual. For instance, resources might include useful information, relationships, the ability to organize groups, employment connections, and more.[17] Do you know anyone who landed a job interview due to the intervention of a friend of a friend? This is an example of social capital at work—especially since jobseekers who know larger numbers of people who already work at high-level jobs are more likely to be able to trade on these connections. Social capital tends to be a limited and protected resource. To return to the golf example, at many country clubs it's not enough just to be rolling in money: You also need to be recommended by current members so that the organization controls (fairly or not) just who gets to hobnob on the links and in the locker room.

Typically, a community is healthier and more desirable when it is able to offer a lot of social capital as an inducement for people to join. Communities build capital through reputation and structure. **Reputational capital** is based on the shared beliefs, relationships, and actions of those in the community such that norms, behaviors, and values held and shared by individuals ultimately support a community reputation. You can think of this like a big, beefy nightclub bouncer who decides who he will admit past the velvet rope. In fact, like exclusive country clubs, **online gated communities** that selectively allow access to only some people may offer a high degree of social capital to the lucky few who pass the test. Consider for example "exclusive" dating sites such as hotenough.org that (at least allegedly) weed out unattractive people. The site's homepage claims, "Through our screening process, we have filtered the masses leaving only your area's most attractive, fit, trendy singles and have now included an exclusive section for our 40+ singles, the "BABY BOOMER SECTION." Hot Enough offers three tiers of hotties, so if you're fit and trendy, then rest assured there is a place for you."[18]

Let's use Foursquare as an example to understand how online social capital works. People visit Foursquare because they can check in at locations and announce their arrivals to their community of friends. Some check-ins can earn members badges and coupons from participating retailers. This networking site is most useful to those who have many friends in the community. Being part of the community makes resources including access to others available to the members. The more people who become involved, the more valuable the community. And involvement grows based on activities that participants value. For instance, people who are into Foursquare crave the status of being designated as "mayor" of a location such as their local Starbucks. As long as people value this title, the Foursquare community will attract enthusiastic participants. If and when people move on to something else, the social capital that flows from being a "mayor" will slow to a trickle. As it declines, the community experiences declines in its own strength as measured by participation, adherence to norms, perceived reputation, and trust among members.[19]

Strong and Weak Ties

Emotional support is one form of social capital. For example, people who struggle to lose weight or fight addictions often prevail because they are part of a group that helps them with these battles such as Weight Watchers or Alcoholics Anonymous. We call this kind of emotional support **bonding social capital**.

This resource easily accrues online because of our accessibility to people who can help us with a variety of issues even though we may not know them personally. In contrast, our **core ties**, those people with whom we have very close relationships, may or may not be in a position to provide solutions to some problems we face (or we may not want them to know about these in some cases).[20] Interestingly, through the course of giving and receiving bonding social capital, we may come to develop core ties, or at least **significant ties** (somewhat close connections, but less so than core ties), with others in the community.

Online communities can also provide support that is not emotional in nature. This is particularly true of those that increase the accessibility of so-called "**weak ties**." This term refers to contacts with whom your relationship is based on superficial experiences or very few connections. For instance, you have a **strong tie** with your best friend. Perhaps you and she went to high school together and so you have a history of shared experiences and friendships from your past. You then attended college classes together and again you were able to share experiences. You also joined the same sorority so you are bound by your relationship in the context of the organization. In this relationship, there are at least three connection streams between you and your friend that extend over several years and multiple shared experiences—we'd say this is a fairly strong tie.

In contrast, you likely have weak ties among your Facebook friends, many of whom are just casual acquaintances or even friends of a friend whom you've never met. Still, these weak ties also have value: They may provide **bridging social capital**, the value we get from others who provide access to places, people, or ideas we might not be able to get to on our own. For instance, consider a recent plea circulated on Facebook to help fund an operation for Memphis, an abandoned pit bull in Cummins, Georgia. His foster family couldn't afford to fund Memphis' surgery so they turned to Facebook to make a plea to their friends, and those friends shared the appeal with their friends and so on. In just a few days, the dog had his surgery. Luckily for Memphis, his owners tapped into bridging social capital—they used nodes build a bridge to otherwise unconnected nodes.

Maintained social capital refers to the value we get from maintaining relationships with latent ties. In fact, many of the connections we make on SNSs are not active ties at all. Rather, they are **latent ties**.[21] Latent ties are pre-existing connections that we've discarded. You've probably heard your parents say they've reconnected with old high school friends on Facebook. This is a perfect example of latent ties—as we move through life, some people stay in our lives, but others lose relevance as we develop and change. SNSs are valuable connectors for latent ties because they represent a low-involvement, low-effort channel to maintain these bonds. In fact, researchers discovered that college students use Facebook as a way to prevent the development of latent ties.[22] Some of your high school friends may have chosen the same university you did. Others went elsewhere. With sites such as Facebook, you are able to easily stay in touch with these friends, despite the shift in lifestyle and geographic location.

Note: Earlier we talked about weak and strong ties in communities. Latent ties are not necessarily weak ties. Your BFF in the sixth grade was once a strong tie, but she might now be a latent one. Before the social media era, it's likely you would have just lost track of her unless you both happened to hobble into your 25th class reunion. Now, you can keep your old connections on the radar screen, even if you don't necessarily talk or write to them on a regular basis. SNSs enable members to maintain relationships across tie types.

Learning
Objective 4
Influencers (known as **power users** in some communities) are those others view as knowledgeable sources of information. They have a strong communication network that gives them the ability to affect purchase decisions for a number of other consumers, directly and indirectly. Five characteristics help to describe them: (1) activists, (2) connected, (3) impact, (4) active minds, and (5) trendsetters.[23] In other words, influencers develop a network of people through their involvement in activities. They are active participants at work and in their communities. Their social networks are large and well developed. Others trust them and find them to be credible sources of information about one or more specific topics. They tend to have a natural sense of intellectual curiosity which may lead them to new sources of information.

Influencers exist in all social communities. It is a natural pattern for some members to be more active and to acquire positions of authority within a community. The source of the influence itself, however, originates from the power bases an influencer may possess. How can someone acquire power? French and Raven explained in their classic article, *The Bases of Social Power*, several sources of power individuals can accrue in organizations.[24] These sources of power include:

- **Reward power:** one's ability to provide others with what they desire
- **Coercive power:** the ability to punish others
- **Legitimate power:** organizational authority based on rights associated with a person's appointed position
- **Referent power:** authority through the motivation to identify with or please a person
- **Expert power:** recognition of one's knowledge, skills, and ability
- **Information power:** one's control over the flow of and access to information

For influencers within social media communities, several forms of power can be developed (and importantly, anyone willing to invest time in accruing power can become an influencer). Influencers begin by actively participating in the community, submitting high-quality content (and possibly also writing original feature content). Over time, the user will develop a reputation as an expert. The user will also spend time commenting on the submissions of influential others. This will build referent power by association. Likewise, the user community will recognize the investment in time and energy heavy users are making to benefit the community, resulting in legitimate power. Eventually, as a user gains power, he or she will begin to influence access to content (information power) and can reward or punish others (reward and coercive power) with the decision of whether or not to support new submissions. Ultimately, the influencers are critically important to the success of a social news marketing initiative. Without support from one or more influentials, the incremental traffic resulting from a social media campaign would be inconsequential.

Word-of-mouth (WOM) is product information individuals transmit to other individuals. Because we get the word from people we know, WOM tends to be more reliable and trustworthy than messages from more formal marketing channels. And unlike advertising, WOM often comes with social pressure to conform to these recommendations.[25]

Ironically, despite all of the money marketers pump into lavish ads, WOM is far more powerful: It influences two-thirds of all consumer goods sales.[26] In one recent survey, 69 percent of interviewees said they relied on a personal referral at least once over the course of a year to help them choose a restaurant, 36 percent reported they used referrals to decide on computer hardware and software, and 22 percent got help from friends and associates to decide where to travel.[27]

If you think carefully about the content of your own conversations in the course of a normal day, you will probably agree that much of what you discuss with friends, family members, or coworkers is product-related: When you compliment someone on her dress and ask her where she bought it, recommend a new restaurant to a friend, or complain to your neighbor about the shoddy treatment you got at the bank, you engage in WOM.

Marketers have been aware of the power of WOM for many years, but recently they've been more aggressive about trying to promote and control it instead of sitting back and hoping people will like their products enough to talk them up. Companies such as BzzAgent have thousands of "agents" who try new products and spread the word about those they like.[28] And many sophisticated marketers today also precisely track WOM. For example, the ongoing *TalkTrack* study reports which brands are mentioned the most by consumers in different categories. Based on online surveys of 14,000 women, it reports that middle-aged (Baby Boomer) women talk about Kraft more than any other packaged goods food brand, and they discuss Olay the most among beauty products.[29]

The influence of others' opinions is at times even more powerful than our own perceptions. In one study of furniture choices, consumers' estimates of how much their friends would like the furniture was a better predictor of purchase than what they thought of it.[30] In addition, consumers may find their own reasons to push a brand that take the manufacturer by surprise. That's what happened with Mountain Dew; we trace its popularity among younger consumers to the "buzz" about the soda's high caffeine content. As an advertising executive explained, "The caffeine thing was not in any of Mountain Dew's television ads. This drink is hot by word-of-mouth."[31]

WOM is especially powerful when the consumer is relatively unfamiliar with the product category. We would expect such a situation in the case of new products (e.g., medications to prevent hair loss) or those that are technologically complex (e.g., laptops). One way to reduce uncertainty about the wisdom of a purchase is to talk about it. Talking gives the consumer an opportunity to generate supporting arguments for the purchase and to garner support for this decision from others. For example, the strongest predictor of a person's intention to buy a residential solar water-heating system is the number of solar-heat users the person knows.[32]

You talk about products for several reasons:[33]

- You might be highly involved with a type of product or activity and enjoy talking about it. Computer hackers, avid football fans, and "fashion plates" seem to share the ability to steer a conversation toward their particular interests.

- You might be knowledgeable about a product and use conversations as a way to let others know it. Thus, word-of-mouth communication sometimes enhances the egos of those individuals who want to impress others with their expertise.

- You might initiate a discussion out of genuine concern for someone else. We like to ensure that people we care about buy what is good for them or that they do not waste their money.

Word-of-mouth is a two-edged sword that cuts both ways for marketers. Informal discussions among consumers can make or break a product or store. Furthermore, consumers weigh **negative word-of-mouth** more heavily than they do positive comments. According to a study by the White House Office of Consumer Affairs 90 percent of unhappy customers will not do business with a company again. Each of these customers is likely to share his or her grievance with at least nine other people, and 13 percent tell more than 30 people about their negative experience.[34]

Node-to-Node Relationships   We refer to connections in a SNS with many terms, including *friend*, *fan*, *follower*, *colleague*, and *contact*. The biggest predictor of whether someone will become active in a social network space, regardless of the site's primary function, is the presence of a critical mass of friends. If your friends are present and active in the space, you probably will be too because you will have someone with whom to interact and to reward you for your participation. Your level of activity is based on a mix of the *people* with whom you are connected, the content (called *artifacts*) you produce on the site, the *feedback* you receive from others, and the *distribution* of the artifacts and feedback throughout the network.[35] Of these four elements of SNS participation, three are dependent upon the nodes in your network. If your contacts are not active in your experience, your own activity in the network will be stunted because you won't have people with whom to interact, you won't receive sufficient feedback, and your content will not be redistributed.

Influence

Word-of-mouth has long been an influence on consumer decision making. Recognizing the ease and speed with which people share brand experiences, recommendations, and product-related opinions with others, both negative and positive, led to marketers to dub the phrase **word-of-mouse**. With the added accessibility to our networks brought about by SNSs, peer-to-peer influence has taken on even more power in terms of the sources that may influence a consumer decision. Some of the brands using social media most avidly are those who recognized early on its value in terms of creating a customer service communication channel and service recovery venue.

These brand-specific conversations also have value in terms of their media equivalent, known as the **ad equivalency value**. In other words, when brands use paid media, they have an estimate of the value of the advertising in the form of the fees they paid to place the ads. But in social media, most of our promotional value comes from earned and owned media. Therefore, we may try to establish a value and relate that value to the cost of buying equivalent paid media. This is the meaning of ad equivalence value—what would the value of the mention be if it had come through a paid advertising placement rather than a volunteered comment?

Forrester Research labeled these brand-specific mentions "influence impressions". We generate influence impressions whenever we discuss brands openly online. In advertising lingo, an **impression** refers to a view or an exposure to an advertising message. In social media, brands may benefit from influence impressions as well as ad impressions. An influence impression is an exposure to a brand via another person—in other words, it's the impressions that are generated through social sharing. Forrester estimates that each year among U.S. consumers 256 billion influence impressions are generated as people talk about their lives with each other, telling stories and experiences that invariably include brands.[36] Further, the brand activity in the social media space, whether it be in the form of tweeting, blogging, social networking, or virtual commerce, encourages people to incorporate this information in their own communication exchanges.

These influence impressions are primarily delivered by—you guessed it—opinion leaders: Only 6.2 percent of social media users are responsible for about 80 percent of these impressions. Forrester calls these influencers **mass connectors**, paying homage to Malcolm Gladwell's popular book *The Tipping Point*. Gladwell posits that three factors work to "tip" a trend, in other words to ignite interest in an idea, behavior, or product: the law of the few, stickiness, and the power of context.[37] The law of the few explains that three types of people help to spread viral messages. **Mavens** are people who are knowledgeable about many things. **Connectors** are people who know many people and communicate with them. **Salesmen** are people who influence others with their natural persuasive power. If an idea is sticky, it has memorable impact. Lastly, Gladwell acknowledges that ideas spread more easily when conditions are right—that's the power of context.[38]

As mass connectors spread influence impressions, the impact of the message grows due to the **momentum effect**.[39] Influencers publish the message through comments made, widgets shared, brand logos placed on pages, and so on. Friends share with friends who share with friends. If a brand is well-liked, relevant, and buzz-worthy, the media value originating from nonpaid, word-of-mouth referrals for the brand can be enormous. This is the essence of the momentum effect. Take, for example, an engagement device used by Travelocity's Roaming Gnome. He was (supposedly) outraged that the Aflac Duck had more friends on Facebook, and so Travelocity created International Gnome Day. On his page, the gnome implored fans to share his plea with their friends in the hopes that he could achieve his goal by the big day.

Why are influence impressions so powerful? People in our personal social graphs are awarded a special form of influence—**social proof**. Social proof works by encouraging consumers to make decisions that mimic those of people in their social network. If friends are favorable toward a brand or making brand purchases, the influenced others are likely to be as well. Morpace, a market research firm, surveyed Facebook users and found that 68 percent were more likely to buy a product or visit a retailer after seeing a referral from a friend. About two-thirds of respondents to another survey said that their opinions of brands were influenced by a friend's interaction with a brand.[40]

The Evolution of Online Communities

Online communities are of course a fairly recent phenomenon. How did these new digital structures form? Historically, physical closeness was key to defining a community; indeed the large majority of people were likely to be born, grow up, and die in the same place so they were likely to see members of their relevant groups (extended families, religious clans, etc.) just about every day.

In fairly recent times, people became increasingly mobile and technologies advanced in ways that shifted personal interactions from outside the home in a neighborhood to inside the home via telephones and computers. As this happened sociologists worried that we would lose the value of communities such as neighborhood and kinship connections. These concerns are not unique to the 21st century, of course. Indeed, back in 1897 the well-known sociologist Emile Durkheim warned of a condition he called **anomie**, a condition of modern industrial life that alienates individuals from society and (potentially) results in suicide.[41]

These concerns were largely unfounded, though many would argue that modern society does make it more difficult to connect with others (hence the popularity of social media dating sites!). Still, over time sociologists recognized that technological innovations actually can help us to maintain and support a number of community relationships despite physical distances and other limitations. Marshall McLuhan, the English professor at the University of Toronto who wrote the seminal work *Understanding Media*, once made the famous statement, "One's village can span the globe." Sure enough, we now define communities in terms of their social networks rather than in terms of the physical space they occupy.[42] One sociologist who has studied communities for a long time observed, "I define 'community' as networks of interpersonal ties that provide sociability, support, information, a sense of belonging, and social identity. I do not limit my thinking about community to neighbour-hoods [*sic*] and villages."[43]

About 10 years ago *Bowling Alone,* a controversial book, warned of a society that is increasingly disconnected from community.[44] As we become more mobile and connected screen-to-screen rather than face-to-face, the book argued that community structures and our involvement in them were in decline. From thousands of interviews, the author showed that people meet less often with others in person and are less involved in community groups. He noted that people even are more likely to bowl alone, rather than in leagues—a clear sign that the digital connections we have do not encourage us to form strong bonds with others.

So, what's the verdict? Are online communities as strong—or stronger—than the traditional kind? The jury is still out. We do know that people can engage in civic activities online and modern political campaigns testify to the power of social media to mobilize voters. (President Obama's 2008 campaign set a new standard for this participation among young people.)

One study of civic engagement and social networks found that online communities neither hindered nor encouraged the sharing of community resources.[45] The Pew Internet & American Life

 ## THE DARK SIDE OF SOCIAL MEDIA

Kids love to gossip and the schoolyard can be a jungle for those who are on the receiving end of rumors and taunts. As young people spend less time hanging at the mall or in each others' rooms and more time texting and posting on Facebook, the viciousness of the schoolyard follows them—but with technology the taunts can hurt even more. **Cyberbullying** is a growing problem; it ranges from texts that tease to group sites where a boy or girl is singled out for sexual harassment. The Cyberbullying Research Center defines these practices as "willful and repeated harm" inflicted through phones and computers—researchers there claim that one in five middle-school students has been a victim. Studies have documented cyberbullying problems as early as the fourth grade. Preteens and teenagers (as we all remember) often have shaky self-concepts and they tend to be overly sensitive to criticism about their appearance or social desirability so negative messages can be especially harmful. It's bad enough to be teased about being overweight or awkward by a couple of kids; when dozens of your classmates register their feelings online the feedback can be excruciating. Platforms such as Formspring.me allow students to post scathing comments to others' mailboxes anonymously; sometimes kids even inflict the pain on themselves as they make these posts available for others to see.

These forms of digital torment are so new that most educators and parents aren't prepared to deal with them. In the United States, 44 states offer regulations about bullying, but only a fraction of those spell out whether teachers or school administrators and guidance counselors are allowed to intervene when these behaviors occur online instead of in the locker room or a secluded hallway. Many new legal issues loom: Can a student be suspended if she posts a YouTube video that slurs a classmate? Can a teacher search a boy's cell phone for damning texts the way he can search his backpack for drugs or weapons? One exasperated principal sent this message to parents (by email of course): "There is absolutely NO reason for any middle school student to be part of a social networking site." He went on to advise parents that if their child is the victim of cyberbullying, "IMMEDIATELY GO TO THE POLICE!"

How can victims, parents, and educators deal with this flood of abuse? Some schools have opened anonymous tip sites where students can divulge information about incidents to help track the source of the problem. The legal system continues to send contradictory messages as some courts uphold the right of schools to punish cyberbullies and others don't; the Supreme Court hasn't yet ruled on the issue of students' online free speech. Along with numerous public service agencies, MTV launched an initiative it calls *A Thin Line* that addresses digital abuse issues. The network has run several public service announcements, and a Redraw the Line Challenge invites young people to submit their ideas for creative solutions to halt the spread of digital abuse. MTV also hosts AThinLine.org, a place where young people can get access to information, resources, and support on issues related to digital abuse. These efforts are great, but kids will be kids—and cyberbullying is not going away.[47]

101

Project offered positive support for the role online networks can play; it noted that the Internet provides us with access to the right people with the right information. In fact, the Pew report even showed that the more we see members of our network in person and talk on the phone, the more likely it is that we will *also* communicate with those people online.[46] The more connected you are, the more connected you will become!

Chapter Summary

What are the characteristics of online communities? How do ideas travel in a community?

Online communities are built on foundations of networks. These networks are made up of nodes connected by ties. The nodes experience interactions and flows of resources, information, and influence occur between nodes. Communities are often built around social objects—objects of mutual interest among community members. Social communities thrive on conversations. They instill a sense of presence for those who participate. Community members share a collective interest and governance is based on democracy. Community members follow standards of behavior that may be presented as rules and as norms accepted by the membership. Participation is necessary for the health of the community but most members are not active. Community participation is typically characteristic of the 80/20 rule whereby only a small percentage of members participate for the benefit of all. Information travels in the community via flows between nodes in the network. When a piece of information enters the general consciousness of the community, it is called a meme.

In what ways do opinion leaders develop in communities? How do these opinion leaders influence others?

Opinion leaders possess sources of social power such as expert power, reward power, and authority power. In addition, the two-step flow model of influence helps to explain how opinion leaders develop and influence others. This model proposes that a small group of influencers are responsible for disseminating information to opinion leaders who then share the information with their large respective networks. The result is that of cascades of information, which we can also think of as influence ripples.

What role does social capital play in the value of social media communities? What types of ties do we have to others in our communities?

Social capital refers to the valuable resources people (individually or in groups) have within the context of a community. The capital may be actual or virtual and can include reputational capital, bonding social capital, bridging social capital, and maintained social capital. People's networks always include strong and weak ties. Both have value. Even weak ties can create social capital for network members.

How has social media leveled the playing field and created a source of power for consumers?

Because everyone who participates in social media can contribute content, including their opinions and experiences, everyone has the potential to spread a message to a potentially large group of people. Though connectors are best able to spread messages, influence impressions can be delivered by anyone participating online.

Key Terms

ad equivalency value	coercive power	cyberbullying
anomie	community	cyberplace
bonding social capital	connectors	democracy
bridging social capital	core ties	expert power
cascades	culture	flaming

flows	network units	significant ties
homophily	niche markets	six degrees
impression	nodes	of separation
influence network	norms	small-world network
information power	object sociality	social capital
interactions	online communities	social contract
latent ties	online gated communities	social graphs
legitimate power	open access sites	social network
maintained social capital	opinion leader	social object theory
mass connectors	passion-centric	social proof
mavens	power users	strong tie
media democratization	presence	ties
media multiplexity	referent power	two-step flow model
meetups	reputational capital	of influence
meme	reward power	vertical networks
momentum effect	salesmen	weak ties
negative word-of-mouth	scale free	word-of-mouse

Review Questions

1. What are the characteristics common to communities, whether offline or online?
2. Explain the meaning of social capital.
3. Are social networks communities or networked individuals?
4. Explain the principles of media and brand democratization.

Exercises

1. Visit the following communities: (1) lugnet.com, (2) ivillage.com, and (3) chatipad.com. What do you see in common among these communities? What's different? Does each so-called community really seem to be a unified group with a common culture? Explain.
2. Review the list of friends you have on Facebook. How many of your friends are "weak ties" and how many are "strong ties?" Identify the relationship bonds you share with those in your strong tie group. Does Facebook help you to strengthen both kinds of relationships? Why or why not?
3. Identify a current meme and track its origin.
4. Search Twitter for hashtags related to a brand (e.g., #dunkindonuts). What kinds of influence impressions appear for the hashtag you searched? Can you identify key influencers who are sharing tweets with this specific hashtag?
5. Discussion: How can the *Six Degrees of Kevin Bacon* game be explained as an example of social network theory?

Notes

1. Barry Wellman, "Physical Place and Cyberplace: The Rise of Personalized Networking," *International Journal of Urban and Regional Research* 24, no. 2 (2001): 227–252.
2. Alexandra Marin and Barry Wellman, "Social Network Analysis: An Introduction," in *Handbook of Social Network Analysis* (London: Sage, 2010).
3. John Coate, "Cyberspace Innkeeping: Building Online Community," 1998, www.cervisa.com/innkeeping, accessed December 31, 2010.
4. T. B. Sheridan, "Further Musings on the Psychophysics of Presence," *Presence: Teleoperators and Virtual Environments* 5 (1994): 241–246.
5. Matthew Lombard and Theresa Ditton, "At the Heart of It All: The Concept of Presence," *Journal of Computer Mediated Communication* 3, no. 2 (1997), http://jcmc.indiana.edu/vol3/issue2/lombard.html, accessed December 31, 2010.
6. "The History of RickRolling: Infographic," *Huffington Post*, June 1, 2010, www.huffingtonpost.com/2010/06/01/

the-history-of-rickrollin_n_596064.html, accessed December 31, 2010.

7. Evelyn Nussenbaum, "The 80's Video That Pops Up, Online and Off," *New York Times*, March 24, 2008, www.nytimes.com/ 2008/03/24/business/media/24rick.html?_r=1, accessed December 31, 2010.

8. Jenna Wortham, "Once Just a Site with Funny Cat Pictures, and Now a Web Empire," *New York Times,* June 13, 2010, www.nytimes.com/2010/06/14/technology/internet/14burger. html?emc=eta1, accessed June 27, 2010.

9. Some of the material in this section was adapted from Michael R. Solomon, *Consumer Behavior: Buying, Having, and Being*, 9th ed. (Upper Saddle River, NJ: Prentice Hall, 2010).

10. Everett M. Rogers, *Diffusion of Innovations*, 3rd ed. (New York: Free Press, 1983); see also Duncan J. Watts and Peter Sheridan Dodds, "Influentials, Networks, and Public Opinion Formation," *Journal of Consumer Research* 34 (December 2007): 441–458; Morris B. Holbrook and Michela Addis, "Taste versus the Market: An Extension of Research on the Consumption of Popular Culture," *Journal of Consumer Research* 34 (October 2007): 415–424.

11. Dorothy Leonard-Barton, "Experts as Negative Opinion Leaders in the Diffusion of a Technological Innovation," *Journal of Consumer Research* 11, no. 4 (1985): 914–926.

12. Herbert Menzel, "Interpersonal and Unplanned Communications: Indispensable or Obsolete?" in Edward B. Roberts, Ed., *Biomedical Innovation* (Cambridge, MA: MIT Press, 1981), 155–163.

13. Meera P. Venkatraman, "Opinion Leaders, Adopters, and Communicative Adopters: A Role Analysis," *Psychology & Marketing* 6 (Spring 1989): 51–68.

14. Everett Rogers, *Diffusion of Innovations*, 4th ed. (New York: The Free Press, 1995).

15. Duncan J. Watts and Peter Sheridan Dodds, "Influentials, Networks, and Public Opinion Formation" *Journal of Consumer Research* 34 (December 2007): 441–458.

16. James S. Coleman, "Social Capital in the Creation of Human Capital," *The American Journal of Sociology* 94 (1988): 95–120.

17. Pamela Paxton, "Is Social Capital Declining in the United States? A Multiple Indicator Assessment, *The American Journal of Sociology* 105 (1999): 88.

18. Quoted on www.hotenough.org, accessed June 27, 2010.

19. Nicole Ellison, Charles Steinfield, and Cliff Lampe, "The Benefits of Facebook 'Friends:' Social Capital and College Students' Use of Online Social Network Sites," *Journal of Computer-Mediated Communication* 12 (2007): 1143–1168.

20. Lee Rainie, John Horrigan, Barry Wellman, and Jeffrey Boase, "The Strength of Internet Ties," Pew Internet & American Life Project, January 25, 2005, www.pewinternet.org/Reports/2006/ The-Strength-of-Internet-Ties.aspx, accessed June 23, 2010.

21. Fred Stutzman, "Activating Latent Ties," May 2007, http://chimp rawk.blogspot.com/2007/05/activating-latent-ties.html, accessed December 31, 2010.

22. Nicole Ellison, Charles Steinfield, and Cliff Lampe, "The Benefits of Facebook 'Friends': Social Capital and College Students' Use of Online Social Network Sites," *Journal of Computer-Mediated Communications* 12 (2007): 1143–1168.

23. Ed Keller and Jon Berry, *The Influentials* (New York: Simon & Schuster, 2003).

24. J. R. P. French and B. Raven, "The Bases of Social Power," in D. Cartwright and A. Zander, *Group Dynamics* (New York: Harper & Row, 1959).

25. Johan Arndt, "Role of Product-Related Conversations in the Diffusion of a New Product," *Journal of Marketing Research* 4 (August 1967): 291–294.

26. John Gaffney, "Enterprise: Marketing: The Cool Kids Are Doing It. Should You?" *Asiaweek*, November 23, 2001, p. 1.

27. Douglas R. Pruden and Terry G. Vavra, "Controlling the Grapevine," *MM* (July–August 2004): 23–30.

28. BzzAgent, http://about.bzzagent.com/word-of-mouth/index/ about-bzzagent, accessed December 31, 2010.

29. Les Luchter, "Kraft, Folgers, Olay Top Baby Boomer Gals' WOM," *Marketing Daily*, November 18, 2008, www.mediapost.com/ publications/?fa=Articles.showArticle&art_aid=95000, accessed November 18, 2008.

30. James H. Myers and Thomas S. Robertson, "Dimensions of Opinion Leadership," *Journal of Marketing Research* 9 (February 1972): 41–46.

31. Ellen Neuborne, "Generation Y," *BusinessWeek*, February 15, 1999, p. 86.

32. Dorothy Leonard-Barton, "Experts as Negative Opinion Leaders in the Diffusion of a Technological Innovation," *Journal of Consumer Research* 11 (March 1985): 914–926.

33. James F. Engel, Robert J. Kegerreis, and Roger D. Blackwell, "Word-of-Mouth Communication by the Innovator," *Journal of Marketing* 33 (July 1969): 15–19; see also, Rajdeep Growl, Thomas W. Cline, and Anthony Davies, "Early-Entrant Advantage, Word-of-Mouth Communication, Brand Similarity, and the Consumer Decision Making Process," *Journal of Consumer Psychology* 13, no. 3 (2003): 187–197.

34. Chip Walker, "Word-of-Mouth," *American Demographics* (July 1995): 38–44; Albert M Muñiz, Jr., Thomas O'Guinn, and Gary Alan Fine, "Rumor in Brand Community," in Donald A. Hantula, Ed., *Advances in Theory and Methodology in Social and Organizational Psychology: A Tribute to Ralph Rosnow* (Mahwah, NJ: Erlbaum, 2005).

35. M. Burke, C. Marlow, and T. Lento, "Feed Me: Motivating Newcomer Contribution in Social Network Sites," ACM CHI 2009 Conference on Human Factors in Computing Systems, 2009, pp. 945–954.

36. "Introducing Peer Influence Analysis: 500 Billion Peer Impressions Each Year," *Empowered*, April 20, 2010, http://forrester.typepad .com/groundswell/2010/04/introducing-peer-influence-analysis .html, accessed December 31, 2010.

37. Malcolm Gladwell, *The Tipping Point* (New York: Little, Brown and Company, 2000).

38. Malcolm Gladwell, *The Tipping Point* (New York: Little, Brown and Company, 2000).

39. "Never Ending Friending: A Journey Into Social Networking," Isobar & Carat, http://creative.myspace.com/groups/_ms/nef/ images/40161_nef_onlinebook.pdf, accessed December 31, 2010.

40. "Consumers Follow Social Brand Referrals," *eMarketer*, April 14, 2010, www.emarketer.com/Articles/Print.aspx?1007630, accessed December 31, 2010.

41. Emile Durkheim, *Suicide* (1897; repr., Glencoe, IL: Free Press, 1951).

42. Marshall McLuhan, *Understanding Media: Extensions of Man* (New York: McGraw-Hill, 1964).

43. Quoted in Barry Wellman, "Physical Place and CyberPlace: The Rise of Personalized Networking," *International Journal of Urban and Regional Research* 25, no. 2 (2002): 228.

44. R. Putnam, *Bowling Alone: The Collapse and Revival of American Community* (New York: Simon & Schuster, 2000).

45. Josh Pasek, Eian More, and Daniel Romer, "Realizing the Social Internet? Online Social Networking Meets Offline Civic Engagement," *Journal of Information Technology & Politics* 6, no. 3&4 (2009).

46. Lee Rainie, "The Strength of Internet Ties," Pew Internet & American Life Project, 2006, www.pewinternet.org/Reports/2006/The-Strength-of-Internet-Ties.aspx, accessed June 23, 2010.

47. Jan Hoffman, "Online Bullies Pull Schools into the Fray," *New York Times,* June 27, 2010, www.nytimes.com/2010/06/28/style/28bully.html?emc=eta1, accessed June 27, 2010; "MTV Launches 'A Thin Line' To Stop Digital Abuse," *MTV.com* December 3, 2009, www.mtv.com/news/articles/1627487/20091203/story.jhtml, accessed June 27, 2010.

Social Community

From Chapter 5 of *Social Media Marketing*, First Edition. Tracy L. Tuten, Michael R. Solomon.
Copyright © 2013 by Pearson Education, Inc. All rights reserved.

Social
Community

LearningObjectives

When you finish reading this chapter you will be able to answer these questions:

1 How do users develop an identity in social networking communities? What are the components of identity?

2 How do social networking communities enable user participation and sharing?

3 In what ways can brands utilize social networking communities for branding and promotion?

GO

Wherever this icon appears in the margin, please go to the website **www.zonesofsmm.com** for an example of the topic discussed.

The Social Community Zone

In this chapter we dive deeper into the zone of social community, the first zone in our model, shown in Figure 1. ALL zones in the social media mix are networked around relationships, technologically enabled, and based on the principles of shared participation.

Let's think of zone 1 as the *relationship zone.* Social media platforms here focus on acquiring and maintaining relationships above all else. The most important channel in this zone is social networking sites. Conversation and collaboration are the principal activities in this zone. In this chapter, we'll begin with a focus on how social networking sites in zone 1 function and how you may use this channel personally. Then we'll take a look at how brands can add value by participating.

Learning Objective 1

Digital You: The Social Profile

Social communities play hosts to members who construct and maintain profiles and participate in site activities. Your profile is the foundation of your participation in social communities. It's basically your digital self—the way you "type yourself into being."[1] The profile includes an image or avatar; a username (i.e., a handle); and descriptors such as age, location, interests, favorite books and movies, and family relationships.

Some profiles are personalizable with **skins** and other decorating components. Skins, also called **themes,** are visual elements people use to change the aesthetic of a web page. They typically include background scenes, colors, fonts, menu styles, and a stylized layout of the page's elements. All of these identity elements enhance our ability to reflect who we are to others in the digital environment.

How do others see us? Social networks strive to design their interfaces in ways that meet the needs of members, and establishing our sense of self online is important. For this reason, communities may offer **identity reflectors:** an option to have one's profile reflected back to them from the perspective of others.[2] Sites may also offer members the opportunity to utilize identity cards. **Identity cards** are the social version of a business card. They are small digital **badges** that people can embed in emails

Figure 1

The Social Community Zone

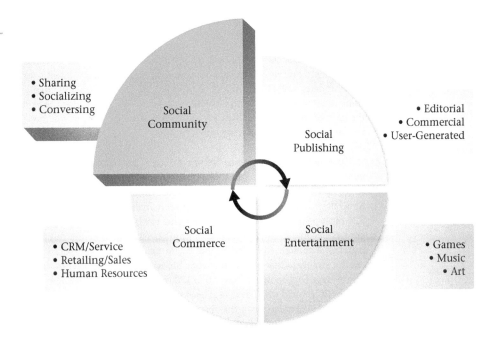

- Sharing
- Socializing
- Conversing

Social Community

- Editorial
- Commercial
- User-Generated

Social Publishing

- CRM/Service
- Retailing/Sales
- Human Resources

Social Commerce

Social Entertainment

- Games
- Music
- Art

and on websites to share their contact information and social affiliations. At some level everyone manages the impressions they make on others and social media is no different. Not only do we want our profiles to reflect our social selves, we might also want to protect our privacy and promote somewhat different personas to different reference groups. People are multifaceted, and this increasingly is reflected in digital profiles. You may have different profiles on different sites or even within the same site such that different reference groups see identity details you customize for them.

Presence is a desirable characteristic of social communities. Presence cues make the community feel more real and engaging. Similarly, individual users often choose to use **presence indicators** that enable them to project an identity more vividly to others within a community. These indicators include:

- *Availability icons:* icons that indicate whether a member is online and available for chat
- *Mood icons:* icons that function much like emoticons, enabling members to indicate how they feel at the time
- *Friend lists:* lists of friends within the network; lists may be customized to highlight specific types of relationships and shared apps on the site
- *Status updates:* posts to the sites' newsfeed; posts are shared with friends in the network; some sites ask a question such as "What are you doing?" to encourage status updates

All of these indicators enhance the perception of **ambient intimacy** we have with those in our network. This term refers to our ability to stay in touch, using digital communications and social media, with people to whom we wouldn't otherwise have access to due to time limitations and geographic dispersion.[3] For example, Facebook lets you see what your friends are doing and thinking even if you have not seen or spoken to them in quite some time. When you do talk with these people, there's no need to ask, "What have you been up to?" because you already know! The social sharing of our daily details enhances our relationships because it increases the amount of information we have available about those in our network.

Learning
Objective 2

Activities in Social Networks

The *Social Media Value Chain* shows that social media support our activities in online spaces. Remember, the social Web is built on participation. Perhaps the two most important types of participation are *sharing* and *content consuming*. If no one shares content, whether that content is video, status updates, wall posts, product reviews, journal entries, or photographs, we'd have nothing to consume when we visit sites. And if we don't visit social sites, consume the content, and offer feedback in the form of comments and likes, eventually the stream of content will die.

Social media sites thrive on conversations, but it's important to distinguish between two types of conversations:[4]

Directed communications are one-to-one interactions on a social network between two users. *Direct messages* (the email of social communities) and *instant messages* are both forms of directed communications. You might think that most of the activity on a network is directed communication, but most users interact only with a very small core of people in their network. Research shows that most people can maintain only around 150 meaningful relationships, online and off—this figure has become known as **Dunbar's number** (named after the researcher who first reported this pattern). Although you may "friend" 5,000 people on Facebook, all but roughly 150 of them are relative strangers that only follow your life with limited interest (sorry to break this news to you). The average Facebook user has 120 to 130 friends; so this leaves room for another 20 or so people in the physical world who haven't (at least yet) started to live digitally.[5]

Consumption describes the rest of our interactions. The reality is that most of the contact we have with the "other" hundreds or thousands of people in our network consist primarily of reading—*consuming*—their feeds. As we read status updates and posts from those in our network, we *feel* that they are communicating with us, even if they posted these updates a while ago. In other words, directed communication is active whereas consumption communication is passive. That's ambient intimacy in action. But it requires the public sharing of content to work because without shared content, there's nothing for us to consume.

In addition to passivity and activity, we can also distinguish between communications in social communities that are synchronous versus asynchronous. Asynchronous communication creates online content that is durable; in other words, we can consume the content at a later point in time. When you post a Facebook update it stays there indefinitely (which is why you need to think about what you post!). In contrast, **synchronous communications** are perishable. They require the active, real-time involvement of two or more people to make sense. For example, if you enter a virtual world in avatar form and strike up a conversation with another avatar you talk as if you are in the "real world"; the other avatar is likely to give up and walk away if it doesn't get a response almost immediately.

Social Networking Sites

Interaction is the currency of social networking sites, but just how do we interact with others on social media platforms? The answer has three parts: we mingle, we chat, and we share. Status updates (called statuscasting) and comments, direct messages (sometimes called a **backchannel**) and instant messages, and "nudges" are ways to engage with others in our network. **Statuscasting** occurs when you broadcast updates to your news feed or activity stream. **Activity streams** are the news feeds or "wall" (as it's known in Facebook) social networks use to establish an ongoing point of connection between network nodes. Status updates and comments about them allow conversations to occur asynchronously much as they would in email exchanges. As people add on new comments, a conversation builds. Direct messages function like private email messages, except within the confines of the social networking site being used. Instant messages are possible when two users are logged in simultaneously and wish to carry on a synchronous conversation. A **nudge** is a tool for reminding someone to socialize. On Facebook, the nudge takes the form of a "poke." Thus, social networking sites enable our interactions with others in several ways.

We can think of social networks as communication hubs; virtually all of them offer users access to a contact list and an interface that makes it easy for people to talk to one another. However, most sites offer more features than these basic ones. The new standard for social networking sites is to offer tools, widgets, applications, and features that encourage **social sharing**; they provide people with the tools they need to reveal elements of their digital identities. These elements include information about us or things that we create—such as our opinions, photos, videos, songs, and artworks. They may also take the form of **secondary content**—things that others create we feel are worth redistributing to our social networks, such as retweets, links to a celebrity blog, or even brands we "like" on our Facebook page. Mark Zuckerberg, president and CEO of Facebook, said this about sharing: "People have really gotten comfortable not only sharing more information and different kinds, but more openly and with more people. [This is a] social norm that has evolved over time."[6]

Social media empowers us and because of it we all have the capacity to share something if we choose to do so. Consider the social consumer segment we call *creators*. Creators are the roughly 20 percent of social media users who actively produce content in the form of video, podcasts/music, stories and articles, and blog posts. They may publish their own website.[7] Creators are a busy bunch—24 hours of YouTube video is posted every minute. The rest of us may not possess the technical skill nor the desire to produce original content. We're happy leaving that work to others—many of whom are professionals. Still, we certainly are avid consumers of the content—YouTube videos alone get 2 billion views every day.[8]

Although not everyone is a creator who develops artifacts such as videos and podcasts for distribution in their social network, anyone *can* join a network, update a status, post secondary content from others, and provide feedback on the content others post in their networks. Remember that analysts estimate lurkers—those people who consume content by reading posts and watching videos, but who do not contribute to the flow of content—make up about 90 percent of any online community.[9]

The act of sharing changes this dynamic, because even lurkers can redistribute secondary content to a larger network of people. In this sense even fairly passive participants can extend their reach well beyond their own social graph. ShareThis, a provider of a widget that enables visitors to easily share content they discover online, found that though almost half of users preferred email for sharing interesting content with others, most of the remainder preferred to use a social media channel to share.[10] Applications such as ShareThis minimize the investment of time and effort necessary to share secondary content to a social network, so it's more likely that content will spread rapidly.

A recent study of social media users found that 75 percent of people are likely to share content via social media channels. The top three reasons people share content "socially" are because they find it interesting and/or entertaining, they think it could be helpful to others, and to get a laugh. Although the content can be virtually anything you can send in digital form, most people reported sharing family pictures and video, news about family and friends, funny videos, news articles and blog posts, and coupons and discounts.[11]

How do social networking sites encourage participation and sharing by members? They make sharing easy. A widget such as the ShareThis application is an example of how sites can make it easy to share. They offer many forms of sharing in addition to just typing a lot of text on a page.[12] Just consider these sharing activities:

- An *activity stream* is an easy tool to share a short piece of content with a network, whether the content reflects a current activity, thought, opinion, idea, or anything else that can be shared in a feed. Your Facebook feed keeps a record of your activities including status updates, mobile uploads, picture posts, group memberships, and within-network interactions.

- **Gift applications** enable members to present virtual gifts to their friends. Even though virtual gifts are not tangible and may have no monetary value, they do reflect an expression of friendship, love, gratitude, and/or thoughtfulness and can be displayed publicly on a profile to visibly reflect the importance of the relationship to others in the network. As we'll see later in the book, these gifts are one kind of **virtual good** that consumers purchase in huge numbers as they continue to spend more of their time in online worlds rather than in the physical world.

- *Ongoing sharing* means working with partners to include activities from other sites in an activity stream on a partnered site. For instance, your Foursquare check-ins can feed directly to Twitter and Facebook. Once the link is in place, the sharing occurs automatically. Many social networking sites and sites with social media applications partner with one another because of the need to provide a constant supply of fresh shared content.

- **Uploading functionalities** are applications that make it easy to share from many locations. You may have an application on your mobile phone that streams a Twitter feed. The camera on your mobile phone might include a share button that automatically uploads your photos to Facebook or Flickr. Your Facebook news feed includes easy share buttons for photos, videos, website links, events, and notes.

- **Embed codes** let people share content where they wish, even on their own distribution networks. Some users like to collect artifacts such as badges, images, and slideshows and display them on their own profiles (or even on other sites, like a personal blog). For example, Adverblog (www.adverblog.com) includes embed codes of YouTube videos and Twitter feeds. This is not only a tool to encourage sharing; it's also a good tool for branding because the artifact may be a brand logo or product image! The distributor creates a snippet of code that the user can copy and paste into his or her blog, activity stream, or other social space.

- Friends can also share experiences with others via social games such as *FarmVille*. Social games refer to online, structured, multiplayer activities based on a social platform. They may exist within a social network or on a separate social platform.

Finally, sites encourage sharing when they reward participation with **reputation indicators**. People like to be acknowledged for their contributions. Sites can award top status to those who contribute the best and most. Reputation indicators broadcast these contributions; they include participation levels, labels, collectible achievements and awards (badges), and points. Some sites maintain a **leaderboard** to highlight the best participants.

These features, and others such as calendar updates, event support, image uploads, and polls, help to make a social network site "sticky." **Stickiness** is a term that explains how well the site can retain visitors during a single session and encourage repeat visits. The more there is to do on a site, the stickier the site is. The trick is not to attract people to your site, but rather to make them want to stay as long as possible once they are there.

Although many people are motivated to contribute so they can accumulate these goodies, it's important to remember that others do so for other reasons. They may like entertaining others or feel that they are nurturing their network. They may do it to validate their own desire to feel important to others. They may try to benefit the greater good.

Ironically, rewarding someone who has an intrinsic source of motivation with an extrinsic reward can lead to reduced participation—just the opposite of what's desired! Amazon learned this lesson. It revised its reviewing system of volunteer reviewers to enable rankings of reviewers based on activity and helpfulness. Some of Amazon's reviewers were hobbyists who responded positively to extrinsic rewards. But many took their roles as reviewers as a responsibility to which they were highly and personally committed. Those reviewers reduced their contributions to Amazon after the extrinsic reward system was implemented.[13]

 # THE DARK SIDE OF SOCIAL MEDIA

The growing power of social networks brings with it the temptation to exploit these networks. Although most companies understand that the value of these loosely connected groups of "friends" lies in encouraging members to share helpful information with others about brands they enjoy, in the early days of social media some marketers still are testing the boundaries in terms of what is appropriate to get consumers to do. Advertising agency Saatchi & Saatchi's campaign to reach young men on behalf of its client Toyota is a case in point. In an effort to convince young men to buy the automaker's Matrix vehicle, the agency's social media team tried to replicate the success of the popular MTV show *Punk'd*. The idea was to enlist a potential buyer to single out a friend who would be the target of a prank. This short-lived project did not turn out well. One woman who was the object of a prank reported that she received a series of emails from a fictitious British soccer hooligan named Sebastian Bowler. This U.K. stalker boasted that he was coming to visit her—with his pet pit bull in tow. In one message she received a fake bill for damage to a hotel room that Bowler allegedly trashed; her name was listed on the bill. Saatchi set up a fake MySpace page where Bowler bragged about "drinking alcohol to excess" and participating in riots. The victim of this prank filed a $10 million lawsuit. She claimed she was so terrified that she slept with a machete by her bed. The ad agency and the automaker defended their actions, claiming that the woman had given "her permission to receive campaign e-mails and other communications from Toyota."[14]

Characteristics of Social Networking Sites

Social networks are the foundation of social media because every form of social media is based on participation from a *community* of members. Still, it is useful to compare and contrast social networks and to understand how their defining dimensions affect our ability to market brands within the social space. Social networking sites all maintain a basic network structure—nodes that interact with one another, flows between node members, and graphs connected to others by way of node relationships. However, social networking sites vary in terms of three important dimensions:

1. Audience and degree of specialization
2. The social objects that mediate the relationships among members
3. Degree of decentralization or openness

Audience Specialization Social networking sites can be internal or external, general or specialized. Internal sites are those a specific organization builds for its own use and limits to members of the organization. Rather than hosting several subcultures within a larger social networking site, an **internal social network** provides a method of communication and collaboration that is more dynamic and interactive. This is a lot like the *intranet* that many companies provide their employees. For instance, Nissan launched a site for its employees called N-Square. The network enables employees to post profiles, maintain a blog, participate in discussion groups, and share files.[15] Microsoft uses a network it calls TownSquare, IBM has the BeeHive, and Yahoo! employees meet in the Backyard. In contrast, an **external social network** is open to people who are not affiliated with the site's sponsor.

Social networks are, of course, about networking—participating in the kinds of activities that enable members to build and maintain their relationships with other people. However, the nature of those relationships also affects the characterization of the social network. LinkedIn is a professional social network that emphasizes career experience and the need to maintain connections to those we know professionally. The primary benefit is to be able to call upon one's network when looking for a consultant, employee, job, or other career-related search. There are several professional networks held together by industry, purpose, and personal career goals. Care2 is a social network for people who want to help with social causes. Focus is a network for business and technology experts. Den provides a social network where architects and designers congregate.

Many of the social networking sites with which you are familiar probably relate to social activities. A primary focus in a truly social platform is the opportunity to build personal relationships. Facebook began as a social networking site, but has evolved into what it calls a social utility. As a social utility, Facebook offers functionality in all zones of the social media mix: networking, group discussion (similar to forums), social publishing and media sharing, social commerce, and social entertainment.

Just because a social network focuses on personal relationships over professional ones doesn't necessarily mean that it has a broad target. For instance, Jdate.com is a dating social network for Jewish singles. Its mission is social, but it still targets a niche audience. There are several networks designed around specific target audiences defined by demographic characteristics including age (e.g., ClubPenguin, Webkinz), marital status (e.g., MarriedLife, MarriedPassions), income (asmallworld.net, affluence.org), and so on.

Social Objects and Passion-Centric Sites In industry terms, sites designed around object sociality, the ability of an object to inspire social interaction, are known as **vertical networks**. The term describes the narrow, deep focus of social networking sites that differentiate themselves because they emphasize some common hobby, interest, or characteristic that draws members to the site. These vertical networks do not attract the same traffic typical of general sites, but one might argue that the members are more involved because of the common interest that initially brought them to the site. They function much like so-called *niche markets* in the physical world; this term refers to marketplaces that offer a relatively small number of items to buyers who tend to be loyal to these outlets.

Decentralization As social media sites continue to proliferate around the Web, they experience "growing pains" because we are still trying to figure out how to manage all of this new activity. Some people seem to spend most of the day just updating their Facebook profiles, responding to email (if they still use that instead of texting), and checking out the *site du jour* that everyone is talking about (today). Can we have too much of a good thing? One of the big issues social media needs to confront is how to let people easily access multiple sites and understand where they go and why.

Openness and Identity Portability Social networks can be closed, gated communities entirely controlled by the vendor that offers the platform. At the other extreme they can be accessible to any members or developers who wish to participate. Many social networking sites require new members to register for membership and to use login specifications to access the community. It often makes sense for a social networking site to keep a record of membership even if anyone is allowed to join. This information can be invaluable for purposes of member management, product development, promoting the site, and utilizing the member data for other purposes. How might social networks utilize member data? Because social networks have access to vast amounts of detailed data about members' preferences, friends, and activities, they may eventually license that data to external marketers who could use the data to target potential customers. For now, the social community site with the most data, Facebook, isn't selling member data, but some speculate that it will.[16]

It's important to recognize that many social networking site members are **social media omnivores**; they eagerly participate in several different platforms. Most people who are involved in social media are members of at least two networks.[17] Think back to your digital footprint—it probably includes your tracks on Facebook, LinkedIn, and other social communities like Twitter and Foursquare. Unless you use a social media dashboard such as HootSuite or an automated feed application, your activity in each community requires an independent and ongoing effort to participate. Many people use such services to manage the time required to participate actively in more than one network. However, using a dashboard also makes keeping different personas separate (e.g., enthusiastic road tripper on TripAdvisor, dedicated career marketer on LinkedIn, avid partier on Facebook) across sites more difficult.

And, what if a new service comes along—which of course happens nearly every day on the social Web? You'll need to complete your profile information yet again. Or you might decide that the new community just isn't worth the hassle required to reenter for the millionth time your username, email address, gender, etc. Ironically, this barrier-to-entry for new services is a boon to established ones because many people are likely to just stick to the service they use the most in order to minimize the hassles of switching.

Complaints about the lack of centralized communities have given rise to the terms **social networking fatigue** and **social lock-in**. The fatigue comes in part from the need to manage multiple community accounts (and to forego some due to the required investment) as well as from the steady streams of content flowing from multiple networks. Rather than experiencing a single social stream, those with multiple networks have several streams flowing at any point in time. Social lock-in occurs when a user is unable to transfer social contacts and content from one social network to another.

This problem is similar to one we often encounter in the physical world when we use a mediocre product, but it's too complicated or expensive to drop it in favor of a better one. For example, a student who has a revelation at the beginning of her senior year that she'd rather be a marketing major than an accounting major may decide to just stick it out with balance sheets because it would require several additional years to complete the course requirements for a new major. Economists would say that in this situation the **switching costs** are too high. It's much the same in the world of social media; once our social graph is firmly engrained in a particular host community, the time and effort to shift may outweigh the benefit we think we will get if we move to a new community service.

How can social media minimize the switching cost problem? One widely discussed solution is to develop a system of **identity portability** such that a single profile would provide access across social networking sites with a single login and shared information. This is the goal of **OpenID**, an authentication protocol that works across participating sites. Unfortunately, OpenID works only on OpenID-enabled sites, limiting the portability for users. Sites can also choose to enable authentication with Facebook Connect, an option that has been more widely adopted.

Open Source   The decision as to whether to grant access to outside developers (and how or if to share in the revenue these applications produce) is one of the most important strategic issues in business today. For example, Apple uses a fairly closed model; the company maintains strict control over "apps" that outsiders can sell for its iPhone and iPad and it takes a hefty commission (30 percent) on each sale. Similarly, Sony shares its code for its PlayStation game with only a selected set of licensed developers.

Other companies follow the **open source model** that turns some of our conventional assumptions about the value of products and services on its head. This model started in the software industry where the Linux system grows by leaps and bounds—even IBM uses it now. Unlike the closely guarded code that companies such as Microsoft use, open source developers post their programs on a public site and a community of volunteers is free to tinker with them, develop other applications using the code, then give their changes away for free. For example, the company that gives out (for free) the Mozilla Firefox Internet browser that competes with Microsoft commands over 20 percent market share among users.[18]

Google believes that the more outside developers it can attract, the faster its business will grow. The company offers what it calls **OpenSocial code**. This term refers to a set of common **APIs** that enable developers to write software for applications that will run on multiple social websites. API stands for *application programming interface*. It's a programming model that enables a piece of software to interact with other software. When private APIs are used, only licensed developers can provide applications. When social networking sites make their APIs freely available, development of tools and features from outside the community can flourish. This has been the case with Facebook; it doesn't use Google's OpenSocial proactively, but it has encouraged freelance developers to contribute to Facebook's community. This has resulted in hundreds upon hundreds of special applications such as Citizen Sports, Where I've Been, Flair, Bumper Sticker, My Family, iLike, Dogbook, and more.

Learning
Objective 3

Marketing Applications in the Social Community Zone

The social community zone focuses on relationships. By becoming an active participant in these channels, brands can leverage social networks to meet several marketing objectives including promotion and branding, customer service and customer relationship management, and marketing research. How? By advertising within the community space, participating in brand-to-consumer relationships within the chosen communities, and engaging consumers interactively. Let's take a closer look.

As social media marketers, we can approach marketing to social networks in terms of both paid media and earned media. Recall that paid media are the paid placements of brand messages. In 2009, advertisers spent $1.2 billion on display advertising on social networks worldwide ($1.2 billion in the United States alone). Facebook alone earned $605 million in advertising revenues in 2010.[19]

In social networks, brands can purchase paid space for advertising and utilize share technologies such as Share This to further leverage the value of the advertising impressions. In contrast, earned media are those messages that are distributed at no direct cost to the company and by methods beyond the brand's control. Brands participate in social networks to generate brand awareness and knowledge and positive word-of-mouth communication. There's an added bonus, too. Links to brand-related online content shared via social media affect the search engine rankings delivered by search engines such as Google and Yahoo! So not only can consumers be influenced by brand interactions and references to brands made by those in their network, they also can be led to branded content via search listings.

Paid Media in Social Networks

Display ads may include text, graphics, video, and sound much like traditional print ads and commercials but they are presented on a website. Whether the ads are text-oriented (e.g., a classified ad in a newspaper), text and graphics (e.g., a print ad in a magazine), or **rich media** (e.g., a television commercial), they are enhanced with a **response device** in that viewers can click the ads (called a **clickthrough**) to reach a target **landing page**. A landing page is the first page that a person sees when he or she clicks through an ad to reach a brand's target site. It's an important page for marketers, in that the content on the landing page will influence whether visitors stay at the site or move on to another page.

Social ads are online display ads that incorporate user data in the ad or in the targeting of the ad and enable some form of **social interaction** within the ad unit or landing page. In these applications, user data (also known as **social data** when collected from information users leave in their digital footprints and lifestreams) are harnessed to deliver messages that should be relevant to the recipients based on their online behaviors. These ads often customize the ad content; they may even incorporate references to friends of the target. The ads are personalized using details from user profiles, images, relationships among users, data gathered from applications, and interactions within a user network. Like other online display ads, they incorporate a response device, enabling interested viewers to click through to a landing page (which could be the brand's social profile). But unlike conventional display ads, social ads are interactive—viewers can play with the ad, share it, or comment.

There are currently three variations of social ads:[20]

1. A **social engagement ad** contains ad creative (image and text) along with an option to encourage the viewer to engage with the brand (e.g., a clickable "Like" button).
2. A **social context ad** includes ad creative, an engagement device, and personalized referral content from people in the viewer's network.
3. **Organic social ads** are shared on a person's activity stream following a brand interaction (such as liking the brand). Organic social ads occur only when people are interacting with the brand and are thought to carry enhanced credibility.

In a study of advertising effectiveness based on 14 ad campaigns run on Facebook, Nielsen found that social ads had strong ad recall and brands featured in the ads benefitted from an increase in awareness and purchase intent.[21] Newsfeed stories of brand interactions, called **derivative branded content**, are just one way to seed content using the network. When organic social ads are combined with social engagement or context ad, effectiveness improved. A limitation is that organic social ads occur only when community members have interacted with the brand's social ads, on the brand's own profile, or with some branded application or game. If few people choose to interact, few organic social ads will be generated. In this case, paid media seeded the interaction necessary to generate additional impressions. But marketers also can utilize seeding to foster consumer engagement and interactivity though nonpaid media activities. In the following, we discuss two key approaches.

BYTES TO BUCKS

How can marketers make the most of relationships and generate earned media? They are tasked with creating and delivering persuasive messages that are relevant, engaging, interactive, personalizable, and shareable. To put it simply, the challenge is to create marketing messages that are so cool, funny, or interesting that people *want* to see them and share them. That's why social media marketers sometimes call the creative design of social media campaigns **experience design**. The term underscores the desire to create more than a passive ad—the goal is launch an experience that people will *want to share*.

Gossip Girl's "What Would Gossip Girl Say About You?" campaign is a great example of creativity that motivates the receiver to get involved with the message and help to spread it to others. Rather than delivering a static commercial (online using paid media or on the CWTV network using owned media) using the interruption-disruption model, visitors to the CWTV.com website were invited to create their own video and find out what Gossip Girl would say about them. The campaign (paid media and promotions on the CWTV website) encouraged *Gossip Girl* fans (and future fans) to create a personalized video using the Gossip Girl app. A fan chose a video storyline. The *Gossip Girl* app pulled personal data from the fan's Facebook page or the fan could answer a series of questions at the CWTV.com site. The personal data were then dropped into designated spots in an interactive video featuring the enticing storylines of the main characters.

The app is a **seed**. It gave *Gossip Girl* fans a reason to interact with the brand and resulted in a segment of produced content that can be shared online using social networks (especially Facebook, which partnered in the app by enabling profiles to feed into the video application), media sharing sites such as YouTube, or email. When the videos are shared, they become earned media. Some of the people who see the videos became intrigued with the *Gossip Girl* story—and maybe, just maybe, they tuned in for the next episode of *Gossip Girl*. The CWTV leveraged the unique attributes of social networks to enhance its marketing communications and meet its objectives.

You can see from the Gossip Girl interactive viral video example the importance of ensuring that paid and earned media support each other. The CW utilized paid media in social networks and earned media in the form of Facebook updates to promote the video app (the seed). Users could take that seed and create their own "What would Gossip Girl say about you?" video on either CW's owned media or on Facebook and then share their influence impressions on Facebook, on YouTube, and by email. Figure 2 illustrates how paid and earned media work together in social media to promote brand messages.

Earned Media and Brand Engagement

Brands earn value in social media when they engage consumers over time (relationship marketing) and when they encourage consumers to interact with the brand and share those interactions with others. Brands stand to benefit from heightened brand loyalty among engaged consumers and a more expansive reach for brand-related messages. The **earned reach** (the breadth and quality of contact with users) gained when people share positive brand opinions and branded content with others is invaluable because of the influence attributed to individual, personalized brand endorsements. Yes, we're talking about word-of-mouth communication.

We can all influence people in our network with our opinions using word-of-mouth (or *word-of-mouse*) communication. Friends and family are important sources of information and influence when we make purchase decisions. According to Razorfish's "Fluent" study of social media consumers, 62 percent of respondents said that they do not actively seek out opinions about brands through social media. Yet these respondents also acknowledged that they learn about brands through their social interactions with others because this information is woven into their everyday conversations.[22] These daily, mostly innocuous comments—possibly as lighthearted as "on my way to Starbucks for a black eye before class"—remind and reinforce brand knowledge. We've introduced this concept—influence impressions—previously. Here we expand the concept by differentiating it from that of influence posts.[23] **Influence posts** occur when an opinion leader *publishes* brand-relevant content

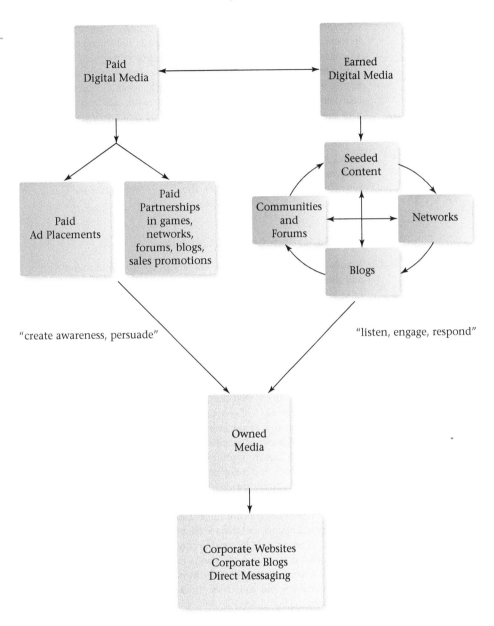

Figure 2

Relationships among Earned, Paid, and Owned Media

such as a blog post in social media. For example, when Girls With Guts (http://girlswithguts.blogspot. com/) blog about a recent restaurant opening, the earned media is known as an influence post.

Influence impressions occur at an outstanding rate—one estimate suggests that people in the United States create 256 billion influence impressions in social communities every year; 62 percent of these come from Facebook.[24] Influence impressions don't always spread virally, but when they do, the impact is substantial. Consider this tidbit from Nielsen Online: It estimates that advertisers created 1.974 trillion online advertising impressions last year, while influence impressions delivered peer-to-peer in social media communities resulted in 500 billion impressions. That's right—peer-to-peer influence is close to a quarter of the influence of online paid media. These impressions occur in conversations held in social communities; in comments to blog posts and shared media; in "likes," "followers," and shares among friends; during conversations surrounding online shopping and group deals; and as people gift virtual branded goods to fellow game players. Anyone active in social media can create an influence impression, but influence is particularly powerful when that person is also well connected—what we've called an *influencer*. The size of a person's network enhances the ability for the message to spread. This goes back to the 80/20 Rule we introduced earlier. In this case under 10 percent of online adults generate 80 percent of the influence impressions.

Word-of-mouth communication isn't new. What *is* new is that when someone talks about a brand, hundreds, thousands, or sometimes even millions of people may also be exposed to the conversation. This is the kind of exposure money can't buy—marketers *earn* it by motivating, sometimes called *seeding*, people to talk about their brands (see the *Gossip Girl* example in the Bytes to Bucks feature earlier in this chapter).

User-Generated Content Campaigns

Brands can seed many forms of content in social communities as they try to boost engagement and sharing. One of the most popular tools is the use of the **user-generated content campaign** (also known as a *UGC contest*). UGC campaigns offer a way for brands to invite consumers to engage and interact while they develop shareable content. The lexicon of online marketers includes many commonly used phrases and accompanying acronyms related to user-generated content, also known as consumer-generated media. **Consumer-generated media (CGM)** or UGC are the catch-all phrases for user content. User content is organic when its creation is motivated by an intrinsic intent on the part of its creator rather than incentivized or guided by the brand itself. Organic brand-oriented UGC, at least when promoting the brand in a favorable light, is valuable and suggests highly engaged customers. For example, a YouTube video espousing one's love for his or her iPad is organic UGC—Apple didn't invite or incent the fan to create and post the content.

A UGC campaign is sometimes called **participatory advertising**. Brands invite content, set mandatory guidelines and specifications, and possibly also provide participants with selected *brand assets* such as footage from prior commercials that ran on TV. UGC contests encourage people in the target audience to develop and submit content related to the campaign. The content is then shared on social sites in the form of a **gallery**, which others can view and pass the content on to their respective networks.

UGC contests engage consumers and spread the message by leveraging consumer networks. It takes work to organize and oversee the process and promotion to activate these contests, but on the other hand they provide interesting content at a relatively low cost to the brand—especially compared to what professional advertisers charge to create commercials! Depending upon the contest design, UGC contests can also offer ways to engage different types of consumers—creators, joiners, conversationalists, and collectors. In addition, they provide content for journalists to include in stories about the brand, so ultimately this enhances a brand's public relations profile.

The most frequently used manifestation of CSM is the "create your own ad" contest, which has been used by numerous brands including Frito-Lay, Dove, and Chevy. Sponsors encourage submissions with incentives such as prize money or the chance for the winning entry to be broadcast on television (possibly during high-exposure events such as the Super Bowl and the Oscars). Doritos used this approach with its *Crash the Super Bowl* campaign.

Social Presence: Brands as Relationship Nodes   In addition to advertising in social networks and engaging consumers in engagement activities, brands also can create a **brand profile** within selected social networking communities. In this way, the brand acts as a node in the network's social graph. Doing so increases the opportunities for interactions with customers and prospects and also encourages people to talk about the brand with each other.

When a brand profile launches on social networking sites, the brands exist much as people do on the sites. Friends can interact with the brands; share information, photos, and videos; and participate in two-way communication. Brands may participate as a corporate entity, as one or more people representing the brand, or as a mascot. Whichever the choice, the brand will develop a profile to represent its persona and then should interact in keeping with that profile—like a good actor, it should "stay in character." Building brand personas strengthen brand personality, differentiate brands from competitors, and set the stage for a perceived relationship. Assuming the brand's persona is likeable and credible, it can facilitate **message internalization** (the process by which a consumer adopts a brand belief as his or her own). It is a natural expansion of the trend for brands to create personalities for themselves, both through the use of creative language—including style, imagery, tone, and creative appeals—and music.

The most social brands in the world might already be among your "friends." Many social network users *like*, *friend*, or *fan* brands. Starbucks has nearly 8 million friends or "fans" as of this writing. Coca-Cola is approaching 6 million. And who could resist being friends with Oreo cookies? That's a friendship that lasts a lifetime! These brands maintain a social presence in online communities as they invite people to interact and share content related to the brand.

Is the social success of a brand tied to the number of people who friend, fan, or like the brand publicly within a social community? Let's just assume that (like in the physical world) being popular matters. If social success is tied to the size of someone's friend or follower list, brands such as Starbucks, Coca-Cola, Skittles, Whole Foods, Oreo, and Red Bull at least for now are the most popular kids in school. Table 1 tells us more about which brands people follow on social networking sites.

Brand Fans   With millions of Facebook fans and thousands of Twitter followers, these brands participate in **friendvertising**, —a brand's use of social networking to build earned media value—and purposefully cultivate **brand fans**. The word "fan" refers to a person who is enthusiastic about something or someone. Fans display their loyalty and affection for celebrities, sports teams, and musicians in the physical world when they buy T-shirts or other licensed products, join fan clubs, and flock to concerts or

TABLE 1

The Most Social Brands

Source: Famecount, www.famecount.com/all-platforms/Worldwide/all/Brand, accessed August 8, 2011. Used by permission of Famecount.

Brand	Facebook Fans	Twitter Followers	YouTube Views
Coca-Cola	33,218,491	340,685	26,877,283
Starbucks	24,225,810	1,598,969	6,811,407
Red Bull	21,819,006	267,437	174,407,903
Oreo	22,590,639	14,265	3,030,000
PlayStation	16,845,503	1,040,162	48,062,300
Converse All Star	20,439,551	—	—
Skittles	18,940,037	15,344	2,188,478
Victoria's Secret	14,791,273	153,335	26,721,220
Pringles	15,140,709	2,446	—
Windows Live Messenger	14,116,083	6,021	—

Note: If no value appears in a cell this brand does not maintain a presence on that social media platform.

stadiums. In a social network, a similar display of loyalty may be as simple as clicking Facebook's "Like" button and "joining" a sponsored page in the networking site. An online fan community is a **fandom**.

For brands to truly leverage social networks as a place to build relationships with customers, fan relationships should strive to mimic those found among strong fan communities such as Trekkers (members of the *Star Trek* fandom) and Gleeks (fans of the television show *Glee*). Fans who define their own individual identities at least in part by their membership in a fandom share five key characteristics.[25]

1. *Emotional engagement:* The object is meaningful in the emotional life of the fan. For example, fans of *Glee* may feel that the program reflects an important aspect of their own life, perhaps related to involvement in the performing arts, a sense of being a misfit, or nostalgia surrounding the challenging days of high school.

2. *Self-identification:* The fan personally and publicly identifies with like-minded fans. *Glee* fans identify themselves as Gleeks and feel a sense of belonging with other Gleeks.

3. *Cultural competence:* The fan has a critical understanding of the object, its history, and its meaning beyond its basic functionality. Gleeks may follow the show on Twitter and Facebook, read the show blog, and participate in Q&A on the Fox Broadcasting Network website.

4. *Auxiliary consumption:* The fan collects and consumes related items and experiences beyond the basic object. Gleeks can buy *Glee: The Christmas Album*, download *Glee* music from iTunes, buy and play the *Glee* iPad app, play the *Glee* Karaoke Wii game, and wear clothes that sport the *Glee* logo.

5. *Production:* The fan becomes involved in the production of content related to the object. Gleeks post their favorite clips (unofficially), and record and post their own renditions of *Glee* tunes to YouTube. Those with the *Glee* iPad app can record their performances and post them to the community of other performers for ratings and downloads. Some Gleeks run their own *Glee*-focused blogs such as Suzie Gardner's Gleeks United blog (gleeksunited.wordpress.com).

It's really too soon to tell whether the fans being amassed by brands active in social networks are true fans who define themselves by their participation in a brand community, or just brand users who are willing to acknowledge some affiliation with a brand. That's because it's become so easy to like, follow, or become a fan. Liking a brand is an easy, low-involvement step and it's one that frequently comes after exposure to an ad requesting the Like as a call to action.

The **fan base** is an indicator of the brand's success in establishing a known presence within a community. But to build brand equity and lasting loyalty, brands need more than brand awareness and recognition or even brand affiliation. As brands embrace social media marketing, they acknowledge that a strong relationship exists between brand and customer when the customer has a high level of **brand engagement**.

We can think of engagement as a continuum. At one end, people may affiliate with a brand online simply because they want to acknowledge the brand. For example, you might affiliate with Oreos because you have a nostalgic connection to the brand based on childhood experiences. It doesn't mean that you plan to buy Oreos now or that you are otherwise engaged with the brand. At the other end, affiliates may want to interact with a brand in meaningful ways, perhaps even working with the brand to develop new products and services. Lego fans, for instance, are infamous for their high levels of brand engagement. And somewhere in between are fans who want special offers and find they benefit from branded content.

Level of engagement makes a big difference in terms of the buying decision process. One study found that purchase intent for a brand with interactive profiles was higher than for brands without such profiles.[26] Another study by Syncapse specifically measured the value of being a brand's Facebook fan. It found that people spend about $72 more on a product for which they have a social network affiliation than for one they do not. Fans are also 28 percent more likely than nonfans to continue using a brand, and 41 percent more likely to recommend a fanned versus nonfanned product to a friend.[27] Fans in the study also said they felt connected to their brands.

Importantly, brands that use social media to develop a relationship with customers need to find ways to provide a **return on emotion** for the fans. Return on emotion conceptually assesses the extent to which a brand has delivered a value in exchange for the emotional attachment fans have awarded it.[28] Traditionally, the relationship between brand and consumer is asymmetric, with more effort invested by the fan. One industry study suggests that for brands to succeed as social friends to consumers, building heightened engagement and loyalty, consumers must feel that their efforts are reciprocated and the relationship is symmetric.[29] To do so, brands should socialize with fans and participate in conversations using a credible and authentic brand voice.

Ultimately, this social media marketing approach seeks to drive awareness and liking of brands while also building earned media. As we suggested earlier, brands should use social spaces to give consumers reason to share positive stories and product information. To encourage this, brands can offer branded assets such as downloads, shareable widgets and wallpapers, and invitations for consumers to co-create branded content. Brands should also be sure to provide value to the fans by using the branded page as an information hub to announce new products, company news, contests and promotions, and career opportunities.

Is the Brand Ready for Social Relationships?

Clearly, there is a lot to be gained for brands operating in social media, and from friending customers in social networks. Managers should ask these questions before deciding whether social relationships will work for a specific brand.

- Is the brand set up for engagement? Mark Kingdon, CEO of Organic, Inc., a digital-marketing agency, said that "Brands have to allow for and anticipate dialogue, because consumers very much want to engage with brands and not all brands are set up for engagement. A lot of brands are simply set up to broadcast their message to an audience."[30] Some brands will be safer with one-way communication.

- If the traditional brand participates in social media, where should the brand be? Should the brand have its own dedicated social network space (e.g., Nike's Joga)? Or will the brand have the best chance at creating consumer dialogue and engagement by using an existing network such as Gather or Facebook? Is there a social networking site that is well-suited to the brand? For example, Purina is perfectly suited to advertising on Dogster, but its message may not be as effective on Glue.

- How can the brand's profiles be developed in such a way as to reflect the brand's personality? With what voice will the brand speak? How will the brand interact within the site?

- If "fan pages" exist among brand loyalists on social networking sites, how can the brand leverage the fan sites to better meet its objectives?

- How can the brand integrate its social network presence into other campaign components? Integration may start with simple steps such as including a Facebook icon in other brand messages and develop into utilizing the social network for sales promotions such as coupon distribution and contest administration.

Chapter Summary

How do users develop an identity in social networking communities? What are the components of identity?

Users develop an identity in social networking communities by completing a profile that includes a picture or avatar, information about their background and demographics, as well as personalization components such as skins, applications, groups, and more.

How do social networking communities enable user participation and sharing?

Social networks encourage participation by providing easy-to-use tools including share buttons, applications, uploading functionalities, embed codes, and activity streams.

In what ways can brands utilize social networking communities for branding and promotion?

Brands have three key ways of utilizing social networking communities for branding. First, social ads can be placed within targeted social communities. Second, brands can engage consumers in these spaces using interactive applications and user-generated contest campaigns. Third, brands can simply participate in the social community and encourage people to become fans of the brand.

Key Terms

activity streams
ambient intimacy
APIs
backchannel
badges
brand engagement
brand fans
brand profile
clickthrough
consumer-generated media (CGM)
derivative branded content
directed communications
display ads
Dunbar's number
earned reach
embed codes
experience design
external social network
fan base
fandom
friendvertising

gallery
gift applications
identity cards
identity portability
identity reflectors
influence posts
internal social network
landing page
leaderboard
message internalization
nudge
open source model
OpenID
OpenSocial code
organic social ads
participatory advertising
presence indicator
reputation indicators
response device
return on emotion
rich media

secondary content
seed
skins
social ads
social context ad
social data
social engagement ad
social interaction
social lock-in
social media omnivores
social networking fatigue
social sharing
statuscasting
stickiness
switching costs
synchronous communications
themes
uploading functionalities
user-generated content campaign
vertical networks
virtual good

Review Questions

1. What social activities are the focus of participation in social communities?
2. How can consumers create identities in social communities?
3. What are the types of social networks in social media?
4. What are the characteristics of social ads? How effective are social ads?
5. How can brands engage consumers in social communities?
6. How are influence impressions different from influence posts?
7. What is earned media? How do brands encourage earned media with their social networking activities?
8. What are the characteristics of brand fans?

Exercises

1. Discussion: Should a social network own our social data? Is it an invasion of privacy for social networks to collect and use the information we leave as we deposit digital footprints in a site and around the Web?
2. Discussion: Is it a good thing to "friend" your professors? Why or why not?
3. Discussion: Are Facebook friends the same as real friends? Are Facebook fans real fans? Explain.
4. Analyze a brand profile on Facebook. Identify all the brand assets on the page. What techniques are being used by the brand to engage consumers? Do the brand fans seem passionate and engaged? Why or why not? How could the brand improve its profile?
5. Interview three people who are passionate about some interest. Document the time and resources they spend to engage with this object. Despite their passion for very different objects, what similarities or common patterns do you observe among them? Do they engage in this interest in social communities?

Notes

1. J. Sunden, *Material Virtualities: Approaching Online Textual Embodiment.* (New York: Peter Lang, 2003), 3
2. "Reflector" (Entry), *Yahoo Developer Network*, July 15, 2009, http://developer.yahoo.com/ypatterns/social/people/identity/reflector.html, accessed December 19, 2010.
3. Leisa Reichelt, "Ambient Intimacy," *Reboot 9.0*, June 25, 2009, www.reboot.dk/page/1236/en, accessed December 20, 2010.
4. Moira Burke, Cameron Marlow, and Thomas Lento, "Social Network Activity and Social Well-Being," ACM CHI 2010: Conference on Human Factors in Computing, Atlanta, GA, 2010, www.facebook.com/data?sk=app_4949752878, accessed December 19, 2010.
5. Robin Dunbar, "You've Got to Have (150) Friends," *New York Times*, December 25, 2010, www.nytimes.com/2010/12/26/opinion/26dunbar.html?_r=1&scp=1&sq=Dunbar&st=cse, accessed December 27, 2010.
6. Quoted in Marshall Kirkpatrick, "Facebook's Zuckerberg Says The Age of Privacy is Over," *Read Write Web*, January 9, 2010, www.readwriteweb.com/archives/facebooks_zuckerberg_says_the_age_of_privacy_is_ov.php, accessed December 21, 2010.
7. Jackie Rousseau-Anderson, "The Latest Global Social Media Trends May Surprise You," *Forrester Blogs*, September 28, 2010, http://blogs.forrester.com/jackie_rousseau_anderson/10-09-28-latest_global_social_media_trends_may_surprise_you, accessed December 20, 2010.
8. "Timeline," *YouTube*, May 2010, www.youtube.com/t/press_timeline, accessed December 19, 2010.
9. Jakob Nielsen, "Participation Inequality: Encouraging More Users to Contribute," *AlertBox*, October 9, 2006, www.useit.com/alertbox/participation_inequality.html, accessed December 18, 2010.
10. Debra Aho Williamson, "Brand Interactions on Social Networks," *eMarketer*, June 2010, www.emarketer.com/Report.aspx?code=emarketer_2000694, accessed December 20, 2010.
11. Josh Mendelsohn and Jeff McKenna, "Social Sharing Research Report," Chadwick Martin Bailey, September 2010, www.cmbinfo.com/cmb.../Social_Sharing_Research_Report_CMB1.pdf, accessed October 15, 2010.
12. Christian Crumlish and Erin Malone, *Designing Social Interfaces*, Sebastopol, CA: O'Reilly Media, 2009).
13. Charla Mathwick, "Influencing the Influencers: Rewarding Social Media Production," Presentation at the Academy of Marketing Science, Portland OR, May 2010.
14. Stephen Baker, "Beware Social Media Snake Oil," *Bloomberg BusinessWeek*, December 3, 2009, www.businessweek.com/magazine/content/09_50/b4159048693735.htm, accessed June 24, 2010.
15. "Nissan Launches 'N-Square' Internal Social Networking Site," *Internal Comms Hub*, November 17, 2007, www.internalcommshub.com/open/news/nissan.shtml, accessed December 20, 2010.
16. Mark Sullivan, "How Will Facebook Make Money?" *PC World*, June 15, 2010, www.pcworld.com/article/198815/how_will_facebook_make_money.html, accessed December 31, 2010.
17. "Social Networks Around the World 2010," InSites Consulting, Social Media Study, www.slideshare.net/stevenvanbelleghem/social-networks-around-the-world-2010, accessed December 19, 2010.
18. Tom Espiner, "IE Slips Further as Firefox, Safari, Chrome Gain," *CNET*, February 2, 2009, http://news.cnet.com/8301-1023_3-10154447-93.html, accessed June 8, 2010.
19. Debra Aho Williamson, "Social Network Ad Spending: 2010 Outlook," *eMarketer*, 2009, www.emarketer.com/Report.aspx?code=emarketer_2000621, accessed December 20, 2010.
20. Jon Gibs and Sean Bruich, "Advertising Effectiveness: Understanding the Value of a Social Media Impression," *Nielsen Company* and *Facebook*, April 2010, http://uk.nielsen.com/site/documents/SocialMediaWhitePapercomp.pdf, accessed December 21, 2010.
21. Jon Gibs and Sean Bruich, "Advertising Effectiveness: Understanding the Value of a Social Media Impression," *Nielsen Company* and *Facebook*, April 2010, http://uk.nielsen.com/site/documents/SocialMediaWhitePapercomp.pdf, accessed December 21, 2010.
22. "Fluent: The Razorfish Social Influence Marketing Report," *Razorfish*, 2009, http://fluent.razorfish.com/publication/?m=6540&l=1, accessed December 21, 2010.

23. Josh Bernoff, "Introducing Peer Influence Analysis: 500 Billion Peer Impressions per Year," *Empowered* (A Forrester Blog), April 20, 2010, http://forrester.typepad.com/groundswell/2010/04/introducing-peer-influence-analysis.html, accessed December 21, 2010.

24. Josh Bernoff and Ted Schadler, *Empowered* (Cambridge, MA: Harvard Business Press, 2010).

25. Robert Kozinets, "Brand Fans: When Entertainment + Marketing Intersect on the Net," in Tracy Tuten, Ed., *Enterprise 2.0: How Technology, E-Commerce, and Web 2.0 Are Transforming Business Virtually* (Santa Barbara, CA: Praeger Publishers, 2010).

26. David Evans and Eden Epstein, "Comparing User Engagement Across Seven Interactive and Social Media Ad Types," *Psychster* and *All Recipes*, 2010, http://psychster.com/library/PSYCHSTER_Allrecipes_Widget_Whitepaper_Mar10_FINAL.pdf, accessed December 31, 2010.

27. "The Value of a Facebook Fan: An Empirical Study," *Syncapse*, June 2010, www.brandchannel.com/images/papers/504_061810_wp_syncapse_facebook.pdf, accessed December 20, 2010.

28. Anna Farmery, "What Is Your Return on Emotion?" *The Engaging Brand Blog*, July 2009, http://theengagingbrand.typepad.com/the_engaging_brand_/2009/07/what-is-your-return-on-emotion.html, accessed December 31, 2010.

29. "Fluent: The Razorfish Social Influence Marketing Report," *Razorfish*, 2009, http://fluent.razorfish.com/publication/?m=6540&l=1, accessed December 21, 2010.

30. E. Steel, "Using Social Sites as Dialogue to Engage Consumers, Brands," *Wall Street Journal,* November 8, 2006, B2D.

Social Publishing

LearningObjectives

When you finish reading this chapter you will be able to answer these questions:

1 What are the channels of social publishing?

2 Who creates the content published in social channels? What kind of content can be published?

3 What content characteristics enhance perceived content quality and value? How can marketers plan and organize their efforts as they embrace a social publishing strategy

4 What is the role of social publishing in social media marketing? How do social media marketers utilize search engine optimization and social media optimization to meet marketing objectives?

5 How can social content be promoted? What role do social news and social bookmarking sites play in content promotion?

GO

From Chapter 6 of *Social Media Marketing*, First Edition. Tracy L. Tuten, Michael R. Solomon.
Copyright © 2013 by Pearson Education, Inc. All rights reserved.

Learning
Objective 1

The Social Publishing Zone

In this chapter, our focus shifts to the second zone of social media. The **social publishing zone** as shown in Figure 1, includes those channels that allow people and organizations to publish content including blogs, media-sharing sites, microblogs, and information and news networks. **Blogs** are websites that host regularly updated content. **Microblogs** are similar to blogs, except that the content is limited to short bursts of text and links. Twitter is one example because it limits posts to 140 characters. **Media-sharing sites** include *video-sharing sites* such as YouTube, Vimeo, and Ustream, *photo-sharing sites* such as Flickr and Snapfish, *audio-sharing sites* such as Podcast Alley, and *document and presentation-sharing sites* such as Scribd and SlideShare. Facebook, as a social utility, also offers multimedia sharing functionality with videos, photos, and links to content.

In this chapter, you'll learn some basic principles of content creation and distribution via blogs and media sharing sites; how marketers can design content for search engine and social media optimization; and how to promote social content using social media press releases, microblogs, and social news and bookmarking sites.

Publishing Content

Content is the unit of value in a social community, akin to the dollar in our economy. Content may include opinions, catchphrases, information, fashion photos, advice, art, or photos from that wild party last week. Although an externally created piece of content like a movie may be the catalyst for a community to form (such as a *Twilight* blog), these collectives are not just sophisticated versions of fan clubs devoted to performers or works of art. Those traditional organizations usually are launched and controlled by the source, such as a movie studio or a record label. In contrast, many online communities we see today operate independently or at least with minimal input from the site's source.

Figure 1

The Social Publishing Zone

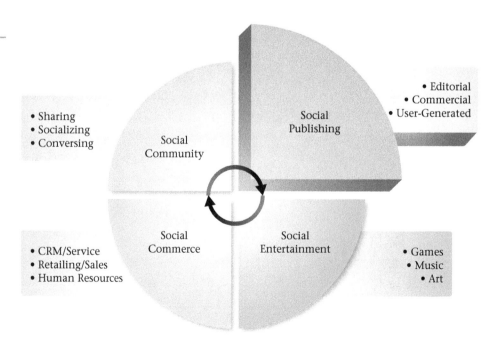

Some even exist to criticize a source, such as **protest sites** like starbucksucks.com or satirical videos people posted on YouTube in reaction to BP's slow response to the massive Gulf oil spill.

Types of Content

Social media content may begin with content published for some other purpose, such as a broadcast commercial, entertainment film, or news story. Or the content may be entirely original contributions that community members produce and publish. Ideally, social media content should do more than repurpose offline content for digital display. Although we often do find this kind of "secondhand content" on some sites, for example, when people retweet a news article they find interesting.

Content appears in a variety of different formats such as:

- Blog posts and feature articles
- Microblog posts
- Press releases
- White papers, case studies, and ebooks
- Newsletters
- Videos
- Webinars and presentations
- Podcasts
- Photos

Content can be any of these and more. Increasingly, however, we see more content that is multi-layered; it offers several applications based on a meme or a piece of factual information. For instance, suppose *Travel & Leisure* magazine publishes an article on fashionable solutions to travel clothing dilemmas. The online magazine site also publishes the article, but now it includes several social features including a comment option, a Share This widget, a bookmarking option, and a game called Pack and Play. The content began its life as a piece of content in the traditional press. It was repurposed for use in the online magazine. But it didn't become social until the content was fortified with interactivity, participation, and shareability. Note too that the social components of the content added *value* to everyone connected to the content. The original publisher gained additional readers through the sharing option and enhanced the stickiness of the site (making the site more attractive to online advertisers) because it offered social features. The readers were able to better use the information in the article because they could share it, store it for later reference, and practice the tips offered in the Pack and Play game application.

Wherever this icon appears in the margin, please go to the website **www.zonesofsmm.com** for an example of the topic discussed.

Channels of Content Distribution

Blogs   Blogs have been around for more than a decade. They began as simple online logs posted in reverse chronological order, and developed into a widely used publishing venue for individual and corporate use. With more than 175 million blogs in existence, blogging is clearly a publishing venue here to stay. However, blogging has evolved: Once a way to simply share opinions via text postings, today many blogs also include video and images. Each year, the blog search engine and media company, Technorati, publishes the *State of the Blogosphere* report. The report is a survey of bloggers (more than 7,000 in 2010) from a range of backgrounds representing hobbyists, part-timers, corporate bloggers, and self-employed bloggers.[1] According to Technorati, the top 100 bloggers publish 500 times the number of posts of the average blogger. As a group, bloggers seek to promote their blogs much as other content providers promote content. To do so, many use Twitter to drive traffic to their blog site.

Blogs offer an opportunity for individuals to express their opinions, share their expertise, make money by selling on-site advertising, and attract clients for consulting work. They also offer opportunities for organizations to establish thought leadership on a topic, increase traffic to targeted websites such an organization's e-commerce site, build links to other corporate sites, and build brand awareness.[2] For example, Heather Armstrong's blog, *Dooce*, established her as a creative writer capable of providing her readers with insight and amusement into the typical life of a woman.[3] David Armano's *Logic + Emotion* blog grew his reputation as a visual thinker and experience designer.[4]

 Media-Sharing Sites Like blogs, media-sharing sites enable individuals and organizations to publish content online. However, whereas blogs are typically in the realm of owned media, media-sharing sites are earned media because their environments are not directly controlled by the person or organization posting the content. Often the choice of which media-sharing site to use is dictated by the type of content to be distributed. For example, Saab maintains a corporate hub for its social media content called the Saab Newsroom, but video content is shared on its YouTube channel, photos are shared on its Flickr photostream, news is shared on its Twitter feed, and Saab iPhone apps are distributed via iTunes. User-generated content is shared on the Saab Facebook page. Reviews are also a form of content that can be published using media-sharing sites.

Learning Objective 2

Content Producers: What Is "Authentic?"

Content can take so many forms that it's sometimes difficult to categorize. This is especially true in the online world, where the lines between what is real and what is not become increasingly blurred. For example, people often share YouTube clips of outrageous or racy commercials with their friends—but in many cases these spots were not produced by the company (sorry to disappoint you). In fact, the proliferation of untruths and exaggerations (or so-called **urban legends**) is so widespread that specialized websites do nothing but verify or refute them. The website Snopes.com is the best-known of these.

This ambiguity also exists when we try to identify the sources or distributors of content. At one time, it was easy to classify a message as either editorial or commercial. An **editorial message** is objective and unbiased; the source expresses an opinion or provides information and does not intend to carry out the agenda of an organization. The most obvious example is the editorial page of a newspaper, where a writer presents an argument that may criticize a government, a company, or a politician. This section of the paper is clearly marked as editorial.

In contrast, a **commercial message** such as an advertisement makes it clear that the intent is to persuade the reader or viewer to change an attitude or behavior; the source has paid a fee to place the message in a medium. So, it's obvious in a traditional newspaper that a half-page plea, say, to pass environmental legislation or carry out sanctions against governments that permit whaling is sponsored and paid for by an identifiable organization.

For news and educational content, traditional *press organizations* hire journalists to research, verify, and write credible, objective, trustworthy stories. These media outlets then deliver that content to a paying audience via newspapers, newsletters, magazines, and radio and television programs. The traditional press controlled the message and the channel, but it adhered to accepted industry guidelines and norms. Similarly, traditional entertainment companies or *production houses* created and distributed their own content. Broadcast networks commissioned the development of programs and movies they showed on the stations they owned. And the transition from editorial to commercial content was clear: "And now a word from our sponsors." Of course even before the explosion of social media these lines blurred—for example, many critics label cartoon shows that feature product-based characters (such as those on popular Yu-Gi-Oh trading cards) as a "program-length commercial."[5]

Though content from traditional media sources is still valuable, today these sources struggle as consumers increasingly turn to other places to access their news and entertainment. People no longer need to subscribe to the local newspaper in order to get credible news. Instead they can read email, Twitter posts, blogs, and updates to social networking sites, all from their smartphones. This seismic shift has forced the closing of media providers around the world as they fail to find new ways to monetize their businesses. Major newspapers such as *The San Francisco Chronicle* have closed, while other traditional media vehicles merge with online companies—for example, the venerable print magazine *Newsweek* recently was acquired by *The Daily Beast.*

 Other traditional content providers adapt to the new media environment as they shift from delivering their messages on a printed page (or, as some new media people like to say, "dead trees") to mobile applications. *Gourmet* responded by evolving into the first mobile magazine. It closed operations late in 2009 due to declining subscriptions and ad revenues. *Gourmet Live* instead delivers articles to foodies on their mobile phones. But, unlike the old dead tree delivery system, this content is also social—subscribers can interact, share, and play games within the application.

In addition to a blurring of the lines between editorial and commercial messages, today we witness an explosion of *user-generated content (UGC)*—which as we've seen is the lifeblood of emerging social media. In many cases everyday people create and post this content for personal reasons rather than to receive financial reward. A proud father shoots video of his son's high school graduation and shares it with the family. An expecting young mother chronicles the story of her pregnancy and birth. A retired couple keeps a photo log of their yearly trips where they explore the world together.

What's new about this consumer-generated content? In one sense, absolutely nothing! People throughout history have written stories, commissioned portraits, kept diaries, and more recently taken photos and videos of family events. What *is* new is that due to the *social media value chain*, people can share this content with those beyond their immediate area. Today they post photos to Flickr or perhaps a less-than-flattering video from last night's raucous party on YouTube. This content is largely shared in the context of social relationships (zone 1), but it is also published content, crossing into the realm of zone 2.

In terms of the content itself, UGC is powerful because it often attracts our attention to things we wouldn't otherwise watch (sometimes it's like watching a train wreck—you know it's terrible but you can't tear yourself away). You may stumble upon this content while you search for specific information about a product or brand, or you may discover it accidentally. And, because of the power of social media, these inputs may well impact what others think or even change a firm's marketing activities. In this form of **cultural co-creation**, co-created meanings (among both producers and consumers) fold back into the culture. Jones Soda, for example, enlists its consumers' input on packages and flavors so that the products it makes are the outcome of a collaboration with its customers. That helps to explain soda flavors such as Blue Bubble Gum and Turkey with Cranberry Sauce, not to mention such favorites as Sweat and Dirt![6]

It's useful to distinguish between UGC that people voluntarily publish and content that appears because some organization has invited contributions from users. **Organic content** is content that a person feels intrinsically motivated to prepare and share. In contrast, **incentivized content** is encouraged by the offer of an *incentive*, such as the chance to win a contest, receive free merchandise, or even earn cold hard cash. In these cases the contribution is a response to a **call to action**. This term refers to a direct request in a marketing message for a specific behavior. You've observed a similar technique in TV infomercials, where a host reminds you to "Call right now. Operators are standing by!" That's a call to action. In social media marketing, calls to action ensure that people participate in the social media campaign.

Consumer-solicited content (CSC) refers to invited but non-compensated **citizen advertising**, which is another way to describe marketing messages that actual consumers create. Sometimes marketers call this approach *participatory advertising;* brands invite submissions, set mandatory guidelines and specifications, and possibly provide participants with selected brand assets such as footage of the brand in use or logos and former commercials. CSC can be incentivized by the sponsoring brand. It functions just as non-incentivized citizen-advertising campaigns except that the sponsor encourages submissions with incentives such as prize money. For Super Bowl XLIV, contributing citizen advertisers had a shot at $5 million in prize money. That seems to have paid off for Doritos in terms of ad effectiveness, with its "House Rules" spot coming in second only to a Snickers commercial featuring Betty White. Other measures pronounced Doritos the winning brand of the Super

Bowl. That's pretty impressive when you remember that the Doritos spots were "homemade" and cost under $100 to create.[7]

Sponsored conversations refer to *paid* consumer content. Consumers are paid for their content creations, and brands may actively seek out certain people like bloggers, videographers, and artists to participate in the campaign. For example, the company PayPerPost pays bloggers to endorse products. Bloggers who post sponsored conversations as their sole reason to contribute to a conversation are known as **spokesbloggers**.

Counterfeit conversations occur when an organization plants content that masquerades as original material an actual consumer posted. The Lonelygirl15 YouTube phenomenon was a planned, strategic marketing ploy to promote the capabilities of its producers who hoped to use their 15 minutes of fame to land other jobs in the video industry. Bree, aka Lonelygirl15, was allegedly a home-schooled 16-year-old. She started a *vlog* on YouTube that for a time was the most viewed video on the site.[8] Eventually the hoax was uncovered, but only after the videos achieved millions of page views and the phenomenon generated several news articles on the story.

So, the lines have blurred and merged among authentic and counterfeit sources. For instance, typically we think of bloggers as independent writers who publish their thoughts, activities, opinions, and information. The blog is historically an online diary of sorts—in fact, its name comes from a combination of the words "web log." Yet many traditional press organizations support bloggers as a part of the information content they provide. The *New York Times*, certainly a stalwart of the traditional press, hosts 69 blogs on its website on topics that range from the cultural *ArtBeat*, the humorous *WordPlay*, and the socially conscious *Green*. These writers are bloggers, but they post on behalf of a commercial publisher.

What's more, even the seemingly independent blogger can shift from noncommercial to sponsored content. If a blogger accepts Google **AdWords** on his or her site so that Google places ads there, or takes freebies or payment to blog about specific topics, that content shifts from editorial to commercial. For example, Walmart established ElevenMoms, a group of independent bloggers who receive free samples and then review the products. These women post on other topics as well, but these sponsored reviews live alongside the other content in their blogs. One important issue for social media is to clearly identify content as either editorial or commercial so that users understand just where it came from and what the poster's intent may be.

Because our cultural expectation for blogs (and other forms of content in the social media space) is that they present independent, non-funded, noncommercial content, the FTC (Federal Trade Commission) introduced specific guidelines for social media content producers. The intent of the guidelines is to protect the public from advertising disguised as a blog post by ensuring that sponsorships are transparent.

Learning
Objective 3

Developing and Organizing Marketing Content

As they develop content to post on social media platforms, there are several guidelines marketers should consider. First, the content must match the brand's overall personality and strategic objectives. To manage workload, authors will need to be appointed and their duties assigned. Content development and responses to content feedback should follow established organizational policies. An important component of social publishing is identifying relevant topics, types of content, publication venues, and a schedule for publication (in the form of an **editorial calendar**). Developing an editorial calendar helps bloggers and other content producers to forecast the time needed to manage the content development process including researching topics, creating content, and promoting the content using the social publishing strategies discussed here. Figure 2 provides an example of such a calendar.

Organizations may have a set of editorial calendars including a master calendar and others for specific activities. The master calendar will provide an overview of all content planned by day and by week over the course of the plan. It will track key dates such as events and activities that could provide topics for sharing with the target audience. It will also consider the planned distribution for content throughout the channels of social publishing.

Figure 2

A Master Editorial Calendar *Source:* Michele Linn, August 16, 2010, "How to Put Together An Editorial Calendar for Content Marketing, http://www.contentmarketinginstitute.com/2010/08/content-marketing-editorial-calendar, accessed September 2011.

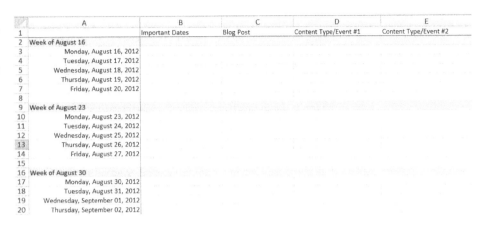

	A	B	C	D	E
1		Important Dates	Blog Post	Content Type/Event #1	Content Type/Event #2
2	Week of August 16				
3	Monday, August 16, 2012				
4	Tuesday, August 17, 2012				
5	Wednesday, August 18, 2012				
6	Thursday, August 19, 2012				
7	Friday, August 20, 2012				
8					
9	Week of August 23				
10	Monday, August 23, 2012				
11	Tuesday, August 24, 2012				
12	Wednesday, August 25, 2012				
13	Thursday, August 26, 2012				
14	Friday, August 27, 2012				
15					
16	Week of August 30				
17	Monday, August 30, 2012				
18	Tuesday, August 31, 2012				
19	Wednesday, September 01, 2012				
20	Thursday, September 02, 2012				

As in any other media, not all content is created equal. Some is trash; some is important. Some content is fun, some inspiring, and some just titillating (anyone for "Keeping Up with the Kardashians?"). As Figure 3 shows, we can characterize content in terms of its originality and substance according to a **content value ladder**.[9] Let's take a closer look at this form of classification.

Figure 3

Content Value Ladder

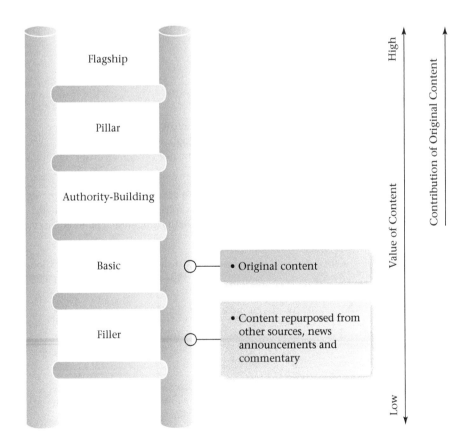

- At the lowest step in the ladder we find the least important type of materials. **Filler content** is simply information that people copy from other sources. A site called ArticlesBase.com is a free online article directory. It hosts articles that have been contributed by authors hoping to expand the reach of their work online. Others can use the articles posted on ArticlesBase at no charge. They just search for the topic of interest, copy and paste the article to their own site, and cite the contributing author. Filler content can also come from other content providers (blogs and posts on media sharing sites) and syndicated sources such as PRNewsWire and the Associated Press.

- All other content on the ladder is **original content**. This level refers to contributions that originate with the poster. At the lowest level, this content is original, but not "weighty" enough to establish the creator as an authority in the topic area or serve as a reference piece for the audience.

- If that original content positions the sponsoring entity as an authority on the subject in question, then we call it **authority-building content**.

- If a source creates a solid foundation of original content, the foundation blocks are known as **pillar content**. Typically pillar content is made up of educational content that readers use over time, save, and share with others. As more and more people refer to these posts, they enable a sponsor to grow in readership, followers, and friends. The content's impact grows over time exponentially as other people share it through reposting, citations, and retweets. Table 1 elaborates on some of the most important kinds of pillar content that blogs can publish.

- **Flagship content** is also authority-building content. This term refers to seminal pieces of work that help to define a phenomenon or shape the way people think about something for a long time. Those pieces of content create a draw for years to come. Tim O'Reilly's 2005 article on "What Is Web 2.0?," which continues to be a reference piece for those who study social media, is an example of flagship content.[10]

TABLE 1

Types of Pillar Content in Blogs

Source: Based on Yaro Starak, "How to Write Great Blog Content—The Pillar Article," *Entrepreneurs-Journey.com*, February 9, 2008, www.entrepreneurs-journey.com/845/pillar-article/, accessed December 25, 2010.

Type	Description	Example
"How-To" Article	This form of content is the most popular type posted, according to an analysis of content shared on several news sites including Digg and StumbleUpon.[11]	*How to Make Brownies in a Crockpot*
Definition Article	This type of post defines a concept. Although this is a straightforward approach, it provides a high level of utility for those interested in the concept being defined	*What is Web 2.0?*
Glossary Article	This form of article includes a series of definitions related to each other and creates a resource guide on the topic.	*A Glossary of Literary Terms*
Theory Article	Theory articles offer some unique insight into a topic but the content is opinion. This is the equivalent to opinion-editorial pieces in your local newspaper.	*Media isn't Social*
List Article	These forms of content use bullets for easy readability and consumption. They may draw on humor or education in detailing the list.	*Top 10 USB Thumbdrive Tricks*

Learning
Objective **4**

Social Publishing Strategies

For marketers there is a twofold goal for social publishing: (1) to increase the exposure to the brand's messages and (2) to use the content to drive traffic to the brand's owned media. The social publishing process is similar to the media planning process we see for traditional advertising campaigns. In those cases the **media plan** designates how the campaign's creative content will be disseminated to the target audience using specific media vehicles such as radio or billboards. The media planner sets specific goals for what is to be accomplished through the ad placements in terms of audience reach, exposure to the message, and desired outcomes. Social publishing works much the same way except the creative content seeking exposure is not necessarily an ad (in the traditional static or rich media formats) and the distribution of that content is accomplished with inbound links or link chains to the content from search engine results, other websites, and social media communities. In other words, traditional media plans utilize paid media to achieve marketing objectives. Social publishing relies upon owned media and earned media online to reach these goals.

Just as traditional media plans vary considerably in terms of complexity and sophistication, so too do social publishing strategies. Marketers must determine what content to publish and where and then develop a strategy to maximize exposure to the content through search engine rankings and social sharing. In fact, we can identify two types of optimization that an organization can use (either individually or in combination) with on-site and off-site optimization tactics. Table 2 summarizes these levels.

Using **search engine optimization (SEO)**, the process of modifying content, site characteristics, and content connections to achieve improved search engine rankings, marketers develop and publish content in ways that improve the likelihood that search engines will rank the sites well in response to search queries. Whereas SEO is all about increasing the prominence of a site on search lists using on-site and off-site tactics, **social media optimization (SMO)** is a process that makes it more likely for content on a specific social media platform to be more visible and linkable in online communities.[12] If the content is valuable and engaging, other sites will link to it. And people will share it, post it, rank it, tag it, and augment it with their own stories about your brand.

All of this linking activity in turn increases the credibility of the marketer's message— exactly the goal of social publishing. SMO not only provides additional visibility for a marketer's message, it benefits search rankings because it increases the likelihood that others will link to it. Thus, SEO focuses on earning higher organic search engine rankings whereas SMO focuses on earning organic links to content. SMO is used by search engine optimizers because those links also improve rankings. The optimization process is so important that it has created an entirely new industry of specialists who help organizations to stay afloat in the growing sea of content. Let's take a closer look at each level of social publishing.

TABLE 2

Media Optimization Matrix

Type of Optimization	On-Site	Off-Site
Search engine optimization	Optimizing content value, tags, keywords, titles, URL	Publishing related content elsewhere with links to original Creating a linkwheel structure
Social media optimization	Including share tools and RSS feed options	Promoting on social news and social bookmarking sites Microblogging Promoting social media press releases

Level 1: Social Publishing and Search Engine Optimization

The first level focuses on ways the brand can increase exposure to its online content and drive site traffic by publishing related components of the content across several social sites. These placements include links back to the targeted site. This cross-promotion to the branded content is accomplished with owned media and the placement of related content on media sharing sites (earned media).

How can a business use different elements of social publishing to multiply its exposure in an inexpensive way? Let's consider the brand SOS (SellOurStuff). SellOurStuff is an eBay reseller of luxury goods. As a promotional tool, SOS might create a **branded article**, an article that is written to promote SOS's expertise in the field, on "7 Ways to Spot Luxury that (re)Sells." The article is a promotional piece that educates the company's prospects on the types of items SOS could auction successfully while it encourages them to retain SOS as their auctioneer.

The article is a good piece of content—but it won't help SOS unless prospects are exposed to it. SOS publishes the piece on its main website at SOS-SellOurStuff.com, and the company also posts a teaser to the article with a link to the original content on the SOS blog. Next SOS takes the images from the article and posts them to Flickr (again with a link to the original) and also creates a Prezi slideshow of the content to share at the Prezi site (with again, you guessed it, a link back to the original). Finally, SOS creates a badge that its top clients can post on their own personal web pages to show visitors that they have an "Eye for Luxury." That is, SOS designates these top clients as people who already know the rules for spotting luxury that resells. The SOS badge also links back to the branded content on the SOS website. In this example, SOS created content that promotes its brand message. It then shared the content on its own site and on other sites where it had some control as to what was presented and how it linked back to the branded content. Publishing in multiple places creates additional "opportunities to see" (OTS) for the target audience and brand-controlled links to the targeted site.

At this point, the brand can utilize search engine optimization to improve how its content is listed in response to search queries. These listings are crucial—as you probably know from experience, most people tend to follow up only on the first few results they get from a query. SEO is a complicated technical process, and it's also a bit of a cat-and-mouse game. For example, #1 site Google uses a secret **algorithm** (a mathematical formula) to decide which sites will appear at the top of a search list. The company changes this formula on a regular basis, so SEO experts engage in a constant contest to figure out the algorithm and then modify their sites to keep up with Google's changes.

Consumers love their search engines. In fact, the Pew Internet & American Life Project estimates that 88 percent of Internet users in the United States use search engines such as Google, Yahoo!, and Bing to find information online.[13] The rankings these search engines generate are crucial because they drive site traffic—and of course traffic is social media's lifeblood. No traffic, no interest. No interest, eventually no site. Sites that attract heavy traffic are valuable for two reasons:

1. A large number of visitors makes it more likely the sponsor will benefit from a higher rate of **conversion** (i.e., the person browsing actually purchases so he or she is *converted* from a browser to a buyer).

2. The more "eyeballs" the site attracts, the more advertising revenue the site can generate (assuming it sells ad space to other advertisers).

SEO is the key tool used for **search engine marketing (SEM)**. SEM refers to a form of online marketing that promotes websites by increasing the visibility of the site's URL in search engine results, both organic and sponsored. Incidentally, there are hundreds of search engines, and some sites that do not feature search as their primary function also offer search engine capabilities. YouTube and Facebook, for instance, are also used for search.[14]

When someone enters a query, the search engine turns to its index for the best matches and then returns a *search results list* to the user. The results list includes the organic results, which are listings

BYTES TO BUCKS

Today it seems that every organization from Product (RED) to the local PTA is going full-stop to enlist as many brand fans on Facebook and other social media sites as possible. Everyone "knows" it's important to build these connections, but how much is each really worth in cold, hard cash? One Atlanta-based firm, Vitrue, claims to know the answer. It conducted research on over 45 million fans of brands on Facebook in its goal to place a dollar value on a fan. Vitrue calculated that one million impressions on the brand's page multiplied by two wall posts per day for 30 days equals 60 million impressions per month. At a $5 **CPM** (cost per 1,000 clicks), those 60 million impressions are worth $300,000 each month, or $3.6 million per year. So, the envelope please: The magic number is $3.60 per fan. This formula makes some assumptions that may be a bit questionable (for example, it assumes that all impressions from all types of sources make an equal impact on the viewer), but at least it's a start. Then again, Burger King arrived at a lower value when it launched its infamous Whopper Sacrifice campaign: In exchange for "unfriending" 10 people on Facebook, you got a coupon for a free Whopper. Let's see . . . a Whopper also costs around $3.60 so each friend is worth only 36 cents. There's no accounting for taste.[15]

ranked in order of relevance based on the search engine's ranking algorithm, and the sponsored results, which are paid advertising links. Why are these search results so important? Believe it or not, search engine use is just as heavy as email use!

How Do People Use Search Results? Let's say you've dreamed of owning a high-end designer handbag—the Hermès Birkin. Celebrities and *fashionistas* carry it, it's always in scarce supply, and a new one can set you back a year's tuition. A brand new Birkin is out—too expensive—but maybe you can find a used one online. You might visit Yahoo! and enter the search query, "hermes handbags." The search results list leads off with **sponsored**, or paid, links. In this case, e-retailers such as DesignerPurseOutlets.com and Bluefly.com have paid for sponsored listings. The search results then provide a series of **organic** listings for Hermès as well as e-tailers such as eBay and The Purse Blog. These sites did not pay to be listed; they are based on the search engine's model for delivering relevant search results. However, in addition to these retailers you may see several merchants that offer counterfeit versions of the bag. Why? Those sites were listed in part because Yahoo!'s algorithm indicated that the content was a good match to your search query. (We'll go into more depth on how this works in a bit.) You might now refine your search, but if it turns out you'd consider a Birkin replica, you might click through to one of the listed sites (and possibly make a purchase, or at a minimum build the site's traffic figures which will help it earn ad revenue).

As you can imagine, it's very important for a brand or site to appear in a search list so that the shopper will at least consider clicking on the link. Although search engine marketers can buy paid listings from search engines, it's preferable to earn organic results. One reason is that these results have no **pay-per-click** fees. These are the fees a marketer pays when someone clicks on an online display ad. Organic results also tend to generate more site traffic, presumably because people view them as more credible referrals from the search engine.

Organic entries, especially the first few, garner most of the attention in a typical search. Click-throughs taper off pretty rapidly, so few people tend to go beyond the first 10 or so. Of course, pages and pages of search results could be returned for any given search—but again, for the most part these won't generate much traffic. For example, the search on Hermès handbags returned a whopping 1,900,000 listings.

We know that people tend to look at the first searches in a list rather than the entire list (few of us would make it to listing #1,900,000 no matter how badly we wanted that Birkin bag). Still, it's helpful to understand more about which links the user is likely to follow. Researchers use **eye-tracking studies** to help identify the characteristics of a search page that determine this. They borrow this method from more traditional advertising researchers, who for many years have hooked respondents to sophisticated devices that follow the precise movements of eyeballs as they scan ads on TV or computer screens.

This method shows clearly that most search engine users view only a very limited number of search results. When typical respondents look at a search page, their eyes travel across the top of the search result, return to the left of the screen, and then travel down to the last item shown on the screen without scrolling. On most screens, this means that every user will view the first three search results, but they may or may not scroll down. Search engine marketers call this space on the screen where listings are virtually guaranteed to be viewed the "**golden triangle**."[16] So the real value—the sweet spot—is in earning a list rank that is on the first page, and preferably one of the top three listings ranked. How can a source enhance the probability that its listing will appear near the top? For many organizations, this is (literally) the million dollar question! And that's exactly the point of search engine optimization.

How Search Engines Work   Search listings are produced by search engines using indexed data and an algorithm that determines a listing's relevance to the search query. Search engines use **web crawlers** (also known as *spiders* and *bots*); these are automated web programs that gather information from sites that ultimately form the search engine's entries. The programs are called crawlers because they crawl websites. They follow all the links, site after site, collecting data until the link network is exhausted. After the bots gather this information, they index (classify) it using labels the sites provide. The **indexed data** include tags and keywords derived from site content. Then, when someone enters a search query, the search engine applies its algorithm to determine the sites that are most relevant to the search query. This algorithm determines which sites are identified in the search listing and the ranking of the sites presented.

On-Site Optimization   You can see that optimizing content in order to improve search engine rankings is an important marketing task. How do marketers optimize? They use one of two key approaches: (1) on-site optimization or (2) off-site optimization. This is because the bots look for cues on-site, especially tags, and for **off-site indicators** such as links from other sites as they index data.

On-site, coders try to optimize certain site characteristics (called **on-site indicators**) that the search bots and the search engine index. In plain English, this means they tinker with elements of the site to make indexing more efficient and ensure that the web crawlers will classify the site the way the developers intend. The primary on-site variables are **keywords** embedded in the page's tags, title, URL, and content.

Keywords tell the bot what information to gather and specify the relevant topic. The bot will collect this information for the search engine to use in indexing. The keywords explain to the search engine when to deliver your site as a search result. Consequently, choosing the right keywords is critical to ensuring a site shows up in relevant searches. Once you have selected your keywords, you will work them into the areas crawled by the bots—the site's tags, title, URL, and body copy (or content).

For example, say your website sells vintage comic books. To ensure that a buyer who wants to snag a pristine copy of *Adventure Comics #77* featuring Superboy and the Legion of Super-Heroes published in 1967 will visit your online store you might code your site with these labels:

- **Meta tag:** Code embedded in a web page. Meta tags are visible to site visitors but only by viewing the source code for the page. Meta keywords should include three or four of the targeted keywords. The meta description should include two or three sentences that summarize the page content. The description is shown with the search engine listing. The vintage comic book store might include meta tags such as adventure comics, Superboy, superheroes, and vintage.

- **Title tag:** An HTML tag that defines the page's title. The title is displayed in the browser's title bar, in search engine results, and in RSS feeds. Title tags should include no more than

12 words, with at least two keywords. For example, your website title tags might read: Comics Direct Sales Rare Comics/Vintage Comic Books—Vintage Comics offers comic book collectors vintage adventure comics.

- **Heading tag:** An HTML tag that is used to section and describe content. Heading tags should include keywords. Tags for heading levels are designated as H1, H2, H3, and so on. Within the web page, major headings (named for keywords) will be designated with code such that the sections are recognizable to the bots. For example, the first heading on the page will be designated "<h1>This is heading 1</h1>".

- **Title:** The title is your headline—the main indicator of your page's content. It should be loaded with keywords. Writing optimized titles may seem difficult to some because the style of an optimized title is quite different from that of a story headline a journalist might write. A traditional headline may be indirect; the idea behind a traditional headline is to engage the audience without giving away the story. For instance, a print magazine article about Hermès Birkin bags and the prevalence of high-quality replicas might be titled "High Fashion Replicas Indistinguishable from the Real Thing." An optimized title might read "Shop Wise: 5 Tips for Ensuring that Birkin is Real, Not Fake, Fashion" to ensure that the search would index on keywords such as Hermès, Birkin, and shop. Another difference is that the title needs to be more literal than the one we might use in an article: Bots are pretty smart, but they don't understand metaphors or puns.[17] "Cute" titles such as "How to Keep Birkinstock" or "Counterfeit Hermès Bags are Birkin up the Wrong Tree" just won't cut it.

- **URL:** The URL is the website address. To optimize the URL, use a static URL and include the title of the article or the keywords in the URL. Static URLs do not change and they do not include variable scripts. **Dynamic URLs** are generated from scripts and change over time, making it difficult for people to return to your content later.

Ideally, you'll have a story or topic in mind around when you devise the content. For example, SOS's owner knew that a story explaining how to determine which luxury items will sell and which will bomb would have high value to eBay hobbyists. The story itself should help to determine the keywords, but it shouldn't be the only source. You will also want to include keywords that reflect popular search terms. Before writing the story, the first step is to research the keywords that will help ensure the bots will index the site's data and the algorithm will show relevance to search queries. So, if your "story" is "Sell your luxury used goods with SOS" you may also want to include more general keywords such as "consignment" to be sure potential resellers find it when they search.

How can you generate a strong list of keywords? **Keyword research!** This process is a critical step to design the content and the site's page for successful search engine optimization. Keyword research involves answering these questions:

- What is the topic of your article? What words and phrases best describe the article?

- What terms are your competitors using as keywords? You can find this out when you analyze their article titles, meta tags, and body copy.

- What words are suggested by **keyword generators** such as Google AdWords Keyword Tool or The Free Keyword Tool?

- What are the derivatives of your keywords? For example, SOS might pick derivatives of handbags such as bags, purses, clutches, totes, and so on. Free SEO tools such as Google Suggest will offer variations on search terms you may not have thought of.

- How much search volume does the keyword generate compared to other keywords you might use? Is it worth using given the resulting search volume? You can check Google Trends to see how much interest there is in your keywords. This useful tool will show how often the keyword was searched and from which geographic regions.

SEO marketers may want to use **long tail keywords**. This term refers to multi-phrase search queries.[18] They are much more targeted than a general keyword because they may say exactly what the searcher wants to find. For instance, the long tail keywords for the keyword topic Hermès handbags might include "finding a gently used Hermès Birkin bag," "identifying a fake Birkin," and "best deals on designer handbags." Because the long tail keywords are actual search queries (and you can use the same tools to find these queries as you did to identify your basic keywords), they help to optimize the site.

Off-Site Optimization   Bots don't look only at site information as they index data and feed information back for the search engine's algorithm. They also use other indicators off-site to determine the value of a site's content. These off-site indicators include the number of links to a website from other sites, the credibility of those sites, the type of site promoting the link, and the link text (called **anchor text**) these sites use. Therefore, search engine optimizers will not stop at tweaking on-site characteristics like the title and meta tags. They will also strive to earn links from high quality sites.

Links are the building blocks of social publishing. The more links to your content, the higher the ranking you will probably receive during a search engine query. There are two approaches to building links. The first approach is to publish related content and links across other sites (branded sites and social media channels). These venues are under the control of the marketer—it is simply a matter of developing the content and identifying where related content and links can be placed to promote traffic to the original site. The second approach is to encourage other, unaffiliated sites to link to the brand's content. This can be accomplished in different ways, such as using **affiliate marketing**, but we'll address how social media optimization builds unaffiliated links when we discuss level two of social publishing.

Building affiliated links to content is an extension of the first level of social publishing in which the brand publishes related content with links back to the main site among several branded sites and social media outlets. This is exactly what SOS did in our earlier example. In addition to using links from related content, the marketer will also strategically formulate these links to form a linkwheel. **Linkwheels** increase the number of links back to a site. They are built on a hub and spoke system that use web properties (i.e., links pages) as spokes to send one link to the home site and another link to the next property. Several properties are set up as spokes; the targeted page is the hub.

Figure 4 shows a sample linkwheel for SOS. The linkwheel system ensures that if a user comes to a site and clicks on a link, that site will connect the user to the next site hub site and to the next spoke site, and so on. The spoke sites also can be used as a hub in a new linkwheel as new content is developed and published. The result of this tactic is that the main site gains links from other sites with branded content using the linkwheel. When other sites link back to the content, it's called a **backlink** or a **trackback**. The site's search ranking benefits then from the increase in the link quantity (this is called **link juice**). Further, all of the new sites used by the main site to promote it can also be indexed and ranked in searches. If done well, a search engine query could produce a results list with several links to sites owned by the same company.

Linkwheels and other SEO tactics can be used appropriately, but there is room for abuse in this system. Have you watched an episode of *Gunsmoke* on TV Land or an old western on Hulu? Cowboy with a white hat—a hero. Black hat—a villain. This Western analogy applies to SEO culture. Social media insiders classify SEO marketers as white, gray, or black hats:[19]

- **White hats** play by the rules of the system, striving to provide good quality content, with the best use of keywords and tags, and earned links at reputable sites. They create site maps so that every page is linked to every other page and search engine bots can crawl every page.
- **Gray hats** take some liberties with the system. For example, they will utilize a keyword density (the number of times the keyword is used in the body of a page) that is beyond

Figure 4

The Linkwheel for the SOS Company

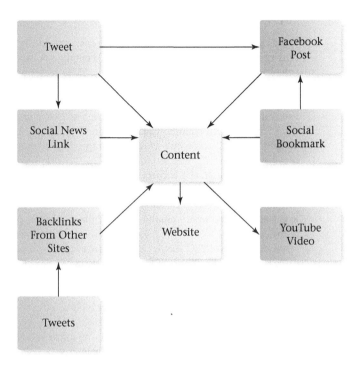

that of the typical usage of keywords, but be below that of true **keyword stuffing** (the insertion of a superficially large number of keywords throughout a site's content and tags). Gray hats also duplicate content at multiple sites and create **link exchanges**, where sites agree to link with each other. They may also utilize **three-way linking**, ensuring that their own sites link to each other in sequence and then back to the original site, and **paid links**, which are considered somewhat unethical in that linking should be the realm of earned media, not paid.

- **Black hats** manipulate the system by utilizing several tactics considered unethical in the realm of search engine optimization. For example, with linkwheels, the more spokes in the wheel, the more links to the hub site. Because the search engines rank in part based on number of links, black hats simply set up a massive number of property sites linking to the hub and using the same anchor text. It works. And, it's easy and inexpensive. Software can be used to automatically build thousands of links using social media properties such as Tumblr and Wordpress while RSS feeds populate the content. Especially for smaller search engines, a black hat linkwheel can send a site soaring to the top in search rankings. Big search engines such as Google combat the black hats by changing the crawler criteria and the indexing algorithm. If Google sees hundreds of links to a site, it will devalue the link, assuming there's a black hat operating behind the scenes.

Black hats also keyword stuff and place keywords in hidden text by making the font color of keywords the same color as the page background. They also may utilize **gateway pages** (pages that real visitors are directed past) stuffed with keywords and **cloaking** (the display of misleading content to search engines). In addition, they utilize **link farms**; groups of websites that link to each other and pages with unrelated links solely for the purpose of creating more links to the targeted pages. Finally, black hats may spam websites with links.

Level 2: Social Media Optimization

Just as SEO tactics optimize a site to increase its exposure (through links) and search engine rankings, social media optimization (SMO) employs tactics to increase the likelihood that others will share and promote content. Essentially, SMO seeks to leverage the network effect to spread endorsements of a brand with links to the brand's content. These shared links are essentially referrals—a form of testimonial from other players in the social publishing zone. Whereas brands use zone 1 to develop relationships and engage consumers to garner influence impressions, the word-of-mouth communication in zone 2 gains *influence posts* and referrals to the brand's content. Influence posts are word-of-mouth content from published sources like bloggers and reviewers.

What's the difference between search engine and social media optimization? Both have the same goals—to support inbound marketing and enable the target audience to find and consume the brand content. But SEO is more about finding ways to ensure search engines index the site and to calculate a good result ranking for the content, whereas SMO is about encouraging the sharing of the content.

In other words, SEO focuses on manipulating the processes controlled by the search engines (because even in this social world, Internet users rely heavily on search engines to find information online). In contrast, SMO focuses on building community. SEO efforts target machines. SMO targets people. SMO is especially valuable to marketers because it improves search engine rankings. This happens because bots prefer links, especially high-quality ones. For now at least, search engines tend to rate social media links as higher quality.

As we've seen, sharing behavior is a cultural norm in most online social communities. Content can be promoted on social networks, blogs, microblogs, and **social bookmarking** and news sites that use **aggregators** such as FriendFeed. People also can share links to content in these channels by email. As a result, the potential impact for a piece of content can be huge. That's because as people share links to content with their network, some of those people will consume the content, and some of those will also share the content with their network, and so on.

How do we optimize for social media? As with SEO, there are on-site and off-site tactics.

On-Site Tactics   SMO is all about encouraging people who are exposed to your content to share, promote, and recommend it. To do this, the content needs to be valuable, interesting, or entertaining enough so that someone wants to endorse it. We're back to the importance of good content, and you'll learn more about developing good social media content a bit later in this chapter. Aside from the issue of good content, though, we can use the title (as we did with SEO) and other site features to encourage endorsements and sharing. Search engines also consider the quality of a linking site and its type. A site will rank better in search engine results listings if independent sites link to it, and if those sites are of high quality and high relevance.

Let's return to SOS for an example of this process. SOS is a reseller of many types of luxury items. Suppose that one of its blog posts on fashion tips for moms on a budget is picked up by *Dooce*, a funny "mommy blog" that's consistently rated among the top 50 parent blogs online. *Dooce* does a post on the tips article with a link to SOS. It's not long before hundreds of other mommy blogs have linked to the SOS post. Because each of these blogs have their own linkwheel to drive traffic, SOS has a lot of potential to further spread the original post beyond this audience. *Dooce*, for instance, maintains a presence on Facebook and Twitter. A reader might link a *Dooce* tweet to her blog, see the SOS reference, and then link to SOS.

SOS has a winner here in terms of quantity of links. But are these links of high quality? The search engine would rather see links from industry-related sites. Since SOS is a luxury reseller, links from other fashion sites such as *The Bag Blog* would hold more value in the indexing algorithm. That's true unless the linking site is a **power site**. This label refers to a site with enormous readership, such as CNN.com. If CNN.com runs a story on how moms increasingly focus on saving money but still wish they could feel fashionable, they might reference SOS as a great site for deals. That link is going to be worth a lot of link juice to the search engine.

Title

Our goal is to persuade people to access our content. How do users initially decide whether a site is worth checking out? The most likely candidate is simple: the title. We can enhance interest in content when we compose a catchy title. Social media pros refer to the careful crafting of a title that markets the content as **linkbaiting**.

To continue the fishing metaphor, let's look more closely at techniques that make linkbaiting effective. You can guess what's coming next: We choose a **hook** that increases the likelihood that the intended audience will click. Hooks are used to position the content for the target audience. For example, consider this blog post title: "Andy Hagan's Ultimate Guide to Linkbaiting and SMM." Andy could have titled the post, "The Basics of Linkbaiting," but he realized that including a full name, the qualifier "ultimate," and the keywords SMM and Linkbaiting would optimize the title and increase clickthrough rates.

- The **resource hook** is a common type in social news sites. It refers to content written with the intent to be helpful to the target audience. For example, the Serta mattress company might create an article entitled "5 Methods to Ensure a Restful Night's Sleep."
- The **contrary hook** refutes some accepted belief. Challenging the belief incites people to read the content if only to argue the point. For instance, Weight Watchers might post an article entitled "Lose Weight with Chocolate"; the company recognizes that this will spark an interest from those who believe chocolate cannot possibly be part of a weight loss plan (just too good to be true).
- The **humor hook** is designed to show that the content will entertain. For example, the *DietBlog* posted a blog called, "Obese Skunk Cuts Out Bacon Sandwiches."[20]
- The **giveaway hook** promises something for free. In other words, it embeds a sales promotion, an incentive offered to encourage a specific behavior response in a specific time period, into the content. For example, our Weight Watchers' article could have been titled "Save $50 Doing What's Good For You!"
- The **research hook** offers a claim about something of interest. For example, our Weight Watchers' article might claim, "66% of Americans are overweight, but you don't have to be."

Share Tools

People are more likely to connect to our content (using that *call to action* we discussed earlier) if we make it easy for them to follow through. **Share tools** are **plug-ins** that appear as clickable icons on a website and enable the viewer to bookmark or share the page with many social networking, social news, and social bookmarking sites. Plug-ins are third-party applications that "plug in" to a main site to add some form of functionality. In this case, the functionality is the ability to easily share the site's content with external sites. Many social media sites offer their own site-specific plug-in (Facebook has a Like plug-in; Delicious has a bookmarking plug-in; Twitter offers a Tweet This button, Digg has a Smart Digg button) or a site may wish to utilize a multi-share tool such as Share This or Sexy Bookmarks.

Social media is about community, so reciprocity matters. Remember the Golden Rule you learned as a child: "Do unto others as you would have them do unto you." You'll want to reward those who link to you by including trackbacks, which promote those who promote your content. When someone links to your site, you'll post a trackback on your site to theirs. The trackback gives attribution to sites linking to you. It can be a method of communication between bloggers but, importantly, it provides an easy way to acknowledge those who send traffic to the brand's site by reciprocating their kindness.

RSS Feeds

Syndicate content with an RSS feed, a tool to automatically feed new published content to subscribers. Enhancing the ease of content distribution with an RSS feed makes it easy for others to consume new content as it is offered by having that content feed directly into their feed reader or email.

Off-Site Optimization   Social media suffers from an embarrassment of riches—there's way too much content available for people to process on their own. Remember that Technorati, a blog search engine, reported more than a hundred and seventy-five million active blogs at the end of 2011. And that's just blogs! There are also corporate white papers, articles from online publishers, and other valuable content available online. Thus, the average consumer can easily be overwhelmed or simply miss valuable sources of information. That's why it's important for social media marketers to optimize their socially published content. We can optimize off-site for social media in three key ways. First, we can publish a social media press release to promote our content. Second, we can use a microblog to encourage sharing of our announcements. Third, the content can be promoted on social news and bookmarking sites.

The Social Media Press Release

A *press release* is an announcement public relations professionals issue to the news media to let the public know of company developments. For social media marketers, a release is also a key tool, but a **social media press release** is structured a bit differently. It should have an optimized title, good keywords and tags, links to the main site landing page, RSS feed options, share buttons, and embeddable multimedia content that can be shared on several networks, in addition to the typical press release content. That's right—a press release is social when it has been prepared in a way that ensures the content is shareable. Figure 5 provides a template for a social media press release.

An organization can publish a social media press release on distribution sites such as PRWeb and Pressit, both social media news release services. In addition, organizations with a corporate blog should also post the social media press release on the blog so that it can be indexed easily by search engines.

Microblogs

Whereas blogs share a story, microblogs share headlines. That's probably one reason that Twitter, the leading microblog service, defines itself as a real-time information network. Microblog posts can be useful for reminder communications and ensuring top-of-mind awareness, but they can also provide valuable links, direct traffic, and build credibility and reputation. Brands can post their own links but social media optimization comes into play when brands figure out ways to encourage others to retweet the message. This may be as simple as offering content valuable enough that others wish to retweet it or asking followers to retweet. Or it may mean offering an incentive to share the links.

Social News and Bookmarking Sites

Have you read current news on Digg or bookmarked online articles for research using Diigo? Digg is one of many social news communities. Social news communities share and promote online news. Diigo is a social bookmarking site. Social bookmarking sites save your bookmarks online so they

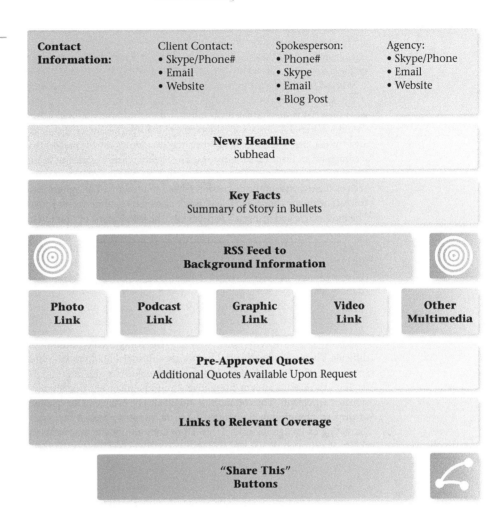

Figure 5

A Template for a Social Media Press Release *Source:* Adapted from *The Social Media Press Release Template*, Shift Communications, www.shiftcomm.com/downloads/smprtemplate.pdf, accessed September 2011.

are always available wherever you have online access. They are social because these bookmarks can be shared and the collective intelligence can promote a bookmark to other interested members. They are very similar with social news focused more on content distribution and social bookmarks more intent upon the organization of content.

Social news and bookmarking communities play an invaluable role, because they filter vast amounts of information into sets that individuals can manage. In many cases this process is as simple as if a trusted friend told you she personally visited 10 ski resorts, and then she suggested the three she was sure you would like. You still might pick and choose among the three, but there's no way you could have considered the original 10 anyway, so you're happy to take her word for it. Imagine how much happier you'd be if five other friends gave you the same recommendations!

Social news websites are social communities that allow their users to submit news stories, articles, and multimedia files including videos and pictures so the submissions can be shared with other users and the general public. Submissions receive enhanced attention and visibility if they get a lot of votes from users. Social bookmarking communities are similar to social news communities in that users can share material from around the Internet with each other and the size and influence of a user's network affects the ultimate influence of the resource in question. However, those who use social news sites put a priority on message promotion, whereas those who use social bookmarking sites place a priority on organizing the links they want to save and store. Users store and organize bookmarks (using tags) to online source materials within the social bookmarking site (instead of storing bookmarks with one's Web browser) to make the information easily sortable, retrievable, and accessible.

These communities uphold the principles of media democratization. Individuals determine what material is disseminated throughout the community as well as the value ratings associated with the material. Users act as editors; they identify what material should be pushed to the featured areas of the site. The process supports the *wisdom of crowds* perspective, in that individual users recommend and vote on submissions. The site then uses algorithms to filter content and determine the popularity of a story. The algorithms include number of votes received as well as other factors such as the richness of the discussion related to the story. The system ensures each individual has a voice, if he or she chooses to use it, but it also enables some voices to be heard louder than others. The most active and respected participants, the influencers, or opinion leaders, come to hold positions of high authority in the community.

Although there's always the potential to manipulate the voting system (like ballot box stuffing in the physical world), the algorithms minimize this threat by seeking to identify **voting campaigns** (in which voters are incentivized to vote for a story). In addition, some social news websites have editorial staff who review stories and award featured positions for relevant, newsworthy stories (though bookmarking sites generally do not). There are more than 100 such sites. Digg, Reddit, Mix, Propell, Diigo, and Furl are some of the major players.

Planning a Social News Campaign   Choosing the communities to seed and target can be difficult. There are several social news sites and social bookmarking sites, just as there are several social networks. Depending on the campaign's objectives and target audience, it may make sense to focus on the leading sites or alternatively to find a niche site that attracts a smaller number of passionate participants. The community should also be evaluated for quality and engagement. Inactive or weak communities will not offer the social support necessary to propel a successful social news marketing campaign. Consider this list of community characteristics when evaluating the desirability of a community target:

1. What is the community's focus (general news, specific topics)?
2. How many active users are involved in the community? What kind of traffic does the site receive?
3. How active are the top users on the site?
4. How many comments on average are generated for each new submission?
5. How many votes are required to earn front page status on the site?
6. Are stories on the site's front page recent? How rapid is story turnover?
7. Are there limitations for branded content in the community's Terms of Service?
8. What have others (such as bloggers) said about the social news site?

Just as journalists receive pitches for content from public relations specialists who pitch stories that promote specific brands, influential social news users may receive pitches for branded content. The influencer's referral is valuable because she provides an unbiased, third-party word-of-mouth endorsement of the content. The process of influencing the influencers follows the traditional public relations model that gets information to be distributed into the hands of those in a position to distribute it to a large number of people. The key to success is to ensure that the content pitched is relevant to the people it targets.

Just as most people do not appreciate only hearing from a friend when she needs a favor, influencers as a group are unlikely to respond well to obvious pitches from social media marketers. Just like a good salesman in the physical world, the effective social media marketer understands that

THE DARK SIDE OF SOCIAL MEDIA

John Chow is a blogger and Internet entrepreneur who lives in Vancouver. He has 50,000 Twitter followers; on a typical day he shared with them a photo of his lunch, discussed the local weather, linked to a new post on his business blog—and then earned $200 by advising his followers where to buy customized M&M's candies. How does he make these hookups? He partners with specialized companies that link his Twitter stream to advertisers that want to plug in to his base. The co-founder of one such firm, Peer2, defends this practice: "We don't want to create an army of spammers, and we are not trying to turn Facebook and Twitter into one giant spam network. All we are trying to do is get consumers to become marketers for us."[21]

It's fine to get employees to "seed" content, so long as they identify themselves as such and avoid **sockpuppeting**. Sockpuppeting is the term used to describe people who take on a fictional identity when promoting content online.[22] Such behavior crosses an ethical line. But is it ethical to "bribe" supposedly objective bloggers to endorse your content with money or freebies? The Federal Trade Commission (FTC) doesn't think so. The practice of compensating bloggers who write product reviews for categories from diapers to movies has become so widespread that the FTC was forced to issue guidelines to regulate it. For example, Microsoft got into hot water a few years ago when it gave away free laptops to potential reviewers. The rationale for the company to hand out valuable hardware is pretty obvious: It's hard to bite the hand that feeds you, so people may be more inclined to post a positive review of a product they got courtesy of the manufacturer.

Now, the FTC says that bloggers must disclose any compensation they receive in exchange for a product review—these rules already apply to broadcast TV, newspapers, and magazines. An FTC official observes, "We look at it from the perspective of the consumer and the principle being that a consumer has the right to know when they're being pitched a product. "It doesn't matter whether it's an email or Twitter or someone standing on a street corner." A blogger who violates this edict risks a fine of up to $11,000 per incident. He'll need a lot of freebies to make that worthwhile. The guidelines don't worry power users who already disclose this information. For example, as we mentioned earlier the ElevenMoms bloggers are a group of moms Walmart put together that receives free merchandise from the retailer's suppliers; they have been flown to special events by Frito-Lay, Johnson & Johnson, and other companies. Christine Young, one of the ElevenMoms, already disclosed these relationships on her posts, and she agrees with the new rules: "The brands and companies directly working with bloggers need to be held accountable. While some companies may choose not to work with us now, I would much rather work with companies that wanted us to be open in the first place." However, other bloggers question the limits of these guidelines. As one observes, "If I get a free tube of toothpaste in the mail and say nice things about it on Twitter, Facebook, or in a PTA meeting, do I have to disclose it as a freebie or pay the $11,000 fine the FTC imposes? What kind of disclosure can one fit into a 140-character Twitter message, anyway?"[23]

it's important to build a relationship with the other person *before* he or she offers a sales proposition. Some care must be taken to introduce oneself, acknowledge the contributions the influencer makes to the community, and flatter the influencer's judgment and expertise in making high-quality content submissions. The influencer will be helping the brand by virtue of the content submission and vote, so it can be useful to help the influencer by offering other content that will be perceived as desirable prior to pitching the branded content. And don't simply send along your social media press release. Instead, a more personal pitch that emphasizes knowledge of the influencer's recommendation patterns and the marketer's relationship to the branded content is likely to be effective.

Chapter Summary

What are the channels of social publishing?

The channels of social publishing include blogs, media sharing sites, microsharing sites, social bookmarking sites and social news sites, as well as owned media sites with social components.

Who creates the content published in social channels? What kind of content can be published?

Anyone can create the content published in social channels. Content can be editorial, commercial, or user-generated. Content appears in a variety of different formats such as blog posts and feature articles, microblog posts, press releases, white papers, case studies, ebooks, newsletters, videos, webinars and presentations, podcasts, and photos.

What content characteristics enhance perceived content quality and value? How can marketers plan and organize their efforts as they embrace a social publishing strategy?

As Figure 3 shows, we can characterize content in terms of its originality and substance. The higher the level of originality and substance, the higher readers will perceive the content's quality and value. The lowest level of quality and value is associated with filler content, which is content resourced from elsewhere. Original content is of higher value than filler content, but can range from basic original content to the highest quality level, called flagship content. Marketers can utilize an editorial calendar to organize their ideas and content across several publishing sites.

What is the role of social publishing in social media marketing? How do social media marketers utilize search engine optimization and social media optimization to meet marketing objectives?

Social publishing enables marketers to distribute branded content. Also called content marketing, this approach helps to bring consumers to the brand's sites. Because consumers utilize search engines to find information online, using search engine optimization to improve search engine rankings is an important marketing task. Thus when we publish content, the content should be optimized for search engines. We also want people to link to our site; a form of referral. This is the goal of social media optimization.

How can social content be promoted? What role do social news and social bookmarking sites play in content promotion?

Social content can be promoted with social media press releases, microblog posts, and social news and social bookmarking sites. The press release and microblog posts encourage sharing among interested people and provide links to the original content. Social news sites enable a way to share links to the content and to promote the content through community rankings. Social bookmarks also enable shared links and a form of content quality ranking.

Key Terms

AdWords	content	giveaway hook
affiliate marketing	content value ladder	glossary article
aggregators	contrary hook	golden triangle
algorithm	conversion	gray hats
anchor text	counterfeit conversations	heading tag
authority-building	cultural co-creation	hook
content	definition article	"how-to" article
backlink	dynamic URLs	humor hook
black hats	editorial calendar	incentivized content
branded article	editorial message	indexed data
call to action	eye-tracking studies	keyword generators
citizen advertising	filler content	keyword research
cloaking	flagship content	keyword stuffing
commercial message	gateway pages	keywords

link exchanges	paid links	sockpuppeting
link farms	pay-per-click	spokesbloggers
link juice	pillar content	sponsored
linkbaiting	plug-ins	sponsored
links	power site	conversations
linkwheels	protest sites	theory article
list article	research hook	three-way linking
long tail keywords	resource hook	title
media plan	search engine marketing (SEM)	title tag
meta tag	search engine optimization (SEO)	trackback
off-site indicators	share tools	urban legends
on-site indicators	social bookmarking	URLs
organic	social media optimization	voting campaigns
organic content	(SMO)	web crawlers
original content	social media press release	white hats

Review Questions

1. What is social publishing? What kinds of content can be published socially?
2. Explain the difference between inbound and outbound marketing.
3. How can social publishing, along with SEO and SMO, help to meet marketing objectives?
4. How can a site be optimized for search engines?
5. Why is it important to achieve a top three ranking in a list of search engine results?
6. Explain the concept of the linkwheel.
7. What are the different types of tags that are used by search engine optimizers to influence search engine indexing?
8. What role does social media optimization play for search engine optimization? How are the two concepts related?
9. Explain the five types of linkbait and why linkbaiting is important.
10. Is there a difference between social news sites and social bookmarking sites? Explain.

Exercises

1. Visit a website of your choice.
   a. Go through the website to identify the components that were strategically optimized using SEO and SMO techniques. What could have been done to optimize the site further? Print out a screen image and label the page for in-class discussion.
   b. Identify the keywords you think would be good tags for the site.
   c. Run a search query using the keywords. Does the site show up in the first page of rankings? In the top three? Why do you think the site was successful (or not)?
   d. While you're on the search results page, take a look at the sponsored and organic results listings. How do they differ? Which would be most influential if you had been conducting a real search?
2. Visit Blogger or WordPress and sign up for a free blogging account. Complete your profile and add the standard blog components to your blog layout.
   a. Now write your first post (your instructor may assign a topic or you can start with one of the review questions).

b. Optimize your post using the techniques described in the chapter.

c. Create your own social media linkwheel with the pages you have in your digital footprint.

d. Try to get your content to spread through the network effect by seeding the content and drawing upon the influencers already in your network.

3. Register for a social bookmarking site and a social news site. You can choose which ones you wish to use. Once you've completed your profiles on the two sites, be sure to add your new activity to your digital footprint.

4. Visit the social bookmarking site you joined and look up a topic of interest for you. Select 10 headlines that have been saved by other users. Classify the headlines according to the type of linkbait used in their title. Anecdotally, does it seem like there is a relationship between the number of users who have bookmarked the content and the type of linkbait used? Explain.

5. Visit Google's free SEO tools. Enter several search terms to see how it presents information to you on keywords, trends, and phrases.

a. Google Suggest

b. Google Keywords

c. Google Trends

6. Read the FTC "Guides Concerning the Use of Endorsements and Testimonials for Advertising" at www.ftc.gov/os/2009/10/091005revisedendorsementguides.pdf. How will the guides affect your own brand mentions in social spaces?

Notes

1. "State of the Blogosphere Report," *Technorati*, November 3, 2010, http://technorati.com/blogging/article/state-of-the-blogosphere-2010-introduction/page-3/, accessed December 25, 2010.

2. "Who's Blogging What: Better Business Blogging in 2011," *HubSpot*, www.hubspot.com/ebooks/better-business-blogging-in-2011/, accessed December 19, 2010.

3. Heather Armstrong, *Dooce*, www.dooce.com, accessed January 1, 2011.

4. David Armano, *Logic + Emotion*, http://darmano.typepad.com/, accessed January 1, 2011.

5. David Silverman, "FCC Increasing Fines for Violations of Children's Programming Rules-Fines As High as $70,000 Per Station Issued," Broadcast Law Blog, May 29, 2010, www.broadcastlawblog.com/2010/05/articles/childrens-programming-and-adve/fcc-increasing-fines-for-violations-of-childrens-programming-rules-fines-as-high-as-70000-per-station-issued/, accessed June 25, 2010.

6. Susan G. Fournier, Michael R. Solomon, and Basil G. Englis, "Brand Resonance," in B. H. Schmitt and D. L. Rogers, Eds., *Handbook on Brand and Experience Management* (Cheltenham, UK and Northampton, MA: Edward Elgar, 2009).

7. Morrissey Brian, "Doritos Wins Super Bowl Web Buzz Battle," *Adweek*, February 8, 2010, www.brandweek.com/bw/content_display/news-and-features/packaged-goods/e3ief7f94880dc0982eb5cad2e8a7e41a77, accessed December 31, 2010.

8. Jon Fine, "LonelyGirl15: A Likely Scenario," *BusinessWeek.com*, August 27, 2006, www.businessweek.com/innovate/FineOnMedia/archives/2006/08/lonelygirl15_th_1.html, accessed December 31, 2010.

9. Chris Garrett, "Diggbait, Linkbait, Flagship Content and Authority," *chrisg.com*, February 11, 2008, www.chrisg.com/diggbait-linkbait-flagship-content-and-authority/, accessed December 25, 2010.

10. Tim O'Reilly, "What is Web 2.0?" *O'Reilly Media*, September 30, 2005, http://oreilly.com/web2/archive/what-is-web-20.html, accessed January 1, 2011.

11. "What Type of Content is Most Popular on Digg, Reddit, Propeller, Delicious, and StumbleUpon," *Social Media Trader*, December 29, 2007, http://socialmediatrader.com/analysis-what-type-of-content-is-most-popular-on-digg-reddit-propeller-delicious-and-stumbleupon/, accessed June 24, 2010.

12. Rohit Bargava, "5 Rules of Social Media Optimization (SMO)," *Influential Marketing Blog*, August 5, 2006, http://rohitbhargava.typepad.com/weblog/2006/08/5_rules_of_soci.html, accessed January 1, 2011.

13. "Trend Data," Pew Internet & American Life Project, http://pewinternet.org/Trend-Data.aspx, accessed July 2, 2010."comScore Releases December 2009 U.S. Search Engine Rankings,"

14. comScore, January 15, 2010, www.comscore.com/Press_Events/Press_Releases/2010/1/comScore_Releases_December_2009_U.S._Search_Engine_Rankings, accessed December 25, 2010.

15. Abe Sauer, "Social Media Worth $3.60 Says Everybody, Nobody," *Brandchannel*, April 15, 2010, www.brandchannel.com/home/post/2010/04/15/Social-Media-Worth-24360-Says-Everybody-Nobody.aspx, accessed July 6, 2010; Nancy Luna, "Burger King: Unfriend 10 Facebook Friends, Get a Free Whopper," *Orange County Register*, January 8, 2009, http://fastfood.ocregister.com/2009/01/08/burger-king-unfriend-10-facebook-friends-get-a-free-whopper/10980/, accessed July 6, 2010.

16. Chris Sherman, "A New F-Word for Google Search Results," *Search Engine Watch*, March 7, 2005, http://searchenginewatch.com/3488076, accessed June 29, 2010.

17. "SEO for Journalists: Headlines & Body Copy," *SEOMoz.org*, April 13, 2007, www.seomoz.org/ugc/seo-for-journalists-head-

lines-body-copy-part-2-of-5, accessed June 29, 2010.

18. "How to Find and Target Long Tail Keywords for More Search Engine Traffic," *Dosh Dosh*, www.doshdosh.com/how-to-target-long-tail-keywords-increase-search-traffic/; accessed July 1, 2010.

19. Linking Strategies, www.webhostingtalk.com/wiki/Linking_strategies#Three-way_linking, accessed December 25, 2010.

20. Ali Hale, "Obese Skunk Cuts Out Bacon Sandwiches," *The Diet Blog*, January 2, 2010, www.diet-blog.com/10/obese_skunk_cuts_out_bacon_sandwiches.php, accessed December 25, 2010.

21. Quoted in Brad Stone, "PING: A Friend's Tweet Could Be an Ad," *New York Times*, November 21, 2009, www.nytimes.com/2009/11/22/business/22ping.html, accessed July 6, 2010.

22. Brad Stone and Matt Richtel, "The Hand That Controls The Sock Puppet Could Get Slapped," *New York Times*, July 16, 2007, www.nytimes.com/2007/07/16/technology/16blog.html, accessed January 1, 2011.

23. Quoted in Amy Schatz and Miguel Bustillo, "U.S. Seeks to Restrict Gift Giving to Bloggers," *Wall Street Journal*, October 6, 2009, http://online.wsj.com/article/SB125475547130664753.html, accessed July 6, 2010.

Social Entertainment

From Chapter 7 of *Social Media Marketing*, First Edition. Tracy L. Tuten, Michael R. Solomon.
Copyright © 2013 by Pearson Education, Inc. All rights reserved.

Social Entertainment

LearningObjectives

When you finish reading this chapter you will be able to answer these questions:

1 What are the characteristics of social games and gamer segments?

2 How can social media marketers use social games to meet branding objectives?

3 Why are social games an effective tool for marketing?

4 What are the characteristics of alternate reality games (ARGs)?

5 What are the advantages and disadvantages of using alternate reality games as a marketing communications channel?

GO

Wherever this icon appears in the margin, please go to the website **www.zonesofsmm.com** for an example of the topic discussed.

The World of Serious Gaming Takes on a Social Flair

Have you played *FarmVille*? Felt addicted to *Bejeweled*? If you are a *Gossip Girl* fan, you may find yourself engrossed in *Social Climbing*. Maybe you get your music fix on MySpace and choose and discuss movies on Glue. The third zone of social media is social entertainment. It encompasses social games, socially-enabled video games, alternate reality games, and entertainment networks such as MySpace and Glue. In addition, there are several entertainment-focused apps and social software services available for online play and mobile devices that include social elements. The social entertainment zone, and especially the social gaming channel, is among the fastest growing areas of social media. The social gaming industry took in $1 billion in revenues in the United States and the United Kingdom in 2010, roughly double that from just 2 years ago.[1] In this chapter, we'll explore several aspects of the social entertainment zone with a focus on games.

Learning Objective 1

Social Games

There is still some uncertainty in the industry regarding just how to define a social game. Because the phenomenal growth of social games is attributed largely to Facebook's game platform and the blockbuster game *FarmVille*, social games are sometimes thought of as games people play within a social network. However, other game formats such as Xbox Live with Kinect also adopt social elements, including the ability to play online with other geographically dispersed players and to share game achievements on social profiles. These developments are quickly changing the parameters of what is or is not a social game.

Take for instance, Adidas's use of a branded game with augmented reality technology. **Augmented reality (AR)** is a form of technology that enables the overlay of digital images and information over a real (physical) environment. The phrase was first coined in 1990 to describe a digital display aircraft electricians used that blended virtual graphics with the physical elements of the aircraft.[2]

Figure 1

The Social Entertainment Zone

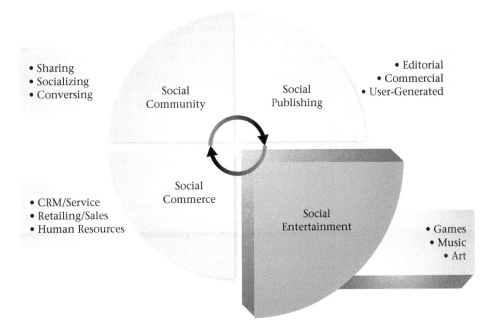

Adidas released a series of shoes (Originals AR) with a QR code built into the shoe's tongue. A **QR code** is a two-dimensional bar code that can be read using a webcam or mobile device equipped with a code reader. QR is an acronym for Quick Response. The code allows the content to be decoded quickly, hence the name. The code unlocks online content that might include information, games, videos, or experiences. In the Adidas example, the code unlocks a protected area of the Adidas website. There, the customer can play games with other players while using the shoes as the game controller.[3]

What makes a game social is largely what makes *any* form of social media social—the existence of and participation in a community and sharing within the community. Games are social when players share their gameplay with others. This means that by definition social games are multiplayer games. The social components of the game will be enhanced if there is communication among the players, tools to share activities and achievements, and methods to encourage others to join in the play. Therefore, we define a **social game** as a multiplayer, competitive, goal-oriented activity with defined rules of engagement and online connectivity among a community of players. Most social games include a few key elements:

- *Leaderboards:* a listing of the leaders in the game competition
- *Achievement badges:* symbols awarded to show game levels achieved and shared to the community
- *Friend (buddy) lists* with chat: a list of contacts with whom one plays and the ability to communicate within the game

The characteristics that appeal to serious gamers—the sense of competition and immersion within a dedicated community of players—can be heightened with the addition of social elements. And, people who once felt games were nothing more than a waste of time for teenage boys who huddle in basements among discarded pizza boxes now find casual, social games an enjoyable way to chase away boredom, spend time online with friends, and, quite simply, play.

Gamer Segments

At one time, we could easily categorize gamers based on the centrality of gaming in their lives. Gamers were either **casual** or **hardcore,** and the games they played reflected this division within the gaming community. Casual gamers played **casual games** and hardcore gamers played **core games**. Casual games are distinguished by low barriers-to-entry. They require only a small amount of time per session, are easy to learn, and are readily available online. For example, someone who wants to play *Bejeweled* can just hop online and start matching gemstones for whatever brief time he or she has available. *Bejeweled* even offers a mobile app for those who want to play while they wait in line at the grocery store.

In contrast, a core game such as *Call of Duty: Black OPS* requires a much larger time investment. Core games typically require extended lengths of time per gameplay session (90 minutes to several hours), are highly immersive, and demand advanced skills for ongoing play. They may be available online, or may have specific hardware and software requirements. Hardcore gamers value realism in the game's contextual clues and challenge in the game's activities; casual gamers value ease of use and immediate gratification. Although the stereotypes of casual versus hardcore gamers still hold some truth, social games are blurring the distinctions between these two types, and indeed they are bringing new gamers (and crossover games) into the mix.

Gaming is not limited to male teens, as most of us assume. Let's take a look at the demographic characteristics of gamers.[4] Today a staggering 67 percent of American households play computer and video games. The gender mix of gamers is skewed male (60 percent), but among casual social games 55 percent are female. As a rule women tend to prefer games that stress relationships (such as *The Sims*), so it's not surprising that as games evolve away from just "shoot 'em up" activities we see the gender mix start to even out.

The average gamer is 34 years old with 12 years of gaming experience. Twenty-six percent of gamers are over 50; this segment is expected to increase as seniors recognize the value of gaming as a social entertainment experience. The majority of American homes now own either a console and/or a computer used to run game software. Historically, casual gamers trend older and female whereas hardcore gamers skew younger and male. Early studies on social gamers suggest that a single profile would paint a picture that looks very similar to that of the casual gamer (and most social games share the characteristics of casual games). That said, the sheer number of people playing social games (eMarketer estimates the number at about 40 million in the United States in 2010) means that social games pull from both types of gamers (as well as recruiting a new breed of gamer who developed an interest in games within the context of social media).[5]

There are differences in the dedication of gamers to their respective games, but overall games exhibit a high degree of *stickiness*. As a reminder, stickiness describes the ability of a medium to attract an audience and *keep* that audience. Gamers as a cohort tend to be dedicated hobbyists who spend countless hours embroiled in intense games (yes, in some cases even while they pretend to work at the office or study in the library). People are passionate about games. In fact, gamers spend more time gaming online than they do on the Internet in all other activities except social networking—which is increasingly linked to game activity.[6] Online gaming even surpasses email in terms of average time spent weekly on the activity.

Casual gamers do spend less time on games each week than do core gamers, but even in these cases eMarketer estimates that 34 percent of gamers spend more than 4 hours a week playing games, 8 percent spend about 3 hours, 17 percent spend about 2 hours, and 9 percent spend 1 hour. That's a lot of game time—and a lot of opportunities for brands to interact with prospective customers.[7]

Gaming involves more than an investment of time, however. These activities require attention and active involvement. Players are not likely to be multitasking during a game or consuming multiple forms of media simultaneously. Gamers aren't texting, talking, or using the remote to channel surf when they're engrossed in killing orcs or acquiring farmland. Many gamers play through *game consoles;* it is important to remember that these devices are permanently connected to televisions in 86 percent of U.S. households. If the game console is on, television programming is not. In-game advertising provides an opportunity to recapture an audience that is not watching TV—and by extension the commercials.

All in all, we can safely say that gaming is a viable medium to market promotional messages. Games meet all of the criteria for viable market segmentation:

- The market is substantial, reachable, and measurable.
- The gaming demographic has broadened so that games are now considered viable vehicles to reach women and older consumers as well as young males.
- Gamers spend sufficient, dedicated time with games to achieve valuable ad impressions.

How We Categorize Social Games

Game design is built upon several layers, including platform, mode, milieu, and genre.[8] In fact, any platform can potentially support a social game environment. If the game can operate as multiplayer and includes online connectivity for communication and sharing among the players, it is social. Let's take a closer look at the dimensions we use to characterize games.

Game Platforms   A **game platform** refers to the hardware systems on which the game is played. Platforms include **game consoles** (consoles are interactive, electronic devices used to display video games such as Sony's PlayStation3, Microsoft's Xbox 360, and Nintendo's Wii), computers (including both online games and those that require software installation on the player's computer hard drive), and portable devices that may include smartphones or devices specifically for game play such as the Sony PSP or Nintendo DS.[9] However, it's important to keep in mind that social games often appear on multiple platforms: Gamers have a strong tendency to use two or more platforms so marketers can reach them as they move back and forth.

Mode and Milieu   **Mode** refers to the way the game world is experienced. It includes aspects such as whether a player's activities are highly structured, whether the game is single player or multiplayer, whether the game is played in close physical proximity to other players (or by virtual proximity), and whether the game is real-time or turn-based.[10] **Milieu** describes the visual nature of the game such as science fiction, fantasy, horror, and retro.

Genres   The **genre** of a game refers to the method of play. Popular genres include simulation, strategy, action, and role-playing. Each of these genre are represented among the game market whether the games are casual, core, or social games.

- **Simulation games** attempt to depict real-world situations as accurately as possible. There are several subgenres including racing simulators, flight simulators, and "Sim" games that enable the players to simulate the development of an environment. Among social games, simulations include the highly popular *FarmVille*, *Pet Resort*, and *FishVille*. Gamers trace most of the innovations in today's simulation games to the pioneering *Sim City* game.

- **Action games** consist of two major subgenres: **first-person shooters (FPS)** where you "see" the game as your avatar sees it and *third-person games*. Contextually there is little difference in these subgenres given the extent to which gamers identify with their avatars. The avatar acts as a virtual prosthetic connecting the player and the environment.[11] Action games are **performative** in that the player chooses an action that the game then executes. The actions may revolve around battles, sports, gambling, and so on. Examples of social action games are *Epic Goal* (a live-action soccer game), *Paradise Paintball* (a first-person shooter social game), and *Texas Hold'Em* (a social gambling game).

- **Role-playing games (RPGs),** games in which the players play a character role with the goal of completing some mission, are closely tied to the milieu of fantasy. Perhaps the best-known RPG started its life as a tabletop game—*Dungeons and Dragons*. Players adopt the identity of a character in the game story and go about completing tasks and collecting points and items as they strive to accomplish the intended goal. **MMORPGs**—*massive multiplayer online role-playing games*—are a type of RPG that truly encompasses the social aspects of gaming. *World of Warcraft* is the largest of these with more than 11 million subscribers. Social RPGs on Facebook include *Haven*, *Mafia Wars*, *Battle Stations*, and *Tennis Mania*.

- **Strategy games** are those that involve expert play to organize and value variables in the game system. These games may involve contextualizing information available from secondary sources outside the game itself, including previous experience with game play. Later in this chapter we will discuss alternate reality games as a game form for marketing. Although these games stand apart from other social games due to their complexity, they also are strategy games that involve the solving of puzzles and the systematic evaluation of new information and choices to be made to continue in the game. **Puzzle games**, a common variant in the realm of social games, are also a type of strategy game. Social strategy games include *Kingdoms of Camelot*, *Highborn*, *KDice*, *Word Cube*, and *Lexulous*. Of course, there is quite a bit of blurring between the genres; you can play other games strategically even though they may best be categorized as sims, action, or role plays.

Learning
Objective 2

Game-Based Marketing

Brands can utilize social games for marketing in several ways—and they should! Games offer a targeted audience, large reach, a high level of engagement, low intrusion methods of promotion, and a way to interact with brand fans. Or, an organization may choose to promote its message in an existing game property. In these cases the brand can advertise in and around the game using display advertising and product placements, sponsor aspects of the game, and integrate the brand into game play. In addition, a brand can take an even bigger step and develop its own **advergame**, a game that delivers a branded message. We'll review each approach.

In-Game Advertising   **In-game advertising** is promotion within a game that another company develops and sells. Marketers can choose from among three general methods for in-game advertising.

1. **Display ads** are integrated in a game's environment as billboards, movie posters, and store-fronts (depending of course on the game's context), or simply as ad space within the game screen. The display advertising may be static or dynamic and include text, images, or rich media. Rich media advertising can run *pre-roll* (before the game begins), *interlevel* (between stages of the game), or *post-roll* (at the game's conclusion), though interlevel is the most common placement.

2. **Static ads** are hard-coded into the game and ensure that all players view the advertising. Bing's display ad in *FarmVille* is an example of an in-game, static display ad. The ad offered players the chance to earn *FarmVille* cash for becoming a fan of Bing on Facebook. In the first day the ad ran, Bing earned 425,000 new fans on Facebook.[12]

3. **Dynamic ads** are variable; they change based on specified criteria. This technique is managed by networks such as Massive (owned by Microsoft) and Google AdWords, which offer insertion technology to place ads across multiple games. The networks contract with game publishers to place advertising in their games. By combining games from several publishers, networks create a large portfolio of in-game media opportunities for advertisers. The network works with publishers to strategically embed advertising, sell the placement to advertisers, serve the ads into the games in the network, and manage the billing and accounting for the process.

   Dynamic advertising is valuable because of the high degree of control and real-time measurement it offers. In addition, this approach makes it possible to develop an ad network within game families. It makes it possible to aggregate numerous games, platforms, and genres into the ad network. Massive Inc. conducted a series of research tests to gauge the impact of dynamic in-game advertising. It found that in games using dynamic advertising, brand familiarity, brand ratings, purchase consideration, ad recall, and ad ratings all increased significantly compared to a control group. The study, which involved more than 1,000 gamers across North America, included tests of several advertising categories including automotive, consumer packaged goods, and fast food.[13]

Product Placement

A **product placement** is simply the placement of a branded item in an entertainment property such as a television program, movie, or game. A placement can be very simple—involving nothing more than having a brand visible in a scene—or it can be heavily integrated into the entertainment property (and then product placement begins to overlap with immersive in-game advertising, which we discuss later).[14]

Screen placements that incorporate the brand into what's happening on the show are the most common form of product placement. In the *Tiger Woods PGA Tour* golf game, for instance, Tiger wears his Nike brand clothing and uses Nike golf equipment (even though the latest edition dropped his image from the cover as the result of his "romantic misadventures").[15] H&M embeds images from its stores in the geo-mobile game *Booyah's MyTown*. When users check in to a location near an H&M, the product images appear along with discount offers for the store.

Script placements take the process one step further: They include verbal mentions of the brand's name and attributes in the plot. For example, in *Madden NFL11*, players are exposed to the Old Spice Swagger, a sponsored rating of a player's personality. Gamers note that product placements that are realistic enhance the game's realism and make the game more enjoyable. However, that hasn't been the case for *Madden NFL 11*—online chatter criticizes the Old Spice sponsorship as product placement gone too far.[16]

Transactional advertising rewards players if they respond to a request.[17] This technique is part product placement, part direct response advertising, and part sales promotion. The offers can be for virtual goods (which players can use in the game or offer as gifts to friends), currency (used to advance in the game), or codes (used to unlock prizes and limited-access player experiences). Players are rewarded with the virtual goods, currencies, or codes if they make a purchase, friend the brand, watch a commercial, or perhaps answer a survey. ProFlowers used transactional advertising as part of a Valentine's Day promotion in Playfish's *Pet Society* game. Players who sent real flowers from within the game were rewarded with Playfish Cash. Netflix offered Farm Cash to *FarmVille* players who registered for a free trial.

Transactional advertising is the fastest growing segment of monetization in the social gaming industry. It's currently worth an estimated $720 million in revenues; marketers love it because, like other forms of direct response marketing, they can obtain valuable feedback about who accepts their promotional offers. Some analysts estimate that virtual goods will make up 20 percent of all game revenues.[18] This is a popular approach to branding in-game, but beware: Some marketers have come under fire for questionable ethical practices related to making offers in exchange for virtual currency. For instance, *FarmVille* has been accused of tricking players into signing up for paid services.[19]

Brand Integration

 In-game immersive advertising opportunities include interactive product placements, branded in-game experiences, and game integration between the game and the brand. In the film industry this is known as a **plot placement**. Plot placements involve situations in which the brand is actually incorporated into the story itself in a substantive manner. Whether a plot placement or some other form of integration, the result is enhanced brand attitudes, recall and recognition, and purchase.

 The campaign to launch the release of the *Public Enemies* DVD illustrates how a brand can integrate its marketing messages very closely with a game. The movie studio that released the film worked with the social game *Mafia War* to create a truly integrated game experience. Players in *Mafia Wars* start their own Mafia family, run their empires, and fight for the position of most powerful of Mafia families. It's played by more than 25 million active users. During a one-week campaign, *Mafia Wars* featured Public Enemies Week. Players could complete tasks to unlock branded virtual goods such as wooden guns and prison stripes. After they completed tasks, players saw movie clips and trivia about the movie characters. A success? You bet. Nineteen million players took part in Public Enemies Week: They completed 44.5 million branded tasks, watched 1.5 million movie clips, and posted 7.6 million news feed posts on game tasks and virtual goods. The promotion also generated 25,000 Facebook "Likes" and 26,000 comments on the *Mafia Wars* Facebook page.[20]

 # THE DARK SIDE OF SOCIAL MEDIA

Gold Farming

Just as in the physical world, unscrupulous people who operate in digital worlds find ways to exploit poor workers who are desperate for money. Yes, the huge demand for virtual goods in games like *World of Warcraft* provides fertile ground for digital "sweatshops," where people work for long hours to accumulate points, game tokens, or virtual goods such as swords. These then are resold to players who want a quick leg up against competitors. There are many thousands of these workshops, mostly in China. The workers, known as **gold farmers**, put in 10- to 12-hour shifts to loot treasures and kill monsters. They must meet daily quotas on behalf of their employers, who then sell these assets to gamers worldwide.[21] See www.youtube.com/watch?v=ho5Yxe6UVv4 for a video documentary of Chinese gold farmers.

Advergames   With advergaming, the game itself is a form of branded entertainment. It is designed by the brand to reflect the brand's positioning statement. Advergames are almost exclusively available online rather than in hard media because of the desire to have a cost-effective method of distributing the game to a large audience. Likewise, they tend to be casual rather than core games because of the costs associated with creating and promoting core games.

The shift to social games is a boon to advergaming given the goal of the game—to spread a branded message. There are developmental costs to be considered, but advergames are sometimes "reskinned" versions of existing games. This means that a game is reprogrammed to contain brand logos or other sponsored images. The key to success in the advergaming market is the quality of the game and the congruence between the brand and the game context. Gamers tend to be thought of as people who eschew traditional advertising, but they welcome a good game, whether or not it appears as an advergame.

Perhaps because advergames are not intended to make money, but rather to serve as a promotion vehicle that builds awareness for the sponsoring brand, many have lagged behind in terms of their technical sophistication compared to social games. However, some success stories illustrate the potential for advergames. Take, for example, Penguin Books Australia. To celebrate its publication of 75 new books in recognition of its' 75th birthday, the publisher launched a social advergame called *Penguin Party*. The game tests a player's knowledge of popular Penguin titles and offers the chance to win branded goods. Players link to the game via Facebook Connect so they can compete and share accomplishments with their friends.

Jane Chen of Ya Ya Media, a video game developer, had this to say of advergaming's potential; "It is one of the few advertising mediums that effectively reaches target audiences in all day-parts—including hard-to-reach at-work hours. . . . The most effective advergames push deeper down the purchase funnel and can serve to qualify buyers and incentivize consumers to visit retail outlets or even purchase directly online. The natural interactivity of games provides the perfect stimulus and ongoing communication channel between brands and their customers."[22]

Learning Objective 3

The Bottom Line: Why Do Social Games Work for Marketers?

Social games have the potential to be a major weapon in a marketer's arsenal. As gaming continues to explode as a consumer activity, we expect to see many more of these vehicles—and you should too. Players tend to be in a receptive mood when gaming and branding efforts result in more positive brand attitudes. In addition, it's possible to finely target users because most games attract a fairly distinct type of player. And, it's relatively inexpensive to use this medium, brand exclusivity is available (where a sponsor is the sole advertiser in a gaming environment), and metrics are available to measure just how well the game works to attract players.

Of course, like any advertising medium games do have some negatives that the industry has to deal with. One is **game clutter**; like the pervasive problem of *advertising clutter* in other formats, this means that there are way too many games out there that compete for players' attention. Facebook alone offers hundreds of social games, and this number multiplies when you consider the massive inventory available on games offered on game networks (such as Pogo.com), microsites, and via consoles and software. Unlike advertising clutter, however, the problem is compounded because of the time investment involved in playing a game. You can either look at or not look at a popup ad on a website and move on, but if you choose to play a game you need to devote time to learning the rules and mastering its tricks. Even for avid game geeks, there are only so many hours in a day (OK, a few more if you skip class to play your favorites). Another issue is available inventory for advertising in-game. Granted there are numerous game titles and genres, but the inventory of space available for display advertising, product placement, and brand integration is still in limited supply.

There are some key characteristics of games—in addition to cost and ease of targeting—that make this domain especially attractive to marketers going forward.

1. *Gamers are open to advertising content in games.* It's not that they're "adverholics"—just that they crave realism and many real-world venues (for better or worse) like stadiums are saturated with marketing messages. In fact, a study by Nielsen Entertainment conducted on behalf of Massive, Inc., revealed that after exposure to in-game ads on Massive's advertising game network, brand familiarity, a measure of brand recognition, increased 64 percent.[23] In addition, the study found that positive attitudes toward the brands studied increased by 37 percent and purchase consideration increased by 41 percent. The advertising itself also performed well; respondents reported an increase in advertising recall and a positive attitude toward the ads they encountered in the games. These results are consistent with other research on the effectiveness of ad placement, which found that placing ads in creative locations such as games over traditional placements such as magazines resulted in positive feelings toward the brand.[24]

2. *Brands benefit when they associate with a successful game.* When players love a game, some of these positive feelings rub off on the brands they encounter within it; we call this spillover a **transference effect**. This is the same thing that tends to happen with event sponsorships. Brands often try to link to sports and music events like the Olympics or a Rihanna concert to gain residual benefits from the brand-event association. The only difference is that a game/brand linkage is more intimate; the player encounters the sponsoring product on his or her screen rather than in an arena packed with 10,000 other fans. Like event sponsorship, a prerequisite for success is congruence between the brand's image and the image and atmosphere the game conveys. It's unlikely that a conservative clothing chain such as Talbot's would sponsor a Lady Gaga tour, and similarly the U.S. Army is probably a better candidate to create a role-playing military game like *Call of Duty* than is, say, the Methodist Church. In other words, there must be a good fit in order to maximize the value of the association. To pick the right game, marketers must choose the game (or game concept) just as they would choose any other media and vehicles for a media plan—they need to consider the demographic profile of game players, the size of the player market, and the quality and content of the game franchise. Ford or Chevrolet in *Grand Theft Auto*? Probably not a great idea.

   Not only do brands benefit from association with the game, but they can also achieve outcomes similar to when they use celebrity endorsers. Famous people who the target audience admires also create a transference effect. That's why companies pay millions to movie stars; they hope that the knowledge that an admired person likes the brand in turn will encourage the star's fans to like it as well. **Internalization** occurs when members of the target market accept the beliefs of an endorser as their own. In a game context, the characters in the game's story and setting can act as brand endorsers.

   The **meaning transfer model** states that consumers associate meaning with the endorser and then transfer the meaning to the brand in question.[25] The consumer first chooses to assign the meaning associated with the endorser to the product or brand. Thus, meanings attributed to the endorser become associated with the brand in the consumer's mind. For game advertisers, the meaning transfer model suggests that a character's attributes can be transferred to a brand a character uses in the game as part of an in-game product placement. The key to using character endorsers successfully parallels the choice of celebrity endorsers. The character endorser should have the appropriate set of characteristics the brand desires.

3. *Players identify with the brands their characters use, and this increases their brand involvement.* Players may be particularly invested in their characters because they spend weeks, months, and even years to build their character identity and develop the attributes that will enable the character to compete at the highest possible level of the game. Even the name of the RPG genre itself, "role-playing," implies just how involved players are with their characters. When brands are embedded using immersive techniques such as enabling players in a racing game

to choose their brand of race car, the players can actively interact with brands during the game experience. This "bonding" results in a heightened sense of brand identification.

4. *Branding within a game's story is an unobtrusive way to share a brand's core message.* In many ways, games approximate the immersive experience of watching a movie. Games, like movies, are capable of transcending barriers of class and culture. However, games offer more than stories told through film and literature, in that they allow the audience to actually participate in the story. When spectators become actors, they are less likely to sit back and think of reasons why the advertising message on the screen doesn't apply to them (psychologists call this common process **counterarguing**). **Narrative transportation theory** explains how even imagined interactivity can build positive brand attitudes. This theory proposes that mental stimulation through narrative storytelling encourages players to become lost in the story. Once immersed in the plot, players are distracted from advertising embedded in the game. They do not counterargue against these messages, and as a result they are more likely to form attitudes toward the brand simply based on the positive feelings the story evokes.[26]

5. *Marketers can measure a game's promotional value.* For both game advertising and advergaming, the game environment creates a higher impression value for the ad compared to that earned from traditional media placements. This is attributed to the frequency of exposure, the potential for interactivity with the brand's message, and the entertainment value of the platform. Millions of advertising impressions can be delivered in just a few weeks of game play at a cost as low as 25 cents per impression. In addition to the low cost, there is little advertising clutter in games, particularly when compared to other media choices. But what's equally or even more important is that marketers know how well a game works to deliver these impressions. Unlike many other forms of advertising, a sponsor can measure who saw the message and in some cases even link these exposures to sales of its product.

Alternate Reality Games: A Transmedia Genre

Learning
Objective 4

So far in this chapter we've focused on social games. But in addition to all the *Mafia Wars* and *World of Warcraft* players out there, other people are getting into an even newer genre that's even more immersive—one that vividly demonstrates the stunning potential of digital media. We refer to **alternate reality games (ARGs)**. Unfiction.com, a leading website for the ARG community, defines an alternate reality game as "a cross-media genre of interactive fiction using multiple delivery and communications media, including television, radio, newspapers, Internet, email, SMS, telephone, voicemail, and postal service."[27] ARGs are still social games, with a community of players who compete and collaborate to solve a complex puzzle. These games are like others of the strategy genre—but on steroids. When a sponsoring brand develops an ARG it also resembles an advergame. And, because ARGs involve two or more different media, they are **transmedia social games**.

All of this sounds pretty complicated, so let's make it simple with a story about a successful ARG. In 2007 the band Nine Inch Nails, fronted by Trent Reznor, released an album entitled *Year Zero*. Reznor observed, "This record began as an experiment with noise on a laptop in a bus on tour somewhere. That sound led to a daydream about the end of the world. That daydream stuck with me and over time revealed itself to be much more. I believe sometimes you have a choice in what inspiration you choose to follow and other times you really don't. This record is the latter. Once I tuned into it, everything fell into place.... as if it were meant to be.... Things started happening in my "real" life that blurred the lines of what was fiction and what wasn't. The record turned out to be more than just a record in scale, as you will see over time."[28] Reznor went on to describe the album: "It takes place about 15 years in the future. Things are not good. If you imagine a world where greed and power continue to run their likely course, you'll have an idea of the backdrop."[29]

The band went on to develop an elaborate game based on Reznor's vision. Players in the game found clues and received phone calls directing them to websites revealing images from "the future." The first clue appeared on the back of a shirt promoting Nine Inch Nails' European tour. On the back of the shirt several letters are highlighted that spell out "I am trying to believe." The words led fans to the website www.iamtryingtobelieve.com, which describes a drug named "Parepin" that, in the Year Zero story, is being added to the water supply to cloud people's minds. The site also contained a blurred image of a hand-like figure reaching down from the sky. This was the first sighting of what was known in the story as the "presence," but it would not be the last. The image of the "presence" served as a primary symbol for gamers tracking clues. It is also the image on the album's cover.

Several of the clues linked back to the band. For instance, at the February 12, 2007, Nine Inch Nails' concert in Lisbon, Portugal, a USB flash drive was found in a bathroom stall. It was later found to hold a single audio file with the title "My Violent Heart." Fans discovered that "My Violent Heart" was a track from the Year Zero album that was slated to be released.

The clues are well-integrated. For instance, gamers noticed static at the end of the audio file found on the USB drive at the Lisbon concert. Using a logarithmic spectrometer to analyze the audio file, the gamers discovered the image of the presence embedded in the file (yes, the people who play these games are hardcore!). A series of clues delivered when players called certain phone numbers led to a set of Web sites such as www.artisresistance.com. This site in turn provided items for fans to download such as icons, printable stickers, stencils, and posters. Physical renditions of these items have since appeared as street art in several locations around the world.

The ARG concluded around the album's release date; players registered at the Open Source Resistance site were invited to meet in Hollywood. At that point, some players were given mobile phones. Days later, the phones rang and gave the players instructions to meet again. They were loaded on a bus and delivered to an abandoned warehouse—the site of a brief performance by Nine Inch Nails. The game finally ended when prerecorded messages on certain phone lines reported, "We've got to go dark for a while, but that is ok—you don't need us anymore."

The Nine Inch Nails campaign is a nicely executed ARG. It featured all of the components of well-designed games, including a good fit between brand, target audience, and plot. The clues were leaked in innovative ways using multimedia and multi-channels. The symbols, including the image of the "presence," the website URLs, and the leaked songs were all integrated into the meaning of the album and into the ARG plot. Players were intensely drawn into the game; many of them stormed the bathrooms when concert gates opened during the Year Zero tour to search for flash drives that might contain additional clues.

Characteristics of ARGs

ARGs begin with a scripted scenario. However, over time an ARG will also become a form of *consumer-fortified media,* as the network of gamers participates in the game by discovering clues, sharing information with others, and literally changing the structure and plot of the game with their responses. In an ARG, players not only share tips, clues, and accomplishments with the player community, they also help to direct how the story underlying the game develops. In fact, that's why sometimes ARGs are referred to as **immersive fiction**. For branded ARGs, marketers have an unmatched opportunity to share a brand story with the audience.

The games unfold over multiple forms of media and utilize many types of game elements, each tailored to specific media platforms. ARGs may utilize websites (story sites and social networking sites), telephones, email, outdoor signage, t-shirts, television, radio play, and more to reveal story clues, compose scenes, and unite gamers.

ARGs are ideally suited to social media because it would be impossible to solve the puzzle alone. Among players, the term "**collective detective**" acknowledges the need for a team approach to solve the mystery. Because players from around the world participate, online communication is a necessary component to play. Many ARGs use other media channels including live events, television, radio, and so on, but social media ensures a hub of communication for the players. We summarize the basic characteristics of ARGs as follows:

- ARGs are based on a fictional story. Game characters, events, places, and plot are imagined and explored by the game writers, known as **puppet masters**.
- ARGs are strategy/puzzle games. The story unfolds as a mystery that invites players to solve clues before more of the narrative is revealed.
- Because they are transmedia social games, ARGs offer clues on multiple platforms that range from traditional media like television and newspapers to text messages and messages hidden in code in movie trailers or even concert t-shirts.
- The story is fictional as are the game characters, but the game space is not. The players are real people and the clues are revealed in real time. Consequently, *real life is itself a medium*. This characteristic has led to the ARG "**TINAG**" credo—"This is not a game!" Telephone numbers, websites, and locations revealed in-game are all real and functioning. Oh—and if you meet an ARG enthusiast, beware. He or she won't take kindly to references to ARGs as games (even though they are).
- Players collaborate to unravel the meanings of the clues offered but they also compete to be the first to solve layers of the mystery. Players are geographically dispersed, sometimes worldwide.
- The story unfolds, but typically not in a linear fashion. The speed of disclosure is influenced by the players' success and speed in solving clues and sharing them with the player population.
- ARGs are organic; the story may not unfold as initially conceived. Because players interact with the game, and player response can dictate the next scene in the story, stories are fluid and unpredictable.
- Players rely on the Internet, and especially social communities including forums, as the hub of communication.
- The desire for players to share information with each other and even for the story to be followed by observers attests to the viral nature of ARGs.

The Vocabulary of ARGs

ARGs have their own vernacular—understanding the lingo is the first step to understanding the culture of alternate reality gaming. The website Unifiction.com is a major clearinghouse for ARG fans. The site summarizes the basic lexicon of alternate reality gamers.[30]

- *Puppet master:* The authors, architects, and managers of the story and its scenarios and puzzles.
- **Curtain:** The invisible line separating the players from the puppet masters.
- **Rabbit hole:** The clue or site that initiates the game.
- *Collective detective:* A term that captures the notion of collaboration among a team of geographically dispersed players who work together to flesh out the story.
- *Lurkers and* **rubberneckers:** Lurkers follow the game but do not actively participate, whereas rubberneckers participate in forums but do not actively play. Consider this common line from brand-sponsored sweepstakes, "You don't have to play to win." From a branding perspective, lurkers and rubberneckers are just as critical to the success of an ARG as are the active players. Unfiction.com estimates that the ratio of lurkers to active players can range from 5:1 to 20:1 depending upon the game.
- **Steganography:** The tactic of hiding messages within another medium; the message is undetectable for those who do not know to look for it.
- **Trail:** A reference index of the game including relevant sites, puzzles, in-game characters, and other information. Trails are useful for new players coming late into a game and to veteran players who eagerly try to piece together the narrative.

The Marketing Value of ARGs

Brands such as Levi Strauss, McDonald's, and Audi have used ARGs for marketing. In fact, to date, the most successful ARGs in terms of participation are brand-sponsored. Most ARGs are tied to entertainment properties such as movies, books, and video games (yes, games to promote games!). It's natural that story-oriented products would promote themselves using a story-based promotional tool, but other brands can benefit from ARGs too. The key, just as with other forms of social games, is to ensure a high level of congruence between the game and the brand.

The movie launch of *A.I.* (Artificial Intelligence) in 2001 started it all with the ARG game *The Beast* that a Microsoft team created. This groundbreaking promotional vehicle was set in the year 2142, 50 years after the events in the movie. This game offered three rabbit holes:

1. A clue hidden among the credits for *A.I.*

2. A trailer for the movie that invited players to call a phone number in order to receive a clue by email, and

3. A promotional poster the producers sent to technology and media outlets that contained another clue.

The prevalence of brand-initiated ARGs is at least in part due to the funding necessary to build an intricate, multimedia, multi-channel narrative with characters and clues spread online and off. Take, for instance, *The Art of the Heist* ARG that Audi used to promote its A3 model. ARG-related expenses ran about $5 million.[31] Compared to television advertising, the cost of an ARG is minimal. Still, the resources required are substantial enough to warrant the need for a brand sponsor. However, this investment can pay off handsomely. For instance, Audi claims that 500,000 consumers, in its target audience of 25-to-35-year-old, upper-income males, participated in its *Art of the Heist* ARG, with average exposure of 4 to 10 minutes spent on numerous websites and pages used to embed game clues.[32] Hits to Audi's website increased 140 percent during the game with the most hits originating from game sites. Its dealers earned 10,000 qualified sales leads, and 3,500 test drives could be attributed to the game.[33]

Although an ARG benefits from a sponsor's deep pockets, many of the games do not identify who is behind the effort. Instead, players play until the mystery is solved (or the sponsorship is inadvertently discovered and leaked to the community) and the brand sponsor is revealed. This type of branded ARG is known as a **dark play ARG**; it's one of the ways that brands can use **dark marketing**, which refers to a promotion that disguises the sponsoring brand. Some say it's an ethical question whether brands should acknowledge their role in an ARG (or other dark marketing promotional stunt), but thus far, both brands and players seem to recognize that the game is best left as pure play space. In the end, players have a sense of gratitude toward the brand for the game experience that translates into more positive brand attitudes, along with potentially stronger brand knowledge because participants stick with the game for days, weeks, or even months before they solve the mystery. Table 1 summarizes the pros and cons of the ARG strategy.

Learning
Objective **5**

Evaluating the Effectiveness of a Brand-Sponsored ARG

How can we measure the effectiveness of ARGs as a branding tool? ARG effectiveness measures are similar to those used for other social media approaches with a focus on site traffic and participation. The most common indicators for ARGs include:

- Number of active players
- Number of lurkers and rubberneckers
- Rate of player registration from launch or from specific game event
- Number of player messages generated
- Traffic at sites affiliated with the ARG
- Number of forum postings (at sites like unfiction.com)
- Average play time
- Media impressions made through publicity generated about the ARG

TABLE 1

Pros and Cons of Using an ARG as a Social Entertainment Branding Channel

Pros	Cons
Reach can be substantial. In addition to active players, lurkers and rubberneckers may also see the messages.	ARGs require a lot of effort from initial conception through planning and execution. And, because the storyline can change depending upon the response from players, ARGs require constant monitoring and input from the game architects through and even beyond (as players are debriefed) the game's end.
The games attract media attention, resulting in earned media in the form of publicity.	Because the game can evolve in ways the architects did not originally plan, there is a risk involved. As fans drive the plot, the game can progress in ways the sponsor didn't anticipate.
Exposures earned last longer than do those for traditional media.	Hardcore brand loyalists may resent the influx of new people who express interest in the game.
ARGs are high-engagement messages. The games pull enthusiasts (players, lurkers, and rubberneckers) into the story and encourage them to seek out new information as it is presented in the game.	ARGs are unlikely to reach the same number of prospects as a brand could attract if it used mass media.
Players welcome brand-sponsored ARGs because they do not invade people's space with a brand message.	

BYTES TO BUCKS

Planning a Successful ARG: *The Lost Ring*

Given the ability of ARGs to engage brand enthusiasts and gamers, and drive publicity and buzz for brands, it's not surprising that McDonald's sponsored one in 2008. Seeking to leverage the spirit and global scale of the 2008 Olympic Games in a way that would encourage consumers to engage rather than tune out traditional marketing messages, McDonald's worked with agency AKQA to develop a global ARG it called *The Lost Ring*. Let's take a closer look at some guidelines for developing a successful ARG, and see how *The Lost Ring* followed each of these:[34]

- *Have a story to tell.* ARGs are first and foremost an interactive story. This story may be closely related to the brand's meaning or may be a **cadet narrative**.[35] The term *cadet narrative* means that the story is not tied to the brand's meaning directly, but rather the story seeks

to intrigue the audience and the brand benefits merely from its sponsorship or association with the story.

> The Lost Ring *is the story of six amnesiac Olympians who competed in an ancient, lost Olympic sport: Labyrinth Running. The story begins with Ariadne (Ari), who wakes up with no knowledge of who she is. Her only clue is a message about a lost ring. She decides to pursue the meaning of the clue, which leads to other clues and the discovery that there are others just like her in other places around the world.*

- *Reveal the story narrative over time using obscure clues and messages that will require player interaction to decipher the scenes.* This will encourage collaboration among players, incite buzz, and generate more interest in the game.

> The Lost Ring *began on March 3, 2008, and ended on August 24, 2008, coinciding with the closing ceremony*

(continued)

Bytes to Bucks   Continued

of the 2008 Beijing Olympic Games. During this period, gamers from all over the world found clues hidden both online in places such as YouTube and Flickr and story microsites as well as in offline locations. Several artifacts were hidden in locations around the world, so the game required participation from geographically dispersed players to solve the puzzle.

- *Utilize a variety of media and carefully design game elements to leverage the characteristics of the delivery medium. There is no limit to the delivery choices. Past ARGs have utilized code on t-shirts and posters, websites identified in video trailers, posts to blogs, email, text messages, and mass media advertising.*

  In The Lost Ring, *several media vehicles were used, including The Lost Ring website, several character-themed microsites, a Facebook quiz, Twitter feed, Google Gadget, podcasts, and video trailers.*

- *Develop an intricate and complex plot that includes a* **back story** *(the pre-game context), the primary narrative, and the* **forward story** *(a plan for how the story will continue, which can be used to foreshadow for future game play), if appropriate.*

  The Lost Ring *was set up with the introduction of the heroine, Ari. We are then introduced to a historian who has information and artifacts that can help Ari solve the mystery, and several other characters who find themselves in the same situation as Ari. To heighten the relationship of the game to the Olympics, the back story includes information on an ancient Olympic sport, Labyrinth Running. The primary narrative is the unfolding of the meaning of*

the Olympic rings as clues are revealed and the story of the game characters, six amnesiac Olympians who competed in Labyrinth Running, as they work through the puzzle with the game players.

- *Include plot lines and story elements that are nonlinear and that can be revealed sporadically. The development of the narrative must not be predictable and must not rely on a linear unfolding of events to make sense. Break the narrative into fragments the players can reassemble. Layer the story and layer the clues. Using layers of clues at various levels of complexity invites collaboration among the players and allows players to play at different skill levels. Chart the flow of the story, clues, and media used for each as a planning tool.*

  In the story, Ari discovers that a historian knows of the Lost Ring. He collects ancient artifacts related to the original Olympic Games, the formation of the modern games, and the true meaning of the Olympic rings. This set the stage for the hunt for the artifacts that could reveal the solution to the mystery. During gameplay, 27 artifacts were placed strategically in locations in the United States, Germany, Australia, China, France, Spain, Switzerland, Japan, Canada, Argentina, England, Singapore, Korea, South Africa, Sweden, Italy, the Netherlands, and Mexico over six stages. Though set into play according to a schedule (see The Lost Ring *Timeline), the timing and rate of discovery of artifacts and their meaning cannot be planned. Consequently, the final story lines were not revealed until the final artifact was discovered.*

Approximate timing for each city:

Group 1 (A2-6) 3/10-3/17	Group 2 (A7-11) 3/18-3/25	Group 3 (A12-16) 3/19-4/2
Berlin	Vancouver	San Francisco
Austin	New York	Copenhagen
Melbourne	Buenos Aires	Toronto
Shanghai	London	Hong Kong
Paris	Singapore	São Paolo
Group 4 (A17-21) 4/3-4/9	**Group 5 (A22-24) 4/10-4/17**	**Group 6 (A25-27) 5/14-5/21**
Lausanne	Seoul	Rome/Venice
Tokyo	Johannesburg	Amsterdam
Bangalore	Stockholm	Mexico City/Rio
Sydney		
Barcelona		

- *Design a story that will enhance the sense of reality in the story.*

  Players communicated with each other and with the game characters via email, forums, and social networks. They became so immersed in the game that they created several social venues for discussing the game and sharing clues and theories. One player-run forum had tens of thousands of posts by the end of game play. A player wiki included 2,238 pages of material edited by players more than 11,000 times. And, without encouragement, players translated game materials and conversations surrounding the mystery into seven additional languages.

- *Ensure that the story and the notion of interacting in a game with geographically dispersed players is appropriate to the brand's image and its target audience.*

  McDonald's is a global company; the Olympics is a global event; The Lost Ring took place in multiple countries and several languages. Although the story did not directly relate to the brand's positioning strategy as a global restaurant, it spoke to McDonald's commitment to the Olympics, a global presence, and the notion of coming together as one.

- *Don't overcommercialize the ARG.* Most ARGs are brand-sponsored and ARG enthusiasts understand this. Still, players want to immerse themselves in a mystery. If the ARG unfolds like a consumer-interactive advertisement, it will offend the ARG community and much of the value will be lost.

  McDonald's followed this principle in The Lost Ring. No mention of McDonald's sponsorship was revealed in the game. Only press coverage of the game as it developed as a global phenomenon eventually revealed the game's actual sponsor. Thus, The Lost Ring was a dark play ARG.

- *Commit to the ARG and its management.* Though the expense is minimal compared to many advertising options, it can be a substantial portion of a brand's ad budget. ARGs take time and continued involvement and management as the story unfolds. The pace of the story may need to be revised, new scenes may need to be developed, responses to player actions may be necessary—the game requires active management throughout. Consequently, brands generally use an agency with ARG experience such as 42 Entertainment, Mind Candy, and AKQA.

  For The Lost Ring, McDonald's worked with AKQA to manage the creative process and run the game. A recognized pioneer and innovator, AKQA has collected more than 100 major awards including the Cannes Lion Grand Prix and was named Agency of the Year three times in 2010 and an "Innovation All-Star" by Fast Company. Its expertise is apparent in The Lost Ring, as the creation and execution was a complex process involving teams at AKQA, lead game designer Jane McGonigal, the International Olympics Committee, and video production house PostPanic.[36]

- *Measure the effectiveness of the ARG based on the objectives for the promotional campaign, not just based on game participation, site visits, and other traffic-based statistics.*

  The Lost Ring official website earned 4.8 million visits. Participants included more than 2.9 million people in 110 countries. The story of the ARG generated tens of millions in impressions in the press in such outlets as The New York Times, USA Today, The Wall Street Journal, and Brandweek. In terms of marketing objectives, McDonald's favorability ratings among customers increased by 6.1 percent.

Chapter Summary

What are the characteristics of social games and gamer segments?

A social game is a multiplayer, competitive, goal-oriented activity with defined rules of engagement and online connectivity among a community of players. Most social games include a few key elements such as leaderboards, achievement badges or buddy lists that allow players compare their progress with other players. Traditionally we distinguished gamers as either casual or hardcore, depending on how much time they spent playing and how important the games were to them. This distinction is blurring as more "mainstream" players get involved. Today there are many women and older people who are avid gamers in addition to the base of young, male players.

How can social media marketers use social games to meet branding objectives?

An organization may choose to promote its message in an existing game property. In these cases the brand can advertise in and around the game using display advertising and product placements, sponsor aspects of the game, and integrate the brand into game play. In addition, a brand can take an even bigger step and develop its own customized advergame that delivers a more focused and pervasive branded message.

Why are social games an effective tool for marketing?

Players tend to be in a receptive mood when gaming and branding efforts result in more positive brand attitudes. In addition, it's possible to finely target users because most games attract a fairly distinct type of player. And, it's relatively inexpensive to use this medium, brand exclusivity is available (where a sponsor is the sole advertiser in a gaming environment), and metrics are available to measure just how well the game works to attract players.

What are the characteristics of alternate reality games?

ARGs begin with a scripted scenario. However, the game changes as the network of gamers participates in the game by discovering clues, sharing information with others, and literally changing the structure and plot of the game with their responses. The games unfold over multiple forms of media and utilize many types of game elements, each tailored to specific media platforms. ARGs may utilize websites (story sites and social networking sites), telephones, email, outdoor signage, t-shirts, television, radio play, and more to reveal story clues, compose scenes, and unite gamers.

What are the advantages and disadvantages of using alternate reality games as a marketing communications channel?

ARGs are ideally suited to social media because it would be impossible to solve the puzzle alone. Because players from around the world participate, online communication is a necessary component to play. The complexity of the game and the desire to help to solve the unraveling mystery insures that players will engage with the application at a high level. On the other hand, those who are not motivated to get so involved will not persevere long enough to learn what happens or to explore more about the brand that sponsors the game. ARGs are best-suited for brands that want to reach people who are willing to invest the time to engage in this kind of activity.

Key Terms

achievement badges
action games
advergame
alternate reality game (ARG)
augmented reality (AR)
back story
cadet narrative
casual gamer
casual games
collective detective
core games
counterarguing
curtain
dark marketing
dark play ARG
display ads
dynamic ads
first-person shooter (FPS)
forward story

game clutter
game console
genre
gold farmers
hardcore gamer
immersive fiction
in-game advertising
in-game immersive advertising
internalization
leaderboards
lurkers
meaning transfer model
milieu
MMORPG
mode
narrative transportation theory
performative
platform
plot placement

product placement
puppet master
puzzle games
QR code
rabbit hole
role-playing game (RPG)
rubberneckers
screen placements
script placements
simulation games
social game
static ads
steganography
strategy games
TINAG
trail
transactional advertising
transference effect
transmedia social games

Review Questions

1. How do casual gamers differ from hardcore gamers? Are social gamers casual, a hybrid of casual and hardcore, or a new segment of gamer all together?
2. What are the four major game genres? Provide examples of each. What is the distinguishing characteristic associated with each genre?
3. What makes a game social? Explain the characteristics of social games.
4. Explain the differences between pre-roll, post-roll, and interlevel in-game advertising.
5. What is an advergame? How do we distinguish it from other social games?
6. How is brand integration and immersive in-game advertising different from other forms of branding in social games?
7. Define transactional advertising and provide an example.
8. Why is the entry clue to an alternate reality game called a rabbit hole? What term refers to the game's writer and director? Why are lurkers and rubberneckers just as valuable to brand sponsors as players?
9. What is augmented reality? What role does the QR code play in enabling AR? What devices are used to unlock the codes?

Exercises

1. Are branded offers in social games ethical? Choose a side and debate this issue with a classmate. Then post your opinions and using polldaddy.com (or another social polling tool) find out what your social graph thinks of this common practice.
2. Choose a social game to play. As you interact with the game, keep a journal of your experience. In particular, note the advertising and branded components and your reactions to them. How does your experience affect your attitude toward the brands?
3. Choose three people you know who play social games. Interview them about the time they spend online as they play social games. Have they responded to branded offers? Write a blog post on their brand experience in social games and their resulting perceptions of the brand.
4. Visit unfiction.com or argn.com to see what ARGs are playing now. Explore one of the current games. Is it associated with a brand (or is it a dark play ARG, with the brand yet to be identified)? Make a list of non-entertainment brands that could use an ARG to tell their story and immerse their brand fans.
5. Visit our website to learn more about *The Lost Ring* and Adidas' use of augmented reality through our shared videos.

Notes

1. "New Survey Reveals Social Gaming Phenomenon in U.S. and U.K.," *PopCap*, February 17, 2010, http://popcap.mediaroom.com/index.php?s=43&item=149, accessed December 21, 2010.
2. Dena Cassella, "What is Augmented Reality?," *Digital Trends*, November 3, 2009, www.digitaltrends.com/mobile/what-is-augmented-reality-iphone-apps-games-flash-yelp-android-ar-software-and-more/, accessed July 13, 2010.
3. Barb Dybwad, "Augmented Reality Turns Show into Game Controller," *Mashable*, January 25, 1010, http://mashable.com/2010/01/25/augmented-reality-adidas-shoes/, accessed July 13, 2010.
4. *Essential Facts about the Computer and Video Game Industry*, Entertainment Software Association, www.theesa.com/facts/pdfs/ESA_Essential_Facts_2010.PDF, accessed July 12, 2010.
5. "Social Gaming Shows Potential," *eMarketer*, June 10, 2010, www.emarketer.com/Article.aspx?R=1007746, accessed December 20, 2010.
6. "What Americans Do Online: Social Media and Games Dominate Activity," *NielsenWire*, August 2, 2010, http://blog.nielsen.com/nielsenwire/online_mobile/what-americans-do-online-social-media-and-games-dominate-activity/, accessed December 21, 2010.
7. Paul Verna, "Video Game Advertising: Getting to the Next Level," *eMarketer*, April 2007, www.emarketer.com/Reports/All/Emarketer_2000386.aspx?src=report_head_info_site earch, accessed December 10, 2007.
8. Thomas Apperley, "Genre and Game Studies: Toward a Critical Approach to Video Game Genres," *Simulation & Gaming* 37, no. 1 (2006): 6–23.

9. *Interactive Advertising Bureau, Game Advertising Platform Status Report: LET THE GAMES BEGIN,* October 2007, http://www.iab.net/media/file/games-reportv4.pdf, accessed August 8, 2011.

10. Thomas Apperley, "Genre and Game Studies: Toward a Critical Approach to Video Game Genres," *Simulation & Gaming* 37, no. 1 (2006): 6–23.

11. Thomas Apperley, "Genre and Game Studies: Toward a Critical Approach to Video Game Genres," *Simulation & Gaming* 37, no. 1 (2006): 6–23.

12. Drew Elliott, "Opportunities for Brands in Social Games," *Ogilvy PR Blog,* May 2010, http://blog.ogilvypr.com/2010/05/opportunities-for-brands-in-social-games/, accessed July 12, 2010.

13. "In-Game Advertising Research Proves Effectiveness for Brands Across Categories and Game Titles," June 3, 2008, http://www.microsoft.com/presspass/press/2008/jun08/06-03adeffectivenesspr.mspx, accessed August 8, 2011.

14. Cristel Russell, "Toward a Framework of Product Placement," in J. W. Alba and J. W. Hutchinson, Eds., *Advances in Consumer Research* 25 (1998): 357–362.

15. Joshua Norman, "Tiger Woods Dropped from Cover of His Own Video Game," *CBSNews.com,* January 6, 2011, www.cbsnews.com/8301-31751_162-20027578-10391697.html, accessed January 7, 2011.

16. Barbara Lippert, "Madden NFL 11: The Ad Game," *AdWeek,* July 11, 2010, www.adweek.com/aw/content_display/special-issues/gaming-special/e3if93da65e51c14c3db939afdb809f3016, accessed July 12, 2010.

17. Andiara Petterle, "Reaching Latinos Through Virtual Goods," *Media Post,* June 10, 2010, www.mediapost.com/publications/?fa=Articles.showArticle&art_aid=129857, accessed July 13, 2010.

18. Gurbaksh Chahal, "There's Real Money in Virtual Goods," *Tech Crunch,* June 23, 2010, http://techcrunch.com/2010/06/23/real-money-virtual-goods/, accessed July 13, 2010.

19. Michael Arrington, "Scamville: The Social Gaming Ecosystem of Hell," *TechCrunch,* October 31, 2009, http://techcrunch.com/2009/10/31/scamville-the-social-gaming-ecosystem-of-hell/, accessed July 12, 2010.

20. "Public Enemies Week on Zynga's Mafia Wars," *AppsSavvy,* www.appssavvy.com/publicenemies/, accessed July 11, 2010.

21. David Barboza, "Ogre to Slay? Outsource It to Chinese," *New York Times,* December 9, 2005, www.nytimes.com/2005/12/09/technology/09gaming.html, accessed July 18, 2010; Nicolas Yee,

"Yi-Shan-Guan," *The Daedalus Project,* January 4, 2006, http://chinesegoldfarmers.com/, accessed July 18, 2010.

22. Dawn Anfuso, "Why You Need to Get In The Game," *iMedia Connection,* July 12, 2007, www.imediaconnection.com/content/15741.asp, accessed December 10, 2007.

23. Jack Loechner, "Advergaming," Research Brief, Center for Media Research, Media Post, October 24, 2007, http://blogs.mediapost.com/research_brief/?p=1550, accessed December 10, 2007.

24. Zachary Glass, "The Effectiveness of Product Placement in Video Games," *Journal of Interactive Advertising* 8, no. 1 (2007), http://jiad.org/vol8/no1/glass/index.htm, accessed December 10, 2007.

25. Grant McCracken, "Who is the Celebrity Endorser? Cultural Foundations of the Endorsement Process," *Journal of Consumer Research* 16, no. 3 (1989): 310–321.

26. Jennifer Escalas, "Imagine Yourself in the Product: Mental Stimulation, Narrative Transportation, and Persuasion," *Journal of Advertising* 33, no. 1 (2004): 37–48.

27. Unfiction, Unfiction glossary, www.unfiction.com/glossary, accessed July 18, 2010.

28. Jon Zahlaway, "Nine Inch Nails' Year Zero Plot Hits the Web," *LiveDaily,* February 22, 2007, www.livedaily.com/news/11570.html?t=102, accessed December 10, 2007.

29. Jon Zahlaway, "Nine Inch Nails' Year Zero Plot Hits the Web," *LiveDaily,* February 22, 2007, www.livedaily.com/news/11570.html?t=102, accessed December 10, 2007.

30. www.unfiction.com/glossary, accessed July 18, 2010.

31. David Kiley, "Advertising Of, By and For the People," *BusinessWeek Online,* July 25, 2005, www.businessweek.com/magazine/content/05_30/b3944097.htm, accessed July 13, 2010.

32. Jim Hanas, "Games People Play," *Creativity* 14, no. 1 (2006): 14.

33. David Kiley, "Advertising Of, By and For the People," *BusinessWeek Online,* July 25, 2005, www.businessweek.com/magazine/content/05_30/b3944097.htm, accessed July 13, 2010.

34. Material provided by Julie Channing, head planner at AKQA for *The Lost Ring* campaign.

35. Grant McCracken, "Transmedia: Branding's New Thing," *This Blog Sits at the Intersection of Anthropology and Economics,* December 9, 2005, http://cultureby.com/2005/12/transmedia_bran_2.html, accessed January 17, 2011.

36. Ken Liebeskind, AKQA's Trailers Launch the Lost Ring Game for McDonald's," *Shoot Online,* April 9, 2008, www.shootonline.com/go/news-view.ev-web2-2772548-1207586779-2.AKQA-s-Trailers-Launch-The-Lost-Ring-Game-For-McDonald-s.html, accessed April 15, 2008.

Social Commerce

LearningObjectives

When you finish reading this chapter you will be able to answer these questions:

1 What is the relationship between social commerce and e-commerce?

2 How do ratings and reviews provide value for consumers and e-retailers?

3 How do social shopping applications and tools affect consumers as they move through the consumer decision-making process?

4 What are the psychological factors that influence social shopping?

GO

From Chapter 8 of *Social Media Marketing*, First Edition. Tracy L. Tuten, Michael R. Solomon.
Copyright © 2013 by Pearson Education, Inc. All rights reserved.

The Zone of Social Commerce

When was the last time you went shopping? Yesterday? Last weekend? Did you go alone or with someone else, or maybe even with a group? Shopping is at its heart a social activity. Doing it with others makes the activity more enjoyable—even when your shopping buddies don't agree with your choices. Our shopping companions, known among marketers as **purchase pals**, help us to think through our alternatives and make a decision. They validate the choices we make. When we don't have a purchase pal with us, we might turn to surrogate pals like sales associates and other shoppers. Shopping together can be a shared activity that strengthens our relationships with others, but it also reduces the risks we associate with making purchase decisions. Perhaps this has been one reason for the prevalence of in-store shopping over online shopping. E-commerce may finally have a solution for those who hate to shop alone but who would still rather browse online while they hang out at home in their pajamas: social commerce.

Social commerce is a subset of e-commerce (i.e., the practice of buying and selling products and services via the Internet). It uses social media applications to enable online shoppers to interact and collaborate during the shopping experience and to assist retailers and customers during the process.[1] Encompassing online ratings and reviews, numerous shopping related apps, deal sites and deal aggregators, and social shopping malls and storefronts, social commerce is the fourth zone of social media (Figure 1).

Historically, wired shoppers have relied heavily on the Internet as an information source during the decision process—but many then turn to offline stores to complete the purchase. Increasingly though, these online researchers are converting to online shoppers—today over 82 percent of those who conduct research online also shop online.[2] Consequently, e-commerce continues to make big strides. Online sales growth surpasses that of traditional retail growth, and by 2014, e-commerce sales in the United States are expected to reach $223.9 billion. Online shopping offers many benefits to shoppers, such as the ability to comparison shop easily and efficiently, convenience, enhanced selection, and cost savings. With advances in social commerce, online shopping can finally offer a shared experience too—the experience of social shopping.

Figure 1

**The Social
Commerce Zone**

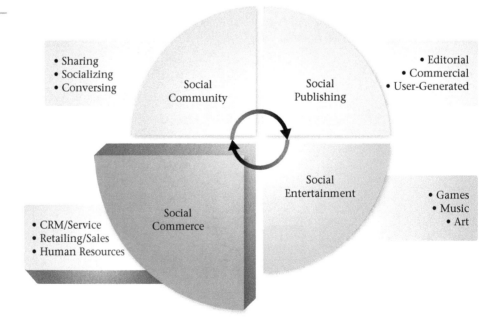

174

Wherever this icon appears in the margin, please go to the website **www.zonesofsmm.com** for an example of the topic discussed.

At its core, **social shopping** refers to situations where consumers interact with others during a shopping event. Of course, just as in the physical world this changes the dynamic of shopping because it opens the door for others to influence our decisions.

Social media applications allow us to share product information electronically; easily post opinions and access the opinions of others; and communicate with friends, family, and associates about shopping decisions without regard to place or time. Whenever consumers navigate product information online using social commerce tools, such as bookmarking their favorite products, e-mailing product summaries, and subscribing to RSS feeds of other users' favorite product lists, they are social shopping. Social shopping provides utility to our shopping experience because it lowers our perceived risk. We can feel more certain, by using social shopping tools, that we got the best price, made the best choice, and know whether our friends will approve of our decision. It's the digital answer to our desires as consumers to shop with others—but with the added convenience and power of online technologies.

Social Commerce: The Digital Shopping Experience

It's a cold day in mid-December, and David is spending some time on Facebook reading about his friends' recent activities. A social ad for 1-800-Flowers appears on the side of his news feed that promotes flowers as a Christmas gift and provides an endorsement that thousands of people like 1-800-Flowers. Remembering that he hasn't yet sent a Christmas gift to his grandmother in Texas, David gets a brainstorm—he really doesn't have the time to spend hours at the mall looking for something for Grammy. He clicks the ad to reach 1-800-Flowers' Facebook page. There he sees a promotion for 20 percent off his order if he "likes" the page and a "Shop Now" call to action. With a click of the Shop Now button on the Shop tab of 1-800-Flowers' page, David can browse flower selections and price points. Not sure whether 1-800-Flowers is the best choice, David first visits 1-800-Flowers' Wall. Comments from past customers fill the page, and David can read the posts from satisfied and dissatisfied customers along with the responses from company service representatives. He chooses three arrangements he likes, but then he posts a message to his two sisters to help him decide which is best. They both respond within 10 minutes (and as usual, they both pick the same one!). Now David is confident he's got a winner, so he returns to the Shop tab where he chooses the arrangement and completes his transaction using Facebook Credits. Share technologies post to David's Wall—"David bought a holiday arrangement at 1-800-Flowers" and "David likes 1-800-Flowers." Once the flowers arrive, David plans to return to the page to share a review on 1-800-Flowers' Wall. From there, the cycle begins again as another individual sees shared posts about the brand and/or social ads. Figure 2 illustrates how David's actions map to the consumer decision-making process—and he went through the whole process without leaving Facebook!

We all know some people who shop simply for the sport of it, and others (like David) whom we have to drag to a mall. Shopping is how we acquire needed products and services, but social motives for shopping also are important. Shopping is an activity that we can perform for either utilitarian (functional or tangible) or hedonic (pleasurable or intangible) reasons.[3]

A shopper's motivation influences the type of shopping environment that will be attractive or annoying; for example, a person who wants to locate and buy something quickly may find loud music, bright colors, or complex layouts distracting, whereas someone who is there to browse may enjoy the sensory stimulation.[4] How such environments translate to social commerce shopping experiences is still unknown. But we can still see where these motives may play a role in social shopping. Hedonic shopping motives include social experiences (the social venue as a community gathering place), opportunities to share common interests with like-minded others, the sense of importance we experience when others wait on us, and the thrill of the hunt.[5] After all, the role of hunter/gatherer has long been ingrained in the human psyche.

Figure 2

Social Commerce on Facebook and the Customer Decision-Making Process

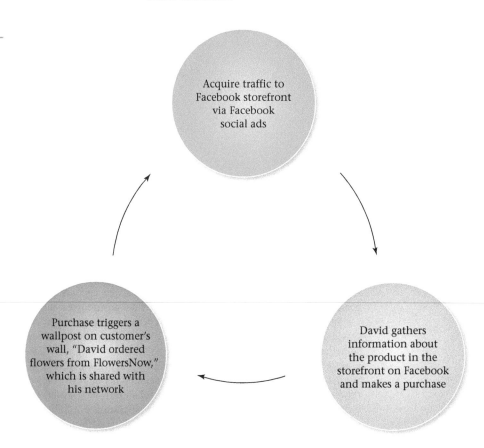

Surely too there are utilitarian motives at play for social shoppers. E-commerce enabled shoppers to find alternatives and a wealth of pricing information with the click of a mouse. Consumers benefit from the convenience and ease of shopping with more choices and better information. Social commerce further enables shoppers to access opinions, recommendations, and referrals from others within and outside of their own social graphs, again potentially improving the ability for consumers to make the most rational and efficient decisions. But there's one more benefit offered by social commerce that was missing from e-commerce—the social aspect of shopping that people got when they shopped in person with their purchase pals. Social commerce provides that missing ingredient to the e-commerce equation. For example, David trusted his sisters' judgment a lot more than his own when choosing a gift for Grammy (though he would probably consult other purchase pals before he buys a new gaming console).

It was only a few years ago that retailers scrambled to figure out how to present their store offerings online and worried as to the effect of e-commerce on their traditional business models. Now, things are changing again as they assess the influence of consumer desires to shop online socially.

Social Commerce and the Shopping Process

At the end of the day, *shopping online is still shopping*. Sure, the way we locate and purchase products may not look the same—but the successful marketer understands that our basic shopping orientations (e.g., to obtain a needed product or service, to connect with others, to stimulate our senses, etc.) are the same as our ancient ancestors (like those who lived in the 20th century and before) possessed.

Furthermore, it's helpful to break down the process of shopping in terms of the stages of consumer decision making. Though some decisions may be made in fewer steps, important decisions require five steps; we move from problem recognition to information search to alternative evaluation to purchase, and finally to post-purchase evaluation. When we look at these stages we realize that what seems at first to be an "obvious" and quick decision ("throw something in the cart") is in fact a lot more complicated. On the bright side, many current social media applications are out there to help consumers make it through each of these stages.

So social commerce is a part of e-commerce, and it leverages social media to aid in the exchange process between buyers and sellers. That seems straightforward enough, but social media is sufficiently complex and broad to influence e-commerce in all five of the consumer decision-making stages. Before we illustrate how social commerce can influence consumers in the stages of the decision-making process, we'll introduce you to the basic components and applications in social commerce.

Learning
Objective **2**

Ratings and Reviews

The first dimension of social commerce is ratings and reviews. **Ratings** are simply scores that people, acting in the role of critics, assign to something as an indicator. The rating may reflect perceived quality, satisfaction with the purchase, popularity, or some other variable. Ratings typically are combined with reviews. **Reviews** are assessments with detailed comments about the object in question. They explain and justify the critic's assigned rating and provide added content to those viewing the content.

The publication of consumer opinions is a powerful and influential form of user-generated content. In fact, one could claim online word-of-mouth communication of product reviews and opinions is the most influential form of user-generated content. Consumer opinions arise as typical people are empowered to express themselves and share these expressions with others, and as typical consumers seek out unbiased, credible information to aid in decision making.

Not all ratings and reviews are user-generated. Some sites provide ratings and reviews from experts. For instance, the popular movie review site *Rotten Tomatoes* summarizes professional reviews of newly released movies and DVDs. However, what really matters when it comes to ratings and reviews is the opinion of other shoppers. Arnold Brown, a writer for *The Futurist*, captured the phenomenon, calling it "zagating the marketplace."[6] Just as the Zagat guide to hotels and restaurants polls actual diners and hotel patrons to create its ratings and reviews, online reviews and ratings provide a venue for people who are experts by virtue of their experience to share their opinions.

The estimated usage of ratings and reviews among online consumers during the buying process varies substantially from source to source, ranging from 42 to more than 70 percent.[7] As you might expect, a relatively small percentage of people also contribute reviews and ratings—perhaps under 25 percent of online consumers.[8] Still, ratings and reviews are the most desired feature people say they look for in a retail website. The *2010 Social Shopping Study* by the e-Tailing Group and Power Reviews found that 72 percent of respondents said customer reviews and ratings were the most important capability for a retail website.[9] In fact, 49 percent of those respondents cited a lack of user-generated customer reviews as a reason they left a website during a product search.

Why are ratings and reviews so important? They serve as a source of research during the information search and evaluation of alternatives stage of the buying process and as a tool to verify a decision before purchase. In addition, users may post reviews and ratings during the post-purchase evaluation stage.

Although shoppers may not always complete their purchases online, many do turn to the Internet to gather information prior to making a purchase. Researching products online makes sense—it can save time, increase confidence, and reduce risk that might be associated with the purchase. It also ensures better, more credible information. Beside using opinions early in the decision process, consumers may also use ratings and reviews as a form of validation just prior to purchase. This is called **verification.**[10] That's right—today buyers seek out information online early in the purchase process, and then many return to validate the decision. Many later also write reviews and rate products in the post-purchase stage. Because reviews are so influential, retailers are inviting customers to rate their experience and write a review soon after products are delivered.

When researching products online, most shoppers start with a search engine (this is why search engine optimization is critical!) and also use retailer sites and brand sites for information. *The 2010 Social Shopping Study* found that customer reviews were more influential than any other source of information on buying behavior—64 percent of shoppers said they spent 10 minutes or more reading reviews prior to making a purchase.[11] Nearly 40 percent reported reading eight or more reviews. In other words, this isn't a casual behavior. Shoppers are intensely studying reviews to improve their purchase decisions.

Of the sources of social media that might influence buyer behavior, ratings and reviews were used more than any other source. Consumers say they trust information provided online by other consumers more than television, magazine, radio, or Internet advertising, more than sponsorships, and more than recommendations from salespeople or paid endorsers.

The Value of a Review   Ratings and reviews are not always useful. Companies like Amazon ask users to rate the reviews according to helpfulness to improve the quality of reviews. *Helpfulness ratings* (yes—a rating of a rating!) give a quality indicator to other users before they invest time reading and also provide feedback to those who complete reviews. What goes into a valuable rating and review? Ratings are a **heuristic**; a mental shortcut consumers use to help them with decision making. For instance, if you want to choose a restaurant near the amphitheatre where you are attending a concert this weekend, you might pull up all the restaurants in the area and then choose the one with the highest average rating. Reviews provide more detailed information for those who want to evaluate the choice at a deeper level. Consequently, a good review should include product information such as features and specifications, an overall impression of the product with a positive or negative judgment, a list of pros and cons, experience with the product, and a final recommendation.[12] With these components, the review will have sufficient information for the readers to judge relevance and credibility and apply the content to their purchase situation.

Benefits to E-Retailers   Product opinions affect shoppers, but that isn't the only way they impact the marketing process. Online reviews generate increased sales by bringing in new customers. Further, people who write reviews tend to shop more frequently and to spend more online than those who do not write reviews. Those who review products make up just a quarter of online shoppers, but they account for a third of online sales.[13] And consumers are willing to pay a price premium for products with higher ratings.[14] For e-retailers, this means that it makes good business sense to host rating and review features. Ratings and reviews also enhance organic search traffic to the website. Organic search results improve because reviewers tend to use the same keywords (tags) in their product descriptions that searchers will use. Petco, a pet supplies retailer, found that having customer reviews on its website generated five times as many site visits as any previous advertising campaign. Those who browsed Petco's Top Rated Products had a 49 percent higher conversion rate than the site average and an average order amount that was 63 percent higher than the site average.[15]

Reviews result in better site stickiness—customers reading reviews will stay at a retail site longer than they would otherwise. They also can enhance the effectiveness of offline promotional strategies. For example, Rubbermaid added review comments from its website to the content included in its freestanding inserts. When reviews were included, coupon utilization increased 10 percent.[16] Lastly, the reviews and opinion posts become a source of research data for the business, highlighting consumer opinions in a frank yet unobtrusive fashion. Some businesses believe the data resulting from online reviews to be more valuable than data from focus group research. Businesses can learn whether consumers like a competitor's brand better and why, how consumers react to positive or negative press, what stories are being spread about the brand, and which customers are being evangelical and which ones are acting as "brand terrorists."

What does this mean for marketers? First, marketers must ensure high standards when it comes to product quality and service if they wish to survive in the world of social reviews. It is so easy for anyone to tell everyone about his or her brand experiences, whether good or bad. That means those experiences had better be good—very good! Those that fail will have their sordid story broadcast to the social world as customers submit reviews and those reviews are shared via social networks. Second, brands should embrace, not hide—because really, online there is no place to hide—from consumer opinions. Instead, organizations can engage in word-of-mouth marketing by actively giving people reasons to talk about the brand while facilitating the conversations. The Word of Mouth Marketing Association (WOMMA) identifies five key components to word-of-mouth marketing on its website, www.womma.org, all of which can be applied to managing online product opinions for brand value:[17]

- Educating people about your products and services;
- Identifying people most likely to share their opinions;
- Providing tools that make it easier to share information;
- Studying how, where, and when opinions are being shared; and
- Listening and responding to supporters, detractors, and neutrals.

In other words, marketers should encourage the conversation by informing consumers about the brand, offering consumers a forum for expressing opinions about the brand and responding (making the communication two-way) to comments consumers make on the forum and elsewhere. Customers can be invited to offer reviews, resulting in more engagement and the propagation of positive word-of-mouth communication about the brand. Perhaps most important is the final component of word-of-mouth marketing—listening. There is valuable information about the need for product improvements like product features and service quality embedded in ratings and reviews.

Many e-retailers encourage reviews on their own sites, using the reviews and ratings as a merchandising tool. But really, ratings and reviews can occur in almost any area of social media— on social networks, blogs, microblogs, review sites, review sections of e-commerce sites—anywhere there is a comment box. One research company recently reported that "53% of people on Twitter recommend companies and/or products in their tweets."[18]

Why Don't All E-Retailers Offer Reviews and Ratings on Their Sites?   Aside from the problem that marketers and advertisers have overlooked their value and influence, the most commonly cited reason given for not allowing online reviews on sites is the fear that dissatisfied customers will use the review feature as a venue to *flame* a brand. Given the old adage that negative word-of-mouth communication is more damaging than positive word-of-mouth communication is beneficial, some retailers have erred on the side of caution when it comes to offering a review feature. The ratio of negative to positive reviews found on various sites suggests that this fear is unfounded. Macy's reported that of the more than 9,000 product reviews posted on www.macys.com, 72 percent of them were positive. Bazaarvoice, a firm that provides a customer review and rating service for e-tailers, reports that 80 percent of its user-generated reviews are positive.[19]

In reality, retailers can benefit from negative reviews and should welcome them. Consumers want to see negative reviews to be able to accurately assess the degree of product risk they face when purchasing. They seek to minimize perceived performance and financial risk associated with purchases. Negative reviews give them the information they need to assess risk. The negative reviews also enhance credibility. Consumers often assume that if the reviews seem too good to be true, they probably are. Lastly, negative reviews give valuable information to the retailer on products that should be improved, augmented, or discontinued. The other primary deterrent for e-retailers is more operational in nature. There are challenges related to acquiring and managing reviews and the review process as well as site maintenance. Companies such as Bazaarvoice and PowerReviews provide solutions; they service retailers by providing the technology to capture and display customer feedback.

Best Practices to Leverage Social Reviews and Ratings Ultimately, it's important to remember that users are reading online reviews because they want to know what people like themselves think of a product. They must be able to trust those reviews; if they can't, the reviews won't be effective. To make the most of the opportunity, marketers should develop a social commerce approach with these characteristics:

- Authenticity: Accept organic word-of-mouth, whether positive or negative.
- Transparency: Acknowledge opinions that were invited, incentivized, or facilitated by the brand.
- Advocacy: Enable consumers to rate the value of opinions offered on the site.
- Participatory: Encourage consumers to contribute posts.

THE DARK SIDE OF SOCIAL MEDIA

Thousands of consumers use social media sites to "vent" about bad experiences they've had with businesses—but can these negative reviews come back to bite them? Justin Kurtz, a student at Western Michigan University, found out the hard way that they can. Justin had a permit to park in his apartment lot, but a towing company hauled away his car anyway. To protest having to pay $118 to get his car back, Justin created a Facebook page he called "Kalamazoo Residents against T&J Towing." Within 2 days, 800 people had joined the group and many shared their own frustrating experiences with the company.

Oops. The towing company filed a defamation suit against the student. It claimed the site was hurting business and asked for $750,000 in damages. The company's attorney claimed Justin's permit wasn't visible and that his accusations had unfairly damaged his client's reputation. However, other lawyers labeled this as an example of a legal maneuver they call SLAPP—a strategic lawsuit against public participation. SLAPP traditionally refers to suits companies and governments use to intimidate critics; they are not necessarily expected to succeed but rather to force defendants to back down rather than face a long and expensive court battle. Many states have anti-SLAPP laws, and Congress is considering legislation to create a federal law banning these actions.

SLAPP lawsuits continue to be filed each year against people who testify at a city council meeting or write an angry letter to their local representative. Now, however, the focus is shifting to situations like Justin's, where negative comments are likely to be viewed by many more people. As one attorney who defends clients against suits based on negative online reviews observed, "In the past, if you criticized a business while standing around in a bar, it went no further than the sound of your voice." Now, however, "there's a potentially permanent record of it as soon as you hit 'publish' on the computer. It goes global within minutes."

Michigan doesn't have an anti-SLAPP law, and Justin's legal battle has turned him into a local celebrity. His Facebook page now has more than 12,000 members. He's countersuing the towing company, claiming that it is abusing the legal process. Justin commented, "There's no reason I should have to shut up because some guy doesn't want his dirty laundry out. It's the power of the Internet, man."[20]

- Reciprocity: Acknowledge the value of the opinions customers offer.
- Infectiousness: Make it easy for users to share reviews on blogs and social networking platforms.
- Sustainability: Online opinions are so influential because they live on in perpetuity. If a consumer tells a friend about a satisfying brand experience on the phone, the story once told is no longer retrievable or trackable. If the opinion is posted in a company-controlled review site (for instance, if you post a review of the leggings you bought from LegLuxe on its review area), the opinions can be moderated and the brand has an option not to publish. However, many reviews are posted in areas that are <u>not</u> the brand's owned media review site—then there's no shut-down option.

Social Shopping Applications and Tools

Social commerce and its consumer counterpart, social shopping, rely on reviews and ratings because consumers seek out information throughout the purchase process. Social commerce makes shopping collaborative—in some cases we can even see purchase decisions as crowdsourced solutions to consumer needs.

In addition to the information that consumers may seek out during the decision-making process, social commerce includes several tools and applications that aid in evaluation of alternatives and purchase, and also enhance the socialness of the online shopping experience. In other words, these applications help us to share information and opinions, organize product information, make decisions, and enjoy shopping together online. In this section, we'll discuss the types of tools available. However, keep in mind that these tools are expanding rapidly; just a few months ago, many of these tools did not exist. Developers are writing applications and widgets with increasing sophistication and creativity, ensuring that marketers and consumers can combine two popular online activities—socializing and shopping.

Recommendations and Referrals **Recommendations** and **referrals** are personalized product endorsements. Whereas ratings and reviews are visible to everyone who wishes to see them, recommendations and referrals originate from the recipient's social graph. This makes them more influential than reviews and ratings because they leverage the social capital of the referrer. In fact, a Harris Interactive poll found that 71 percent of respondents said recommendations from family and friends have substantial influence on their purchase decisions.[21] And while we tend to trust reviews from strangers, we are more trusting of recommendations from people we know; 90 percent in the survey said they trust an online recommendation from someone in their network, but just 70 percent trust reviews from unknown users.[22]

Recommendations from friends and family are all around us, and the prevalence of social media in the lives of wired consumers heightens our ability to share these opinions. WOMMA claims that the average consumer mentions specific brands in conversations with others more than 90 times a week.[23] Just imagine how those influence impressions can travel when shared via social networks. This number could increase as people use social media to seek out recommendations. A study from researchers at Penn State found that 20 percent of Twitter posts were from people asking for or providing product information.[24]

Recommendations and referrals can be simple or integrated in their execution. Facebook's "Like" button, now available on millions of external web pages, is a form of recommendation. When you click it, you publicly announce that you recommend the content on the page. While others can see the total number of Likes, anyone in your network can also see that you personally made the recommendation.

Referral Tools Marketers Can Use Marketers can develop integrated referral programs as part of their social media strategy. These work much like typical referral programs where friends refer friends, in exchange for premium benefits and offers. The referred friends also receive some form of special benefit such as access to scarce information or special deals.

Google has successfully used referral programs to encourage usage of its products. As it introduces a new service in beta, Google will issue a limited number of invitations. Those new users are then allowed a limited number of invitations they may share with others. The use of a referral program enhances the perceived value of the product while it also builds adoption through a credible network.

In addition to recommendation agents and referral programs, several more social commerce applications are useful to e-retailers:

- **Pick lists:** item lists such as wish lists and gift lists; pick lists usually also offer a sharing feature
- **Popularity filters:** filters that enable the shopper to show products by most popular, most viewed, most favorite, or most commented
- **Share Your Story:** tools for publishing customer testimonials; includes video testimonials and narratives submitted by customers

  User forums: group of people who meet online to communicate about products and help each other solve related problems

  Deal directories: collections of special offers; sometimes maintained and updated by user submissions
- **Deal feeds:** a stream of offers made by participating businesses to followers/friends
- **Group buy:** opportunities for people to join together to qualify for volume discounts; some communities have developed around the concept of group buy such as Groupon or LivingSocial
- **Geo-location promotions:** sales promotions including coupons and special offers delivered via geo-location services such as Gowalla and Foursquare
- **Social media storefronts:** applications that enable businesses to conduct transactions with customers from within social network sites; these work with applications like Payvment to complete transactions within the social networking site. In Facebook, payment can even be made in-network with Facebook Credits. Facebook Credits enable people to shop online much like PayPal.
  - Share and **ask your network** tools: share and query tools within e-commerce sites that enable one to post product information and ask friends for advice prior to purchase
  - **Shop together:** an application that allows shoppers to log in to an e-commerce site and then interact and collaborate throughout the e-commerce site; includes the ability to see purchase pals' movement throughout the site, discussion, and sharing
  - **User galleries:** a virtual gallery where users can share their creations, shopping lists, and wishlists; these exist outside of social commerce but may include galleries that feature products for sale
  - *Social bookmarking* for products: shopping-oriented bookmarking sites like Snipi enable online shoppers to bookmark products they like and share the lists with others
  - **Social shopping portals:** sites that enable shoppers to shop multiple stores (like when at a mall) using several social shopping tools

You can see from our discussion that there are social commerce implications at every stage of the consumer decision-making process. Table 1 summarizes the decision-making stages and illustrates some of these social media and social commerce tools that already are changing how we shop (but again, not *why* we shop!).

	Decision Stage	Social Commerce Tools
TABLE 1 **Social Commerce Tools for Purchase Decision Stages**	Problem Recognition	Social ads on social networking sites Shared endorsements from friends posted in activity streams Preprogrammed reminders in networks (e.g., Hallmark's Social Calendar) and on smartphones Location-based promotions (e.g., Shopkick, Foursquare) Social games (e.g., *FarmVille*) indicating need to level up
	Information Search	Comments (influence impressions) throughout social channels (opinions posted on a brand's Wall, tweets about an experience, etc.) Queries and responses within social networks (e.g., LinkedIn and Facebook) Ratings and reviews posted on sites (e.g., Yelp, Zagat, Citysearch) Product and pricing information available (QR readers, Google Goggles, and other apps—mobile and otherwise) Deal directories Wish lists, gift registries
	Evaluation of Alternatives	Bar code scanning/price comparisons Recommendations, testimonials, recommendation agents, and popularity filters ("ask your network" apps, video testimonials such as VideoGenie, and Top lists from retailers such as Amazon) Referrals
	Purchase	Shop within network options (e.g., Payvment, Social Storefront) Social stores and social shopping malls (e.g., Levi's) Micropayments (e.g., Facebook Credits) Social gift cards (e.g., Facebook Credits and participating retailers like Starbucks) E-couponing (and especially the new wave of group-oriented deal aggregators/coupon sites like Groupon)
	Post-Purchase	Share posts in activity streams Ratings and reviews on review sites Comments with networks and microblogs Reviews and product experiences posted on blogs

Learning
Objective **4**

The Psychology of Social Shopping

Social media marketers who want to win customers find it helpful to understand what we know more generally about the **psychology of influence**—the factors that make it more or less likely that people will change their attitudes or behavior based on a persuasive message In particular, some social shopping tools play to our **cognitive biases**. This term refers to the "shortcuts" our brains take when we process information. Unlike computers that impassively process data and produce the same result each time (when they work!), humans aren't so rational. Two people can perceive the same event and interpret it quite differently based on their individual histories, gender, and cultural biases. For example, our reactions to colors are partially "colored" by our society, so a North American might interpret a woman in a white dress as an "innocent bride" while an Asian might assume the same woman is going to a funeral since white is the color of death in some eastern cultures.

Cognitive biases are important when we look at purchase decisions, especially because they influence what we may pay attention to and how we interpret it. Even though consumers have access to more information than ever before when it comes to purchase decisions, they are also faced with the limitations of **bounded rationality**. Bounded rationality captures the quandary we face as humans when we have choices to make but are limited by our own cognitive capacity.[25] As consumers, we typically approach an identified need with information search followed by alternative evaluation. In a world of search engines and social media, though, our information search could potentially be limitless. With thousands of online retailers carrying products, millions of product reviews to sort through, and hundreds of "friends" to ask for recommendations, online commerce is fraught with **information overload**; there's simply too much data for us to handle.

When consumers are confronted with more complexity than they can manage comfortably, bounded rationality kicks in. We adjust to the overload by finding ways to make decisions without considering all the information for an optimal choice. Instead, we often **satisfice**—this means we expend just enough effort to make a decision that's acceptable but not necessarily the one that's "best." We call the shortcuts we use to simplify the process **heuristics**. This term describes "rules of thumb" such as "buy the familiar brand name" and "if it's more expensive it must be better."

This process of using heuristics to simplify the decision-making process is sometimes referred to as **thinslicing**, where we peel off just enough information to make a choice.[26] When we thinslice we ignore most of the available information; instead we "slice off" a few salient cues and use a mental rule of thumb to make intuitive decisions. Research on the psychology of influence identifies six major factors that help to determine how we will decide.[27] Let's review them and illustrate how social shopping applications and tools harness these heuristics.

Social Proof

We arrive at many decisions by observing what those around us do in similar situations. When a lot of people select one option (e.g., a clothing style or a restaurant), we interpret this popularity as **social proof** that the choice is the right one. There are several ways that marketers use social proof. For instance, identifying brands as the #1 choice, market leader, and so on, all point to evidence of social proof. In social commerce applications, tools can enable shoppers to see the social proof related to the product. As more people jump on the bandwagon a **herding effect** can occur.[28] Herd behavior occurs when people follow the behavior of others.[29]

Although in every age there certainly are those who "march to their own drummers," most people tend to follow society's expectations regarding how they should act and look (with a little improvisation here and there, of course). **Conformity** is a change in beliefs or actions as a reaction to real or imagined group pressure. In order for a society to function, its members develop **norms**, or informal rules that govern behavior. Without these rules, we would have chaos. Imagine the confusion if a simple norm such as stopping for a red traffic light did not exist.

We conform in many small ways everyday—even though we don't always realize it. Unspoken rules govern many aspects of consumption. In addition to norms regarding appropriate use of clothing and other personal items, we conform to rules that include gift-giving (we expect birthday presents from loved ones and get upset if they don't materialize), sex roles (men often pick up the check on a first date), and personal hygiene (our friends expect us to shower regularly).

We don't mimic others' behaviors all the time, so what makes it more likely we'll conform? These are some common culprits:[30]

- *Cultural pressures:* Different cultures encourage conformity to a greater or lesser degree. The American slogan "Do your own thing" in the 1960s reflected a movement away from conformity and toward individualism. In contrast, Japanese society emphasizes collective well-being and group loyalty over individuals' needs.
- *Fear of deviance:* The individual may have reason to believe that the group will apply *sanctions* to punish nonconforming behaviors. It's not unusual to observe adolescents who shun a peer who

is "different" or a corporation or university that passes over a person for promotion because she or he is not a "team player."

- *Commitment:* The more people are dedicated to a group and value their membership in it, the greater their motivation to conform to the group's wishes. Rock groupies and followers of TV evangelists may do anything their idols ask of them, and terrorists willingly die for their cause. According to the **principle of least interest,** the person who is *least* committed to staying in a relationship has the most power because that party doesn't care as much if the other person rejects him or her.[31] Remember that on your next date.

- *Group unanimity, size, and expertise:* As groups gain in power, compliance increases. It is often harder to resist the demands of a large number of people than only a few—especially when a "mob mentality" rules.

- **Susceptibility to interpersonal influence:** This trait refers to an individual's need to have others think highly of him or her. Consumers who don't possess this trait are *role-relaxed;* they tend to be older, affluent, and to have high self-confidence. Subaru created a communications strategy to reach role-relaxed consumers. In one of its commercials, a man proclaims, "I want a car …. Don't tell me about wood paneling, about winning the respect of my neighbors. They're my neighbors. They're not my heroes."[32]

In Table 2 you can see that several of the social shopping tools we covered earlier influence shoppers with social proof. Any content that we can share with others includes a social proof component. When you choose items for an online wish list and then share that list with your network of friends, you've given your friends social proof that the items listed are desirable. And, **testimonials** have long been a source of social proof that a product is the right one to choose. New social tools such as *VideoGenie* make it possible for customers to share their stories with video clips they record with their mobile phones or web cams. At one time, testimonials were limited to those of typical person endorsers, celebrity endorsers, or word-of-mouth communication. Now, users can share testimonials with a written story, comments, or with a video.

Authority

The second source of influence is authority. **Authority** persuades with the opinion or recommendation of an expert in the field. Whenever someone has expertise, whether that expertise comes from specialist knowledge and/or personal experience with the product or problem, we will tend to follow that person's advice. We can save time and energy on the decision by simply following the expert's recommendation. In advertising, we see the use of authority in ads for pain relievers that state "9 out of 10 doctors recommend." A doctor should know which medicine is best for pain, and the copy in the advertisement delivers this advice.

However, the use of authority is also in play when we see ads from someone who has experience with choosing a product for a specific functional need. For example, when Mia Hamm or Peyton Manning endorses Gatorade products, it's based not on credentials in the area of nutrition, but rather on their personal experience with needing a beverage that can rehydrate them efficiently. We listen to them because, as elite athletes, they ought to know which product is best. In the realm of social media, authority can be activated in several ways including referral programs, reviews (from experts as well as from existing customers who can speak with the voice of experience), branded services, and user forums.

Although citizen endorsers are not paid agents representing a brand, they do hold a position of authority in the minds of other consumers. Professional experts and reviewers, whether book critics, movie critics, doctors, or lawyers, have authority in specific, relevant product categories but so do citizen endorsers who have actually used the product. In other words, one's experience with the product serves as the source of authority.

TABLE 2

Social Shopping Tools and Sources of Influence

Social Shopping Tool	Social Proof	Authority	Scarcity	Affinity	Consistency	Reciprocity
"Ask your network"				*	*	
Brand butler services					*	*
Deal directories			*			
Deal feeds			*	*		*
Filters	*					
Group buy			*			*
Lists	*			*	*	
Recommendations	*	*		*	*	
Referral programs	*	*	*	*		*
Reviews	*	*			*	
Share tools	*			*		
Shop together				*		
Storefronts				*		
Testimonials	*	*				
User forums	*	*				*
User galleries	*			*		*
Geo-location promotions			*		*	

Affinity

Affinity, sometimes called "liking," means that people tend to follow and emulate those people whom they find attractive or otherwise desirable. If we like someone, we are more likely to say yes to their requests or to internalize their beliefs and actions as our own. We talked about how advertising often uses endorsers as a source of authority. They can also be used as a source of affinity. While Peyton Manning is an expert when it comes to whether Gatorade is the best choice for hydration during times of physical exertion, he is simply a likable celebrity when he endorses Timex watches. With social media, affinity is almost always present because the social shopping is tied to your social graph—to your friendships. Some tools that leverage affinity as a source of influence are "ask your network" tools that enable shoppers to request real-time recommendations from their friends, *deal feeds* (where friends share deals), shopping opportunities posted in friends' news feeds, pick lists, referral programs, sharing tools, and shop together tools.

Scarcity

We tend to instinctively want things more if we think we can't have them. That's the **principle of scarcity** at work. Whenever we perceive something as scarce, we increase our efforts to acquire it—even if that means we have to pay a premium for the item and buy it before we would otherwise have wanted. Marketing promotions that use scarcity as an influence tool might focus on deals that are time-sensitive, limited edition products, or products that are limited in supply. In social commerce, scarcity applications include deal feeds, news feeds with special offers, group buy tools, referral programs, and deal directories.

Reciprocity

The **rule of reciprocity** basically says that we have an embedded urge to repay debts and favors, whether or not we requested the help. Reciprocity is a common norm of behavior across cultures. We reciprocate kindnesses in part because we feel it is the fair and right thing to do (a social contract we have with others) and in part because reciprocation is important to well-functioning relationships. Reciprocity influences daily interactions all around us. It may be as simple as choosing a birthday present for someone for whom you wouldn't normally buy a present, but you do because they gave you a gift on your birthday. Marketers activate the rule of reciprocity to encourage consumers to choose a specific brand and to show loyalty to the brand over time. The key is to initiate an offer of some kindness, gift, or favor to the target audience. The targeted consumers will then feel compelled to respond in kind.

This is the basic principle behind the sales promotion technique of **sampling**; where a marketer offers a free trial of a product to consumers. The free trial illustrates the relative advantage of the product, but it also creates the perception of having received a gift in the minds of consumers. Consequently, sales of sampled products are higher than those of products that are not sampled. Some retailers send birthday and holiday cards to their top clients. Even something as simple as a greeting card can be perceived as a kindness that should be reciprocated. In social commerce, several tools can be perceived as a favor or kindness offered by the brand. These include deal feeds, group buy, referral programs, and user forums.

Consistency

People strive to be consistent with their beliefs and attitudes and with past behaviors. When we fail to behave in ways that are consistent with our attitudes and past behaviors, we feel **cognitive dissonance**, a state of psychological discomfort caused when things we know or do contradict one another. For example, a person may believe it's wrong or wasteful to gamble, yet be drawn to an online gambling site. To avoid this discomfort, we strive for consistency by changing one or more elements in the situation. Thus our gambler may decide that he or she is betting the house only due to "intellectual curiosity" rather than due to the thrill of betting. The need for consistency is a fairly broad source of influence because it can be activated around any attitude or behavior. Marketers may instigate the need for consistency with image ads, free trial periods, automated renewals, and membership offers. Some of the social shopping tools that include a consistency component include ask your network tools, social games, pick lists, share tools, shop together tools, reviews, forums, and galleries.

BYTES TO BUCKS

F-Commerce

Facebook offers consumer and business applications in every zone of social media. Whether you want a network for reaching out to old friends, an online site for gaming, a place to publish your pictures and videos, or a one-stop shop for your online shopping needs, Facebook has an offering in that zone. Industry insiders call Facebook's version of social commerce **F-commerce**. And chances are it will be one of the primary ways social consumers learn to shop with social tools. That's because Facebook has made the process of creating a social storefront easy for retailers. Using applications from Facebook-affiliated developers like Payvment and Storefront Social, retailers

can set up a Shop Tab on their Facebook pages in a matter of minutes. Facebook members don't need to leave the site to place their order. With Payvment and Facebook Credits, the entire transaction can take place without ever leaving Facebook.

Social shopping on Facebook is likely to be a winner for retailers. Facebook is a site that people don't want to leave—it's sticky enough that while brands are getting fans, they can't get the fans to leave to go to the e-commerce sites. Facebook's shopping-cart applications, like Payvment, help retailers take social media marketing beyond an approach that can build awareness and image to one that can direct store traffic and increase sales.

Benefits of Social Commerce

So far we've talked about the ways that marketers can approach social commerce. But what benefits does social commerce offer to marketers?

1. It enables the marketer to monetize the social media investment by boosting site and store traffic, converting browsers to buyers, and increasing average order value.
2. It solves the dilemma of social media ROI. Some criticize social media for its lack of accountability, but linking sales to social media eliminates this criticism.
3. Social commerce applications results in more data about customer behavior as it relates to the brand.
4. Social shopping applications enhance the customer experience. They make online shopping fun and functional, which should mean higher levels of customer loyalty and better long-term customer lifetime value.
5. Social shopping makes sharing brand impressions easy. The brands earn referral value with these easy to use word-of-mouth tools.
6. Brands can keep up with the competition, and maybe differentiate themselves from others in the e-commerce space.

Chapter Summary

What is the relationship between social commerce and e-commerce?

Social commerce is a subset of e-commerce (i.e., the practice of buying and selling products and services via the Internet). It uses social media and social media applications to enable online shoppers to interact and collaborate during the shopping experience and to assist retailers and customers during the process. Encompassing online ratings and reviews, applications, numerous shopping related apps, deal sites and deal aggregators, and social shopping malls and storefronts, social commerce is the last zone of social media.

How do ratings and reviews provide value for consumers and e-retailers?

Ratings are simply scores people, acting in the role of critic, assign to something as an indicator. The rating may reflect perceived quality, satisfaction with the purchase, popularity, or some other variable. Reviews are assessments with detailed comments about the object in question. They explain and justify the critic's assigned rating and provide added content to those viewing the content. Both serve as a source of research during the information search and evaluation of alternatives stage of the buying process and as a tool for verifying a decision before purchase. For retailers, reviews generate increased sales by bringing in new customers. Further, people who write reviews tend to shop more frequently and to spend more online than those who do not write reviews. Consumers are willing to pay a price premium for products with higher ratings too. Ratings and reviews also enhance organic search traffic to the website.

Explain how social shopping applications and tools affect the consumer decision-making process.

Table 1 indicates which social shopping applications primarily affect each stage of the consumer decision-making process. Many of these applications are influential in the information search and evaluation of alternatives stages, but to some extent social shopping is relevant throughout the process.

Describe the psychological factors that influence social shopping.

Research on the psychology of influence identifies six major factors that help to determine how we will decide; these can be applied to social commerce. These sources of influence include social proof, authority, affinity, scarcity, consistency, and reciprocity. Social proof occurs when we can see what others would choose or have chosen. Authority persuades with the opinion or recommendation of an expert in the field. Professional experts and reviewers, whether book critics, movie critics, doctors, or lawyers, have authority in specific, relevant product categories but so do citizen endorsers who have actually used the product. Affinity, sometimes called "liking," means that people tend to follow and emulate those people for whom they have an affinity. With social media, affinity is almost always present because the social shopping is tied to your social graph—to your friendships. We tend to instinctively want things more if we think we can't have them. That's the principle of scarcity at work. In social commerce, scarcity applications include deal feeds, news feeds with special offers, group buy tools, referral programs, and deal directories. The rule of reciprocity basically says that we have an embedded urge to repay debts and favors, whether or not we requested the help. In social commerce, several tools can be perceived as a favor or kindness offered by the brand. These include deal feeds, group buy, referral programs, and user forums. The final source of influence is our tendency to be consistent. People strive to be consistent with their beliefs and attitudes and with past behaviors. Some of the social shopping tools that include a consistency component include ask your network tools, social games, pick lists, share tools, shop together tools, reviews, forums, and galleries.

Key Terms

affinity	norms	Shop Together
ask your network	pick lists	social commerce
authority	popularity filters	social media
bounded rationality	principle of least interest	storefronts
cognitive biases	principle of scarcity	social proof
cognitive dissonance	psychology of influence	social shopping
conformity	purchase pal	social shopping portals
deal directories	ratings	susceptibility to interpersonal
deal feeds	recommendations	influence
geo-location promotions	referrals	testimonials
group buy	reviews	thinslicing
herding effect	rule of reciprocity	user forums
heuristics	sampling	user galleries
information overload	Share Your Story	verification

Review Questions

1. Explain the concept of purchase pals. Do you pull your offline and online purchase pals from the same pool of friends and family, or are they different somehow?
2. How is social commerce related to e-commerce? In the future, will e-commerce be able to exist without social applications? Why or why not?
3. What are the benefits that accrue to businesses implementing social shopping applications?
4. Explain the two dimensions of social commerce. How do they relate to the three pillars of social media?
5. How are reviews different from recommendations?
6. Why are ratings an important cue to include with a review site?
7. Explain the concept of bounded rationality as it relates to social shopping.
8. Which stage of the decision-making process is most affected by the dimensions of social commerce? Explain.
9. What is thinslicing?
10. Explain the six sources of influence prevalent in social commerce applications.
11. Is F-commerce the future of social commerce? Why or why not?

Exercises

1. Search Facebook for brands you like until you find one with a Social Storefront (Shop Tab). Explore the Shop Tab. Is a recommendation tool included in the page? Can you add products to your shopping cart and check out from within the page? What could make the Social Storefront more effective in your opinion?
2. Which is more influential—reviews from experts or reviews from customers? Explain.
3. Review the list of social shopping applications presented in the chapter and visit some of the sites that use these applications. Social shopping applications provide functionality for customers such as enhanced organization, price comparisons, risk reduction, and access to product information, but they also make the shopping experience more fun. Tag the list of applications based on the benefit the application provides—utility or fun. Which aspect of social shopping is most important to shoppers?

Notes

1. Adapted from "Simple Definition of Social Commerce (With Word Cloud & Definitive Definition List) Updated June 2010," *Social Commerce Today*, Nov 17, 2009, http://socialcommerce-today.com/social-commerce-definition-word-cloud-definitive-definition-list/, accessed July 28, 2010.
2. Jeffrey Grau, "US Retail E-Commerce Forecast: Room to Grow," *E-Marketer*, March 2010, www.emarketer.com/Reports/All/Emarketer_2000672.aspx, accessed July 28, 2010.
3. For a scale to assess these dimensions of the shopping experience, see Barry J. Babin, William R. Darden, and Mitch Griffin, "Work and/or Fun: Measuring Hedonic and Utilitarian Shopping Value," *Journal of Consumer Research* 20 (March 1994): 644–656.
4. Velitchka Kaltcheva and Barton Weitz, "When Should a Retailer Create an Exciting Store Environment?" *Journal of Marketing* 70 (2005): 107–118.
5. Mark J. Arnold and Kristy Reynolds, "Hedonic Shopping Motives," *Journal of Retailing* 79, no. 2 (2003): 77–95.
6. Arnold Brown, "The Consumer is the Medium," *Futurist* 42, no. 1 (January 2008).
7. Quoted in Social Commerce Statistics, *Bazaarvoice*, www.bazaarvoice.com/resources/stats, accessed July 30, 2010.
8. Reineke Reitsma, "The Data Digest: How Consumers Use Ratings and Reviews," *Forrester Blogs*, July 16, 2010, http://blogs.forrester.com/reineke_reitsma/10-07-16-data_digest_how_consumers_use_ratings_and_reviews, accessed July 29, 2010.
9. "2010 Social Shopping Study Reveals Changes in Consumers' Online Shopping Habits and Usage of Customer Reviews," *The e-Tailing Group*, May 3, 2010, www.e-tailing.com/content/?p=1193, accessed July 29, 2010.
10. "New Research Reveals Best Approach to Harness the Power of Online Influence on Purchase Behavior," *Cone*, www.coneinc.com/consumers-confirm-recommendations-online, accessed July 29, 2010.

11. *5 Social Shopping Trends Shaping The Future of Ecommerce*, Power Reviews and the eTailing Group, 2010, www.powerreviews.com/case-studies.php, accessed January 1, 2011.

12. Warren Barnes, "5 Components a Written Product Review Must Have," http://ezinearticles.com/?5-Components-a-Written-Product-Review-Must-Have&id=4160024, accessed July 29, 2010.

13. "Leading Retail Analyst Shows Retailers Can Gain Market Share Through Consumer-Generated Product Ratings and Reviews," *Bazaarvoice,* August 15, 2006, www.bazaarvoice.com/about/press-room/leading-retail-analyst-shows-retailers-can-gain-market-share-through-consumer-generated-product-rati, accessed January 1, 2011.

14. "Online Consumer-Generated Reviews Have Significant Impact on Offline Purchase Behavior," *comScore*, November 29, 2007, www.comscore.com/Press_Events/Press_Releases/2007/11/Online_Consumer_Reviews_Impact_Offline_Purchasing_Behavior, accessed July 30, 2010.

15. Don Davis, "Customer Reviews Help Cut Product Return Rate at Petco," *Internet Retailer*, June 26, 2007, www.internetretailer.com/2007/06/26/customer-reviews-help-cut-product-return-rate-at-petco, accessed July 30, 2010.

16. "Rubbermaid Products with Reviews Show Increased Revenues," *Bazaarvoice* Case Study, January 2010, www.bazaarvoice.com/resources/case-studies/rubbermaid-products-reviews-show-increased-revenues, accessed July 29, 2010.

17. "An Introduction to WOM Marketing with Definitions," *WOMMA*, http://womma.org/wom101/, accessed January 1, 2011.

18. Quoted in "ROI Research for Performance June 2010, Social Commerce Statistics," *Bazaarvoice*, www.bazaarvoice.com/resources/stats, accessed July 30, 2010.

19. "Leading Retail Analyst Shows Retailers Can Gain Market Share Through Consumer-Generated Product Ratings and Reviews," *Business Wire*, August 15, 2006.

20. Quoted in Dan Frosch, "Venting Online, Consumers Can Find Themselves in Court," *New York Times*, May 31, 2010, www.nytimes.com/2010/06/01/us/01slapp.html?pagewanted=1&ref=general&src=me, accessed January 5, 2011.

21. Quoted in "Social Commerce Statistics," *Bazaarvoice*, www.bazaarvoice.com/resources/stats, accessed July 30, 2010.

22. Jake Hird, "Online Consumers Trust Real People, Not Companies," *eConsultancy*, July 8, 2009, http://econsultancy.com/blog/4175-online-consumers-trust-real-people-not-companies, accessed July 30, 2010.

23. "Buyers Guide," *WOMMA, The Keller Fay Group*, http://buyers.womma.org/companies/keller-fay-group/, accessed July 30, 2010.

24. "20% of Tweets about Brands," *Social Media Today*, September 14, 2009, www.socialmediatoday.com/SMC/123878, accessed July 30, 2010.

25. Gerd Gigerenzer and Reinhard Selten, *Bounded Rationality: The Adaptive Toolbox* (Cambridge, MA: MIT Press, 2002).

26. Paul Marsden, "How Social Commerce Works: The Social Psychology of Social Shopping," *Social Commerce Today*, December 6, 2009, http://socialcommercetoday.com/how-social-commerce-works-the-social-psychology-of-social-shopping/, accessed July 29, 2010.

27. Robert Cialdini, *Influence: The Psychology of Persuasion* (New York: Collins, 1998).

28. J. H. Huang and Y. F. Chen, "Herding in Online Product Choice," *Psychology & Marketing* 23, no. 5 (2006): 413–428.

29. Wenjing Duan, Bin Gu, and Andrew Whinston, "Analysis of Herding on the Internet—An Empirical Investigation of Online Software Download," Proceedings of the Eleventh Americas Conference on Information Systems, Omaha, NE, USA August 11–14, 2005, www.hsw-basel.ch/iwi/publications.nsf/bc26b92ec161bc8fc12572180036eb62/592d 9e78196c07fec125722e00292418/$FILE/VIRTCOM01-1424.pdf, accessed July 20, 2010.

30. For a study that measures individual differences in proclivity to conformity, see William O. Bearden, Richard G. Netemeyer, and Jesse E. Teel, "Measurement of Consumer Susceptibility to Interpersonal Influence," *Journal of Consumer Research* 15 (March 1989): 473–481.

31. John W. Thibaut and Harold H. Kelley, *The Social Psychology of Groups* (New York: Wiley, 1959); W. W. Waller and R. Hill, *The Family, a Dynamic Interpretation* (New York: Dryden, 1951).

32. Bearden, Netemeyer, and Teel, "Measurement of Consumer Susceptibility to Interpersonal Influence"; Lynn R. Kahle, "Observations: Role-Relaxed Consumers: A Trend of the Nineties," *Journal of Advertising Research* (March–April 1995): 66–71; Lynn R. Kahle and Aviv Shoham, "Observations: Role-Relaxed Consumers: Empirical Evidence," *Journal of Advertising Research* (May–June 1995): 59–62.

Social Media for Consumer Insights

From Chapter 9 of *Social Media Marketing*, First Edition. Tracy L. Tuten, Michael R. Solomon.
Copyright © 2013 by Pearson Education, Inc. All rights reserved.

Social Media for Consumer Insights

LearningObjectives

When you finish reading this chapter you will be able to answer these questions:

1. What types of data are used in social media research?

2. What are the qualitative approaches to social media research?

3. How can we apply quantitative methods to social media research?

4. What are the common errors and biases associated with social media research?

GO

Learning
Objective 1

Wherever this icon
appears in the margin,
please go to the
website **www.zonesofsmm.com**
for an example of the topic
discussed.

The Role of Social Media in Research

To plan a social media marketing strategy that will meet objectives, marketers need to understand their consumers and their environment. They need to know the answers to questions about consumer personalities and past experiences, motives and fears, responses to campaigns, brand loyalties, and media usage. Why? Because every decision we make as marketers is based on what we know about the target audience. From the product benefits to the brand image to the creative strategies used in the campaign to the media placement of the message, we make decisions based on what we know. And, we make better decisions when we understand the environment within which we compete. Gathering market insight and competitive intelligence are critical steps to develop strategy. Relying upon research—market, competitive, and consumer—to make more informed marketing decisions is standard practice for marketers. None of that changes when we work in social media—only the techniques that we use to collect this information.

Social media has expanded the outlets for consumer expression; it shifts the importance of utilizing user-generated content to a higher level. Content is shared by many users across many forms of social media communities. The content includes opinions, experiences, and facts expressed in text, audio, and video. Conversations are built around the content. As conversation has increased in quantity, quality, location, and format, it has also become more useful and significant to marketers.

What can researchers monitor? Anything that's publicly available in the social media space. That means marketers can utilize content shared across all four zones of social media including conversations in social networks and forums, blog posts and comments, product reviews, photos shared in sites such as Flickr, videos shared on sites such as YouTube, social bookmarks and comments, and microblog posts. This content can be very useful, because it offers insight marketers can use in segmentation, needs analysis, and customer profiling. Conversations that include influence impressions provide information about brand awareness, attitude toward a brand, competitive advantage, and more because these **brand mentions** are explained in the context of an online discussion.

Marketers rely on several variants of marketing research to make decisions. Our options include both secondary and primary research. **Secondary research** is information already collected and available for use. It may be internal, published publicly, or available via syndicated sources. Secondary data might include background on the market, industry, competitors, and the brand's history. In contrast, **primary research** is collected for the research purposes at hand. Primary data can help marketers to understand consumers in the market, including psychological makeup, spending and media consumption patterns, and responsiveness to message appeals and offers. We conduct primary research via exploratory, qualitative methods such as observation, focus groups, and in-depth interviews; descriptive techniques such as surveys; or with experimental techniques such as simulations and test markets.

Social media research can include both secondary and primary research. As we participate in the social media zones, we leave residual evidence of our activities and opinions (our social footprint). Such residue can become rich sources of secondary data (this is currently the main focus of social media researchers). In addition, we can utilize social media channels as modes for data collection, conducting interviews, focus groups, surveys, and experiments within social channels.

After we collect data, regardless of the technique used, our next task is to analyze the results. Unlike a lot of traditional survey research which is quantitative (i.e., in numerical form), much of the data we need to analyze are qualitative. Typical types of data include **verbatims** (the actual comments people post in English or other languages) as well as other identifying information such as the time the item was posted and the site on which it appeared. Multimedia posts can also be analyzed, but those entries require special attention. Once collected, the data are analyzed using frequency counts and descriptive statistics, sentiment analysis, and content analysis.

We're not going to go into detail about the foundations of marketing research in this chapter (are you relieved?). However, we will highlight some of the tools that social media platforms provide to improve an organization's ability to understand what its customers want and how they relate to its offerings. Social media provides new sources of data and information that were once difficult to collect or altogether unavailable. In this chapter, we discuss the developing area of **social media research** and how social media marketers can utilize social content as a valuable source of marketing information. Social media research is the application of scientific marketing research principles to the collection and analysis of social media data such that valid and reliable results are produced.[1]

Learning
Objective 2

Qualitative Social Media Research

Observational Research

Observational research involves recording behavior or the residual evidence of behavior. Researchers in offline contexts have done this for years; they watch people as they shop in stores, or perhaps count the number and type of candy wrappers people throw out after a party to see what they're eating. Depending upon the residual evidence and how that evidence is measured and recorded, observational research may utilize small samples and suffer from a high risk of subjective bias. But the organization goal is to listen and respond, more so than to pursue systematic research.

Organizations can approach **social media listening** (as the approach is known in the industry) anecdotally or more systematically. At the early stages of maturity, many organizations essentially just listen to what users say in cyberspace. Analysts collect content haphazardly and inconsistently as they try to track the comments people post about their brand. For instance, they may compile a list of comments people make on a brand's Facebook fan page or the company blog. At times, they may run searches using tools such as Twitter Search and Blog Pulse to get a sense of how many times their brand is mentioned in posts. But as organizations recognize the value of residual data shared in social channels, their approaches are likely to become more systematic and grounded. At that point, social media listening and monitoring services can be used to enhance and/or automate the collection of this information. The social web is rich in tools for searching social conversations. The following list highlights the top tools for simple social media listening.

- Technorati (blog search)
- Google Blog Search
- Blog Pulse
- Twitter Search
- OneRiot
- Kosmix
- Scour
- Social Mention
- Same Point
- WhosTalkin
- BoardTracker (forum)
- Omgili
- BackType
- TalkDigger
- HowSociable
- Google Alerts
- Google Trends
- Trendrr
- Trendpedia
- Hashtags

It is important to keep in mind that searches of social content may not be systematic or exhaustive. They may not be representative of the possible sites where relevant content is posted. In research terms, this form of search is akin to a *convenience sample*; the information we get is suggestive, but it's difficult to generalize it to the broader population. Though there are vast amounts of content available for analysis, we must also remember that many conversations about consumer needs and brands are still held offline—some estimate that as much as 90 percent of word-of-mouth conversations potentially of interest to marketers is conducted offline.[2]

What consumers talk about online in social channels and offline may vary considerably. One study of offline and online conversations of 700 brands in 10 product categories over a 3-year period found that online conversations gravitated heavily to media and entertainment products, technology products and services, and cars.[3] In contrast, offline conversations included heavier coverage for beverages, food and dining, cars, and technology but with no specific areas dominating the discussions. Table 1 illustrates the percentage of discussions by category offline and online.

One more warning about using social content as data in marketing research: It's labor intensive and time consuming. To "listen" to social media chatter, individuals (more so than machines and software) usually have to read and sort the data, thus the process is cumbersome and can't accommodate large volumes of responses.

TABLE 1

Category Distribution of Offline and Online Word-of-Mouth for the 700 Most Talked About Brands

In a study of online and offline conversations of 700 of the most discussed brands, researchers found that what is talked about varies considerably. Offline, there are product categories that make up a large percentage of the overall conversation, but no one category dominates the discussions. Online, however, things are a bit different. A third of all conversations relate to media and entertainment brands, and cars and technology make up another third. There is very little conversation about the other product categories.

Category Distribution of Offline and Online Word-of-Mouth

	% of offline	% of online
Beauty products	5%	1%
Beverages	13%	3%
Cars	10%	17%
Children's products	2%	0%
Clothing products	7%	3%
Department stores	5%	4%
Financial services	4%	2%
Food and dining	12%	4%
Health products and services	3%	1%
Home design and decoration	1%	1%
Household products	2%	0%
Media and entertainment	9%	32%
Sports and hobbies	3%	8%
Technology products and stores	13%	17%
Telecommunications	9%	7%
Travel services	3%	1%

Source: Renana Peres and Ron Shachar, presentation at the Cross-platform and Multi-channel Customer Behavior Conference, Marketing Science Institute and Wharton Interactive Media Initiative, December 2010, reported in Ed Keller, "Wharton Study Shines New Light on Online Versus Offline Word of Mouth," *MediaBizBloggers.com*, December 16, 2010, www.mediabizbloggers.com/media-biz-bloggers/111949889.html, accessed December 27, 2010.

Technically we could measure anything anyone is talking about in social spaces, but one of the most common searches is for *brand mentions*. Exploring social media research by monitoring mentions of a brand name and/or tag line is one of the simplest approaches to using social media data. Brand mentions can be used to measure buzz, assess **viral spread** (i.e., the speed and intensity of a message across the online population), and identify service satisfaction issues. In this way, listening to social media conversations is a key activity for marketers involved in social CRM tactics. For instance, customer service teams can monitor social media to detect posts by people who write to vent about a "disservice" experience they had with a company. If an organization learns about complaints quickly, it can respond quickly as well. It may have a chance to salvage a customer relationship it would have lost if the wound had been allowed to fester.

As an added bonus, it may actually turn lemons into lemonade because word spreads about the positive actions the organization took to address the problem. Consider this real-life example: A man took his car for servicing at the auto maintenance shop at a Sears in Honolulu, Hawaii. When he picked up his car he found it in a decidedly different condition from when he first dropped it off. Snack wrappers and empty water bottles were in the car and, interestingly, it had less gas! It seems someone had decided to joyride in his car during its stay at the Sears shop. Appalled, he tweeted about his experience on Twitter. Within hours, a Sears service representative reached out to him, made an offer to make things right, and arranged a time for the man to bring the car in for detailing. How does this customer feel about Sears now? He's one of the retailer's biggest fans.[4]

Even at this simple stage, an organization can find out a lot of valuable things. If it monitors brand mentions over time, it can assess changes in the velocity of brand mentions (i.e., the rate of growth or decline in the number of brand mentions), location of mentions, and determine whether the shift in mentions could be associated with other events like a promotional campaign or competitive move. Speaking of competitors, market researchers can also track brand mentions on competitors' brand names. Tracking brand mentions of key competitors and comparing those points to those for the brand enable marketing managers to learn how the brand is positioned in the marketplace.

Ethnographic Research

When marketing researchers want to understand how "real" consumers use their products, they may conduct field research where they visit people's homes and offices to observe them as they go about their everyday lives. For example, a team of researchers that wanted to learn about how teenage girls actually talk about beauty care products sponsored a series of sleepovers where they sent (female) employees to hang out overnight and record what they learned when conversation turned to cosmetics, skin treatments, etc.

Now, some social scientists adapt these methods to rigorously study online communities.[5] **Netnography** is a rapidly growing research methodology that adapts ethnographic research techniques to study the communities that emerge through computer-mediated communications. Like monitoring, the approach uses information available through online forums such as chat rooms, message boards, and social networking groups to study the attitudes and behaviors of the market involved. The primary difference is based on how the study takes place. In monitoring, data are collected passively. Web crawlers scour the sites designated in the sampling frame to collect the relevant content and save it to our database.

Netnography is an unobtrusive approach to research with a key benefit of observing what is likely to be credible information, unaffected by the research process. Many marketers already use a very informal and unsystematic form of netnography by simply exploring relevant online communities. However, to minimize the limitations of netnography, researchers should be careful in their evaluations by employing triangulation to confirm findings whenever possible.

THE DARK SIDE OF SOCIAL MEDIA

Is It Ethical to Mine Social Conversations?

Social media research is a relatively new area of market research. Ethical guidelines for best practices don't yet exist. The following are some issues to think about.

When researchers conduct research with human subjects, they operate under a policy of **informed consent.** Participants are made aware of the research and its benefits and implications, and they are given the opportunity to withdraw or move forward. In social media environments, monitoring is akin to data mining of residual traces of consumer behavior, except the traces include opinions, stories, photographs, and videos. Given the often personal nature of the content shared, should researchers seek permission to collect and analyze content? Is it even feasible to acquire the equivalent of informed consent in social media communities?

How should you handle the attribution of comments analyzed and quoted? When it comes to social media research, the data may come entirely from unsolicited comments. Assuming identity can be identified, would the original source want attribution or prefer to have his or her identity protected?

In some situations, the researcher may engage in social media communities to have access to data (passive data collection) and perhaps also to tease out conversations on particular topics of interest (social media's version of "man-on-the-street interviews"). In the passive version, the monitoring requires membership to access the content in closed communities. The researcher lurks or eavesdrops by playing the role of community member. But once a member, the researcher can also pose questions and post opinions that may elicit responses from others. Should researchers disclose their affiliations to such communities?

As a start toward developing ethical guidelines for social media researchers, one blogger has proposed a set of rules he adapted from the guidelines a major marketing research organization (ESOMAR) applies to members who collect observational (or passive) data in the physical world:[6]

- If content has been posted to a truly public domain (i.e., there is no gate to viewing data such as registration), it can be used by the researcher.
- If content is posted in a "gated community" to be available to members only, researchers should announce their presence and request cooperation. Researchers should never pretend to be something or someone they are not when they interact in social communities.
- Assess whether the data to be collected includes personally identifiable and/or sensitive information. If it does, take steps to comply with relevant policies and protect the interests of the affected individuals. Processing of personally identifiable data should require informed consent, or at a minimum the implication of deemed consent.
- Prior to reporting and sharing of data, analysis, or results, all data should be made anonymous.
- Take steps to ensure that no harm is done due to researcher behavior or research uses.

How can we use netnography? One researcher recommends the following steps:[7]

- Identify online venues that could provide information related to the research questions.
- Select online communities that are focused on a particular topic or segment, have a high "traffic" of postings, have a relatively large number of active posters, and appear to have detailed posts.
- Learn about the group's culture including its characteristics, behaviors, and language.
- Select material for analysis and classify material as social or informational and off topic or on topic.
- Categorize the types of participants involved in the discussions to be analyzed.
- Keep a journal of observations and reflections about the data collection and analysis process.
- Be straightforward with those in the online community about your purpose for participation by fully disclosing the researcher's presence in the community as well as his or her intent.
- Utilize "member checks" following content analysis of the discourse to ensure that members feel their attitudes and behaviors have been accurately interpreted.

Quantitative Social Media Research

Try this simple exercise: Visit Twitter and search the term "Starbucks." How many hits did you get? Hundreds of mentions even within the past hour, most likely. For a brand like Starbucks, listening is a challenge. There are simply too many conversations going on to monitor them on an individual basis—to do so would probably require hundreds of employees who would need to drink a lot of lattes to keep up with the torrent of comments. When organizations have more complex research needs and/or face managing potentially hundreds of thousands of incidences of conversation around specific terms, they will likely shift to a more advanced use of social media research.

Monitoring and Tracking

In stage 2 of social media research, the level of listening shifts to **social media monitoring**. This is one of the most popular approaches to social media research. It works with the aid of software that systematically searches key words it finds in social spaces such as blogs, social networks, and forums. By carefully choosing and searching the appropriate key words and the relevant social communities, the researcher can gather insight into customer decision making, perceptions of the brand, perceptions of competitors, and more. The difference between listening and monitoring is in the consistency of the approach to the process; listening is done on an ad hoc basis, whereas monitoring occurs more systematically. An automated monitoring service may be retained to crawl the web (much as search engine bots do), collecting conversations according to established criteria (called **scraping**) for inclusion in a database. From that database, conversation volume, source, and sentiment can be gauged. At this point, analysts have access to both quantitative and qualitative data.

Monitoring explains what was said, when, by whom, and how many times. Thus this process answers four basic questions:

1. How many times was the search term found?
2. When was the search term found?
3. Where was the search term found?
4. Who mentioned the search term?

Like listening, the content of the data collected using monitoring is of great use to marketers. Positive comments can turn into customer testimonials for use in retailing and promotions. Comments about competitors serve as competitive intelligence. Conversations among like-minded groups of friends and connections provide consumer insight that's useful for targeting and positioning. But it gets even better: Monitoring results in the development of a detailed database that analysts can use to create more insights as they synthesize the comments of hundreds or even thousands of people.

At this stage, the research program ideally will take a step beyond listening and simple monitoring. Instead, it will specify more rigorously just who the researchers want to speak to, where these people will be found, and in some cases questions they will be asked to answer. This approach requires the specification of a formal **research design** before any data are collected. The research design specifies a plan to collect and utilize data so that desired information can be obtained with sufficient precision and/or so that hypotheses can be tested properly. It includes decisions on the study approach (exploratory, descriptive, or experimental), the sampling plan to be used and procedures for data collection, and data analysis decisions. This in turn gives the researchers more confidence if they wish to generalize their findings to a larger population (e.g., many or all of their customers). When we apply a scientific approach to gathering data for social media research, we plan a research design to maximize the reliability and validity of our study. In addition to collecting data systematically using software that can collect and scrub relevant content, we pay special attention to the minimizing sources of error that could create bias in our results. We do so as we consider our research design decisions and set data collection protocols. Next we discuss some of these specific approaches such as text mining, sentiment analysis, and content analysis.

Sentiment Analysis

Whereas research at stage 1 primarily tracks and counts simple brand mentions, data collected at the monitoring stage and beyond can be used to assess **sentiment**. This term refers to how people think or feel (especially feel) about an object such as a brand or a political candidate. Sentiment is heavier on emotion than reason but it captures an opinion about something. In that regard, collecting and analyzing sentiment data can provide an alternative to attitudinal surveys of consumers—if, and it's a big if, people are talking about what you need to know in social spaces.

How can marketers use sentiment analysis? They can analyze product reviews to obtain insight into the mix of features people want, and the product's strengths and weaknesses. News mentions of a company can be analyzed to indicate perceptions of the company in terms of product quality, service quality, performance, and value. Customers can use sentiment analysis to systematically utilize reviews when they make purchase decisions.

Sentiment analysis is at its core attitudinal research. In fact, sometimes it is called **opinion mining**. In the context of social media conversations, it means at a very basic level to analyze content to determine the attitude of the writer. When we employ social media research to assess attitudes toward a brand, we essentially seek to determine whether the relevant conversations are positive or negative. Certain emotions are strongly related to specific words. When people feel a particular way they are likely to choose certain words that tend to relate to the emotion. From these words, the researcher will create a **word-phrase dictionary** (sometimes called a *library*) to code the data. The program will scan the text to identify whether the words in the dictionary appear. The words and phrases in the dictionary are also used as text classifiers, in that once data are retained for further analysis, the data can also be classified according to the words and phrases in the dictionary. That might sound simplistic, but it doesn't mean it's easy to analyze sentiment. It's incredibly labor-intensive when analyzed by human coders and complex when analyzed with text mining software.

Consider this example based on Canon's PowerShot A540. A review on *Epinions*, a product review site, included this statement, "The Canon PowerShot A540 had good aperture and excellent resolution." A sentiment analysis would extract the entities of interest from the sentence, identifying the product as the Canon PowerShot A540 and the relevant dimensions as aperture and resolution. The sentiment would then be extracted for each dimension; the sentiment for aperture is "good" while that for resolution is "excellent." Of course, at this level, the coding is probably managed by text mining software. Many users post assessments; the individual sentiments are obtained and stored in a database for further analysis and reporting. Let's review the steps to conduct a sentiment analysis.[8]

Step 1: Fetch, crawl, and cleanse. Data from the sources are collected using **web crawlers**. These simple applications move through the designated websites and collect and store the content they find. These are the same types of programs search engines use to catalog web pages. Using the word-phrase dictionary, the crawlers select only the content that appears to be relevant based on matches with the dictionary. This process is called **fetching** or **web scraping**. The scraped data need to be cleansed to eliminate unnecessary formatting prior to moving forward. A **text classifier** (from the dictionary) is then applied to the data to filter any irrelevant content that made it into the data set.

Step 2: Extract entities of interest. From this filtered set of content, relevant posts are extracted. Remember, a blog post might contain information on several brands, not just the ones of interest in the study. The data are filtered again using rules to tag the entities of interest and further narrow the data set.

Step 3: Extract sentiment. From there, the analyst can begin sentiment extraction using **sentiment indicators**. These are words or other cues used to indicate positive or negative sentiment. In what proximity to the brand mention must they be to serve as an indicator? Accuracy is best when proximity is close. That's one reason why sentiment analysis of tweets tends to be more accurate than that of blogs; the message intent is easier to interpret when the data per content piece are smaller.[9] A **sentiment**

dictionary specifies sentiment indicators and rules to be used in the analysis. For instance, if the word "high" is in close proximity to the word "price," the sentiment may be scored as negative. The rules are in place in part to deal with sentence structure patterns. For instance, *negation words* such as "no," "not," or "never" can totally transform the meaning of a sentence; the analysis will need to be programmed to properly extract the sentiment intended.

Step 4: Aggregate raw sentiment data into a summary. Raw sentiments are then aggregated creating a sentiment summary.

However, as with any technique there are challenges associated with sentiment analysis.

- First and foremost is accuracy in gauging sentiment with automated tools. The sheer volume of conversation creates an information overload issue for most brands wanting to use social media monitoring and research. The solution is the use of an automated system, but these systems still struggle with accuracy in the coding of meaning.

- Cultural factors, linguistic nuances, and differing contexts all make it difficult to code text into negative, neutral, or positive categories. Consider this example: A search on attitudes toward the movie *Julie & Julia* revealed a positive sentiment score from 77 percent of tweets related to the movie. But some tweets may have been miscoded. A tweet reading "Julie and Julia was truly delightful! We all felt hungry afterwards" was coded as negative.[10] The word "hungry" was used as a sentiment indicator for negative. A person could understand that this statement was positive for the movie, but the software program couldn't. Linguistic nuances make it difficult for mining software to achieve better accuracy levels. A chocolate torte described as wickedly sinful would be coded as negative, when it fact the descriptor is positive.

- Defining the sentiment dictionary can also be a challenge, ultimately affecting whether the right words are extracted. Words can have many meanings. Take BP, for instance. As the oil spill in the Gulf of Mexico created a public relations crisis for the company, measuring sentiment before and after recovery steps and announcements is a useful tool to gauge damage control for the brand's image. But in a world of acronyms, BP may mean blood pressure, border patrol, business plan, Brad Pitt, or bipolar disorder.

- Accuracy in the categorical data needed to make better use of data is also an issue. It's difficult to gauge who is making comments (which segments they represent) in terms of demographic and geographic descriptors. Conversation origin may be identifiable using the URL, the IP address, or the language used, but all of these methods have flaws. The URL and IP address are not always helpful (take Facebook, for instance, with users around the world). Language indicators likewise leave a lot to be desired.

Content Analysis

Sentiment analysis is a form of **text mining:** the gathering and analysis of text data from relevant sources. Sentiment analysis uses a bottom-up approach to extract patterns from text. Human coders identify the sentiment indicators and interpret patterns, but the emphasis is on software manipulation of the data based on extraction rules.

In contrast, **content analysis**, an analysis approach used to identify the presence of concepts and themes within qualitative data sets, uses a top-down approach that applies theory or empirical evidence to the coding process. For example, a researcher might test a hypothesis that TV commercials reinforce traditional sex-role attitudes by sampling a large number of ads that aired during a certain period of time and comparing the occupations that male versus female actors portrayed.

Both sentiment analysis and content analysis can include quantitative analysis, but the intent is to enable the researcher to make inferences about messages in the content relevant to the research questions. Because content analysis is used to study the meanings relayed through content, the

BYTES TO BUCKS

Text Mining for Dove

When Unilever launched its Pro•Age skincare line for mature women, it developed a series of television commercials featuring mature women in the nude. Network television stations refused to air the commercials and a censored version was created for broadcast instead. The toned-down version encouraged viewers to visit the Pro•Age website to watch the original version and to participate in an online dialogue about beauty and aging. Response to the campaign was strong, in part driven by media coverage of the network refusals to run the original commercials. *Entertainment Tonight* and *Oprah* ran coverage of the story. Online at the Dove Pro•Age message boards, comments poured in. Unilever quickly realized it had an opportunity to analyze the wealth of data provided in those comments and conversations. What was being discussed? Who was participating and what motivated them to speak out online? How were the commercials received? How did the participants feel about beauty and aging? What should be the focus of future campaigns to this audience?

Unilever didn't need a web crawler to gather data—the data were all there on its own message boards! But it did face a daunting challenge: how to make sense of the vast amount of qualitative data available. Qualitative data including customer comments are typically read and coded by individual analysts following the procedures for content analysis, but in this case, the sheer volume of data combined with the importance of the issue made that approach less desirable. Unilever turned to Anderson Analytics, one of the leading providers of sentiment analysis research. Anderson first "scraped" the message board to collect the posts as well as meta data including time stamps and categorical information about the participants. Anderson's analysts then used its proprietary text mining software to identify meaningful word combinations, sentiment, and other relevant measures. The results? Not only were the commercials well-received by Unilever's target audience; it also learned that mature women are concerned about more than aging. The forums were home to discussions of inter-generational concerns, society, and media influence on culture.

content used as sources is broadly defined. It is most often text-based but may include multimedia. The content could originate from books, essays, interviews, newspaper headlines and articles, speeches, advertising, and so on. For social media researchers most content originates from social conversations and user-generated content posted online. The primary *unit of analysis* is the word.

To conduct a content analysis, the text is coded, or broken down, into manageable categories on a variety of levels—word, word sense, phrase, sentence, and theme—and then examined further for interpretation. Using **codes**, labels that classify and assign meanings to pieces of information, analysts can use the comments to determine any themes that are reflected in the comments. Table 2 summarizes major coding categories researchers use and provides examples to illustrate each.[11]

TABLE 2

Coding Categories for Content Analysis

Type of Code	Purpose
Context codes	Provide information on the source of the comment
Respondent perspective codes	Captures the general viewpoint revealed in the comment
Process codes	Indicate when over the course of the campaign a comment occurred
Relationship codes	Indicate alliances within social communities
Event codes	Indicate unique issues in the data
Activity codes	Identify comments that require response

Caution! Research Errors and Biases

When we look at research results, it's tempting to jump to quick conclusions about what is going on "out there." However, we need to be very careful about doing so because a variety of potential other explanations for the results exist. Numerous biases and errors may complicate the story. Every study has a certain amount of error that we cannot precisely specify; our goal as researchers is to minimize that error. Ultimately we want our research to provide as close an estimation of the truth as it possible.

Let's briefly review several types of errors that are particularly dangerous for social media research. Market researchers should remain vigilant against potential sources of bias that could interfere with the reliability and validity of the research outcomes. Though numerous errors are possible at every stage of research, our focus is on minimizing coverage error, sampling error, measurement error, and nonresponse error. Interpretation error is also an issue for social media research, but we will address that error in the section on analysis.

Coverage and Sampling Errors

One of the first decisions we must make (after we identify the need for research information and our research approach) is to establish the population from which we need to collect data. If we were collecting primary data using survey research or interviews, we would specify the units of interest, likely the people or families to which we wish to generalize the study results. This is known as defining the **population**. That's because we want to select participants for our study who represent the people in our population. If we were to study the whole of the population rather than a subset (known as a **sample**), this would be called a **census** (like the one the U.S. government undertakes every decade). We would then define a **sample frame**, an available list that approximates the population and from which we draw a sample to represent the population.

Alas, in social media research it generally isn't possible to identify unique people as units in a defined population, though we still want to ensure that our content is representative. It also isn't possible for us to scour the entire Internet every day for every single brand mention to conduct a census of brand mentions. Instead, we define the population as the social communities to which our audience belongs. We create a sampling frame of selected social communities and websites based on their descriptions; these include membership demographics, purpose, location, and activity. In other words, rather than identifying a population of consumer units that matches our target audience and then defining a sampling frame that provides a list from which to draw access to that population, we define a population of relevant communities for those consumer units.

The sample refers to the units of content we draw from the frame for inclusion in data analysis. In this case the sampling plan should also include specifications on identifying relevant content and the time period in which content is drawn. For example, let's say we want to understand how our new video game product fares in relation to other games that are similar. We define our population as members of gaming sites such as *GamesForum* and *Gaming Bay*. Our sampling frame could be all members who post on these two forums over a 4-week period, including 2 weeks prior to and 2 weeks post video game launch.

The first source of potential error we need to address is **coverage error**. This occurs when there is a failure to cover all components of a population being studied. It represents a gap between the sampling frame we use and the population we define. For social media research, the researcher must ask, "Which social media platforms and sites should be (and can be) included in data collection?" We are limited in coverage by the need to access publicly posted commentary. For instance, tweets are largely public content, so Twitter is one platform researchers commonly include in social media research studies. Coverage error occurs if we fail to specify the places where the people we want to study choose to hang out. It would be hard to justify a sample of hard-core gamers that did not include members of the *GamersTalk* forum. If we failed to include this group, our sample may suffer from coverage error.

Sampling refers to the process a researcher uses to select specific cases from a sampling frame for inclusion in a study. It is almost always used in research because in most cases it is financially or logistically impossible to use a census. That's especially true for social media that literally includes several platforms, thousands of sites, millions of pages and profiles, and zillions of individual pieces of content that could serve as data. A well-devised sampling plan helps ensure that a small portion of the data in the sampling universe can provide as accurate a depiction of the truth as we could get if we actually took a census of the entire population. The issue is, what is the truth? **Sampling error** is the result of collecting data from only a subset, rather than all, of the members of the sampling frame; it heightens the chance that the results are wrong. In our example, we would commit a major sampling error if we somehow sampled only female gamers who are in their fifties.

In survey research, sampling error is associated with how we draw our sample, using either a probability or non-probability method. For social media research, we will utilize these guidelines in collecting data, but two situations create additional concerns in the area of sampling error for social media researchers: (1) the **echo effect** and (2) the **participation effect**. The actual number of conversations may not always be what it seems.

The echo effect is also called "**online echo.**" It refers to the duplication in conversation volume that tends to occur in social media spaces. Online echo exists because people who share content online tend to share it in more than one community, and people in the sharer's network may then also share the same content. In Twitter, this is called *retweeting*, but sharing another person's content is common (and encouraged) throughout social media. Thus the question is how should retweets and reposts be counted in a study?

There also are other forms of irrelevant content that can create sampling error. **Spam** is increasingly common in social communities and signature lines but it does not represent real conversations we should include in the data set. Further, some marketers pay bloggers and other social media influencers to discuss their respective brands. These paid brand mentions could also be collected during the sampling process, but again, they do not reflect real conversations. To make it even more complicated, organic conversations could grow around these paid brand mentions. Some content is also duplicate content that is simply retweeted automatically by bots programmed to spread messages with specific keywords.

How should researchers handle these issues in the collection of data? The solution to these issues is not as simple as creating a rule to not include duplicate content. If a comment is shared by other people, the extent of sharing is an indicator of increased exposure of the message and sentiment in that someone felt the message worthy of passing along, even if they didn't express an original thought. How we handle different types of mentions and duplicates is something that we must agree to before we start the study.

Nonresponse Bias

There is the potential for **nonresponse bias** in social media research due to the participation effect. In survey research, nonresponse error is the potential that those units that were not included in the final sample are significantly different from those that were. If there are relevant differences, the results based on participating units may not accurately reflect the population of interest. For example, people who are willing to take a 30-minute phone survey may be different than those who aren't.

In social media research, we can sample from any public content posted on the sites we specify in our sampling frame. So why are we concerned about nonresponse bias? Because we've specified our population based on the communities where our customers are likely to be, but our ultimate interest is the attitudes and behaviors of people, not sites. Our specification of social media communities served as a proxy for access to the people. But not all people who are members of social communities participate actively or at the same level. Some people consume content, some join and lurk, and some are not active in social communities at all. That means there are people who may use a brand but who are not represented in the social media research analysis.

Also, the content people share varies for different forms of social sites. Those who post tweets on Twitter are far more vocal than those who share feedback to videos they see on YouTube, but both sites may be included in our sampling frame. This issue must be addressed and can be managed after data collection by using weighting. **Sampling weights** are adjustment factors applied to adjust for differences in probability of selection between cases in a sample. For example, less than 9 percent of all Internet users are on Twitter, but Twitter generates up to 60 percent of content that social media monitoring tools monitor. This means that to get a more accurate picture of all users we might want to sample relatively fewer tweets than other kinds of posts. Without weighting, the data will be skewed based on the sites we choose for data collection.

Providers of Social Media Monitoring and Analytics Services

Marketers can utilize many social media monitoring tools like those identified in Table 1 for little to no cost, but for those who need more help, there are several paid services. Some of the major providers follow.[12]

- *Radian 6* provides broad coverage of social media channels (public conversations in the most popular social networks and posts and comments in 100 million blogs) and offers Topic Analysis, which breaks each mention down by the words within them; Trending Analysis, which shows how mentions change over time; and Sentiment Rankings, which automatically determines whether a post is positive or negative. Users gain access to a dashboard that can be used for queries and reports. Prices begin at $600/month.
- *ScoutLabs* covers less content than Radian (just 12 million blogs) but is more affordable at a starting price of about $250/month. Analyses include buzz volume, customer sentiment, and competitive share of voice. ScoutLabs also provides a Quotes application that highlights key verbatims relevant to the brand.
- *Sysomos* offers a similar service including sentiment ratings, user activity charts, most-active keywords, influencer ratings, demographics, and more, starting at $500/month. Sysomos offers one unique feature that provides a differential advantage compared to other services—a Facebook Fan Page report.
- *NetBase* draws data from 95 million online sources to create a comprehensive database of conversations. Its NLP (Natural Language Processing) engine boasts an 80% accuracy rating in gauging sentiment and emotion.

Primary Social Media Research

Thus far in this chapter, we've introduced two approaches to marketing research using the residual data that people leave behind as they interact in social channels. These sources of data are valuable because they provide marketers with insights into consumer opinions, interactions, and behaviors. Importantly, as secondary data, these traces are readily available and inexpensive for organizations that choose to mine the social web. However using residual data is not the only approach marketers can take to social media research. Organizations can collect primary data in social spaces, too. The possible approaches include the use of consumer diaries, interviews and focus groups, surveys, and experiments—all conducted within channels of social media.

 For instance, Firefly MB, a global qualitative research company, conducted a global study of consumer views of social media and social media marketing.[13] Participants from 15 countries were recruited using message boards, Facebook, Twitter, and Craig's List. Firefly's research design included asynchronous one-to-one interviews conducted via consumer blogs, focus groups conducted within Facebook Groups, and a hybrid approach using a proprietary online community, IDEABlog, to engage participants in a multi-day forum.

The company's report, *The Language of Love in Social Media*, touts the benefits of the Firefly approach (not surprisingly). Though the participants were queried on specific topics, Firefly notes several advantages to hosting the process in social channels.

- The participants were comfortable being in an environment they frequent regularly, and the community setting led to a feeling of trust and camaraderie during the group sessions. While it can be a challenge to encourage respondents in traditional research studies to open up, the context of social media is already framed with the expectation of sharing.

- Traditional market research is sometimes criticized for its reliance on so-called professional respondents, so this approach filters out these people.

- It's easier to reach people in niche groups. Recruiting can often be a challenge, but the many specialty communities and groups in social media make finding participants with specific characteristics easier.

Harris Interactive, another large market research company, pursues another approach to gathering social media insights. Remember when we said that social media monitoring relies upon public content posted in social channels? The public aspect can be a detriment to market researchers because it may not reflect the whole truth. Many people may post only to those in their networks, and they maintain a wall of privacy around the content they share. The Harris Interactive Research Lifestreaming approach solves this issue of access to private content. Harris Interactive maintains a large panel of participants who have agreed to respond to surveys periodically. By asking these panel members if Harris Interactive could "friend" the members (on Facebook, Twitter, LinkedIn, and Bebo), Harris Interactive gained access to content that was otherwise protected. Harris Interactive still scrapes and mines content, but this content is content otherwise unavailable because of network privacy settings. In addition, because the Research Lifestreaming data are collected from people who have agreed to participate in surveys, Harris Interactive can supplement what it finds in the social content with survey data.

Chapter Summary

What are the types of data used in social media research?

Social media research can include both secondary and primary research. As we participate in the social media zones, we leave residual evidence of our activities and opinions. Such residue can become rich sources of secondary data (and currently the main focus of social media researchers). In addition, we can utilize social media channels as modes for data collection, conducting interviews, focus groups, surveys, and experiments within social channels.

What are the different methods of qualitative social media research?

Organizations that engage in social media listening monitor what users post about them. They may simply collect these comments or conduct a more systematic analysis. Netnography adapts ethnographic research techniques to study the communities that emerge through computer-mediated communications. Like monitoring, the approach uses information available through online forums such as chat rooms, message boards, and social networking groups to study the attitudes and behaviors of the market involved. The primary difference is based on how the study takes place. While social listening techniques collect data passively, netnography requires the researcher to take a more active role by identifying relevant communities and opinion leaders to explore how they think about a brand.

How can we apply quantitative methods to social media research?

Social media monitoring uses software to systematically search key words it finds in social spaces such as blogs, social networks, and forums. By carefully choosing and searching the appropriate key words and the relevant social communities, the researcher can gather insight into customer decision making, perceptions of the brand, perceptions of competitors, and more. Sentiment analysis is a similar approach that emphasizes how people think or feel about an object such as a brand or a political candidate. Content analysis identifies the prevalence of concepts and themes within data sets; it uses a top-down approach that applies theory or empirical evidence to the coding process. Analysts assign codes to classify pieces of information they gather so they can determine any themes that are reflected in a lot of users' comments.

What are the common errors and biases associated with social media research?

Social media research is prone to coverage error, sampling error, measurement error, and nonresponse error. Coverage error occurs when there is a failure to cover all components of a population being studied. Sampling error is the result of collecting data from only a subset, rather than all, of the members of the sampling frame.

Key Terms

census	participation effect	social media
codes	population	monitoring
content analysis	research design	social media research
coverage error	sample	spam
echo effect	sample frame	text classifier
fetching	sampling	text mining
informed consent	sampling error	verbatims
netnography	sampling weights	viral spread
nonresponse bias	scraping	web crawlers
online echo	sentiment	web scraping
opinion mining	sentiment dictionary	word-phrase dictionary

Review Questions

1. What is social media research? Would you qualify it as primary or secondary research? Exploratory or descriptive?
2. What are the levels of social media research?
3. What is the value add for researchers to approach social media research systematically rather than anecdotally?
4. What sources of error are common in social media research?
5. Explain the steps in sentiment analysis.
6. When should a researcher use content analysis versus sentiment analysis?

Exercises

1. Visit Social Mention and run an analysis on a brand of interest to you. Do you agree with the analysis? Read the information provided from Social Mention on the sites from which it pulls data. Should you be concerned about coverage or sampling error in the analysis revealed?
2. Identify five videos on YouTube that include mentions of a single brand. The videos should include at least one corporate piece but the others may be user-generated. View the videos and read the accompanying comments; then conduct a content analysis of the material you find. What insights are you able to glean?

Notes

1. Home page, *Conversition*, www.conversition.com, accessed September 2, 2010.

2. Ed Keller, "Wharton Study Shines New Light on Online Versus Offline Word of Mouth," *MediaBizBloggers.com*, December 16, 2010, www.mediabizbloggers.com/media-biz-bloggers/ 111949889.html, accessed December 27, 2010.

3. Renana Peres and Ron Shachar, presentation at the Cross-platform and Multi-channel Customer Behavior Conference, Marketing Science Institute and Wharton Interactive Media Initiative, December 2010, reported in Ed Keller, "Wharton Study Shines New Light on Online Versus Offline Word of Mouth," *MediaBizBloggers.com*, December 16, 2010, www.mediabizbloggers.com/media-biz-bloggers/ 111949889.html, accessed December 27, 2010.

4. Personal communication. January 13, 2011.

5. Robert V. Kozinets, *Netnography: Doing Ethnographic Research Online* (London Sage, 2009); Robert V. Kozinets, "The Field Behind the Screen: Using Netnography for Marketing Research in Online Communities," *Journal of Marketing Research* 39 (February 2002): 61–72.

6. *Guidelines for Social Media Monitoring*, adapted from Ray Poynter's The Future Place Blog at http://thefutureplace.typepad.com/ the_ future_place/2010/01/what-are-the-ethical-guidelines-for-blog-and-buzz-mining.html, accessed August 7, 2011.

7. Robert Kozinets, "E-Tribalized Marketing? The Strategic Implications of Virtual Communities of Consumption," *European Management Journal* 17, no. 3 (1999): 252–264.

8. Mukund Deshpande and Avik Sarkar, "BI and Sentiment Analysis," *Business Intelligence Journal* 15, no. 2 (2010): 41–50. See also Robert V. Kozinets, *Netnography: Doing Ethnographic Research Online* (London Sage, 2009); Robert V. Kozinets, "The Field Behind the Screen: Using Netnography for Marketing Research in Online Communities," *Journal of Marketing Research* 39 (February 2002): 61–72.

9. "Turning Conversations Into Insights: A Comparison of Social Media Monitoring Tools," *FreshMinds*, May 14, 2010, http://shared.freshminds.co.uk/smm10/whitepaper.pdf, accessed August 19, 2010.

10. Alex Wright, August 24, 2009, "Mining the Web for Feelings, Not Facts," *New York Times*, August 24, 2009, www.nytimes.com/2009/08/24/technology/internet/ 24emotion.html, accessed December 27, 2010.

11. R. B. Bogdan and S. K. Biklin, *Qualitative Research for Education: An Introduction to Theory and Methods,* Third Edition (Needham Heights, MA: Allyn and Bacon, 1998).

12. Tracy DiMarino, "Social Media Monitoring Tools Comparison Guide," *PR 20/20*, August 11, 2010, www.pr2020.com/page/social-media-monitoring-tools-comparison, accessed December 27, 2010.

13. "The Language of Love in Social Media," Firefly MB, 2010, personal communication, COO Cheryl Stallworth-Hooper and presented at Ad Tech 2010 New York, November 3, 2010.

Social Media Metrics

From Chapter 10 of *Social Media Marketing*, First Edition. Tracy L. Tuten, Michael R. Solomon. Copyright © 2013 by Pearson Education, Inc. All rights reserved.

Social Media Metrics

LearningObjectives

When you finish reading this chapter you will be able to answer these questions:

1. What is the role of metrics in social media marketing programs?

2. What are the steps in the DATA approach to measurement?

3. What characteristics do most commonly used social media metrics share?

4. How do we calculate social media ROI?

5. How do we assess the costs and benefits of a social media marketing program?

6. How do we track social media results?

GO

The Numbers Just Don't Add Up

A funny thing happened on the way to the CMO's office.

Between the realization of an eye-opening, game-changing insight gleaned from advertising test results and Web behavior data, the report you're gleefully ferrying to the C-Suite wilted, turns brown at the edges and starts to dribble a slimy substance with a conspicuous stench.

The CMO immediately develops a nose-squint. The VP of Corporate Communications has that "Oooo, you're in for it!" look in her eye and the VP of Advertising nudges the Director of Direct Marketing and says *sotto-voce*, "The golden boy is about to find out his day in the sun has turned him to toast."

The CMO points to (but does not touch)

- a traffic report from comScore
- a traffic report from Hitwise
- a chart from Compete.com
- an ad banner report from Atlas
- a traffic report from Omniture and
- another from Google Analytics

"It's like the old joke," she said with no humor at all. "If you take all the economists in the world and line them up end-to-end, they all point different directions. What the hell is going on with these numbers? Are we getting thirty two and a half million people on our Web site or forty-four million?"

The first time you ran into this nest of nettles, you hopped over to the white board and cheerfully explained all about

- cookie deletion
- cookie blocking
- multiple machine browsing
- multiple browser browsing
- multiple people on the same cookie
- non-human traffic
- dynamic IP addressing
- page caching
- javascript loading
- called pixel placement

You didn't even get to the good stuff about comparing miles to gallons and how

- different tools using
- different date cut-off routines and
- different methods to capture
- different types of data to store in

- different kinds of databases with a
- different method of data cleansing and
- different slicing and dicing segmentation to produce
- different kinds of reports that ended up in
- different feed for integration into
- different data warehouses

…before you were thanked for your help and shown the door—permanently.

You don't fall for it this time.

This time you explain that the world of online marketing has been suffering from a delusion of precision and an expectation of exactitude.

You tell them that we live in a world of statistics and probabilities. We can't count all the stars in the sky, so we don't try. We don't try to get an actual count of

- television watchers
- radio listeners
- magazine readers
- billboard readers
- bus poster readers
- floor sticker readers
- airline ticket jacket readers
- sandwich board readers

Instead, we count some and estimate the rest.

You share the good news that we can do this better than any of the above—and we've got some astonishing tools and techniques for dynamically targeting the audience and optimizing each one's experience.

You say, "We get 36.3 million people coming to our Web site."

The CMO lowers her half-glasses and gives you the look you last saw when caught using the office copy machine for party invitations. So you add, "With a 4% margin of error and it's a benchmark we can compare month over month from now on."

"So somewhere between 34 and a half and 38 million," she says.

"Pretty much right between them, in fact."

Disparagingly, she asks, "You really can't give me a more accurate number of how many people saw this digital marketing masterpiece that costs me tens of millions a year?"

"I can tell you whether our digital visitors are more engaged with our brand, come back more often, buy from us and discuss our products with their friends. How many people buy our products who saw our ads on CNN and 'Oprah' that cost you hundreds of millions a year?"

The VP of Advertising makes himself visibly smaller.

"I came here to show you a way that could save four million dollars of search marketing while boosting online sales by 6 to 8%," you say.

> The scowl leaves the CMO's face. The odor of dubious data dissipates. Her eyes narrow as she leans forward and says, "Show me."
>
> The numbers don't have to be precise—just compelling.

Source: Jim Sterne, "The Numbers Just Don't Add Up," *Media Post*, October 2, 2009, www.mediapost.com/publications/?fa=Articles .showArticle&art_aid=114723, accessed October 15, 2010. Used by permission of Jim Sterne, Founder of the eMetrics Marketing Optimization Summit and Chairman of the Web Analytics Association.

Learning Objective 1

What Matters Is Measured

Brands can benefit when they participate in the social media space. With social media, brands can engage consumers, enhance brand reputation and image, build positive brand attitudes, improve organic search rankings, service customers, and drive traffic to brand locations, both online and off. But no social media marketing campaign will conclude unless objectives are set and effectiveness has been assessed. The challenge is to identify the right measures to use. It's harder than it sounds— in fact, marketers continue to wrestle with these decisions as they seek concrete ways to illustrate the value of these techniques to others in their organizations who hold the purse strings.

Not that long ago, social media marketers felt that there were no standard metrics we could apply to social media marketing campaigns. Some believed that applying metrics to something as organic as social media was "mission impossible"—the metrics were bound to be meaningless at best because social media was not about quantitative monetary accomplishments. Social media is meant to be about participation and relationships between brands and consumers. In a short period of time, we've developed a host of valuable metrics, but these also come with an important caveat. The metrics we use must be appropriate for the objectives we set for the campaign. Counting followers and fans, retweets, and blog comments is only relevant if those behaviors relate to the goals of the brand's social media activity.

In many ways, social media marketing mimics online advertising in terms of the viable metrics available to measure how effective these messages are. Advertisers can measure **reach** (the number of people exposed to the message) and **frequency** (the average number of times someone is exposed), and analyze *site stickiness* (the ability of a site to draw repeat visits and to keep people on a site) and the **relative pull** (a comparison of how well different creative executions generate a response) of creative advertising. Brands can monitor *clickthroughs* (the number of people exposed to an online ad or link who actually click on it), **sales conversions** (the number of people who click through who go on to purchase the product), and **viewthroughs** (the number of people who are exposed and do not click through, but who later visit the brand's website).

A First Date or a Marriage?

Some metrics such as number of unique visitors, page views, frequency of visits, average visit length, and clickthrough rates may be irrelevant or simply fail to capture information appropriate to the reasons we use them. When we want to demonstrate the value of what we're doing, we love to count— we count impressions, visitors, friends, posts, players, even how often we count! There's no doubt that numbers are important. For instance, when we know the number of community members involved in brand-related conversations this measure can serve as an indicator of exposure, and the number of message threads and lines of text within a thread can serve as proxies of conversation depth.

However, simply counting the quantity of interactions consumers have with a brand doesn't tell us much about the *quality* of these touchpoints. We also need to know the degree of **engagement** people feel during and after the interaction, and how these exposures influenced their feelings about

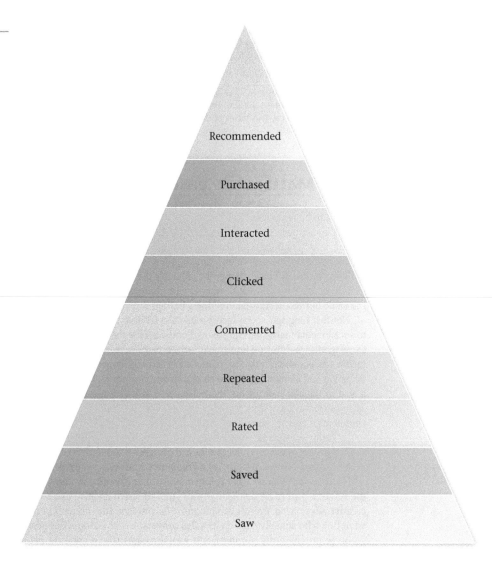

Figure 1

The Engagement Food Chain

Source: Based on "The Engagement Food Chain," Jim Sterne, 2010, *Social Media Metrics*, p. 109,

Recommended

Purchased

Interacted

Clicked

Commented

Repeated

Rated

Saved

Saw

the brand. For this reason we also try to collect other numbers that are a bit more diagnostic, such as measures of brand likeability, brand image, brand awareness, brand loyalty, brand affiliation, congruency, and purchase intent. Hershey's Bliss, a brand we will look at closer later in this chapter, may have more than 32,000 Facebook friends, but what does the number of friends tell us about how the target audience *feels* about Hershey's Bliss chocolate? As one analyst observed, "Four thousand two hundred and thirty-one is a measurement. Without context, it is merely a number. When compared with your personal best, company expectations, or your competitors' efforts, that number becomes a metric. It is now indicative of value, importance or a change in results."[1]

Engagement is a complex construct made up of several individual accomplishments. The Engagement Food Chain illustrates the hierarchy of effects we seek from our target audience as they reach increasing levels of engagement with our brand. Figure 1 above demonstrates how we look for different outcomes depending upon the consumer's level of engagement with the brand.

Figure 2

A Sample Social Media Campaign Timeline

Source: Based on Oliver Blanchard, "Social Media ROI – Part 8: An Introduction to Timelines," *BrandBuilder*, http://thebrandbuilder. wordpress.com/2009/07/21/ social-media-r-o-i-part-8-an-introduction-to-timelines/, accessed December 27, 2010.

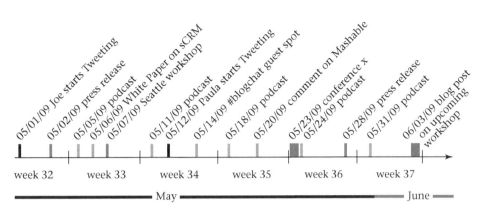

Because engagement is such a complex phenomenon, we need to be choosy about just what measures we collect and which ones are important. **Key performance indicators (KPIs)** are those metrics that are tied to organizational objectives.[2] But, there's a catch: In order for KPIs to be valuable, we first must be sure the objectives they're supposed to measure are well-defined. As the old geek saying goes, "Garbage in, garbage out." To review where we are so far:

- Measurements within a defined context are metrics.
- Measurements require context to provide useful feedback.
- Metrics that are tied to objectives are key performance indicators.
- Objectives must be well-defined before we can identify key performance indicators.

Wherever this icon appears in the margin, please go to the website **www.zonesofsmm.com** for an example of the topic discussed.

Campaign Timelines and Metrics

To make matters a bit more complicated (uh oh!), it's important to remember that the metrics we use may shift as a campaign progresses. For example, in the early days just following launch we primarily may be interested in awareness—are people in cyberspace tuning in to what we're doing? As the campaign progresses, we may not be so impressed with that as the pressure builds to show tangible results such as a boost in sales. For example, when Gap ran a group deal with Groupon offering $50 of Gap apparel for $25, it was excited to sell 441,000 Groupon coupons in a single day—$11 million in revenue. But Gap's social commerce tactic wasn't meant to act solely as a single sales promotion to improve sales revenue and deplete inventories. Gap also wanted to remind consumers about the Gap brand and encourage consumers to utilize Gap's website. Later measures of the campaign showed that 70 percent of the Groupon users went on to browse Gap online, meeting a key objective for the tactic.[3] Figure 2 provides a sample campaign timeline to illustrate how a campaign evolves over time. Metrics should be tied to each stage in the campaign timeline.

Learning Objective 2

The Evaluation and Measurement Process: DATA

When it comes to social media marketing—or any form of marketing, for that matter—measurement isn't optional. It's a necessity for organizations that are serious about adjusting their strategies and tactics to better meet their objectives. Some may feel intimidated about specifying what it is they want to see happen when it comes to their social media activities; perhaps they believe this sets them up to fail because they're not sure they can actually define or attain specific goalposts. Others may still be in the early stage of the social media maturity life cycle; because they're still "playing" with social media, they don't yet feel the need to define what results they would like to see. But ultimately social media will have to answer to the same masters as other kinds of traditional media—the bean counters that need to see value for their money. The investment in social media marketing will require justification. Strategists will want to understand what's working and what isn't in order to decide if a campaign needs fixing or if it's worth continuing at all. Welcome to the cold cruel world of budgets!

In reality, devising a measurement plan is a relatively straightforward process (at least on paper!). We organize our plan according to a four-step process known as the **DATA approach:**[4]

1. *Define:* Define the results that the program is designed to promote.
2. *Assess:* Assess the costs of the program and the potential value of the results.
3. *Track:* Track the actual results and link those results to the program.
4. *Adjust:* Adjust the program based on results to optimize future outcomes.

Let's dive deeper into each of these four steps.

Define

Our first—and arguably most critical—task is to define just what we want to occur and what we need to measure. Quite simply we have to define the objectives of the social media marketing campaign. After all, if we don't have clear objectives, how do we know when we've reached them? The specific objectives we might identify can vary dramatically from brand to brand but it's likely they will include three overarching issues:

1. *Motivating* some behavior from the target audience (such as visits to a website or purchases of the product),
2. *Influencing* brand knowledge and attitudes (particularly among those who are likely to spread the message to their own networks), and
3. *Accomplishing* the first two objectives with fewer resources than might be required with other methods.

For instance, if we use Twitter to identify customer complaints early on and resolve those complaints online like the Best Buy Twelpforce does, we can potentially influence attitude toward the brand, inspire the customer to share the experience with others, and do so online at a cost far

BYTES TO BUCKS

Hershey's Bliss

Hershey's Bliss worked with the agency House Party to create a campaign with both offline and social online components. The campaign sought to make female consumers aged 25 to 49 who love chocolate aware of the three varieties of Hershey's Bliss chocolate and to position the brand as an everyday indulgence. Further, they wanted to ensure product trial during the campaign and encourage word-of-mouth communication in social communities and on blogs. To pursue this goal, House Party planned 10,000 real parties in the homes of consumers they identified as influentials. Party hosts received a House Party Pack filled with products, gift bags, themed cocktail napkins, and a party photo album. Party hosts and attendees were asked to share the Hershey's Bliss experience online at the House Party microsite and to further share that content with their networks.

less than it normally takes a call center to resolve. Remember that organizational objectives will tie directly to the applications they've selected. If social media are being used as a customer service venue, we will identify service-oriented results in this step. If social media are a part of the brand's promotional strategy, we will identify communication objectives. If social media are a source of data for customer insight, we specify research objectives.

Are Your Objectives SMART? How can we be sure our objectives are clear enough that we can adequately measure them? The key is to state them so they have SMART characteristics:

- Specific
- Measurable
- Appropriate
- Realistic
- Time-oriented

To understand how objectives can be SMART or not, consider the following two examples.

> *"We will tell everyone we can about our new Facebook page and see if they like it so much they'll buy more of our product."*

> *"We will promote our new Facebook page in print advertisements we will place in the June issues of* Rolling Stone, Sports Illustrated, *and* Maxim. *On July 15 we will count the number of Facebook users who 'like' our brand and compare sales to the same period last year."*

The second objective is SMART; the first, not so much. However, defining objectives in a specific manner is not as easy as it sounds. Even the most desirable of outcomes (brand engagement and cost-efficiency, for instance) must be clearly defined if they are to be useful in assessment. It may seem difficult to shift from thinking about the benefits we can derive from social media marketing to ways we can measure those values. The benefits may seem intangible ("create lots of buzz!"), so an early step is to find a way to quantify results that may not lend themselves to numerical measurement. Here are some examples:

- One benefit of hosting a blog is that the target audience may use it to educate themselves about the company's product line. It is difficult to measure the value of consumer education, but there are tangible benefits we should see from greater knowledge about a brand. Assuming that people like what they see, these efforts should move blog visitors to the e-commerce site and from there to transactions. Thus the benefit of consumer education is valuable if it results in increases in site traffic and sales.

- Another common goal of social media marketing is search engine optimization. We can see whether our site is optimized when we test the search rankings we achieve. In addition, better search results should lead to higher traffic to the site. Aha! Something we can measure.

- Reaching a specific audience with our brand message is a valuable outcome. Here we may need to measure impressions, but we can also compare the cost of reaching the target audience with social media to the cost of doing so using traditional media. Social media are valuable for showing responsiveness to consumer concerns, but what is the value of the increased responsiveness? We can track customer satisfaction and retention to assess this value.

Metrics The next step is to decide on the *metric*, or specific standard of measurement, we will use to measure the objective. When we specify our metrics we need to match these to the results we are concerned about—whether attitude shifts and behavioral responses from our target audience or efficiency and profitability measures resulting from cost savings and/or increased sales. Table 1 lists some of the most commonly-used metrics.

TABLE 1

Commonly-Used Social Media Metrics

1. WOM Metrics Buzz volume
   a. Number (volume) of posts, comments, retweets/shares, bookmarks by channel
   b. Frequency, momentum, recency, seasonality
2. Asset popularity, virality
   a. Sharing, viewing, bookmarking, downloads, installs, and embedding of branded assets such as videos, pictures, links, articles
   b. Changes over time
3. Media mentions (earned media)
4. Brand liking
   a. Fans, followers, friends
   b. Growth in fans, followers, friends
   c. Likes, favorites, ratings, links back
5. Reach and second degree reach (influence impressions from others)
   a. Readers, viewers
   b. Subscriptions
   c. Mentions, links
6. Engagement
   a. Comment volume
   b. Uploads, contest participation
   c. Subscriptions (RSS, podcasts, video series, document series)
   d. Registrations
   e. Time spent with social pages
7. Quality
   a. Ratings, bookmarks
8. Search engine optimization
9. Web site effectiveness (traffic, clicks, conversions, viewthroughs)
10. Share of voice in social media and overall
11. Influence
12. Sentiment
    a. Nature of comments, tag attributes
    b. Attitudes
13. Customer value
    a. sales changes online, offline;
    b. customer lifetime value shifts, customer retention, lower customer acquisition costs

Based on David Berkowitz, "100 Ways to Measure Social Media," *MediaPost Social Media Insider*, November 17, 2009, www.mediapost.com/publications/?fa=Articles.showArticle&art_aid=117581, accessed October 15, 2010.

Learning Objective 3

A Social Media Marketing Metrics Matrix The list of possible measures applicable to social media can be overwhelming. Applying a framework to manage the types of measures is useful. The matrix shown in Table 2 illustrates the types and characteristics of social media metrics. The three types of metrics include activity metrics, interaction metrics, and return (financial) metrics.

- **Activity metrics** measure the actions the organization takes relative to social media. For instance, an organization might set goals in terms of the number and timing of blog posts, white papers, tweets, videos, comment responses, and status updates it may contribute in social venues. Hershey's Bliss House Party campaign set activity metrics for number of parties held, party attendance, blog posts, and content quantity uploaded to the microsite.
- **Interaction metrics** focus on how the target market engages with the social media platform and activities. Interaction measures include the number of followers and fans, comments, likes, recommendations and reviews, and the amount of shared content. Interactions are essentially made up of all the ways in which users can participate in a social media relationship with the brand.

TABLE 2

**A Social
Media Metrics
Frame1work**

Source: Adapted from Mike
Brown, July 14, 2010, 6, "Social
Media Metrics You Should Be
Tracking," *Social Media Today*,
http://www.socialmediatoday.
com/mikebrown1/146589/6-
social-media-metrics-you-
should-be-tracking, accessed
September 2011.

Category/Characteristic	Quantitative Measures	Qualitative Measures
Activity (input)	Number, frequency, and recency of Blog posts Updates/posts Comments/reply comments White papers Photo posts Video posts Activity across media channels	Creative messaging and positioning strategy Resonance/fit of campaign appeal Social media involvement
Interaction (responses)	Number, frequency, and recency of: Registrations Bookmarks/favorites/likes/ ratings Comments/posts/mentions/ tags Links/trackbacks Downloads/installs/embeds Subscriptions Fans/followers/friends Share/forward/invite/refer Reviews/testimonials Traffic/visits/views/ impressions Time spent on site Profile development UG content contributed Discount/deal redemption rate Echo effect/virality	Sentiment Engagement Influence effects Recommendations Buzz/virality
Performance (outcome)	Cost/prospects Lead conversion rate Average new revenue per customer Cost efficiencies across marketing functions Customer lifetime value Earned media values Shifts in average sales/site Traffic/search engine ratings Share of voice Return on investment	Attitude toward the brand Brand loyalty Customer satisfaction Service quality perceptions

Source: Adapted from Mike Brown, "Social Media Metrics You Should Be Tracking," *Social Media Today*, July 14, 2010, www.socialmediatoday.com/
mikebrown1/146589/6-social-media-metrics-you-should-be-tracking, accessed January 1, 2011.

Hershey's Bliss House Party included interaction metrics in its' measurement plan too. Brand analysts measured the quantity of shared content and the sentiment of these posts.

- **Return metrics** focus on the outcomes (financial or otherwise) that directly or indirectly support the success of the brand. They include return on investment measures, cost reduction measures, and other performance metrics. In addition to these categories, social media data can be characterized as qualitative or quantitative. Using both forms provide the hard numbers that CFOs (chief financial officers) require to fund investments in social media strategy while also valuing the soft benefits of social media such as stories, buzz, and image. Hershey's Bliss House Party didn't disclose its return metrics or the cost of the campaign, but you can bet these figures were calculated. The agency would be sure to calculate the cost to reach 10.1 million consumers in the target audience and the 77 million impressions the campaign earned when it reported return estimates to the client.

Learning
Objective **4**

A common metric to gauge success is **return on investment (ROI)**. ROI is a measure of profitability. It captures how effective a company is at using capital to generate profits. To determine ROI we assign a financial value to the resources we use to execute a strategy, measure financial outcomes, and calculate the ratio between inputs and outcomes. Return on investment answers the question, "How much income was generated from investments in the activities?" When we apply this concept to a brand's investment in social media marketing we call the measure **social media return on investment (SMROI)**. SMROI answers the question, "How much income did our investments in social media marketing generate?"

It's natural to want to quantify the value of a corporate activity and to use that value as justification to continue and expand the activity. The challenge when it comes to social media is the qualitative, viral, pervasive nature of the outcomes of social media advertising. Investments in social media generate goodwill, brand engagement, and momentum, and analysts must define how those constructs will be assessed.

Analysts have proposed several ways to calculate SMROI that are appropriate to measure the financial return on social media depending on the objective that is relevant. In addition to SMROI, we can view other returns that may be generated as a result of social media marketing efforts. Let's review some other approaches.[5]

- The **return on impressions model** demonstrates how many media impressions were generated by the social media tactics employed. An impression is simply an "opportunity to see" for the target audience. When a brand buys advertising space, it purchases opportunities for the target market to be exposed to the ad. Social media also provides impressions but the media space is not purchased. The costs are different. The opportunity for exposure to the brand message might be delivered as part of a virtual world event, on a social networking profile site, and with consumer-generated ads, product reviews, and so on. Impressions are valuable, according to this model, because we assume that impressions lead to changes in awareness, followed by changes in comprehension, changes in attitude, and ultimately changes in behavior (sales). Using the percentage of people reached who ultimately purchase as a way to calculate sales value, we can then determine a return on impressions by taking the gross revenue estimated minus the cost of the social media advertising program divided by the cost of the program. For example, if we estimate that Dunkin' Donuts earns $500,000 in gross revenue due to its Twitter presence, at a cost of $100,000 in time investment, the ROI for the microblogging activity is 400 percent.

- The **return on social media impact model** attempts to track coverage across media and in different markets against sales over time. It requires the statistical technique of *advanced multiple regression analysis* to analyze variables that may affect sales, including the mix of advertising and promotional tools used at each time and place. This approach offers the greatest potential for social media marketers, because it can include lagged measurements that control for time order of events taking place online (for instance, the timing of an event in a social world, the point at which a profile was activated, the timing of a contest conclusion, and subsequent posting of consumer-generated ads). Return on social media impact promises to determine how sales can be attributed to each element in a marketing mix and for tactics within the social media advertising strategy. Content generation and consumption is tracked and assigned algorithm scores to dictate weight of relative influence. Sales are also tracked at the same intervals and then statistical analysis is used to determine how sales trends shifted according to the timing of the social media marketing.

- The **return on target influence model** relies upon survey data to assess the effectiveness of social media marketing. Surveys assess whether participants were exposed to the social media tactics and what perceptions they formed as a result of exposure. The model then calls for calculating the change in the probability of purchase based on the exposure.

- The final approach is that of **return on earned media model**. This approach uses a metric called advertising equivalency value to equate publicity in news media outlets to its paid advertising equivalent. In other words, if a brand had paid for a mention in a specific space, what would it have cost? For social media advertising, an AEV would attempt to equate source authority, source prominence, depth of brand mention, and recommendation with a paid advertising value. To calculate advertising equivalency, the cost to purchase a display ad on a site would be used to assign a dollar value to the impressions achieved socially. For example, if a display ad on Facebook costs $50,000, we could assign an earned media value of $50,000 to a thousand page views of our brand profile on Facebook. The value can also be adjusted by the subjective importance of the earned media in question. For example, one might believe that profile visits are more valuable than a display ad rotation because it suggests that visitors sought out the brand interaction. The earned media value can be adjusted to account for variables such as the popularity of the location, the relative influence of the source, and so on. The ROI calculation is then based on the difference between the AEV and the cost of the social media advertising program divided by the cost of the program. If the AEV for the Facebook profile is $50,000 but it cost $5,000 in time for its development and maintenance, the incremental gain is $45,000. The gain divided by the cost of the program expressed as a percentage reveals an ROI of 900 percent. This measure may be among the easiest to execute for those social media spaces that also sell display advertising. However, it is not truly a return on investment measure so much as it is a measure of effective resource utilization.

Assess

As you've begun to see from the discussion of returns, we need to know something about costs and values in order to calculate outcome measures. This is the second step in the measurement planning process—to identify the investments required for specific activities and how to value the outcomes. What does it take to participate in social media marketing and what is it worth? What is the value of a customer or of a lead? What is the cost to gain a lead or a customer? What does it cost to maintain a blog? To promote and manage a social game? To maintain an active Twitter presence? What is the value of an ad impression? These are the kinds of questions an organization must answer in order to calculate returns. Here are some of the costs we need to consider:

- **Opportunity cost:** What else could employees or volunteers have done if they weren't spending time contributing to the brand's social media activity? For example, what's the time value of the person tasked with creating content for the corporate blog or posting responses to irritated customers on Facebook when without these tasks they could have spent time on other revenue-generated tasks?

- **Speed of response:** Social media enable companies to identify crisis situations quickly and respond quickly. It can be difficult to quantify the value of speed, but we know it is valuable.

- **Message control:** Brands accept a risk that the brand's message will be shared or manipulated in ways that the brand would rather not have happen. But if we want to capitalize on the value of virality and the *echo effect*, then we also have to be willing to sacrifice some control. For example, Comcast Cares grew out of negative tweets customers made about the brand on Twitter. Comcast took those tweets as an opportunity to right wrongs and ensure customer satisfaction.[6] But some brands may take the approach that they'd rather not have customers speaking openly about their experiences. In fact, many businesses set their Facebook walls to "Brand only" posts so that contributions from others are hidden to visitors. Unfortunately, these brands won't benefit in the same way that Comcast did.

Learning Objective 5

A simple approach to assessing costs and value is to develop a cost-benefit analysis table. Table 3 illustrates an example of a cost-benefit analysis to start and maintain a corporate blog.[7] The analyst needed to make several assumptions about value, and he or she researched costs to complete the assessment. The possible value associated with the corporate blog has been included and financial figures have been estimated for those benefits. If the assumptions are correct, the brand should pursue the corporate blog because the benefits outweigh the costs to maintain it.

TABLE 3

Cost-Benefit Analysis of a Corporate Blog

Estimated Costs	
Start-up costs	
Planning and development	$ 25,000
Training for blogger	10,000
Ongoing costs (annual)	
Blogging platform	25,000
Brand-monitoring service	50,000
IT support	3,000
Content production	150,000
Review and redirection	20,000
Total costs (Year One)	**$283,000**
Estimated Benefits	
Advertising value (visibility/traffic based on 7,500 daily)	$ 7,000
PR value (24 stories at 10,000 each)	240,000
WOM value (370 posts at $100 each)	37,000
Support value (50 calls daily avoided at cost of $5.50/call)	69,000
Research value (5 focus group equivalent at $8,000 each)	40,000
Total benefits (Year One)	**$393,000**
Net value for Year One	**$110,000**

The brand could also calculate the return on investment for maintaining the blog using the figures in the table or it could calculate the blog's **Blog Value Index (BVI)**.[8] The BVI is a simple equation that enables a company to assess whether the blog adds more value than it costs. If the BVI is under 1, the blog costs money, but if it is greater than 1, the blog yields a profit. The cost of software and hosting is assumed to be zero because presumably the organization is already covering the cost of website hosting and additional costs for the blog would be negligible.

$$BVIa = [adh (aay/1,000)] \div [abt \times ehw]$$

where

adh = average daily hits

aay = average advertising yield

abt = average number of hours spent per day blogging

ehw = employee hourly wage of the blogger

The equation itself is straightforward, but sometimes our input figures are difficult to assess in social media. For instance, it can be a challenge to identify how many unique blog readers one has. Feedburner, a service from Google that enables blog subscriptions and tracks analytics, reports a measure of *reach;* the total number of people who have taken action on the content in your feed. It also includes a *subscriber measure* of how many people are subscribed to your feed. But readers can also view blog content via a news filter site or blog search engine, which can limit the accuracy of the reach figures.

Learning Objective **6**

Track

In the tracking stage we collect and organize the data we will use to determine our results. The tracking step in the DATA process involves the following components:

- Identify tracking mechanisms
- Establish baseline comparisons
- Create activity timelines
- Develop transaction data
- Measure transaction precursors
- Overlay timelines and look for patterns

Tracking is not only concerned with determining how we will collect the data we need to make assessments. It is also concerned with organizing the data in a way that enhances their utility. There are three approaches to tracking that reflect different ways to do this: (1) forward tracking, (2) coincident tracking, and (3) reverse tracking:[9]

1. **Forward tracking** means that the tracking mechanisms are developed prior to launching the activity or campaign. Forward tracking is the most accurate approach because it enables the account team to develop a mechanism for tracking exactly the data desired. Ideally, then, the measurement plan will be created as part of the strategic social media campaign plan and the tracking mechanisms identified up front. If the organization has set SMART objectives, forward tracking should already be in place.

   For instance, the Hershey Bliss House Party campaign sought to promote 10,000 in person home parties for the launch of Hershey's Bliss chocolate. The social media aspect of this campaign was a microsite where participants could post and share stories, video, and photos about the parties. While 150,000 people would attend the parties, that's a drop in the proverbial bucket for a national campaign for a major brand. Rather, the real value would be in the impressions delivered via the shared social content posted on the microsite. Therefore, the campaign planned to track uploads of consumer-generated media and share commands (using *Share This* buttons)

THE DARK SIDE OF SOCIAL MEDIA

In order to assess the effectiveness of social media, we need to track if or how people interact with our messages. As you might suspect, the downside of evaluating performance is that the greater the need to track people's activities, the greater the risk of violating their privacy. Lotame Solutions Inc. is one of many companies that uses sophisticated software called a "beacon" to capture what people type on a website—whether they comment on something fairly innocent like the latest Brad Pitt thriller, or perhaps something a bit more intimate like feminine hygiene products. These companies don't release the names of individuals, but they do sell their profiles to interested marketers. A recent *Wall Street Journal* study discovered that the nation's 50 top websites on average installed 64 pieces of tracking technology onto the computers of visitors, usually with no warning. A dozen sites each installed more than a hundred.

The researchers found new tools that scan in real time what people are doing on a web page, then instantly assess location, income, shopping interests, and even medical conditions. Some tools surreptitiously re-spawn themselves even after users try to delete them. For example, Microsoft's web portal, MSN.com, obtains data from users that allow it to predict the person's age, ZIP Code, gender, income, marital status, presence of children, and home ownership. Other sites track health information and serve up ads based on the types of sites people browse. A visitor to Encyclopedia Britannica Inc.'s dictionary website who looks up entries related to depression, bipolar disorder, or overactive bladder might see Healthline ads for depression treatments on that page—and then also on pages viewed elsewhere.[11]

The companies that collect this data do so anonymously; they strip out information that identifies an individual before they sell it. However, this practice may create a sense of false security—someone who is determined (and smart) can potentially trace profiles back to real people. Recently two computer scientists at the University of Texas–Austin did just that. They developed an algorithm that looks at relationships among all the members of a social network to retroactively pinpoint individuals. The professors found that one-third of those who are on both Flickr and Twitter can be identified from the completely anonymous Twitter graph. Even though it's estimated that there is only about a 15 percent overlap between the two platforms, members of each have many other common members in their social network, so there was no hiding from the computer.[12] Although not everyone is (or knows) a high-powered computer scientist, companies that track our online behavior will need to be held to greater scrutiny as the pressure mounts to follow our online journeys.

---

for the posts over the campaign period. The campaign was a success; it generated 15,000 blog posts and consumers uploaded 24,000 videos and photos. The content was shared 7.2 million times, resulting in a combined reach of 10.1 million and impressions of 77 million.[10]

2. **Coincident tracking** begins during the activity or campaign. Coincident tracking can be effective in that it relies on residual data (like that we utilize for social media research) left at the point of interaction or point of sale. It doesn't necessarily require that a unique tracking mechanism be developed. However, it is interaction or outcome oriented because it occurs only when someone leaves traces of their activity or opinions. The Hershey Bliss House Party team, for instance, could have decided to monitor comments made in social communities once the campaign began in addition to tracking the activity on the microsite. Many parties may have shared photos on Facebook and tweets on Twitter in addition to uploading to the site. This is an imperfect approach. Searches won't necessarily reveal relevant information unless the consumer posting used keywords or hashtags.

3. **Reverse tracking** is conducted after an activity or campaign has concluded. Reverse tracking also uses residual data and may include primary data collection such as surveys to assess the effects of the campaign. In the Hershey Bliss example, some of that data could have been tracked after the fact. For instance, it would be simple to count the number of pieces of content uploaded to the microsite. However, without forward tracking in place, the microsite would have been missing key share technologies, making it more difficult to track the shared content originating from the site.

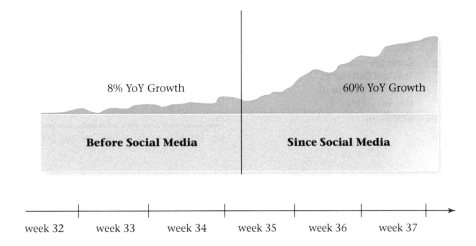

Figure 3

A Baseline Graphic

Note: YoY = Year over Year

8% YoY Growth

60% YoY Growth

Before Social Media

Since Social Media

week 32   week 33   week 34   week 35   week 36   week 37

Baselines   One useful way to track a campaign's effectiveness is to construct a **baseline**. This is a metric (often expressed visually) that allows a marketer to compare its performance on some dimension to other things such as how competitors are doing or how its own efforts fluctuate over time. Figure 3 provides a simple baseline comparison between a marketer's efforts pre-social media campaign and post-campaign.

Measurement Maps   A **measurement map** displays the types of branded messages produced and distributed (e.g., written vehicles like blog posts and white papers; ads in the form of display ads or rich media video; podcasts) and invitations for consumer engagement with the brand (e.g., games, consumer-generated advertising contests, promotions, and interactive brand experiences) as well as the online location for these materials.[13] It should also include online locations where content relating to the brand may be distributed by others. Here are some examples of opportunities to create measurement maps:

- Are there viral videos on YouTube that highlight the brand? Are there product reviews on sites like Epinions.com?
- Are there MySpace pages with brand icons and information posted?
- Are there bloggers writing about the brand?
- Are members of Delicious tagging the brand's website and are Digg members voting for branded content?

Once the analyst identifies all the sources of brand information, the map should sketch out the chain of potential touchpoints. Figure 4 illustrates several different examples of measurement maps. Each provides a vivid visual report about some aspect of the campaign's performance.

Adjust

The final step in the process is adjusting. There is little value in measuring without a process for applying what is learned to future activities and investments. In the Hershey Bliss House Party example, Hershey Bliss has continued to engage its House Party participants and their friends. A Facebook page boasts more than 32,000 friends, and the House Party microsite provided contact information for later use. Hershey Bliss met its goal to reach females aged 25 to 49 with an introduction to its three varieties of Hershey's Bliss chocolate. Had the results differed, the Hershey Bliss House Party team would have analyzed what could have been done differently and what should happen next.

Figure 4

Measurement Maps Illustrate Changes in the Tracked Outcomes over the Course of the Social Media Campaign

Source: Adapted from Oliver Blanchard, "Social Media ROI–Part 8: An Introduction to Timelines," *BrandBuilder,* http://thebrandbuilder. wordpress.com/2009/07/21/ social-media-r-o-i-part-8-an-introduction-to-timelines/, accessed December 27, 2010.

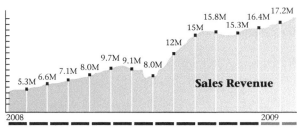

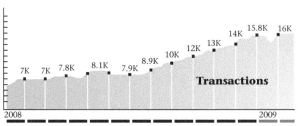

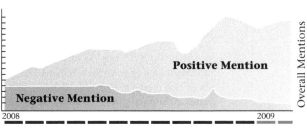

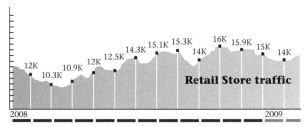

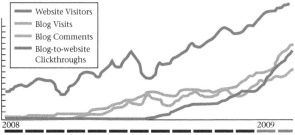

Simple Ways to Start Measuring

Clearly, we can choose from a variety of criteria, approaches, and tools to measure the effectiveness of a social media campaign. Some marketers, however, will want a simple start before they dive in and develop a full measurement program for their social media marketing campaigns. This list highlights a few metrics that provide a good start:[14]

- *Content consumption:*Who is interacting with and consuming the brand-generated and consumer-generated content? Is it who you want to consume your content?
- *Content augmentation:*Who is adding to or changing your content by continuing the conversation with response posts? In what ways is the content augmented? Is it consistent with what you want from the campaign?
- *Content sharing:*At what rate are those exposed to the brand messages sharing the content with others using Share tools? Does the rate of sharing suggest campaign momentum?
- *Content loyalty:*How many consumers have subscribed to branded content with RSS feeds or by registering for site access?
- *Content conversations:*Who is discussing the brand? Who is linking to brand websites? What is the comment-to-post ratio?
- *Content engagement:*Is the number of friends to brand profiles growing? Are people contributing content like comments and photos?

Chapter Summary

What is the role of metrics in social media marketing programs?

Metrics are measures to which marketers can compare results that relate to specific marketing objectives. Metrics allow us to determine the extent to which our strategies have been successful, if at all. Without metrics, we would be unable to assess the effectiveness of our campaigns.

What are the steps in the DATA approach to measurement?

We organize a measurement plan according to a four-step process known as the DATA approach: Define, assess, track, and adjust. This process allows us to clearly specify what the program should accomplish for the organization and then confirm the plan works. If it doesn't, the DATA approach encourages the organization to modify the plan to make it more likely it will yield the desired results.

What are characteristics the most commonly used social media metrics share?

One way to describe social media metrics is in terms of what they measure: Activity metrics measure the actions the organization takes relative to social media. Interaction metrics focus on how the target market engages with the social media platform and activities. Interaction measures include the number of followers and fans, comments, likes, recommendations and reviews, and the amount of shared content Return metrics focus on the outcomes (financial or otherwise) that directly or indirectly support the success of the brand. They include return on investment measures, cost reduction measures, and other performance metrics.

How do we calculate social media ROI?

ROI is a measure of profitability. It captures how effective a company is at using capital to generate profits. To determine ROI we assign a financial value to the resources we use to execute a strategy, measure financial outcomes, and calculate the ratio between inputs and outcomes. Return on investment answers the question, "How much income was generated from investments in the activities?" When we take this concept and apply this concept to a brand's investment in social media marketing we call the measure social media return on investment (SMROI). SMROI answers the question, "How much income did our investments in social media marketing generate." We calculate SMROI with one or more of the metrics listed in Table 2.

How do we assess the costs and benefits of a social media marketing program?

Social media marketing programs have the potential to provide direct and indirect benefits to organizations. In some applications the returns will be direct and fairly easy to measure because a campaign will cause consumers to buy the product as a result. Other applications are more indirect and may only be evident in the long-term; these include buzz-building and awareness campaigns that motivate people to talk to one another about a brand or to seek out more information about it. Social media programs overall tend to be less expensive than traditional marketing campaigns, but they also contain hidden costs. In particular, they may require the organization to allocate employees' time to monitor so personnel costs need to be included in the budget.

How do we track social media results?

Forward tracking requires the analyst to develop tracking mechanisms prior to launching the activity or campaign. Forward tracking is the most accurate approach because it enables the account team to develop a mechanism to track exactly the data desired. Coincident tracking begins during the activity or campaign. This method relies on data we gather at the point of interaction or point of sale. Reverse tracking is conducted after an activity or campaign has concluded. This approach also uses residual data and may include primary data collection such as surveys to assess the effects of the campaign.

Key Terms

activity metrics	key performance indicators (KPIs)	return on investment (ROI)
baseline		return on social media impact model
Blog Value Index (BVI)	measurement map	return on target influence model
coincident tracking	message control	reverse tracking
DATA approach	opportunity cost	sales conversions
engagement	reach	social media return on investment (SMROI)
forward tracking	relative pull	
frequency	return metrics	speed of response
interaction metrics	return on earned media model	viewthroughs
	return on impressions model	

Review Questions

1. What is a metric?
2. Explain the meaning of SMART objectives.
3. How can marketing managers apply the DATA process to evaluate social media marketing efforts?
4. Describe the differences among activity metrics, interaction metrics, and return metrics.

Exercises

1. Identify a student organization that uses social media to promote its activities and membership opportunities. Briefly review the social media zones in use by the organization and define three SMART objectives for the organization's use of social media.
2. Using the SMART objectives developed in Exercise 1, identify two metrics appropriate to measure the success of each objective.

Notes

1. J. Sterne, *Social Media Metrics* (Hoboken, NJ: Wiley & Sons, 2010), p. 4.

2. J. Sterne, *Social Media Metrics* (Hoboken, NJ: Wiley & Sons, 2010).

3. Zachary Sniderman, "5 Winning Social Media Campaigns to Learn From," September 14, 2010,http://mashable.com/2010/09/14/social-media-campaigns/, accessed December 27, 2010.

4. J. R. Roy, "Marketing Metrics and ROI: How to Set Up a Measurement System that Can Double Your Profitability," 2009, www.marketing-metrics-made-simple.com/index.html, accessed September 19, 2010.

5. Fraser Likely, David Rockland, and Mark Weiner, "Perspectives on the ROI of Media Relations Publicity Efforts, Institute for Public Relations," Institute for Public Relations, 2006, www.instituteforpr.org/research_single/perspectives_on_the_roi/, accessed December 26, 2010.

6. Rebecca Reisner, "Comcast's Twitter Man," *BusinessWeek*, January 13, 2009, www.businessweek.com/managing/content/jan2009/ca20090113_373506.htm, accessed December 26, 2010.

7. Charlene Li and Josh Bernoff, *Groundswell* (Boston, MA: Harvard Business Press, 2008), p. 113 (note that *Groundswell* includes similar tables for calculating the ROI of ratings and reviews and of a forum).

8. Jason Stampler, "The ROI of Blogging, and Whether Jonathan Schwartz's Blog Pays for Itself," *Computer Business Review*, April 4, 2006, www.cbronline.com/blogs/technology/the_roi_of_blog, accessed December 27, 2010.

9. J. R. Roy, "Marketing Metrics and ROI: How to Set Up a Measurement System that Can Double Your Profitability," 2009, www.marketing-metrics-made-simple.com/index.html, accessed September 19, 2010.

10. Case provided by House Party.

11. Julia Angwin, "The Web's New Gold Mine: Your Secrets," *Wall Street Journal*, July 30, 2010), http://online.wsj.com/article/SB10001424052748703940904575395073512989404.html?mod=dist_smartbrief, accessed October 19, 2010.

12. Arvind Narayanan and Vitaly Shmatikov, "De-anonymizing Social Networks," presented at IEEE Security & Privacy '09, http://randomwalker.info/social-networks/, accessed October 19, 2010.

13. Chris Brogan, "Measuring Social Media Efforts." September 24, 2007, www.chrisbrogan.com/measuring-social-media-efforts/, accessed December 27, 2010.

14. Michael Brito, "Measuring Social Media Marketing: It's Easier Than You Think," *Search Engine Journal*, June 30, 2007, http://www.searchenginejournal.com/measuring-social-media-marketing-its-easier-than-you-think/5397/, accessed August 7, 2011.

CASE

Wherever this icon appears in the margin, please go to the website **www.zonesofsmm.com** for an example of the topic discussed.

Increasingly, brands are integrating social media into their marketing communications campaigns or creating stand-alone social media campaigns to meet marketing objectives. Here we showcase examples of social media marketing by three organizations to illustrate how social media can be used in regional, national, and global initiatives.

Brand: Saab
Agency: In-House

Featured Zone: Social Publishing

Saab, the premium car manufacturer of Sweden, experienced a turbulent 2009 with the potential demise of its brand and a sense of uncertainty among even its most loyal fans. It sought to generate awareness of the brand and to build trust among those who loved the brand, but who may have lost faith in it. Saab is now owned by Dutch sports car manufacturer Spyker Cars NV.

Saab has several brand pillars—aircraft heritage, Scandinavian origins, independent and innovative thinking—and these are reflected in its promotional materials that target its key audience of independent-minded individuals who value design authenticity and the freedom to make statements through unconventional choices.

Facing a turbulent product period, Saab's communication and PR departments faced serious challenges. Saab addressed the promotional needs of this difficult period with three separate but coordinated campaigns: the "Trust Building" campaign (Spring 2009), the "Changing Perspective" campaign (Fall 2009), and the "Anything But Ordinary" campaign (Spring 2010). Though each campaign had a different focus based on the challenges at that specific point in Saab's rebuilding, all three campaigns were built around the Saab Newsroom.

The Saab Newsroom is a social media website that serves as the hub for all things Saab—at least all of Saab's social media and online promotional efforts. The Newsroom is open to enthusiast blogs and automotive sites; these linkages allow Saab to benefit from experts and fans with knowledge of the automotive industry and Saab's unique strengths. Links are included to dedicated Saab social media channels (Facebook, YouTube, Twitter, Flickr) and international press coverage. The site is social, with customer comments enabled.

The Newsroom also allowed Saab to publish content and to generate content from its fans. The Saab Newsroom now hosts the *SaabMagazine* online, as well as videos, photos, comments, official news, and more. It presents feeds from all of Saab's various social media channels including Flickr, Facebook, YouTube, and Twitter.

Saab used Google Analytics and Facebook Insight tools as standard reporting measures, which provided metrics on volume of traffic as well as traffic trends.

The following results illustrate the effectiveness of the Saab Newsroom approach:

- 1,500,000+ page views on Saab Newsroom since start (8,000 views/week)
- 42,700+ fans on Facebook (50,000 reached organically mid-December 2010)
- 1,000,000+ views on YouTube channel prior to developing a dedicated YouTube channel for "SaabCarsOfficial"
- 2,000+ followers on Twitter
- 30,000+ downloads of Saab's iPhone/iPad app

From *Social Media Marketing*, First Edition. Tracy L. Tuten, Michael R. Solomon.
Copyright © 2013 by Pearson Education, Inc. All rights reserved.

These results were all generated solely using social media, primarily through options focused on the social publishing zone, but supported with efforts in the community-building zone. No separate media investments were made to support the campaigns.

For Discussion

1. Visit the Saab Newsroom and assess the content and connections provided on the site. Is it an effective hub for the brand's global social media efforts? Why or why not?

2. Develop a profile for the Saab target audience that includes social media usage and trends. Based on your analysis, how would you evaluate Saab's strategy?

3. Build a linkwheel diagram that reflects the optimization tactics Saab utilized to link to and from the Newsroom hub to other social media sites. Are there other actions Saab could have taken to further optimize its Newsroom site? Explain.

4. Saab shares branded content and user-generated content on the Newsroom site and elsewhere. Based on your evaluation of the content, how would you categorize the type of content (based upon the value ladder and the types of content) Saab posts?

5. Brands can utilize owned, paid, and earned media in their promotional efforts. With the three campaigns tied to the Newsroom social media hub, on which forms of media is Saab relying?

CASE

Wherever this icon appears in the margin, please go to the website **www.zonesofsmm.com** for an example of the topic discussed.

Increasingly, brands are integrating social media into their marketing communications campaigns or creating stand-alone social media campaigns to meet marketing objectives. Here we showcase examples of social media marketing by three organizations to illustrate how social media can be used in regional, national, and global initiatives.

Client: New Belgium Brewing's Mighty Arrow Pale Ale
Agency: Friend2Friend

Featured Zones: Social Community and Social Entertainment

New Belgium Brewing (NBB) turned to social media marketing company Friend2Friend to develop a cause-related Facebook marketing campaign on behalf of its popular Mighty Arrow Pale Ale. NBB sought to raise awareness of the Mighty Arrow spring beer launch and ultimately increase beer sales, raise brand awareness of New Belgium Brewing brands generally, and increase the fan base on Facebook. In addition, NBB wanted to illustrate its commitment to dogs and to support the Humane Society.

Why the focus on dogs for a brewer? Mighty Arrow, NBB's seasonal spring beer, is named for Arrow—New Belgium CEO Kim Jordan's beloved Aussie/Border Collie mix. Jordan's faithful dog is famous for patrolling the brewery grounds.

Friend2Friend set out to create a co-branded Facebook application for NBB's Mighty Arrow Pale Ale that focused on "dogs, beer, and the outdoors" using photos and video. The application needed to be consistent with the brand image for NBB and its magazine partner, *Outside*, a magazine focused on outdoor activities. You can learn more about *Outside* at www.outsideonline.com. Friend2Friend's strategy relied on tapping into the love beer enthusiasts have for their dogs, and using that emotion to engage the target audience on NBB's Facebook page.

The creative team's ideation stage of the campaign development yielded the following concepts:

- Create fun, short online vignettes of dogs (e.g., dog getting beer from fridge, dog taking a tour of the brewery).
- Include historical content about Arrow, the dog behind NBB's commitment to canines.
- Highlight the best dog-friendly bars, as a way to link enthusiasts' love of beer and love of dogs.

Privacy was also an issue. Friend2Friend, NBB, and *Outside*. are aware of the latest privacy best practices and are committed to transparency in all Facebook applications. Users' names and information are not shared with other organizations.

The resulting app enabled fans to post photos and videos of their own moments with their favorite canines for a chance to win weekly prizes. For every participant, NBB and *Outside* donated $1 to the Humane Society, up to a maximum of $10,000. The campaign can be found on NBB's Facebook page (www.facebook.com/newbelgium?v=app_120904631311748).

The application lived on the NBB and *Outside* Facebook pages as a tab and was supported with regional media buys (40 ads) and Facebook ads. Both websites promoted the application on their respective homepages and it was promoted on the back label of NBB beer bottles.

The campaign, which ran until early March, marked Friend2Friend's fourth campaign on behalf of NBB, working in tandem with NBB's agency of record, Backbone Media. The inaugural

From *Social Media Marketing*, First Edition. Tracy L. Tuten, Michael R. Solomon.
Copyright © 2013 by Pearson Education, Inc. All rights reserved.

campaign, in 2009, invited consumers to submit their favorite "follies," upload a picture (possibly taken while engaging in their folly), and browse those of fellow New Belgium fans. The 2010 "Bike Yourself" campaign invited guests to place their picture on the Facebook-posted photo of the New Belgium Brewery's iconic bike diorama. This promotion allowed fans to share a souvenir photo "from the brewery." Through this approach New Belgium has built a fan base of over 200,000 fans across its Facebook pages.

For Discussion

1. New Belgium Brewing used cause marketing in its social media marketing campaign, which relied on a Facebook application. This strategy links a brand or company to a charitable organization. Would you say is the use of social media consistent with the cause-related marketing strategy? Why or why not?

2. What metrics could NNB apply to measure the effectiveness of the campaign?

3. New Belgium Brewing has continued to update its Facebook presence with a series of apps for its fans. How important is it to continue to spend time and money to update this content?

BUILD A SOCIAL MEDIA MARKETING PLAN

From *Social Media Marketing*, First Edition. Tracy L. Tuten, Michael R. Solomon.
Copyright © 2013 by Pearson Education, Inc. All rights reserved.

Build a Social Media Marketing Plan

Here's a handy template that serves as a road map both to develop a social media marketing plan and to guide you through the course.

1. The first column provides the basic social media marketing plan **OUTLINE**.

2. The second column gives you **QUESTIONS** you must answer in each of the sections of the social media marketing plan.

The Social Media Marketing Plan OUTLINE

A. CONDUCT A SITUATION ANALYSIS AND IDENTIFY KEY OPPORTUNITIES

1. Internal Environment

2. External Environment

3. SWOT Analysis

B. STATE OBJECTIVES

C. GATHER INSIGHT INTO TARGET AUDIENCE

D. SELECT SOCIAL MEDIA ZONES AND VEHICLES

1. Social Relationship Zone Strategies

2. Social Publishing Zone Strategies

3. Social Entertainment Zone Strategies

4. Social Commerce Zone Strategies

E. CREATE AN EXPERIENCE STRATEGY ENCOMPASSING SELECTED ZONES

F. ESTABLISH AN ACTIVATION PLAN

G. MANAGE AND MEASURE

QUESTIONS the Plan Addresses

- What activities exist in the overall marketing plan which can be leveraged for social media marketing?
- What is the corporate culture? Is it supportive of the transparent and decentralized norms of social media?

- What resources exist which can be directed to social media activities?
- Is the organization already prepared internally for social media activities (in terms of policies and procedures)?

- Who are our customers? Are they users of social media?
- Who are our competitors? What social media activities are they using and how is social media incorporated in their marketing and promotional plans?

- What are the key trends in the environment (social, cultural, legal and regulatory, political, economic, and technological) which may affect our decisions regarding social media marketing?

- Based on the analysis, what are the key strengths, weaknesses, opportunities, and threats (SWOT)?

- What does the organization expect to accomplish through social media marketing (promotional objectives, service objectives, retail objectives, research objectives)?

- Which segments should we select to target with social media activities?
- What are the relevant demographic, psychographic, and behavioral characteristics of the segments useful in planning a social media marketing strategy?

- What are the media habits, and especially the social media habits of the segments?

- What approach to social networking and relationship building should we use? How will we represent the brand in social networks (as a corporate entity, as a collection of

corporate leadership, as a brand character)? What content will we share in this space?

- What content do we have to share with audiences? Can we develop a sufficient amount of fresh, valuable content to attract audiences to consume content online?
- What form should our blog take?

- Which media sharing sites should we use to publish content? How should we build links between our social media sites, owned media sites, and affiliates to optimize our sites for search engines?

- What role should social entertainment play in our social media plan? Are there opportunities to develop a customized social game or to promote the brand as a product

placement in other social games? Is there an opportunity to utilize social entertainment sites such as MySpace as an entertainment venue?

- How can we develop opportunities for customer reviews and ratings that add value to our prospective customers?
- Should we develop retail spaces within social media sites? If we socially enhance our own e-retailing spaces, what applications should be used?

- How can we utilize social commerce applications like group deals to increase conversions?

- How can we develop social media activities that support and/or extend our existing promotional strategies?
- What message do we want to share using social media?
- How can we encourage engagement with the brand in social spaces?

- How can we encourage those who engage with the brand socially to act as opinion leaders and share the experience with others?
- In what ways can we align the zones used as well as other promotional tools to support each other? Can we incorporate social reminders in advertising messages, in store displays, and other venues?

- How do we make the plan happen?
- Who is responsible for each aspect of implementing the plan?
- What is the timing of the elements in the plan?

- What budget do we need to accomplish the objectives?
- How do we ensure that the plan is consistent with the organization's overall marketing plan and promotional plan?

- How do we measure the actual performance of the plan?

Index